Dimensions of Diffusion and Diversity

Cognitive Linguistics Research

Editors
Dirk Geeraerts
Dagmar Divjak
John R. Taylor

Honorary editors
René Dirven
Ronald W. Langacker

Volume 63

Dimensions of Diffusion and Diversity

Edited by
Janice Fon

DE GRUYTER
MOUTON

ISBN 978-3-11-073530-7
e-ISBN (PDF) 978-3-11-061089-5
e-ISBN (EPUB) 978-3-11-060823-6
ISSN 1861-4132

Library of Congress Control Number: 2018952443

Bibliographic information published by the Deutsche Nationalbibliothek
The Deutsche Nationalbibliothek lists this publication in the Deutsche Nationalbibliografie;
detailed bibliographic data are available on the internet at http://dnb.dnb.de.

© 2020 Walter de Gruyter GmbH, Berlin/Boston
This volume is text- and page-identical with the hardback published in 2019.
Typesetting: Integra Software Services Pvt. Ltd.
Printing and binding: CPI books GmbH, Leck

www.degruyter.com

Contents

Janice Fon
Introduction —— 1

Part I: Language variation from a linguistic perspective

Po-Ya Angela Wang and Shu-Kai Hsieh
1 Characteristics of lexical conventionalization in Chinese —— 9

Satoko Imaizumi
2 Typological study on expressions of possibility and their related meanings in English, Chinese and Japanese – How modality and voice intersect —— 56

Li-chiung Yang
3 Rhythmic synchrony in conversation —— 83

Part II: Language variation from a nonlinguistic perspective

A Variation in speakers' cognitive capability

Karlien Franco and Dirk Geeraerts
1 Botany meets lexicology: The relationship between experiential salience and lexical diversity —— 115

Ching Chu Sun, Peter Hendrix, Harald Baayen and Michael Ramscar
2 The price of knowledge: A bilingual paired associate learning study —— 149

Cheung Hin Tat
3 The use of cognitive state verbs in narratives of school-age Cantonese-speaking children with and without language impairment —— 177

B Variation in the general context

Thomas Van Hoey and Chiarung Lu
1 Lexical variation of ideophones in Chinese classics: Their implications in embodiment and migration —— 195

Chihkai Lin
2   A case study of accent shift in the Ryukyuan languages —— 227

Hsin-yen Chen and I-wen Su
3   Textual patterns of modern western paintings: A cognitive multimodal exploration —— 260

Index —— 277

Janice Fon
Introduction

Language universality has always been a holy grail for linguists in their endeavors to understand how language functions in and interacts with the human mind. Throughout the years, researchers from all subfields, be it phonetics/phonology, morphosyntax/semantics, or pragmatics/discourse, have been vigorously attempting at the quest in order to see through the mist of multiplicity that language has to portray and understand its essence. However, if one pores through the linguistic literature, one would find that there are only a few candidates that have been proposed, and even fewer that are unanimously agreed upon. Naturally, much of this has to do with our lack of understanding of the languages that had been, have been, or will be spoken around us. Despite the collective effort of linguists, there is still a disproportionate quantity of the unknown as opposed to the known.

However, if there is one commonality about languages that all linguists would have to admit regardless of the theories they believe in, the training they received, and the methodologies they employ, language evolvement would have to be among the top of the list. In other words, languages not only vary, in all possible imaginable and unimaginable aspects, but also evolve, albeit at an oftentimes glacial pace imperceptible to their contemporary users. Of the very little we know about languages around the world, one could hardly find a linguistic system in equilibrium so stable that no change at all is taking place. Changes are especially volatile for burgeoning pidgins and endangered languages, but they are also ubiquitous for fully-developed, robust systems.

Naturally, this has to do with the essence of language, as it does not exist in void, but is instead reflective of the complexity of the human mind and interacts with the multiplicity of the human culture. Even the seemingly simplistic social network in a conservative tribal hamlet could not prevent its language from evolving into some state of heterogeneity. The urbanization of industrialized megacities certainly only accelerates and intensifies the process exponentially. In other words, variation and change are not only a universal norm of languages, but also define us of what we are as cognitive and social beings.

In this volume, we would like to invite the readers to delve deeper into this issue with us on the dimensions that underlie language variation and change. By doing so, we believe that a more profound understanding of the human mind

---
Janice Fon, Associate Professor, Graduate Institute of Linguistics, National Taiwan University

could be achieved, and a more well-rounded appreciation of the human society could be attained. It is only through rigorous research of this kind that we could be more adequately equipped to think critically about how language variation intertwines with our everyday lives.

As language plays an indispensable role in our daily routine, it is not surprising that one of the main dimensions underlying language variation and change is linguistic. However, since linguistic dimensions never exist in vacuum, but are rather reflective of the cognitive complexity and cultural sophistication of the human nature, a second set of nonlinguistic dimensions is necessary in order to make the picture more complete. This volume thus inspects a wide range of possibilities, some more commonly studied, some less, in both linguistic and nonlinguistic dimensions.

There are three contributions from the linguistic perspective. Using a computational and corpus linguistic approach, Wang and Hsieh studied the underlying factors determining the "survival rate" of Mandarin novel words by examining three time periods, before 1950, after 1950, and words from the web (i.e., approximately after 1970). They found that words arising before 1950 behave differently from words arising after that. Older words tend to be monosyllabic, and the number of pragmatic connections for a given word is the deciding factor for its survival rate. For newer words, however, they are more multisyllabic, and their survival rates are more determined by their syntactic connections. In other words, words that have lived longer are more likely to be correlated with the rich experiential world knowledge, with which they have interacted for a long time, while those that have been newly coined are more dependent on their immediate syntactic compatibility. This is surprisingly parallel to the developmental stages of human beings. As children, we are more dependent on our immediate family members in order to survive the adversities of life. However, as we become physiologically and psychologically more mature, our social connections would more determine our level of well-being in the society instead. Being a system that is created, adopted, and manipulated by man, the lexicon that have survived through time remarkably mirrors how well-rounded longevity could be achieved in human life.

In the second paper, Imaizumi attempted at constructing a three-dimensional semantic map on the concept of possibility across three different languages, Mandarin, Japanese, and English, in the hope of integrating what was traditionally considered as two separate fields, modality and voice, into a continuum. Her results showed that the two could be represented through an intersection of controllability and speaker orientation. Of the three languages examined, Mandarin and English side with each other and uphold the importance of speaker orientation in determining their semantic continuity, while Japanese values event orientation more and thus controllability seems to be more essential to the language. The author argued that this cross-linguistic difference is correlated with the differential construal styles each language prefers, as Mandarin and English prefer objective construal, while Japanese prefers subjective construal. However, since the corpus is based on a Japanese novel that has been translated into Mandarin and English, some confounding effects might have occurred, as the former is a native text, while the latter two are translated ones. It would be interesting to see whether such an observation still holds when more native texts are involved.

Finally, shifting the focus from written to spoken, Yang investigated how speakers use feedback markers and F0 peaks to build rapport and mutual understanding in unplanned Mandarin dialogues. Based on two hour-long conversations, she found that feedback markers showed a gender-dependent distribution. Males use more affirmative markers such as *dui4* ('right'), while females use more conversation supporting markers such as *oh* and *umhum*, reflecting the gender-dependent social-cultural expectations in the Asian society of males being more authoritative and females being more supportive. On the other hand, synchrony and asynchrony of F0 peaks are not randomly distributed, but instead reflect whether speakers are "in sync" in their conversation. Exchanges between strangers typically start with asynchrony in their F0 peaks, as speakers are still fishing for common grounds. However, as conversations gradually unravel, and topics of common interest are identified, F0 peak alignment starts to appear, mimicking a singing duet of songbirds. The patterning dichotomy between feedback markers and F0 alignment has interesting implications for the functions of linguistic and paralinguistic cues in conversational dyads. It seems that social-cultural factors are more likely reflected in the former while pragmatic factors are more dominant in the latter.

The set of nonlinguistic dimensions underlying language variation and change could be further divided into two subgroups, one pertaining to the cognitive capability of speakers themselves, and the other to the more general context in which speakers are situated. There are three contributions for each subgroup. The first paper regarding the effect of cognitive capacity has to do with experiential frequency. Using a corpus linguistic approach, Franco and Geeraerts studied how cognitive familiarity molds our lexicon by comparing flora distribution in Northern Belgium with the number of linguistic labels Dutch speakers use for these plants. Results showed that although in any given community, a plant can have more than one lexical label, there is a trend for globally and locally more frequent plants to be lexically less variable. This has intriguing implications for the standardization of the lexicon. Although standardization is often achieved via a process that is instigated by headstrong political forces, this study showed that cognitive familiarity can perhaps foster this process in a milder and smoother fashion that would likely encounter less resistance from language users. In other words, the degree of lexical variability much reflects the delicate balance between meeting the human need for successful communication and that for building self identity. For familiar concepts, the former far outweighs the latter, as one would inevitably be in need of communicating the concept across to a larger population group, and a common form would certainly facilitate such a process. However, for less familiar concepts, there is less of a need to conform to a general common norm, as one only needs to cater to a smaller group of audience, with which unanimity is easier to achieve, and variance more likely to be tolerated.

Using a paired-association task, Sun et al. also studied the effect of speaker experience, yet from a different perspective. They argued that what is commonly observed as an age-related performance decline is in fact not due to cognitive degeneration, as is often conjectured, but is rather a reflection of experience accumulation. As elderly speakers would naturally have more experiences with the language and thus have accrued more information than younger ones, they would inevitably have higher information processing demands when dealing with linguistic input, which would take a heavier and heavier toll on their processing efficiency as they age. In their experiment, German monolinguals and Mandarin learners of German showed an expected pattern of elderly speakers being outperformed by younger ones for German and Mandarin item-pairs, respectively. However, elderly German-Mandarin bilinguals performed better than their younger counterparts and also their age-matched German monolinguals for the German pairs. This is in line with the argument that elderly speakers are only in disadvantage in their L1 due to a higher processing load, but not necessarily in their L2, for which they could have a processing load comparable to that of the younger L2 speakers. The results of this study are interesting, and even comforting for those of us who are becoming more and more aware of the effect of life's wear and tear on us. However, as the "elderly" group in this study was only in their 40s, which is far younger than what one would define as "old" in both the layman's and academic sense, it would be interesting to see whether such results could be replicated for more senior language users, since having a better understanding of healthy aging is crucial to the well-being of the human society.

The interaction between language and cognitive ability could be further demonstrated in the last paper of this set, which dealt with a population that has been identified as suffering from specific language impairments (SLI). This particular disadvantaged group is academically of interest because children with SLI demonstrate no other obvious physiological (such as hearing loss) or cognitive disabilities (such as nonlinguistic developmental delays), and are clinically defined only by significant impediments in the mastery of linguistic skills. Cheung studied narratives from Cantonese-learning 6-to-8-years-olds with SLI and their age-matched controls, and found that there was a major difference in their use of two types of complement-taking cognitive state verbs. For perception verbs (e.g., *kin3* 'see'), there was little difference between the two groups. Both showed a big jump in using the verbs with a complement clause between ages 6 and 7. However, for mental state verbs (e.g., *jing6 wai4* 'consider'), children with SLI generally showed less usage of such, even though both groups showed an increase in using them with a complemental clause between ages 7 and 8. This implies that mental verbs are in general cognitively more difficult for children to acquire, but are especially challenging for children with SLI. Since mental verbs in narration require a shift in perspective and a reconstruction of others' minds, this seems to suggest that contrary to the common clinical definition of the deficit, there is at least some cognitive capabilities that have been compromised in the SLI population, and the linguistic deficits they display are merely a reflection of such.

The second set of nonlinguistic dimensions focuses on how language interacts with its ambiance. Adopting a corpus linguistic approach and GIS mapping techniques, Van Hoey and Lu correlated the usage of ideophones in Classical Chinese with the geographical surroundings in which they occurred. In particular, three variants of *mangmang* 'vast, boundless' in Tang poems were chosen for their prominent watery imagery, along with three other control ideophones that lack such imagery. Results showed all three *mangmang* variants aligned with major river courses. the oldest form 芒芒 occurred neatly along the two major rivers, the Yellow River and the Yangtze River, the former of which is thought to be the cradle of Chinese civilization. The second oldest form 茫茫 also occurred along the Yellow River, but had a more diffuse pattern along the north-south axis, likely reflecting the southeastward migration waves that have occurred repeatedly throughout history due to warfare. The newest form 蒼茫 showed the most different pattern. It first appeared near the mouth of the Yangtze River, and travelled inward and southward along major river channels. For the three control ideophones, the distributions did not pattern with waterways at all. This study thus showed that the course of lexical diffusion is neither homogeneous nor unidirectional, but is rather a result of a complex interaction among the direction of human migration, the immediacy of the ambient environment, and the morphology of the lexicon. Language as a heritage is forever a dynamic selection process in which elements that more truthfully reflect the immediate surroundings have a better chance to be passed on to the generations to come.

Lin studied the interaction between language and environment from the perspective of sound change. In particular, he examined the accent shift in proto-Ryukyuan languages on five islands in the Ryukyu archipelago, including Amami, Okinawa, Miyako, Yaeyama, and Yonaguni, from north to south. Results showed that there seemed to be a rightward accent shift starting from Amami all the way to Yonaguni. For example, *hair* was reconstructed as accentless $*k^hï$: in proto-Amami, as $*k^hï$┐: with a penultimate moraic accent in proto-Okinawa, as $*\_ki$:┐ with a low initial register and a final moraic accent in proto-Miyako, as $*^-ki$:┐ with a high initial register and a final moraic accent in proto-Yaeyama, and finally, as accentless/$^-k^hi$:/

with a high initial register in Yonaguni. This corresponds nicely with the archeological evidence of the north-to-south migration pattern of the ancient Ryukuan people. As pitch accent is oftentimes viewed as a primitive tonal system consisting of only H and L tonal targets, this study sheds some light on the nature of tonogenesis. In particular, the evolvement of tonal and atonal systems might form a cycle. Tones can be derived from atonic languages, and atonicity can also be derived from tonal systems. However, as there are no other comparative data to serve as a reference, it is unclear whether the left-to-right directionality is a fixed parameter for such an accent arrival and accent change, and there are some cognitive bases supporting a rightward shift preference, or whether this directionality is merely a random coincidence, and language-dependent preferences are the major force for determining the direction of the shift. Future studies would be needed in order to more clearly understand this matter.

The last paper made a novel turn from linguistic data to visual arts. In particular, Chen and Su examined titles and their pictorial contents of nonrepresentational modern western paintings ranging from figurative to abstract to see if some kind of 'visual grammar', as was proposed by Kress and van Leeuwen's 2006 book *Reading Images: The grammar of visual design*, could be applied. Results showed that figurative paintings generally follow a tendency of displaying a left-to-right directionality, which parallels that of western writing systems, by placing given information on the left and new information on the right. Such a tendency was drastically diminished in semi-figurative paintings, and virtually nonexistent in abstract paintings. Instead, the latter two painting styles are more easily understood using the principles of Diagrammatic Iconicity, as was proposed by Masako Hiraga in her 2005 book *Metaphor and Iconicity*, which are commonly adopted to examine nonlinguistic visual texts. The results of this study implied that language, being a figurative system, may have more underlying cognitive commonality with other modes of figurative communication systems, than what we have originally imagined. Whether this left-to-right directionality preference is writing-system-dependent and thus culture-specific, or whether it stems more from a deeper cognitive need and is thus culture-general, would await further studies on paintings from drastically different cultures, with extremely different writing systems.

The nine contributions in this volume form a unique combination, as not only a wide range of dimensions underlying language variation and change is displayed, but a broad spectrum of languages is covered, including not only the more commonly studied languages like English, German, Dutch, Mandarin, and Japanese, but also some less studied ones like Cantonese, Ryukuan, and classical Chinese. It is hoped that such a rich variety could help us form a more complete and well-rounded view of how language evolves and interacts with human cognition.

Part I: Language variation from a linguistic perspective

Po-Ya Angela Wang and Shu-Kai Hsieh
1 Characteristics of lexical conventionalization in Chinese

Abstract: Language variations and changes have been widely investigated since they are encapsulated phenomena involving many linguistic factors. The notion of conventionalization, which is regarded as the diachronic process subject to normal constraints on language change, can refer to the newly coding of conceptual categories in the synchronic sense, or the process of adopting into the lexicon in the diachronic sense. To better capture the dynamic nature and underlying cognitive mechanism of conventionalization in Chinese, this paper presents the quantitative profile of a set of target lexical items based on large corpus, and provides a cognitive-functional linguistic explanation. The experimental results of linear regression model show that pragmatically world knowledge as well as structurally syntactic compatibility play statistically significant roles respectively in the establishment of words at different temporal stages. In addition, five linguistic variables are identified to distinguish newly diffused words and words having existed for centuries. Third, "number of types co-occurring before target words" is a key factor in predicting latent fluctuation of present diffused words based on the testing result of machine training with the accuracy of 63%. Hence, linguistic factors influencing conventionalization and statistically significant features of conventionalization are identified and well testified with a prediction model.

Keywords: conventionalization, life cycle of words, neologism, internet language, language change, quantitative linguistics, corpus lexicology

1 Introduction

Mental lexicon is "the cognitive system that constitutes the capacity for conscious and unconscious lexical activity" (Jarema and Libben 2007). It is dynamic in its continually giving birth of new words and forming new connections, which is

---

Po-Ya Angela Wang, Graduate Institute of Linguistics, National Taiwan University, differe94nt@gmail.com
Shu-Kai Hsieh, Graduate Institute of Linguistics, National Taiwan University, shukaihsieh@ntu.edu.tw

https://doi.org/10.1515/9783110610895-002

largely different from a fixed dictionary, so how to capture this dynamic and reflect the collective mental lexicon in a speech community should be the goal lexicography aims at for further application in language teaching as well as resources for natural language processing.

An adult may possess a vocabulary size with around 50,000 actively used in her/his mental lexicon (Aitchison 2003). From the viewpoint of lexicographers, Barnhart (1978) claimed that there are nearly 500 new words recorded in dictionary every year, while Metcalf (2002) proposed that in English there are 10,000 words coined in each day. Given the dynamic nature of word usage, the life cycle of words remains a mystery. Scant attention has been paid to understand factors contributing to how lexical items are adopted into lexicon from both quantitative and qualitative perspectives. Linguistically, we propose that frequency-effect takes the lead and entrenchment drives the effects; nevertheless, how frequent should a word's occurrence be claimed to be entrenched remain a question. Besides, it is even harder to tackle with the issue in Chinese since the notion of wordhood is still in great controversy.

Over the past years, though the motives for emergence of words have been qualitatively discussed in a wealth of works (Chao 1976; Keller 1994; Hudson 1996; Aitchison 2001; Hickey 2003; Love 2006; Halliday 2007; Milroy 2008), and many linguistic insights can be found in the literature of neologisms studies (Fischer 1998; Hsu 1999; Kjellmer 2000; Metcalf 2002), there has been less experimental or empirical evidence in grounding the arguments. On the other hand, while there are some quantitative observations or proposed formula to delineate life stages and predict how a word may possibly survive after being coined (Chang and Ahrens 2008; Wang 2010; Altmann 2011, 2013; Antoinette 2013; Kerremans 2015), their definitions on survival are inappropriate. As we will argue in this study, a lexical item comes into existence once it is coined, the only difference lies in whether it will be passed on to the next generation or not. Meanwhile, even a lexical item is less stabilized in current usage, it still has the potential to revive in the future.

Chang and Ahrens (2008) used normalized frequency within a year to decide whether a once diffused new word is conventionalized in usage or failed to be captured, however, we argue that such one-year normalized frequency cannot properly reflect conventionalization, for it may be the result of temporary burst. Being conventionalized or not should be viewed from more longitudinal temporal information and cross-timing points' stabilization. Alternatively, the Constant U proposed by Wang (2010) in evaluating textbook words seems to be more appropriate. However, this measure should not only be used in defining whether a word is activated or not, but to observe the stabilizational process of a word. The linguistic factors underlying this surface behavioral constant use has not been delineated in the study of Wang (2010), and should be further explored for the deeper understanding of the mechanism regarding how our mental lexicon cognitively incorporates new words. Moreover, target words perceived in these studies, except Chang and Ahrens (2008), are easily fluctuated nouns. The words included are *biased* as the sources are either only words from the Internet or occur in textbooks and dictionaries. And, rare studies have evaluated cognitive factors and disparate linguistic aspects which influence a word's usage.

Overall, based on previous proposals and limitations, the purpose of this paper is set to sketch linguistic characteristics catalyzing lexical conventionalization from both qualitative and quantitative perspectives. In order to realize the underlying factors for a lexical item in entering into our mental lexicon, and to be used in real life communication, three types of words from different temporal points (words having existed for more than 50 years; words coined around 50 years ago; and words newly diffused about 10 years back) are included. 18 linguistic features are evaluated to help understand underlying linguistic factors contributing to the process of conventionalization. The generality and temporal information of included target words are carefully controlled based on available resources.

2 Literature review

This section reviews related lexical studies and illustrates the findings among them, to sew together these insights for the understanding of factors influencing the fluctuation of lexical items. Given the fact that what we concern is around the occurrences of a lexical item along with temporal fluctuation, how historical linguistics tackles with the diachronic development of lexical items and how lexical semantics investigates the synchronic emergence of new expression are reviewed. Following that, studies paying attention on "life cycle" of lexical items as well as proposed features for words to be "survival" are introduced, whose insights are further utilized to guide the design of our current study.

2.1 Qualitative Discussion from Historical linguistics and Lexical Semantics

In order to decipher the birth (and death) of a word, the reason why certain words can survive over decades while some others die so early are all important issues to be paid attention to. A panorama of the *life cycle of a word*: its birth, in-use, settling-down, death, and re-birth should shed lights on the secrets of words, and the cognition of human. To approach these issues, we cannot just focus on newly coined words, but also have to bring our attention to the words stored in our lexicon over generations. Related diachronic studies on how words sustained and expanded their meanings and functions as well as how words fluctuate are reviewed with the attempt to explore the life journey of lexical units.

Grammaticalization is a well-known topic related to our concern here. Instead of proposing rules, the focus on grammaticalization path gives insights into the emergent properties of language and its changing tendency (Fischer 2000; Jucker 2010). *Metaphorical Extension* and *Invited Inferencing* are two main approaches commonly adopted in the study of grammaticalization. They are proposed separately by Heine and Traugott, and are so coined by Evans and Green (2006). De-grammaticalization, lexicalization, and exaptation are some counter-examples of grammaticalization (Lipka 1990; Lehmann 1995 [1982]; Wischer 2002; Evans and Green 2006) *De-grammaticalization* stands for two different situations. The first refers to prototypical cases of end-stage in grammaticalization, the other involves cases that the changing direction violates the uni-directionality of grammaticalization. *Lexicalization* is viewed as the way to enrich the lexicon. Lipka (1990) has defined it as "…the phenomenon that a complex lexeme once coined tends to become a single complete lexical unit, a simple lexeme." It may employ "conversion" as a strategy to use grammatical items as other parts of speech. Lehmann (1995 [1982]) and Wischer (2002) indicate that there is intersection of grammaticalization and lexicalization, for lexical phrases must be first lexicalized (frozen) before they go into grammaticalization. *Exaptation* refers to the situation that a form is given with a new function. It is widely discussed in studies on language evolution (Hurford, Studdert-Kennedy and Knight 1998), and in historical morphosyntax (Lass 1990, 1997; Vincent 1995; Norde 2002). Traugott (2004) has pointed out that some terms have also been used with reference to similar phenomena, such as "regrammaticalization" (Greenberg 1991), "functional renewal" (Brinton and Stein 1995), "degrammaticalization" (Norde 2002; Heine 2003), and "hypoanalysis" (Croft 2000).

Based on the above-mentioned discussion on grammaticalization, de-grammaticalization, lexicalization and exaptation, we propose that instead of viewing them as counter-examples, they reflect different stages of words' change. They also imply the relations between form and meaning. We would like to argue that grammaticalization is the long-living secrets for lemma. It derives pragmatically enriched functions from existing senses. Degrammaticalization and Lexicalization can be perceived as the birth of new sense or function. Exaptation illustrates the reviving of old forms. The reviving mechanisms include: an old lemma +brand new sense (dissociated with original sense), an old lemma + its original sense, or the reviving of one of less significant usage that has once appeared in past but became marginal for competition with another usage. Our proposed examples for "life cycle" of lexical items are going to be exemplified in Methodology section with uniting other views from different linguistic branches on life of words.

Historical linguistics provides insights into the semantic development and reviving of stabilized senses and lemmas. It describes how a lexicalized frozen word, a coded meaning, leads its life after settling down. However, how these expressions are "born" remain unclear. Neologisms, for instance which may be newly-coined word forms or new senses of an existing word form, have constantly appeared (Algeo 1980; Lehrer 2003). In the intertwining field of lexical semantics and corpus linguistics, neology has gained a lot attention. Antoinette (2013) classified neology into three types: semantic, lexical and grammatical neology. Semantic neology is concerned with emergent senses, whose identification can be probed with collocational environment because the new sense of an existed word would collocate with different words from its original sense. Lexical neology is about the formation of new words, which can be identified in diachronic corpus. Grammatical neology probes issues like lexical conversion, so it can be studied via post-processing with parts of speech tagging.

Comparing with recent emergent expressions, early words that have started their lives since emergence of language should own different communicative motivations. As indicated in Wang and Minett (2004) with the development of language, there are increasing needs to express more complicated meanings. Thus, it is hypothesized that lately coined words bear richer presuppositions in their senses, or more unique senses to compensate or balance semantic network. For example, 打臉 'hit face' in Chinese uses two syllables to concisely lexicalize the complicated concept that "A person says or does something that contradicts to what he or she has said." In this case, this verb lexicalizes an experience in our flux of life, and it owns unique status in this lexicalization. Boulanger (1997) proposed eight factors on comparing survived words and fade-away words, which is defined by observing words which appeared in English new-word dictionary in 1990 and its inclusion in general dictionary several years later. The proposed factors include: *frequency, popular referent, non-specialized register, particular notional fields, variety of genre, cultural prominence, synonymous competition, and Taboo association*. However, the decision on inclusion is solely determined by lexicographers' looking-up in recording of dictionary, which is a relatively indirect method. Details on proposed features we used for the understanding of stabilization would be covered in section of methodology.

As shown in above reviews, studies on neology have had rich insights in probing issues about the paths new words are born, the rules to coin new words, the characteristics of new words, the reviving of old usages, or comparisons on new born words; however, the reasons and constraints for new words to be born, the reasons for lexicalization, and the diffusion or step down of expressions should all be deeper analyzed. Hence, in order to fill this gap in our knowledge, this study investigated probable factors influencing fluctuation of lexical items.

2.2 Quantitative Analysis on "Life Cycle" of Lexical Items

Aside from the birth and recycle of lexical items from the results of qualitative analysis, there are some quantitative investigations about the "Life Cycle" of lexical items. Approaches in corpus-based studies in delineating stages of lexical items from either newspaper or web as well as computational methods in modeling fluctuation of words by external social indexes of internet community all shed light in possible living appearances of lexical items, and illustrate external influences on words.

Renouf (2013) used 1.2 billion words from UK mainstream newspaper texts spanning from 1989 to 2011 to understand the life-cycle of proper nouns (e.g. "Arab Spring"). These nouns are easily influenced by the events occurring in the external world. The result indicates that the life cycles of words should include: *Birth, Increase in Frequency, Orthographic Adjustment, Lexical Productivity, Creativity, Settling Down, Obsolescence, Death, Semantic neology, and Re-birth or Revival*. However, we argue that Renouf (2013) has mistaken the factors influencing birth, settling-down, obsolescence, death, and re-birth for the stages of life cycle of words. The reasons are as following. First, increase in frequency may be the indicator of being born and settling-down. The threshold of what kind of increase in frequency should be called settling-down needs further discussion. Second, just like the situation of rising words discussed, the increase in frequency may be influenced by different factors. Third, orthographic adjustment may be one of the reasons for the fade-away use being re-born with new appearance. Fourth, Lexical productivity and creativity should be viewed as the characteristics of the words that influence their birth, death, and length of life span, too. Finally, the semantic neology should be one of the paths for reviving of lemma.

Different from the proposal of Renouf (2013), Kerremans (2015) with her construction in automatic crawlers for detecting non-sense new words has highlighted the role conventionalization plays. The proposed four stages of conventionalization are: *(1)Non-conventionalization(2)Transitional conventionalization (3) Recurrent semi-conventionalization (4) Advanced conventionalization.*

Kerremans (2015) illustrated these 4 stages by using 44 neologisms retrieved from the Internet between October 2009 and January 2011. The *transitional conventionalization* is defined as momentary conventionalization of lexemes with a sudden burst in overall frequency contributed from extralinguistic events. This phenomenon highlights the necessity of long-term observation on the frequency cycle of words. As stated in Kerremans (2015), whether an item, originally belonging to transitional conventionalization, is able to enter into advanced conventionalization depends on its topicality. Kerremans (2015) further claimed that "[...] it requires a high frequency of occurrence within a longer time span." The emphasis on conventionalization and the recognition on reviving correspond to our assumptions; however, her investigation ignored the type of new words being investigated as well as lacked quantifying indexes in defining the stages.

In profiling "life stages" of lexical items quantitatively, Chang and Ahrens (2008) proposed threshold for deciding whether a word is "survived" or "died" with reference to developmental trend in slope and normalized frequency. In their study on non-sense-neologism fashion verbs, they collected the year-by-year frequencies in UDN (United Daily News) from 1996 to 2006. The threshold includes normalized ratio in 2006 and slope of the normalized ratios throughout the years. The retrieved frequency is normalized to the frequencies per 10,000 characters. Words' actual survival or failure is based on normalized ratios in 2006. A word fails to survive when its normalized ratio is less than or equal to 0.3 in 2006 (e.g., 哈草, ha1 cao3, 'to smoke,' normalized ratio=0.11). A word is considered to be "success" if it is with normalized ratio greater than 3 (e.g., 抓包 zhua1 bao1,'(to be) caught doing something,' normalized ratio=4.24). In addition to normalized ratio, developmental tendency is used. Thus, only words with a slope less than -0.06 would be counted as failures. However, frequency can only highlight the activation aspect of a lexical item. A lexical item may be high in total frequency due to the fact that it has been used frequently within a short period, which does not signify its stabilization in use for it may be a flush in the pan. Hence, when understanding conventionalization we should not just focus on the activation aspect, but should also take diachronic temporal information into consideration.

The accumulated temporal information can be captured in the formula proposed by Wang (2010). The more temporal points included, the more stringent the measurement is. By calculating seasonal mean frequency divided by standard deviation of frequency, called as **Constant U** in Wang (2010), sudden burst in frequency can be distinguished from stabilization, for with more fluctuation in the passage of time, the value of Constant U would become smaller. However, the words used in Wang (2010) are selected Chinese Words in textbooks with reference to Newspaper Corpus, so these target words are the easily fluctuated noun[1] and a detailed analysis on linguistic factors driven behind has also been ignored.

In addition to life stages a word may go through, the underlying factors influencing the fluctuation of a word draw a lot of attention in quantitative studies. Recently, there has been wide interest in tracking the changing status of novel words across decades in the field of lexical semantics and corpus linguistics (Renouf 2013). It is believed that the deeper understanding of the mechanism underlying the life-cycle of a word, including its birth, settling-down, death, even its re-birth, etc., will shed new light on the coevolution of language and culture, as well as development of human cognition. Previous research touched upon this issue mainly focused on the frequency in diachronic dimension. Altmann et al. (2011) held interest in the mystery on why some words live long life, while the others "died" soon. They proposed that along the historical time scale, word frequency is the factor of word success; however, in short time scale the frequency of a word is determined by the amount of being used by different individuals (*indexicality*) and the range of being used in different topics (*topicality*).

Altmann et al. (2011) discussed not only the secret of being survived, the secret of brewing the birth of a word was also probed by analyzing the rising words. The rising words are words that are not used during the first year of the group, but are consistently used for at least some years thereafter (Altmann et al., 2011). Altmann et al. (2011) aimed to probe deeper into the understanding of what brews the birth of a word. They tackled this issue by analyzing the rising words: *product words (P-words)* and *slang words (S-words)*. The difference between product words and slang words is that the rise of P-words (e.g. Iraq) is driven exogenously by events that are external to the group, such as product releases or political policies, but the use of S-words (e.g. lol) is more endogenously influenced by the social values and language patterns of the communication group. Slang words are different from other words for being used to "establish or reinforce social identity or cohesiveness within a group or with a trend or fashion in society at large" (Eble 1996). The result indicates that for general words, if they are less frequently used by different individuals (indexicality) and in different topics (topicality), then they will decline in frequency, but, interestingly, different from the fate of general words, even with low indexicality and low topicality the frequencies of P-words and S-words still rise. The rise of P-words notes that exogenous forcing, social event, is efficient, and the rise of S-words shows that the endogenous forcing, social value, is also efficient comparing with the fate of

---

[1] Wang has also proposed exploratory study on verbs. However, there is no response from my written e-mail for permission in taking reference on this related study.

words in general, which is predicted to be dead if they are less used by different individuals and in different topics. This also shows that it is just similar to the life of human beings the life of a lexical item is also influenced by the events in the world. The strong influence from the events in the world and the endogenous social value are identified. This result highlights the important role of social events and the social value in influencing the rise of words.

Chesley and Baayen (2010) conducted a study to propose prediction model for entrenchment of borrowings by predicting loan words' 10-year later frequency with their 10-year ago frequency in French newspaper corpus. This is similar to the aim of this thesis; however, its scope is limited in loan words and the features proposed *(frequency, dispersion, sense pattern, cultural context, donor language)* are hard to be reduplicated, for there is a lack of ideal available diachronic newspaper corpus for Chinese. For works exploring not just loan words Kjellmer (2000) and Metcalf (2002) separately proposed theoretical hypothesis on conditions influencing words' stabilization on being passed down over generation. Kjellmer (2000) presented thirteen conditions in assessing potential words. These conditions have been reselected and divided into five categories in our study: semantic, phonological, morphological, and graphematic conditions, and others, such as prestige. Kjellmer (2000) emphasizes on "pre-existing semantic pattern" such as the suffix " –able: capable of being V-ed." However, factors like this may not be suitable for linguistic context in Chinese.

Metcalf (2002) proposed FUDGE scale to rank new words from level 0 to level 2 in each factor and sum up the total scores in the end. The higher the scores are, the more likely the new words are able to survive over time. The FUDGE is acronym of its five conditions: *(1) frequency of the words (2) unobtrusiveness: a successful word should not be exotic or too cleverly coined (3) diversity of users and situations (4) generation of other forms and meanings, namely the productivity of the word (5) endurance of the concept, related to the concept's reference to a historical event.* Although Chang and Ahrens (2008) have evaluated predictors from Kjellmer (2000) and Metcalf (2002) empirically in predicting Chinese novel verbs, it needs some reconsideration on experimental design and on selection on appropriate corresponding linguistic behaviors. Besides, it is necessary to choose more linguistic driven factors and to be aware of calculating methods. For example, Barnhart (2007) has used multiplication on factors proposed in investigations (Sheidlower 1995; Barnhart 2007; Hargraves 2007; Metcalf 2007) as indicator for understanding importance of a new word for including in a dictionary. The factors include: *"number of forms of target words," "frequency," "number of sources the target word occurs," "number of genres a target word occurs," "time span a word has been observed."*

As discussed in above literature review, most of the previous studies proposed life stages a word may go through. Other studies hypothesized or evaluated possible factors affecting the fluctuation of words' life cycle. Nevertheless, we did not find any publications that reported the linguistic factors contributing to the process of conventionalization. There was a noticeable absence of research projects tackling words that are not easily fluctuated with the changes of the world. Thus, in order to bridge this gap, we evaluated general words in different life stages with a variety of possible linguistic factors to find out contributors related to conventionalization of a word.

3 Method

3.1 Proposed life stages

As reviewed previously, past historical linguistics or neology studies provide diverse angles in understanding a lexical item. It still remains unclear what words have gone through before they are incorporated into the mental lexicon, a process defined in this article as being passed from one generation to another. Thus, potential stages words may iterate through are proposed to be explored in this work.

The "life cycle" of words described from previous studies may be overlapped in proposed stages or biased to their target words. Some may focus on mechanisms leading to conventionalization (Ke, Jinyun, et al. 2002), others may pay attention to types of conventionalization (Kerremans 2015), and still others may take separate perspectives in discussion (Schmid 2008). In this study the complicated delineation on a words' life proposed from previous studies is abstracted as a continuum including stages of "Birth," "Diffusion," "Conventionalization," and "Inactivation". It is assumed that the relationship of life stages of words is more like a cycle, so words which are inactivated may be re-activated once the speech community decides to adopt it again.

Though this study is not going to touch on this issue in depth, we suppose that the path for inactivated words to be re-activated again should be called as "**reviving**," which includes three situations. The first one is when old lemmas are revived with a new meaning as in the case of 囧 which signifies "bright" in the first place, but in its reviving in recent years 囧 signifies "embarrassed," for it looks like an embarrassing face. This type should correspond to "Exaptation" captured in Historical Linguistics. The second type is when old lemmas with original meanings are revived for the need of speech community. For example, 中肯 means to recognize "precise saying," so it gets its popularity in PTT. Opinion exchanging in posts or comments is important on PTT, thus it is common to see people use 中肯 to recognize others' opinions. This reviving is different from the first one, for the reviving of 中肯 is due to its precise meaning, namely, its useful function in response is the reason why it is chosen to be popularly used on PTT. The third type is the reviving of those which once existed, but its function has not been in use as time passes by. For example, the "present perfect aspect" function of "有" once existed in ancient Chinese, but got lost; however, it has revived in present days.

Words belonging to the stage of "**Birth**," proposed here include lexical neology, morphological neology, and reviving old lemma (the "exaptation" proposed by Vincent (1995)). This proposed stage corresponds to "individual innovation" proposed by Wang and Minett (2004). However, this stage is hard to be captured. Unless they reach certain threshold to be diffused into larger community, they are only sporadically used in individual corpus, so we are not going to study their characteristics.

Words in diffusion should receive attention on studies of neologisms because Fischer (1998) has defined neologism as "A neologism is a word which has lost its status of a nonce-formation but is still one which is considered new by the majority of members of a speech community." Losing nonce-formation is reached if the speaker is aware of having used or heard the form (Bauer 1983). Kerremans (2015) described the attributes of "conventionalization" and "diffusion": "...conventionalization refers to the dynamic socio-pragmatic process by means of which a linguistic innovation becomes established in the language and the speech community..... diffusion denotes the dynamic spread of novel formations across the language and its speakers; it is therefore as much a socio-cognitive as a linguistic process, affecting both society and the language." The proposed definition to "**Diffusion**" here is that the words in this stage should be those that can be comprehended by certain groups of people and are highly activated in certain registers. Namely, diffused words should be the fashion words that have been widely comprehended and used in contemporary. In this aspect, it is similar to what is described as transitional conventionalization in Kerremans, but "diffused words" defined here should not be limited to those born from social events. Hsu (1999) proposed that we should observe words that have existed for around ten years. On the contrary, Guo (qtd. in Hsu 1999) has highlighted that new words should be those with freshness. Present study supposes that different study highlights different aspects of new coming expressions. The fresh words should be those which are just newly born, namely, the individual innovation named in Wang and Minett (2004). What Xu (1999) have identified should be more diffused ones. We suppose that the diffused ones are actually the focal point in studying neologisms, for neologisms are not just about new words but those which have lost their nonce status in formation as well as are becoming established in language and used by most members in speech community (Fischer 1998; Hohenhaus 2005).

"**Conventionalization**" proposed here is different from the complicated levels in Kerremans (2015), but is closer to the "language acquisition" proposed in

Wang and Minett (2004). Wang and Minett (2004) adopt computational linguistic method in simulating how the first word emerged. They describe stages of emergent words as: individual innovation→diffusion→language acquisition. Present work proposes that the stage of "language acquisition" means that expressions are recognized to enter into the lexicon, for they are conventionalized and can be passed from one generation to the next generation. Namely, conventionalized words should be passed from generation to generation. Kerremans (2015) has proposed that transitional conventionalization is characterized by a sudden significant increase in frequency and diffusion into various types of source and fields of discourse. The frequency curve shows one steep rise and declines within a short period. Most occurrences are strongly linked to the coinage event. Such words may then become inactivated, or re-appear because the same or similar events occur (semi-conventionalization). There is no clear quantitative threshold between diffusion and recurrent semi-conventionalization, though Kerremans (2015) has pointed out that whether the diffused words become established as recurrent semi-conventionalized words depends on the regularity of recurrence and the degree of intensity. However, we argue that words behave this way are only observed in a short time period, so they should be categorized as diffusion words for an increase in use does not indicate its being stabilized. **"Conventionalization"** is proposed here to be defined as words being stably used across different registers and across generations. The other stage proposed is **"Inactivation,"** which should be those which are comprehensible but less active in being used. On the other hand, stabilization in use, which is usually viewed as one of stages in many studies, is assumed here to be the behavioral indicator of whether a word is conventionalized or not, for stabilization in us indicates not only activation in frequency but also temporal information. Thus, a highly activated word does not resemble its being conventionalized, for it may be just a momentary burst in frequency. Similarly, if a lexical item is less active in its total frequency, but is stably used over time, then it is conventionalized, though it may be inactivated. But, it should be notable that the observational resource used is the synchronic PTT corpus, so the diffused words may reflect similar stabilized situation as the highly conventionalized lexical items, for the diffused words are in fact diffused in this speech community. Thus, the distinction between diffused and conventionalized words will be further evaluated statistically.

To sum up, to sketch linguistic characteristics distinguishing conventionalized and diffused words we would like to focus on the two stages, "Diffusion" and "Conventionalization." The former is defined as the situation where the words can be comprehended by certain groups of people and are highly activated in certain registers. The latter is proposed here to be defined as words being stably used across different registers and across generation.

3.2 Scope of study

While words are the observation targets in this study, it is hard to give a satisfactory definition of words for all languages (Cruse 2001). Word segmentation in Chinese is an issue that is still under debate. Evert (2005) has illustrated that even in English-speaking countries the "knowledge-free" approaches that segment words based on white-space and punctuation can have inconsistency such as in variants like "whitespace," "white-space," or white space." Chinese owns unique properties in syntax and in lexicon (Tang 1989; Yip 2000). This study assumes that every lexical item is encoded as one single semantic bearing unit. Given the fact that expressions used in real languages are diverse, instead of pre-defining the unit of observations, we adopt a functional angle in including expressions only if the expression can independently conduct functions in conveying meanings. That is, as Evert (2005) put in defining an umbrella term for multi-word expressions (MWE), "... whose semantic and/or syntactic properties cannot be fully predicted from those of its components, and which therefore has to be listed in a lexicon." Namely, a "word" is defined as a generic term for any minimalist independent construction that is used to convey communicative information, which is similar to what is proposed in Huang (2005). On the other hand, words encoded in written characters are important in natural language processing. Chinese characters own its unique status in meaning and sound bearing from its diachronic development. Hence, written forms in Chinese should not be excluded from being part of an important feature in studying Chinese language. Discussion of the variants of written forms would be included.

In addition to observation units, different from the focus of subjects in studying product words (P-words) and slang words (S-words) (Altmann et al., 2011), we will pay more attention on predicates. Verbs and nouns have been proposed to be classified by anchoring their distributional syntactic behaviors or semantic classification. Givon (1984) has proposed that nouns like "rock, tree, house" are "most time-stable concepts," and verbs like "die, run break" are "least time-stable concepts." However, we suppose that while core nouns or basic terms like kinship terms or body parts are long life, as reviewed in Section 2 most nouns may be easily affected by external factors, as shown in the potential influence from indexicality and topicality delineated in Altmann et al. (2011), the studies in Antoinette (2013) as well as in Kerremans (2015) (P-words, S-words, proper nouns, or fashion words instigated from popularity). Their target words more easily fluctuate due to external factors. Hence, the scope of this study focuses on non-nouns, the predicates from a syntactic angle. We include non-nouns in our list of target words. Without selecting on purpose most of words are verbs. In Chinese, some studies argue that verbs should not be distinguished from adjectives or adverbs. Verbs are relatively hard to be automatically detected for its significance in present core information in sentences (Aitchison 2003; Cook 2010). Though verbs are with significance in building sentences, verbs are three times less than nouns in amount (G.A. Miller and Fellbaum 1991). Similar amount gap is also shown in Chinese in our exploratory study on data from Google Books Ngram Corpus (GBNC).

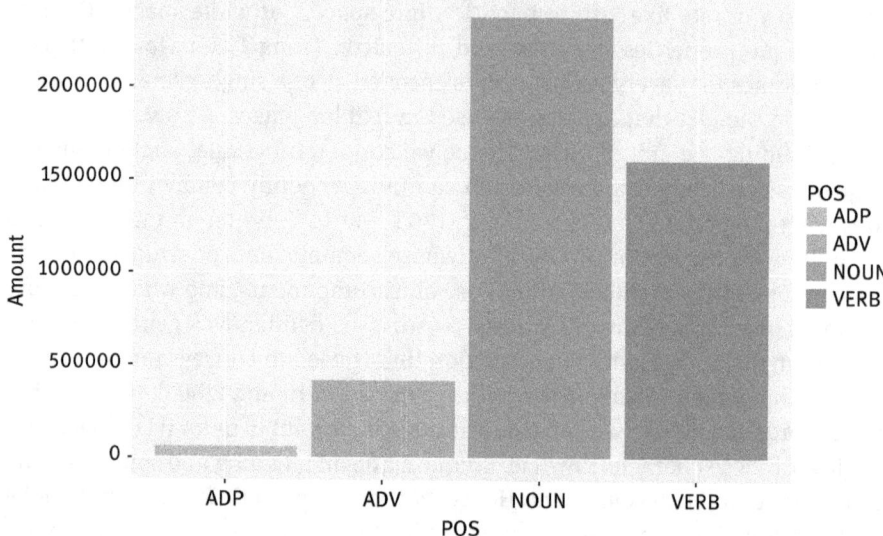

Figure 1: Distribution of POS in GBNC. Raw data for producing this graph are retrieved from http://storage.googleapis.com/books/ngrams/books/datasetsv2.html Copyright 2013 by Google.

According to the exploratory of data in temporal information provided by GBNC, it has further shown that the average "living span" for verbs is right skewed with extreme high outliers stocked around 400 to 500 years. This may imply that the emergence of newly created verbs is rare, and that the once created "elder" verbs are reliable in uses over centuries.

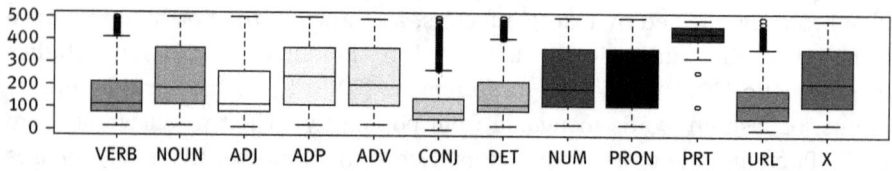

Figure 2: "Lifespan" of all parts of speech in GBNC. Raw data for producing this graph are retrieved from http://storage.googleapis.com/books/ngrams/books/datasetsv2.html Copyright 2013 by Google.

Additionally, verbs conceptually hold special status. As proposed in Schmid (2005), those who really create concepts are not those concrete nouns that denote already bounded objects, but the event nouns or abstract nouns carve segment from the flux of ongoing events. Thus, verbs are assumed to hold special functions in capturing experiential presuppositions from daily lives.

In addition to POS, temporal information, sense number, and syllable number are also taken into consideration in sampling target words. In order to include words as general as possible, words that originated in different time points, words with different number of senses and words with different number of syllables are all included. Syllable plays a role in Chinese. Words with richer senses or being homophonic are mostly monosyllabic ones, while words with precise senses are mostly multi-syllabic because the increase in component number in constituting the lexical item increases the appropriate selection of a particular sense. For example, the sense of 打 can be precisely anchored at the sense of "calling" in the multi-syllabic expression 打電話 with 電話 (telephone) composing this lexical unit.

To capture life situations of words it would be great if we have resources to see how a word fluctuates from its birth to its later development as in the way of Chesley and Baayen (2010) in comparing the first appearance frequency and 10-year later frequency of words. However, there is a lack of available diachronic corpus as the newspaper corpus they use, so we decide to compensate for this by selecting target words from a variety of sources, and then track down their fluctuation from the contemporary synchronic PTT corpus built by Liu (2014).[2] By doing so, we can ensure the diversity of our sampling as well as avoid weighted effects coming from external events. The retrieved sources and types of words we selected are introduced as the following.

Word type 1: Words once are new words

Resource 1: Wordlists adopted in Kim (2006) and Chang and Ahrens (2008)

The wordlists provided by Kim (2006) and Chang and Ahrens (2008) are those which first appeared 17 years ago, so they provide the opportunity for us to examine their situations of stabilization and inactivation from the present perspective, namely, their fluctuation. Meanwhile, they are good candidates as test data for testifying the representative and prediction ability of our proposed features because we are clear about its life situation before and after 17 years. These

---

2 http://lopen.linguistics.ntu.edu.tw/PTT/concordance/

words are "Collection of Neologisms I" updated by National Languages Committee around 1998 to enlarge the dictionary proposed by Ministry of Education. We select compound verbs with a single meaning in our target wordlist. The list includes both loan and non-loan verbs.

Resource 2: Newspaper
United Daily News (UDN), a well-known and well-run newspaper published in Taiwan since 1951. We consulted texts in 1951 and 2000 in UDN database to be inspired with words that were used over the past half century and words popping out in recent years in order to enlarge the generality of selected words.

Word type 2: Words in formal writing

Resource: Google Books Ngram Corpus (GBNC)
Formal writing, with the intention to be understood by readers, should be more careful in using words that can be comprehended by the audience of that generation, so the words used are more representative of that generation. Besides, formal writing is more stringent in using words and less easily in giving away words, so if words in such register have been lost, then they would also no longer be used in oral condition. Thus, we can have the chance to understand the potential common ground between new words and words that have fallen out of usage. We have adopted our words from Google Books Ngram Database (GBNC, Michel et al. 2011). GBNC has been available online since 2010, which supports data query across many languages. The huge dataset originates from the "Google Book Project," which aims to digitalize books from 1500s, around the Ming Dynasty to the present, and has facilitated many researches of digital humanities since its publication. As described in Lin et al. (2012), the new edition of GBNC contains data from 8,116,746 books, or over 6% of all books ever published. Data included in the corpus are only those n-grams that appear over 40 times across the books, where an ngram refers to the consecutive sequence of n items from texts (n = 1, 2, 3, etc.). Google Books Ngram performs tokenization and sentence boundary detection for Chinese with a statistical system. We removed the non-Chinese tokens that have been collected in books, so the number of tokens is 8,535,128, and the number of types is 57,089. The data were tagged with the universal POS tagset described in detail in Petrov et al. (2011). It should be noted that for the Chinese section, the data were retrieved from the books published in Mainland China in simplified Chinese. The data were transformed into traditional Chinese when adopted in current study.

Word type 3: Recently created words

Resource: Web

The words collected from GBNC are different from contemporary new words, which may cater for the new communicative needs in modern society, and are built up based on existing semantic representation, so recent more new words are formed via compounding. The collection of new born diffusion words mainly come from PTTpedia,[3] which records frequently used terms in PTT and PTT events. The Internet Fashion terms reported in news[4] are also included, though some of words are words that have already been recorded in Ministry of Education around 1998. As discussed in Kerremans (2015) Internet language has become the bed for giving birth of new words. Besides, Internet may even become the sources of news to the formal register like newspaper. Thus, the target diffusion words studied here may highly focus on new words from Internet.

Word type 4: Words bearing world knowledge

Resource: Chinese Wordnet

We assume that world knowledge a word bearing plays an important role in sustaining the life of a lemma and in giving birth of new expressions. World knowledge can be reflected in the paradigmatic contexts a word in, or the world knowledge connected to this word (number of competitive synonyms, number of antonyms, built on embodiment etc.). In order to cope with this issue, we choose Chinese WordNet (CWN) to collect needed information, for WordNet, compared with FrameNet, inclusively contains synonymous information (Baker 2009). We select words matching following qualities: (1) Words in different sizes of synsets (2) Words with variation (3) Antonymic or near-synonymous words (4) Words from the same embodied experiences. Synsets with large members is adopted to understand the potential competitions in lexical items. The largest two verb synsets were chosen, and two of the rest of synsets were randomly chosen. Besides, verbs in similar paradigmatic contexts may still have different behavioral characteristics, so we also include words from the same synset. One set of variation words is included. Meanwhile, words derived from "hot" and "cold" are also included to understand the potential semantic connection between antonymic or near-synonymous words and words from the same embodied experiences

---

3 http://zh.pttpedia.wikia.com/wiki/PTT%E9%84%89%E6%B0%91%E7%99%BE%E7%A7%91
4 http://dailyview.tw/Daily/2014/10/20

because competitions among synonymous lexical items have been largely proposed (Boulanger 1997).

3.3 Categorization on target lexical items

In order to understand factors contributing to conventionalization, words in different life stages proposed in previous part should be included. That is, our target words should include diffused words, words once diffused, and words which have lived over years. The words collected from resources mentioned above are divided into these three categories in order to meet our research purpose. "**Diffused words**" are those used on Web, so they are collected from either PTTpedia or news about Internet language. The once diffused ones are those which have been through the stage of diffusion, and may or may not be conventionalized nowadays. They are named as "**words After 1950**," for they can be first traced around 1950 in our resources. Words used centuries are for understanding elements sustaining the "living span" of words, and for easy comparison they are labelled as "**words before 1950**." The number of three types of target words is shown as in Figure 3.

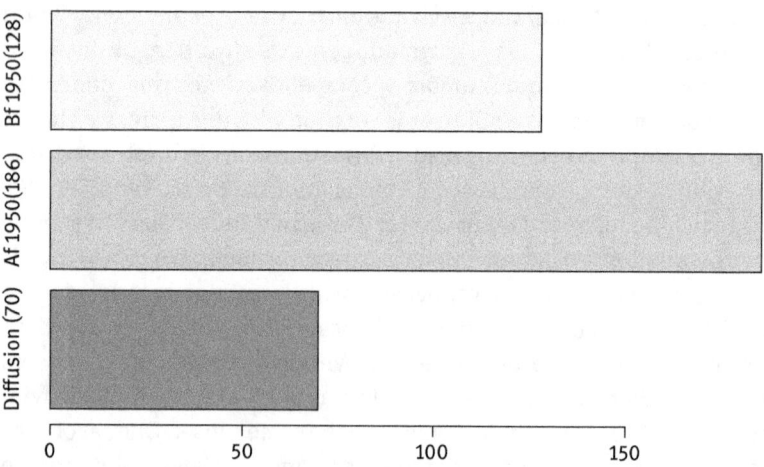

Figure 3: Number of three types of target words.

3.4 Operational value of stabilization

Frequency has been highly relied on as reference of inclusion for dictionaries (Cook 2010). Previous studies have taken frequency as one of the predictive features (Kjellmer 2000; Metcalf 2002), or as the threshold for deciding being survival or not (Chang and Ahrens 2008). Though frequency in the aspect of performance behaviorally represents the need of usage, it can also reveal information about our comprehension. The highly frequent used ones are also those comprehensible ones. Additionally, frequency represents not only the output result, but also the input influence, "frequency of complex words significantly influences the way in which we process and store them." (Plag 2006). McQueen and Cutler (1998) proposed that our mental lexicon can be accessed either by 'whole word route' (directly access to the whole word representation), or by 'decomposition route' (access to the decomposed elements). Degree of decomposability of a given word (Hay 2002) depends on relative frequency of the derived word and its base: the ratio of the frequency of the derived word to the frequency of the base.

If the frequency of derivatives is higher than that of the base, then it means the derivatives are no longer taking the decomposition route, but the whole word route, which seems to be a good indicator for defining being conventionalized or not; however, it is hard to be adopted in present study. The first reason is that in Chinese the definitions on "base" are still controversial. Besides, the elements for constituting disyllabic words are also included as target words in this study, so the f values of them are hard to retrieve appropriately based on this formula. Third, momentary total frequency may be hard to capture real stabilization in use over time. Neologisms are relatively less frequent for their "freshness" in coinage (Cook 2010), so to focus solely on frequency may not be reliable. In addition, though frequency does imply valuable information, stabilization is the real one that embraces both activation of words and information about temporal aspect of activating, so it is more suitable to be the target predicting value for modeling. Hence, we decide to adopt the Constant U from Wang (2010) to understand whether a word is stabilized or not.

Wang (2010) measures seasonal Constant U for words in teaching wordlists. She has claimed that with more temporal points in measuring, value of Constant U will be smaller, so the filter threshold would be stringent. Thus, instead of calculating Constant U by seasons, the values used here would be calculated by month. It is termed as Revised Constant U in the following discussion. For every lexical item its total frequency "x" (summed up from each month) is divided by the sum of total months in the data to yield an average $\bar{x}$. Revised Constant U is calculated as the average frequency being divided by standard deviation of "x", as shown in following formula:

$$\text{Revised Constant U} = \frac{\bar{x}}{\text{stdev}(x)}$$

It is found in our data that the correlation between Revised Constant U and total frequency is quite low, which signifies that these two values highlight different aspects of words. This corresponds to our assumptions that being used frequently does not mean being stabilized, for it may be just a flash in the pan. Meanwhile, small value in total frequency does not entail the word is not stabilized, for it can still be constantly used across temporal periods or when certain event occurs. The Revised Constant U captures the phenomenon named "Recurrent semi-conventionalization" in Kerremans (2015). The differences in the values of Constant U in posts and in comments measured monthly or yearly are briefly summarized as below. The correlation of Constant U in posts by year or by month is highly correlated (0.85203), which is similar to the situation in comments: the correlation of constant U by year and by month in comments is 0.9297476. The by-year correlation in comments and posts is less correlated (0.5964252), but by-month correlation is still high (0.7099764). The words captured as being used in posts are more than those in comments. The by-month Revised Constant U in comments is chosen as the threshold value in quantitatively modeling stabilization in present work, for we assume that posts may be closer to formal written register in its larger context of arranging information structure, but relatively instant comments may be closer to spontaneously instant response in oral conversation. In order to capture how language is used in a spontaneous way, the proposed **Revised Constant U calculated in comments by-month** is taken as the indicator of behavioral performance in stabilization.

3.5 Proposed linguistic predictors for understanding stabilization

Chang and Ahrens (2008) computed three prediction models on judging words' survival and failure. The first two are separately based on factors of Kjellmer (2000) and of Metcalf (2002), and the third one is the hybrid of the two. We adds extra features to complement the original proposed ones. The features used in the three models and corresponding or new features used here are summarized in following tables.

For clear understanding, operational definitions on features adopted in present work will be illustrated in the discussion. Six linguistic dimensions (phonology, morphology, syntax, semantics, pragmatics, and sociolinguistics) are all included. Under each aspect several features are quantified to evaluate. There are 18 features in total. When evaluating the features, we choose GBNG to retrieve morphological information due to the fact that it provides more longitudinal accumulation angle to reflect the activation of roots. To explore semantic relationships, we take CWN as the informative consulting resource. As for other pragmatic, syntactic or sociolinguistic factors, PTT is used for its rich contextual information (register, userID, topic types, complete sentential texts, temporal information etc.) There are 9 themes included: Games, Gender, Mood, Sport, Lifestyle, Business, Story, Ask, and Geography. The themes are incorporated from 22 boards. The 22 boards are: LoL, ToS, PuzzleDragon, MenTalk, WomenTalk, Boy_Girl, Hate, happy, Sad, NBA, Baseball, movie, Food, BuyTogether, home_sale, Stock, StupidClown, joke, ask, Kaohsiung, Keelung, and TaichungCont. Over one hundred million tokens are retrieved from PTT to evaluate our proposed linguistic factors.

4 Discussion

In regard to quantitative profiling, we have obtained about one hundred million entries of data from 2000 to 2014, including posts on twenty popular boards as well as all of the comments in these posts. Multifarious topics are included: games, gender issues, emotions, economics etc. Linear regression, logistic regression, and prediction model are the three dimensions probed in this study to profile the quantitative characteristics.

4.1 Revised Constant U in three types of targets

The overall distribution of the Revised Constant U for all target words shows that there is a peak for those with a zero Revised Constant U, which leads to the left skew of the distribution. Namely, according to our definition, many retrieved words are not stabilized. Having this information in mind, we look closer at lexical items as three types: Words Before 1950, Words After 1950, and Diffused Words.

Comparing the distribution pattern of the top 10 frequent words in these three sets of words from Figure 4 to Figure 6, it shows that **Words Before 1950** are used stably across time frame than the other two sets. **Words After 1950** behaves more sporadically than other word sets. The stabilization pattern of **Diffused Words** in Figure 6 is similar to that of **Words After 1950** in Figure 5, but words in the former are generally more activated in single temporal point. Comparing with Figure 4, the **diffused words** are less activated than lexical items that have existed over a century. This may imply that facilitated by the Internet community they originate from, the diffused words are being stably used, but they are still less stable than those which have existed over a century.

Table 1: Predictors used in current study and their correspondence to previous models.

Phonology	Proposed Features	Included in present work or not
Present Work	Number of syllable	Y
Features in Kjellmer (2000)	Ph1. It has phonological parallels in the language.	N: Do not meet characteristics in Chinese
	Ph2. It is easy to pronounce.	
	G2. Its spelling agrees with its pronunciation	
Features in Metcalf (2002): FUDGE	Unobstrusiveness	N: Do not meet characteristics in Chinese
Features in Chang (2008)		
Features in Kerremans (2015)		

Morphology	Proposed Features	Included in present work or not
Present Work	MO1: Component Richness of the monosyllabic verb or of the elements in the dissyllabic verb constructions	Y: Source of Data: Google Book N-gram Corpus (GBNC)
	MO2: Number of graphematic variation	Y
	MO3: Be encoded by Chinese character or not	Y
	MO4: Mixed originated morphemes or not	Y
Features in Kjellmer (2000)	M3. Its derivative affix is highly productive.	Y: Incorporated in MO1 of present work
	G1. It has graphematic parallels in the language.	Y: Incorporated in MO2 of present work
	M1. It has morphological parallels in the language.	Y: Incorporated in MO3 of present work
	M2. It follows morphological principles.	
	M4. Its derivative affix is compatible with the stem.	Y: Incorporated in MO4 of present work

Features in Metcalf (2002): FUDGE	"Generating new forms (level 2)" of "Generation of Other Forms and Meanings"	[Y] Incorporated in MO1 of present work
Features in Chang (2008)	Productive Affixes	[Y] Incorporated in MO1 of present work
	Words should not have morphemes of mixed origins	[Y] Incorporated in MO4 of present work
Features in Kerremans (2015)		
Semantics	Proposed Features	Included in present work or not
Present Work	SE1: Number of synonym	[Y]
	SE2: Number of near synonym	[Y]
	SE3: Number of antonym	[Y]
	SE4: Number of holonym	[Y]
	SE5: Number of hyponym	[Y]
Features in Kjellmer (2000)	S1. It has semantic parallels in the language. O2. It is concise	[Y] Incorporated in SE1 and SE2 of present work
	S2. It is transparent to the layman.	[N]: This can be reflected in the dissemination across language users and number of senses, for to investigate the meaning is morphological or metonymic originated is not so meaningful because based on frequency effect as well as studies on mental lexicon once the sense of the form has been highly activated, then it becomes automation, so there is no significant activating differences in reaction time as in those cases of entrenched metaphors.

(continued)

Table 1 (continued)

Semantics	Proposed Features	Included in present work or not
Features in Metcalf (2002): FUDGE	"Generation of Other Forms and Meanings"	[Y] Incorporated in SE1 and SE2 of present work
	Unobtrusiveness	[N]: as stated in the response to "S2. It is transparent to the layman." in Kjellmer (2000)
Features in Chang (2008)	Semantic Gaps	[Y] Incorporated in SE1 and SE2 of present work
	Transparency: we adopt identical operational definitions as in Metcalf's model, i.e., the meanings of transparent words	[N]: as stated in the response to "S2. It is transparent to the layman." in Kjellmer (2000)
Features in Kerremans (2015)	if there are no competing synonyms, then we consider the word filling up a semantic gap.	[Y] Incorporated in SE1 and SE2 of present work
	H1: Semantic ambiguity	[N]: as stated in the response to "S2. It is transparent to the layman." in Kjellmer (2000)

Syntax	Proposed Features	Included in present work or not
Present Work	SY1: Co-occurrence	[Y]
	SY2: Parts of Speech	[Y]
Features in Kjellmer (2000)		
Features in Metcalf (2002): FUDGE	"Generation of Other Forms and Meanings"	[Y] Incorporated in SY1 of present work
Features in Chang (2008)	Productivity: words having more than ten collocates would be scored as two; those with less than ten collocates but having more than three would be considered moderately productive and scored as one; those with less than ten collocates and having less than or equal to three would be scored as zero	[Y] Incorporated in SY1 of present work

		Included in present work or not
Features in Kerremans (2015)	H6: The early development of syntagmatic lexical networks, represented by collocations in the present study, promotes conventionalization.	Y Incorporated in SY1 of present work
Sociolinguistics	**Proposed Features**	**Included in present work or not**
Present Work	SO1: Loan words or not	Y
	SO2: Dissemination across users	Y Number of User IDs/total frequency
Features in Kjellmer (2000)	O1. It has prestigious and/or exotic connotations.	Y Incorporated in SO1 of present work
Features in Metcalf (2002): FUDGE	Unobtrusiveness	Y Incorporated in SO1 of present work
	Diversity(variety of users and situations)	Y Incorporated in SO2 of present work
Features in Chang (2008)		
Features in Kerremans (2015)		
Pragmatics	**Proposed Features**	**Included in present work or not**
Present Work	PR1: Number of Conceptual Relation Type	Y (ConceptNet)
	PR2: Number of Related Concept Words	Y (ConceptNet)
	PR3: Activeness in Different Writing Styles	Y Total frequency and Slope in PTT Posts: Excluding Gossiping for its inclusiveness in various topics
		Total frequency and Slope in PTT comments: Excluding Gossiping for its inclusiveness in various topics

(continued)

Table 1 (continued)

Pragmatics	Proposed Features	Included in present work or not
	PR4: Activeness in Different Themes	[Y] Number of Activation Themes: Total frequency and Slope in different theme boards (posts) (Including Gossiping for its inclusiveness in various topics) Posts take the lead in directing themes, so the information retrieved from posts.
Features in Kjellmer (2000)	O3. It has humorous connotations	[Y] Incorporated in PR2 of present work
Features in Metcalf (2002): FUDGE	Unobtrusiveness	[Y] Incorporated in PR2 of present work
	Frequency of Use	[Y] Incorporated in PR3 and PR4 of present work
	Diversity(variety of users and situations)	[Y] Incorporated in PR3 and PR4 of present work
	Endurance of the Concept	[N] This is reflected in Constant U
Features in Chang (2008)	Frequency: normalized ratio in the year 1996 in order to simulate the prediction process	[Y] Incorporated in PR3 and PR4 of present work
Features in Kerremans (2015)	H5: The nameworthiness of the represented concept or its salience in society promotes conventionalization.	[Y] Incorporated in PR3 and PR4 of present work

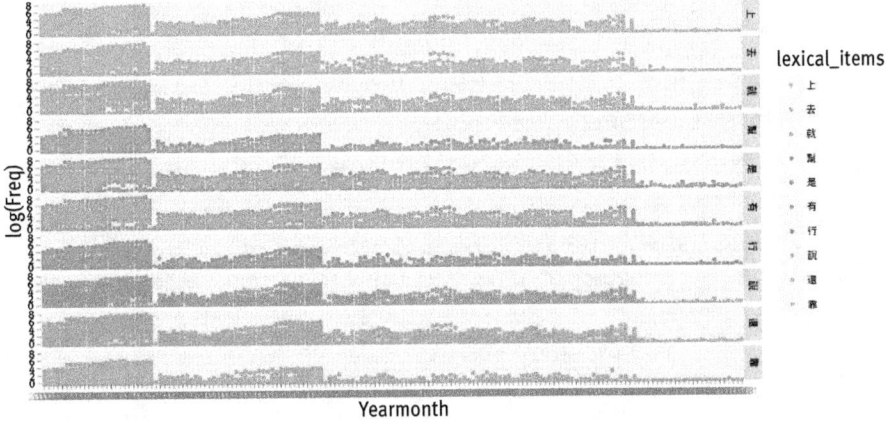

Figure 4: Cross month frequency distribution for top 10 target words before 1950.

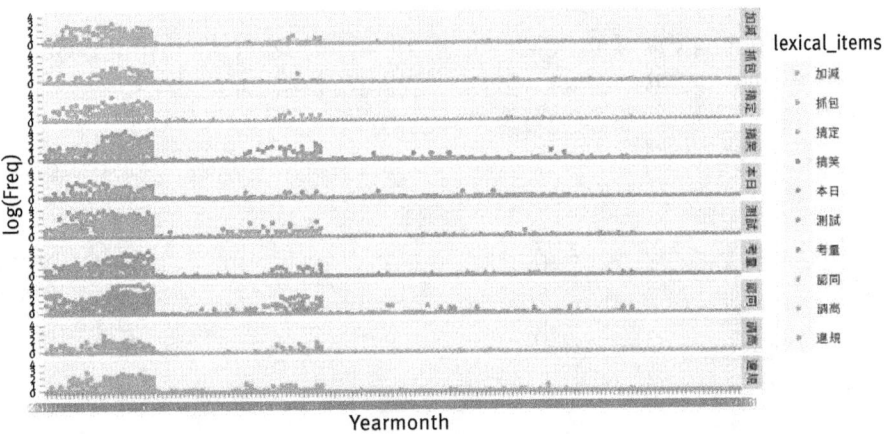

Figure 5: Cross month frequency distribution for top 10 target words after 1950.

Comparing the Revised Constant U in these three groups in Figure 7 we can observe that lexical items existing over a century are stabilized in nearly normal distributed way, but the diffused words are slightly right skewed and the words existed over 50 years are sort of left skewed. The boxplot shows that the maximum stabilization value of lexical items traceable after 1950s locates around the median part to the lexical items existing over a century. Those words that have existed around 50 years have the potential for resembling possible future situations of the presently diffused words. This implies

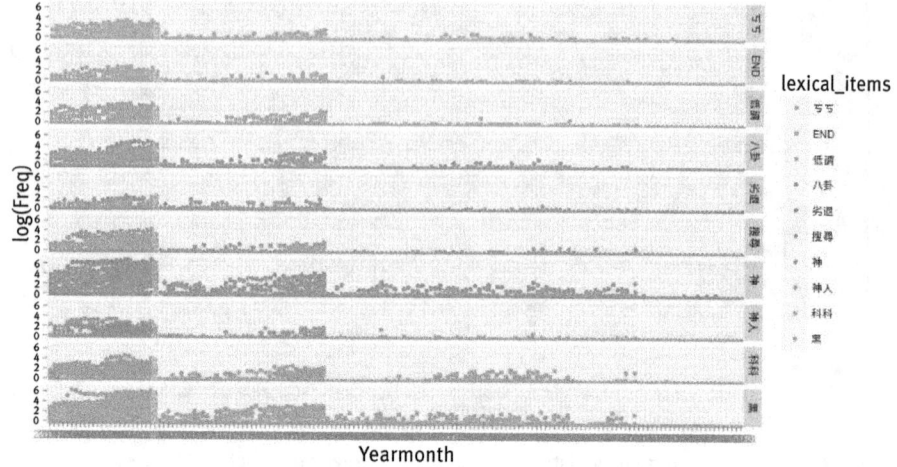

Figure 6: Cross month frequency distribution for top 10 diffused words.

the different degrees of stabilization distribution among the lexical sets. The lexical items traceable after 1950s are relatively less stabilized than those which have existed over a century.

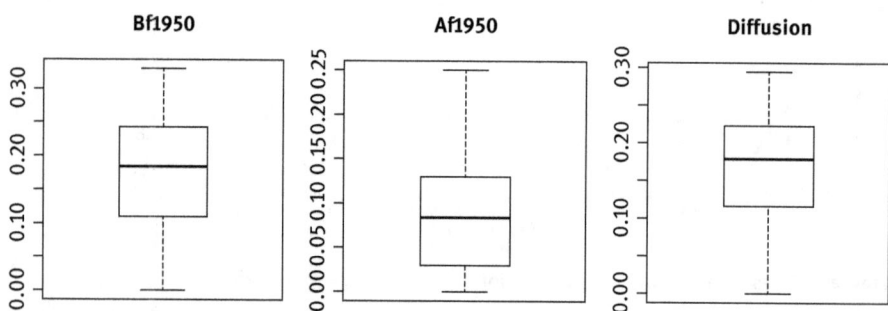

Figure 7: Distribution of Revised Constant U of three sets of target words.

4.2 Linear regression models of different linguistic aspects

In the previous section, the stabilization distributions of different sets of words are presented, and thus in this part with the aid of linear regression model we are going to probe into the distinguished differences and the linguistic factors driven behind.

Density plots of Revised Constant U for words born before 1950, born after 1950, and diffused words are explored based on synchronic PTT corpus. All of them are not normal distributed, so the log transformation is adopted as in Figure 8, which is still slightly left skewed though.

Such result is similar to the prediction model Chesley and Baayen (2010) built for understanding entrenchment of loan words. There is also non-normality in our response variable, the Revised Constant U. However, we still decide to adopt regression models to understand linguistic factors driven behind Revised Constant U based on following reasons. First, the non-parametric random forests conducted by Chesley and Baayen (2010) did show the reliability of the results from regression model. Second, we explore the issue with 384 lexical items and 19 predictors under 6 proposed linguistic aspects, which is different from their solely focus on main effects and two-way interactions. Third, given the fact that six linguistic aspects are testified separately here, the less ideal in residual plots of every model should be reasonable, for a single linguistic aspect is hard to solely account for the surface performance in Revised Constant U.

With the aid of quantitative model we can sketch different linguistic factors working behind these three sets of words and understand what factor can account for the stabilization of conventionalization. With concern on degree of freedom, the models are built separately for each linguistic aspect.

The result of the linear regression model for each linguistic aspect (phonology, morphology, semantics, pragmatics, sociolinguistics, syntax) is presented respectively followed with discussion on possible reasons driven behind.

The linear regression between Revised Constant U and **Phonology** of different target words indicates that number of syllable plays a relatively crucial role in explaining variations to words before 1950 (Multiple R-squared=0.3106) than words after 1950 (Multiple R-squared=0.163) or diffused ones (Multiple R-squared=0.05621).

One possible reason for this may lie in number of syllable. Different the other two sets, Words before 1950, as shown in Figure 5, are more monosyllabic words, which can bear complex meanings as a single unit. This difference may reflect the fact that the diachronic change of vocabulary formation, instead of creating more new sounds, people tend to either extend meanings of existed sounds, or to combine existed sounds into multisyllabic words to convey information. This explanation is in agreement with the angle of memory processing, for unit with shorter length is advantageous to be memorized. This finding may imply that there is certain limitation on sound creation, or more generally, the facilitating strategy of cognition, so instead of creating new sounds, we tend to use the rearrangement of existing ones to bear more complicated concepts.

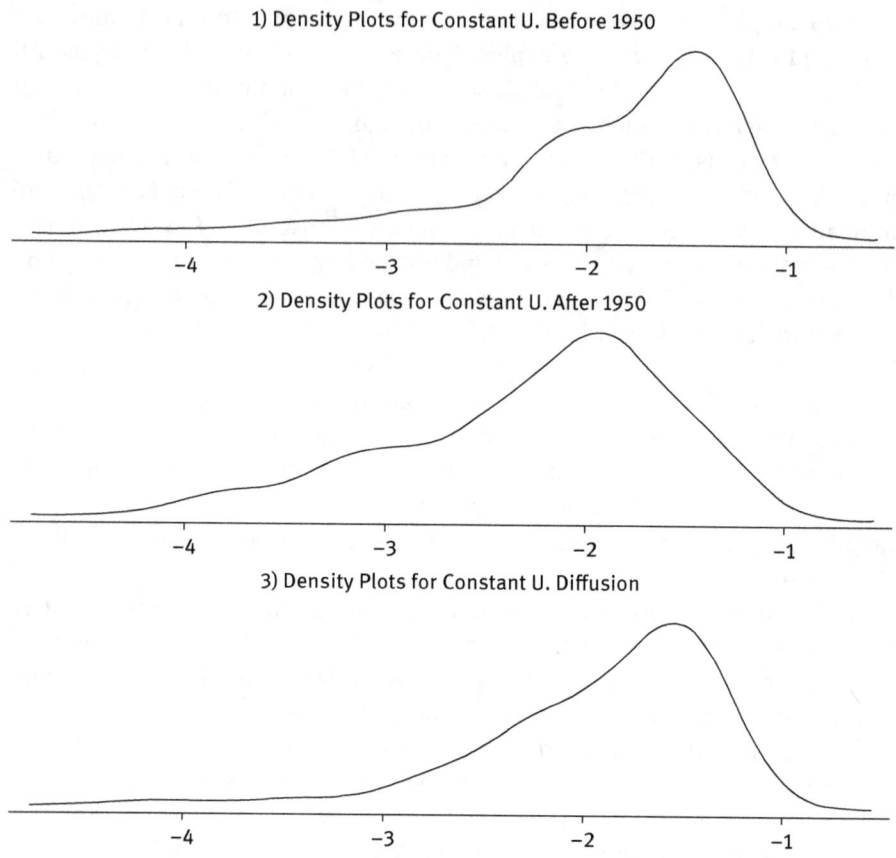

Figure 8: Density plots for Constant U of 3 Sets of Words: From top to the bottom shows separately the distribution of log transformation of Revised Constant U in Words Before 1950, Words after 1950, and diffused Words.

In exploring the linguistic aspects with more than one predicting factors (morphological aspect, semantic aspect, syntactic aspect, pragmatic aspect, and sociolinguistic aspect), backward variable selection starting with main effects and interaction for all predictors in each aspect is performed, and the Akaike Information Criterion (Akaike 1974) is used to eliminate superfluous predictors. The yielded formula of powerful predictors in each linguistic aspect for different target word types is different.

Morphological variables also show advantageous explanation ability to words before 1950 (Multiple R-squared=0.2012) than words after 1950 (Multiple R-squared=0.03522) or diffused ones (Multiple R-squared=0.1575). Among the predictors the relative important ones are type-token ratio of component richness as well as interaction between type-token ratio of component richness and realized productivity of component richness.

The realized productivity and token-type ratio are calculated with the assumption that a lexical item is easier to be passed down over generations if its components have constituted in other lexical items. This is due to the hypothesis that if one component, usually with rich senses, is being used to form disyllabic or more syllabic lexical items, then the sense of the new formed word should base on the sense the component owns. Thus, the highly activated in being used in consisting other lexical items reflect both the activation in this morpheme as well as importance in its sense.

Fernández-Domínguez (2010) compared the morphological productivity of lexicalized ones and new-formed non-lexicalized compounds. The same formula is used here: number of individual lexical unit being divided by the sum of frequency of the lexical units. Previous discussions all stand from the point of view of affixation or compounding in Indo-European languages, but there is less discussion in the compounding productivity or affixation in Chinese. To simplify this issue and to meet characteristics of Chinese, the measuring unit used here is syllable-based. Every syllable is viewed as a morpheme and its value is calculated. The quantitative result is not in line with the result of Fernández-Domínguez (2010). Their resulted values are relatively higher in non-lexicalized ones, the new words, than in lexicalized ones. It seems that in Chinese words before 1950, the more lexicalized ones, are more explainable by morphological aspect. New words in Indo-European may correlate with affixation or compounding, but in Chinese realized productivity plays a more significant role in the stabilization of lexicalized words.

Semantic variables also show significant explanatory ability to words before 1950 (Multiple R-squared=0.6074) than words after 1950 (Multiple R-squared=0.1042) or diffused ones (Multiple R-squared=0.3048). The linguistic properties involved here are sense number and semantic relationships.

When probing semantic factors, previous studies highly focus on the semantic transparency in comprehension: "S2. It is transparent to the layman," (Kjellmer 2000) and the "Unobtrusiveness" (Metcalf 2002). "Unobtrusiveness" has been interpreted as "the meanings of transparent words should not be specialized and must be clearly inferable from the form" in Chang and Ahrens (2008), and it corresponds to the "H1: Semantic ambiguity" in Kerremans (2015). However, these assumptions should be reconsidered for following reasons. First, in real language use, semantic ambiguity could be solved by contextual information. Second, transparency can actually be reflected in the range of use and in number of senses. Third, sense is tricky in its activation. For example, due to frequency effect, a sense of a form can become automatic, if only it has been highly activated, no matter whether it is morphological or metonymic originated. Namely, there are actually no significant activating differences in reaction time as in those cases of entrenched metaphors. When the metaphorical meaning is entrenched enough, its reaction time can be no later than the reaction time of activating its literal meaning. The quality or origination of a sense may not be the core factor influencing its being adopted or not because once adopted in use it is in use. With this in mind, in semantic part we pay more attention on the number of senses, or the relationships with other lexical items. Hence, the statistics may imply that the richness in senses and in semantic relations may be correlated to the constant use for words existing over centuries.

Similar to previous models, **pragmatic** aspect shows explanatory ability to words before 1950 (Multiple R-squared=0.7606) than words after 1950 (Multiple R-squared=0.3012) or diffused ones (Multiple R-squared=0.5003). Besides, the statistic requirements in residual plots are somewhat met compared to the residual plots in other linguistic aspects. Among the factors, the quantitative evaluation indicates that experiential conceptual relations, writing styles, and themes are important contributors in this linguistic aspect.

This finding shows that for words before 1950, pragmatics plays more significant role than other linguistic aspects. Different from semantic relations, pragmatically conceptual experiences are habitually linked, so this habitual entrenchment plays a key to revealing human cognition. The experiential concepts the lexical items involved can be achieved by retrieving data from ConceptNet5.[5] ConceptNet5 originally is built for computers to learn the world by constructing a knowledge representation network. Relationships among these words are not just based on lexical definitions but also include the general common knowledge, namely, the related experiences lexicalized in natural language. For example, knowledge about "jazz" should not just lexical defining like "Jazz is a genre of music," which is caught in the IsA relation defined in ConceptNet5, but also includes facts like AtLocation: "Jazz comes from New Orleans," or UsedFor: "Saxophone is used for jazz." There are total 21 types of relationships. The different types of relationships the target words used in this study are captured, so for words existing over centuries, accumulation of related experiences is quite significant in accounting for stabilization.

Information of writing styles and themes used in the present study is to realize the feature "Diversity (variety of users and situations)" proposed from Metcalf (2002). The source for different writing styles lies in posts and comments in PTT.

---

5 http://conceptnet5.media.mit.edu/

If thinking of genre as a continuum with one end as the written register, and the other end as the oral register, we assume that posts are closer to the written style, for posts are mostly intended for presenting information, but comments are more communication-oriented to give dialogue-like feedbacks, whose instant-response quality is more like what we do in oral conversation. Thus, the register a word is accepted to be used influence whether it is conventionalized or not.

Activeness in different themes provides information in exploring possibility of theme-bonding words, which is similar to idea of "topicality" in Altmann et al. (2013), but the calculating method adopted here is much closer to the way Kerremans (2015) adopts in calculating the number of themes that are activated. The judgement on activeness is based on the normalized accumulative frequency and slope proposed in Chang and Ahrens (2008). The long-existing words are more active in different themes.

In brief, conceptual experiences signify the cognitive importance of a word. When a word is able to connect to richer existed experiences or human daily activity, the chance to be conventionalized is enhanced. Similarly, being used in wider written style and being active in different themes indicate the applicability of a word. The quantitative testified evidence revels that words with applicable meaning that can be connective to human cognition are those which may be more easily conventionalized.

Sociolinguistic predictors show higher explanatory ability to words before 1950 (Multiple R-squared=0.4768) than words after 1950 (Multiple R-squared=0.2891) or diffused ones (Multiple R-squared=0.2599), but they are not so significant as pragmatic factors.

Dissemination of users is the factor taken into consideration in this linguistic aspect. Similar to the calculation of indexicality in Altmann et al. (2011) the dissemination is calculated by dividing the amount of users by the total frequency of the use of the words. This information is based on post author across different boards with the assumption that if a word can be highly disseminated across posts, then it should be significant in some way. On the other hand, though a single person may have multiple IDs in writing posts, the amount of data used is huge enough to minimize this bias. Thus, it shows that how diverse a word is in being used in different situations and by different people contribute a lot in conventionalization.

Different from previous models, **syntactic** predictors show explanatory ability to words after 1950 (Multiple R-squared=0.6629) than words before 1950 (Multiple R-squared=0.5029) or diffused ones (Multiple R-squared=0.5522). The main effects and the interaction among the three variables: parts of speech, number of before-word co-occurring type, and number of after-word co-occurring type are all significant in the model.

One significant meaning for this result is that members in Words after 1950 behave differently from the other two sets in cross month frequency as in Figure 6 and Revised Constant U distribution as in Figure 8. They are obviously less stable, but since they are once diffused words, parts of them are being gradually conventionalized, and parts of them are no longer in use, which makes them very representative in understanding factors accounting for whether words can enter the stage of conventionalization. Thus, the quantitative results indicate that parts of speech and co-occurrence play special roles in explaining words that are not fully conventionalized as well as are no more diffused.

Syntactic factors are less discussed in previous studies, but the attributes categories of words own should be taken into consideration because parts of speech may denote the specific functions and behavioral distributions of a word. Though there are other non-noun lexical items in our target words, most of which are verbs. Verbs are highly related to syntactic structure, and thus more complicated than nouns as indicated in aphasic studies (Hand et al., 1979). The proposed inclusion of parts of speech shows its significance, which implies that non-nouns hold quite distinct status in understanding word creation. As proposed in Schmid (2005), those who really create concepts are not those concrete nouns that denote already bounded objects, but the event nouns or abstract nouns carve segment from the flux of ongoing events. This is reasonable for non-nouns are usually less fluctuating for external events, but are created to satisfy specific concept illustration. For example, in Chinese we have the new verb phrase, 打臉 which denotes the concept of demolishing one's own words. Different from the functions of nouns, like 臉 'face', 天氣 'weather', or *KTV*, to denote a single concrete reference, non-nouns bear more complicated abstract concepts. Therefore, parts of speech could matter for influencing conventionalization of a word.

On the other hand, "co-occurrence" is also employed. Collocational links may be those optional candidates that are commonly associated as in, "rude adolescents," or "fresh-faced youths." Some frequent associations may become fixed order as in "bride and groom," or become clichés (Gibbs and Gonzales 1985; Fenk-Oczlon, 1989). Evert (2005) has introduced that "Collocation" can be explored mainly in two approaches: distributional approach and intensional approach. The former one proposed by the Neo-Firthians is to define collocations with observable quantity. This also becomes reference for corpus-oriented lexicographic in the United Kingdom (Sinclair 1991; Lehr 1996; Williams 2003). The latter one may meet requirements like "semantic non-compositionality, syntactic non-modifiability, and the non-substitutability of components by semantically similar words" (Evert 2005). Evert (2005) has termed distributional notion as "cooccurrences," which employs co-occurring frequency information and statistical association. Cooccurrences may be positional or relational (Evert 2005). Positional cooccurrences are co-occurred words within certain distance, the collocational span (Sinclair 1991). Relational cooccurrences are concerned with linguistic views in the structural relationship involved by co-occurring words. The issue is simplified here by calculating number of different types of co-occurrences to illustrate the horizontal connections of the lexical items. The co-occurrence used here refers to co-occurred words without setting arbitrary threshold on co-occurring frequency due to the fact that the co-occurrence phenomenon of some newly emergent expressions with low frequency may be easier to be filtered out, for it is hard to compute meaningful association scores for less frequent data (Evert 2005; Cook 2010). The same 22 boards are used for calculating co-occurrence from comments in PTT.

The result of co-occurrence quantitatively verifies the H6 in Kerremans (2015), "The early development of syntagmatic lexical networks, represented by collocations in the present study, promotes conventionalization." Process of developing syntagmatic lexical networks in mental lexicon is called as network-building in Aitchison (2003). Its importance is shown from how children deal with words in similar sigmatic context, such as those near synonyms or antonyms. For both children and adults, collocations show certain degree of importance in words' identification and learning (Aitchison 2003). Thus, though some linguistics may devalue the importance of collocation by emphasizing selectional restrictions/preferences, and take the lexicon as a list of interchangeable words (Evert 2005), from our experiential result it is hard to deny what Firth (1957) has said, "You shall know a word by the company it keeps!" Namely, word meaning can be learned or reinforced from the words come alongside. This explains why the co-occurrence should be important in deciding whether a word will enter the stage of conventionalization. If it is able to co-occur with more different types of words, then it is more functional and acceptable to the existing mental representation.

To sum up, the quantitative model illustrates that linguistic aspects proposed here are more explanatory about words before 1950. Given the fact that words before 1950 are the conventionalized ones, we can find out the linguistic characteristics distinguishing conventionalized words and non-conventionalized words. The stabilization of words existing over centuries can be explained by phonological, morphological, semantic, pragmatic and sociolinguistic aspects. Some may argue that it is a words' constancy in use that give chances to establish various relations, to extend rich senses, and to accumulate pragmatic world experiences;

nevertheless, there are a large number of words created in every generation, but only a few of them are passed down. There must be some unique characteristics of the surviving words; their conceptual significance, for example, that leads to constant as well as irreplaceable use. In other words, it is the linguistic nature of the word that contributes to its being conventionalized to pass down to the next generation. Hence, the linguistic features of the word should be the causes of conventionalization rather than the effects brought forth by temporal accumulation of being conventionalized.

Meanwhile, except from syntactic variables, most of the linguistic factors are related to the conventionalized words, so it shows that linguistic cause to whether a coined word can be passed down and adopted into mental lexicon does exist. When comparing all of these factors, we can discover that words born before 1950 can be best statistically accounted by pragmatic factors, which account 76% behavioral performance of Revised Constant U. Differently, for words born after 1950, those which exist only about 50 years, syntagmatic predictors show explanatory ability. These two results imply that words existing over centuries are highly correlated with rich pragmatic experiences accumulated in daily life as well as relevant to used contexts selected by language users. Thus, possibility of habitual experiential association plays an important role in understanding whether a word can live longer and be used from generation to generation. To be used in a variety of contexts highlights the adoptive ability of the word in language and its important role in conveying messages. On the contrary, for words coined in more recent years the syntactic compatibility is the key. Types of word collocating with the target become an important indicator. With the temporal information and the correlated linguistic features we may conclude that the usability of lexical expressions may first be decided by their compatibility with already existing words. Such compatibility is more than being paradigmatically antonymous or synonymous, but more about whether the target words can cooperate with other words semantically and syntactically.

To sum up, a word with stronger structural compatibility means that the word is more likely to be accepted by the lexicon. Then, the further sustainability relies on deeper entrenchment with world knowledge as well as suitability in being used in different registers as indicated by the results of Words before 1950. The results in this section show that as the days progress the important factor influencing life of a word may move from more context-limited syntactic relation to broader pragmatic information related to world knowledge we have entrenched with the word. A word is more than a sign carrying literal meanings, but a crystal of human cognition, experience, and world knowledge.

4.3 Logistic regression model for features of conventionalized words

In the previous section, we have evaluated linguistic variables driven behind conventionalization. However, when facing the issue of conventionalization, the difference between conventionalized words and diffused words still remain unclear. A logistic linear regression model is conducted, in which words before 1950 are viewed as conventionalized, and diffused words are viewed as not conventionalized in order to look deeper in statistically significant features of conventionalized words.

The main effects are evaluated except the total number of semantic relations because it is statistically collinearity with other semantic variables. According to the parametric statistic Wald test, "number of syllables," "number of synonymic relations," "number of near synonyms," "whether it is actively used in content of comments," and "whether it is from other language" are variables statistically significant in distinguishing these two sets of words. In logistic model, R^2 indicates how accurate the predictions of the model are. The R^2 in our model is higher than 0.5, so the accuracy concurred. C is the index for concordance between predicted probability and observed responses. If its value is above 0.8, then it may indicate the model has real predictive capacity. D_{xy} is a rank correlation between predicted probabilities and observed responses, which is 0.751. The values R^2, C, and D_{xy} are high. They are gauging values of building a model, so the conclusion drawn from this model may have its reliability. The bootstrap validation test also indicates reasonability of the current model. The fast backwards elimination algorithm reports that all predictors are retained. This indicates that though behaviorally with similar performance on Revised Constant U, these two sets of words are different in linguistic aspects. Hence, "number of syllables," "number of synonymic relations," "number of near synonyms," "whether it is actively used in content of comments," and "whether it is from other language" are indicators to sketch the differences between conventionalized words and not conventionalized ones.

Figure 9 illustrates the different characteristics between conventionalized words and not conventionalized ones. The conventionalized words are more monosyllabic words, but the recent diffused words are with various syllabic combinations. On the contrary to what we find in number of syllable, the distribution of loan words has signified that loan words are more in not conventionalized words. This indicates that loan words are important contemporary source of inviting new words.

Results of semantic relations indicate that words born before 1950 are with more near synonyms, antonyms and hypernyms than others. The synonymic relations also show similar trend with richer information for words existing over

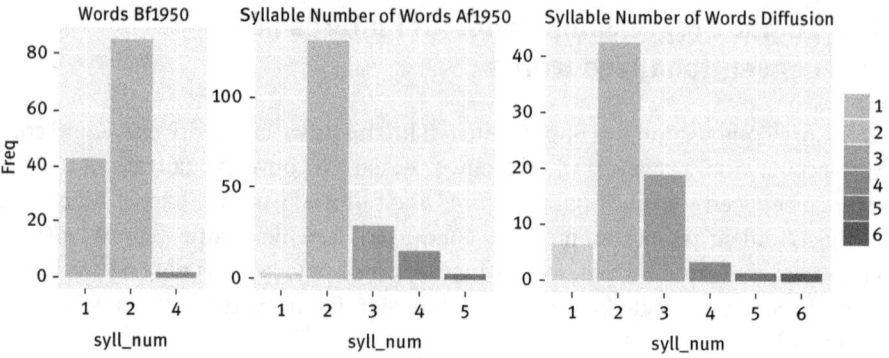

Figure 9: Number of syllables for three sets of target words.

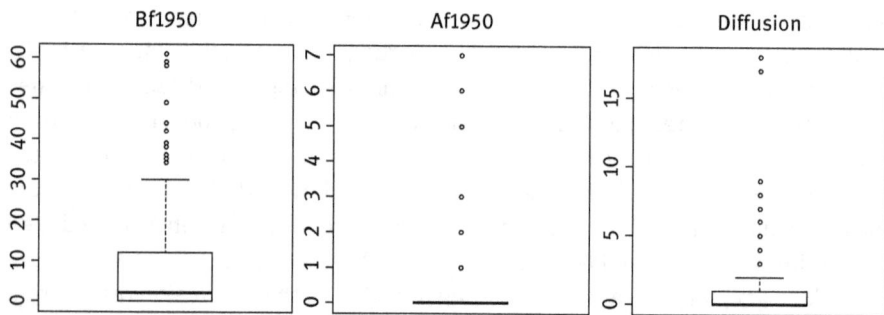

Figure 10: Distribution of number of involved synonymous relation.

centuries as in Figure 10. This is reasonable for conventionalized words may develop their semantic network as time goes by.

Activeness in posts and comments shows differences across sets of words. The activeness defined here refers to the threshold value proposed by Chang and Ahrens (2008). If the target word is active in one of the retrieved themes in posts or comments, then it will be categorized as active in that writing style. It shows that words before 1950 are relatively higher than others in both writing style, especially in post style. Diffused words tell a different story. They are relatively active in both styles than words after 1950, but less active than words before 1950. The more active style for them is in comments. This may imply two points. First, different usages of words in different oriented writing styles may exist. Second, if we regard posts as with information structure closer to formal writing, and view comments as with information structure closer to casual feedback-oriented dialogue, then it may imply that diffused words are more correlated in oral style and "diffused" in interaction.

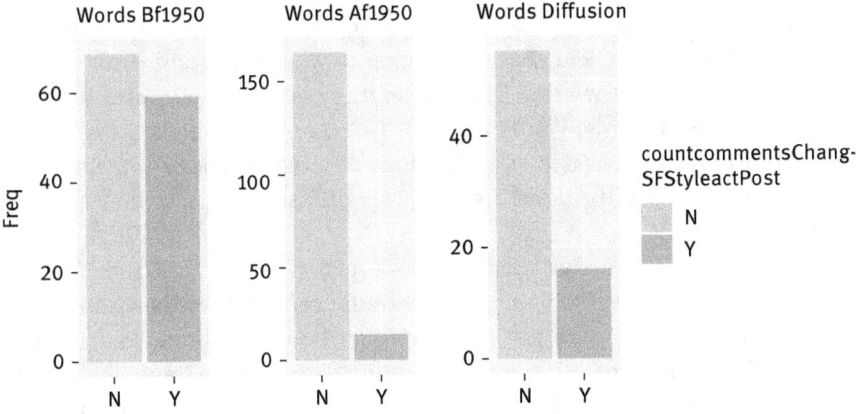

Figure 11: Actively used in posts or not.

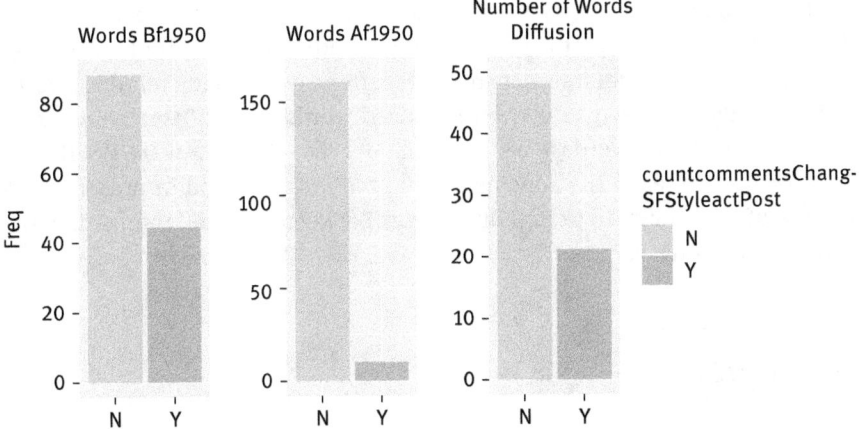

Figure 12: Actively used in comments or not.

To conclude, in addition to sketching what can account for conventionalization, we also illustrate the significant distinguishing characteristics: phonological syllable, semantic aspects, pragmatic writing style, and sociolinguistic loan words. These are statistically significant factors making conventionalized and not conventionalized words different.

4.4 Application: Conventionalization prediction

We decide to use a quantitative prediction model to testify the applicability from our analysis on conventionalization. It may be inappropriate to build a single model to all target words because the diversity of words included in the present work. Words born before 1950 are those similar to what Wang and Minett (2004) called as "first emergent words." They are earlier coined for purposes different from recent diffused words. Words born after 1950 are characteristically similar to recent diffused words as shown in previous discussion. They can better shed lights in understanding the future life of present diffused words, so they are used for a logistic model.

Words after 1950 are classified into two sets. Words with a zero Revised Constant U are considered to be not conventionalized, and words with Revised Constant U higher than zero are considered to be conventionalized. Among the total 180 lexical items, 37 are unconventionalized and 143 are conventionalized. Though this is a small data set, they are still randomly split into test data and training data. With stepwise back selection it shows that the number of co-occurring words before target word is singly good enough as a predictor. The accuracy on test data is 0.7955. This result could further ensure that syntactic feature hold eminent status in anchoring whether a word could be conventionalized. In order to make sure its real effect from syntagmatic relation, words born before 1950 are used as conventionalized words and diffused words used as unconventionalized words to testify the model. The accuracy is 0.6335. Hence, we may be able to reach the conclusion that the factors found in present work are explanatory enough to sketch differences between conventionalization and unconventionalization.

5 Conclusion

Little research in the past has been done to delineate the picture of fluctuation of lexical items. The generality of included target words, their temporal information and other linguistic aspects have rarely been considered in exploring the conventionalization of a word. Therefore, this study contributes to provide quantitative profiling along with qualitative linguistic interpretations for the understanding of factors involved in the process of conventionalization.

Linear regression model is used to highlight the significant linguistic predictor variables for words at different temporal points. The result indicates that pragmatic information can best account for behavioral performance of words over a century, while syntactical one best captures those which were once diffused words sixty years ago, but now fluctuate differently in use. This implies that words that live longer may be correlated with rich experiential world knowledge, but for those which are newly coined, their structurally syntactic compatibility plays vital role in deciding their future fluctuation in use. Logistic regression model is constructed to sketch differences between words over a century and diffused words. It is found that "number of syllable," "number of near-synonym," "number of synonym," "activeness in used in comments," and "borrowing from other language or not" are five statistically significant features of conventionalized words. On the other hand, words coined after 1950 and diffused words show similarities in their linguistic characteristics. That is, words coined after 1950 are once diffused words, so their later fluctuations are able to suggest possible future fluctuating conditions present diffused words may meet. Thus, prediction model based on training data from words after 1950 is built to foretell potential life of diffused words. It shows that "number of types co-occurring before target words" is statistically valued. To further testify, words that have existed over hundreds of years, and recent diffused words are taken as test data. The accuracy of the test result yields up to 63%.

Though there are still many directions for further studies ahead, factors influencing conventionalization, statistically significant features of conventionalized words, and results of a prediction model all throw some light on how linguistic characteristics driven behind lexical conventionalization.

References

Aitchison, & Lewis. 1996. *The mental word web: Forgeting the links.* Svartvik.
Aitchison, J. 2001. *Language change: progress or decay?* Cambridge University Press.
Aitchison, J. (2003). Words in the mind: an introduction to the mental lexicon. Oxford: Blackwell.
Aitchison, J. 2012. *Words in the mind: an introduction to the mental lexicon.* Chichester, West Sussex; Malden, MA: Wiley-Blackwell.
Akaike, H. 1974. A new look at the statistical model identification. *IEEE Transactions on Automatic Control 19.* 716–723.
Algeo, J. 1980. Where do all the new words come from. *American Speech 55*(4). 264–277.
Altmann E.G., Zakary L. & Whichard Motter A.E. 2013. Identifying Trends in Word Frequency Dynamics. *Journal of Statistical Physics 151*(1–2). 277–288.
Altmann E.G., Pierrehumbert J.B. & Motter A.E. 2011. Niche as a determinant of word fate in online groups. *PloS one 6*(5).
Baayen R. H. 2009. Corpus linguistics in morphology: morphological productivity. In *Corpus linguistics. An international handbook.* 900–919.
Baker, Collin F., and Christiane Fellbaum. "WordNet and FrameNet as complementary resources for annotation." Proceedings of the third linguistic annotation workshop. Association for Computational Linguistics, 2009.
Barnhart 2007. A calculus for new words. *Dictionaries*(28). 132–138.
Barnhart C. 1978. American lexicography, 1945–1973. *American Speech 53*(2). 83–140.
Bauer. 1983. *English Word-formation.* Cambridge University Press, Cambridge.

Betz W. 1949. *Deutsch und Lateinisch: Die Lehnbildungen der althochdeutschen Benediktinerregel*. Bonn: Bouvier.

Boulanger V. 1997. *What Makes a Coinage Successful?: The Factors Influencing the Adoption of English New Words*. University of Georgia.

Brekle H. 1978. Reflections on the conditions for the coining and understanding of nominal compounds. In U. Wolfgang & W. Meid (eds.). *Proceedings of the 12th International Congress of Linguists*. 68–77. Innsbruck: Universitätsverlag Innsbruck.

Brinton L. 2002. Grammaticalization versus lexicalization reconsidered: on the 'late' use of temporal adverbs. In T. Fanego, L.-C. M.J., & J. Pérez-Guerra (eds.). *English historical suntax and morphology: selected papers from 11ICEHL*. 67–97. Amsterdam: Benjamins.

Brinton L. & Dieter S. 1995. Functional renewal. In *Andersen, Amstertam studies in the theory and history of linguistic science series*. 33–47.

Caramazza, A. 1997. How many levels of processing are there in lexical access? *Cognitive Neuropsychology*(14). 177–208.

Ceng, W.-X. 2013. Huayu baqian ci cihui fanji yanjiu [Classification on Chinese 8,000 Vocabulary]. *Teaching Chinese as Second Language*. 23–35.

Chang, P, & Ahrens, K. 2008. Towards a Model for the Prediction of Chinese Novel Verbs. *PACLIC*. 131–140.

Chao, Y. 1976. *Aspects of Chinese sociolinguistics: essays (Vol. 9)*. Stanford University Press.

Charles,W. & Miller G. 1989. Contexts of antonymous adjectives. *Applied Psycholinguistics*(10). 357–375.

Chesley, P. & Baayen, R. H. 2010. Predicting new words from newer words: Lexical borrowings in French. *Linguistics 48*(6). 1343–1374.

Choueka Y., Klein, S. & Neuwitz E. 1983. Automatic retrieval of frequent idiomatic and collocational expressions in a large corpus. *Journal of the Association for Literary and Linguistic Computing 4*.

Church K. W. 1990. Word association norms, mutual information, and lexicography. *Computational Linguistics 16*(1). 22–29.

Church K., Gale W. A., Hanks P. & Hindle, D. 1991. Using statistics in lexical analysis. In *Lexical Acquisition: Using On-line Resources to Build a Lexicon*. 115–164. Lawrence Erlbaum.

Cook P. 2010. *Exploiting linguistic knowledge to infer properties of neologisms*. University of Toronto.

Croft, William. 2000. Explaining Language Change. An Evolutionary Perspective, ch. 5. Form-function reanalysis. Harlow: Longman, 117–144.

Cruse. 1992. Antonymy revistited: Some thoughts on the relationship between words and concepts. In *Frames, Fields, and Contrasts*. 289–306. Hillsdale, NJ: Lawrence Erlbaum associates.

Cruse. 2001. The lexicon. In Mark Aronoff and Janie Rees-Miller. In *The Handbook of Linguistics*. 238–264. Blackwell Publishers Inc., Malden, MA.

Cruse. 2011. *Meaning in Language: An Introduction to Semantics and Pragmatics*. Oxford:Oxford University Press.

Donovan R. & O'Neil M. 2008. A systematic approach to the selection of neologisms for inclusion in a large monolingual dictionary. *Proceedings of the 13th Euralex International Congress*. 571–579. Barcelona.

Duckworth D. 1977. *Zur terminologischen und systematischen Grundlage der Forschung auf dem Gebiet der englisch-deutschen Interferenz*.

Eble, Connie C. (1996): Slang and Sociability. In-Group Language among College Students. Chapel Hill/London.
Evans V. & Melanie G. 2006. *Cognitive Linguistics An Introduction*. Edinburgh:Edinburgh University Press.
Evert S. 2005. *The statistics of word cooccurrences: word pairs and collocations*.
Evert, Stefan. "The statistics of word cooccurrences: word pairs and collocations." (2005).
Farrar S. & Langendoen D. 2003. *A linguistic ontology for the semantic web*. Glot International.
Fellbaum C. 2014. Large-Scale Lexicography in the Digital Age. *International Journal of Lexicography*.
Fellbaum L. 1995. *Morphological Aspects of Language Processing*. Hove:Lawrence Erlbaum.
Fenk-Oczlon, G. 1989. Word frequency and word order in freezes. *Linguistics*(27). 517–556.
Fernández-Domínguez J. 2010. Productivity vs. Lexicalization: Frequency-Based Hypotheses on Word-Formation. *Poznań Studies in Contemporary Linguistics*, 46(2). 193–219.
Firth J. 1957. A synopsis of linguistic theory 1930–55. In *In Studies in linguistic*. The Philological Society, Oxford.
Fischer. 1998. *Lexical Change in Present Day English: A Corpus-Based Study*. Gunter Narr Verlag, T¨ubingen, Germany.
Fischer O., Rosenbach, A. & Stein, D. 2000. *Pathways of change: grammaticalization in English (Vol. 53)*. John Benjamins Publishing.
Fromkin. 1971. The non-anomalous nature of anomalous utterances. *Language*(47). 27–52.
Geeraerts D. 2010. *Theories of Lexical Semantics*. Oxford: Oxford University.
Gibbs & Gonzales. 1985. Syntactic frozenness in processing and remembering idioms. *Cognition*. 243–259.
Giuliano V. 1965. The interpretation of word associations. In M. Stevens, V. Giuliano, & L. Heilprin (eds.). *Proceedings of the Symposium on Statistical Association Methods For Mechanized Documentation 269*. 25–32. Washington,DC: National Bureau of Standards Miscellaneous Publication.
Greenberg Joseph H. 1991. The last stages of grammatical elements: Contractive and xpansive desemanticization. In Heine & Traugott, *Approaches to grammaticalization*. 301–314.
Gross D. & Miller K. 1989. Adjectives in WordNet. *International Journal of Lexicography*(3). 265–277.
Halliday M. & Webster J. 2007. *Language and society 10*. Bloomsbury Publishing.
Hand, C. Rebekah, John D. Tonkovich, and Jean Aitchison. "Some idiosyncratic strategies utilized by a chronic Broca's aphasic." Linguistics 17.9-10 (1979): 729–760.
Hargraves, O. 2007. Taming the wild beast. *Dictionaries*(28). 139–141.
Harley T. 2005. *The Psychology of Language*. New York: Psychology Press.
Harris A. & Lyle C. 1995. *Historical Syntax in Cross-Linguistics Perspective*. Cambridge, UK: Cambridge University Press.
HaugenE. 1950. The analysis of linguistic borrowing. *Language*(26). 210–231.
Hay, J., & Baayen, H. (2002). Parsing and productivity. In G. Booij & J. Van Marle, *Yearbook of morphology* (pp. 203–35). Dordrecht/Boston/London: Kluwer.
Heine B. 1997. *Cognitive Foundations of Grammar*. Oxford: Oxford University Press.
Heine B. 2003. *(De)grammaticalization*. Kate Burridge and Barry Blake.
Heine B., Claudi U. & Hünnemeyer F. 1991. *Grammaticalization: A Conceptualframework*. Chicago: The University of Chicago.
Hickey R. 2003. *Motives for language change*. Cambridge University Press.

Hohenhaus P. 2005. Lexicalization and institutionalization. In *Handbook of word-formation*. 353–373. Springer Netherlands.

Hong, J.-f., Wu, Y. & Huang, C.-R. 2005. yitizi yu yiti ci cihui yuyi chutan [Probe on Variants in Chinese Characters and Lexical Items]. *CLSW2005*.

Hsu, F.-h. 1999. *tai wan dang dai guo yu xin ci tan wei* [Exploring the Contemporary Mandarin New Words in Taiwan]. National Taiwan Normal University.

Hsu, F.-h. 2006. *Taiwan dangdai guoyu xin ci tan wei* [Probe on Neologisms of Taiwan Modern Chinese].

Huang, C.-R. 2005. Hanzi zhishi bi oda de ji ge cengmian: Zi, ci, yu ciyi guanxi gailun [Ontology of Chinese Characters in Several Perspectives: Characters, Lexical Items, and Semantic Relations]. *International Conference on Chinese Character and Gobalization*. Taipei.

Hudson, R. 1996. *Sociolinguistics*. Cambridge University Press.

Hunston, S. 2002. *Corpora in Applied Linguistics*. Cambridge: Cambridge University Press.

Hurford, J. R., Heasley, B. & Smith, M. B. 2007. *Semantics: a coursebook*. Cambridge University Press.

Hurford, J., Michael, S.-K. & Chris. 1998. *Approaches to the Evolution of Language*. Cambridge, UK: Cambridge University Press.

Jarema, G. & Libben, G. 2007. Introduction: Matters of definition and core perspectives. In G. Jarema & G. Libben, *The Mental Lexicon: Core Perspectives*. 1–7. Oxford: ELSEVIER.

Jenkins. 1970. The 1952 Mnnesota word association norms. In Postman & Keppel, *Norms of word association*. 1–38. Academic Press New York.

Johnson-Laird. 1983. *Mental Models*. Cambridge:Cambridge University Press.

Jucker A. H. & Taavitsainen I. (eds.). 2010. *Historical pragmatics*. Walter de Gruyter.

Keller R. 1994. *On language change: The invisible hand in language*. Psychology Press.

Kerremans D. 2015. A Web of New Words: A Corpus-based Study of the Conventionalization Process of English Neologisms.

Kerremans D., Stegmayr, S. & Schmid, H. J. 2011. The NeoCrawler: identifying and retrieving neologisms from the internet and monitoring ongoing change. *Current Methods in Historical Semantics*(73). 59.

Ke, Jinyun, et al. "Self-organization and selection in the emergence of vocabulary." Complexity 7.3 (2002): 41–54.

Kessler B. 2001. *The significance of word lists*. Center for the Study of Language and Inf.

Kim, H. (2006). *Xiandai hanyu xin ci yanjiu* [Sutdy on Neologisms of Modern Chinese].

Kim H. 2007. *Xiandai hanyu xin ci yanjiu* [Sutdy on Neologisms of Modern Chinese].

Kjellmer G. 2000. Potential Words. *Word*(51). 205–228.

Klein D. E. 2001. The representation of polysemous words. *Journal of Memory and Language*(45). 259–282.

Kövecses Z. 2000. *Metaphor and Emotion*. Cambridge: Cambridge University Press.

Kreidler. 1998. *Introducing English Semantics*. London: Routledge.

L'Homme M. C. (2014). Why Lexical Semantics is Important for E-Lexicography and Why it is Equally Important to Hide its Formal Representations from Users of Dictionaries. *International Journal of Lexicography* 27(4). 360–377.

Lakoff G. & Kövecses Z. 1987. The cognitive model of anger inherent in American English. In D. Holland & N. Quinn, *Cultural Models in Language and Thought*. 195–221. Cambridge: Cambridge University Press.

Lakoff, George & Mark Johnson. 1980. *Metaphors We Live By*. Chicago:University of Chicago Press.

Langacker R. 1987. *Foundations of Cognitive Grammar, Vol. I: Theoretical Prerequisites*. Stanford, CA: Stanford UP.
Lass R. 1990. How to do things with junk: exaptation in language evolution. *Journal of Linguistics 26*. 79–102.
Lass R. 1997. *Historical Linguistics and Language Change*. Cambridge, UK: Cambridge University Press.
Leech G. 1981. *Semantics*, 2nd edn. Harmondsworth: Penguin.
Lehmann C. 1995[1982]. *Thoughts on Grammaticalization (originally published as Thoughts on Grammaticalization: A Programmatic Sketch, Vol. 1. University of Cologne: Arbeiten des Kölner Universalienprojekts 49)*. Munich: LINCOM EUROPA.
Lehrer A. 1996. Kollokationen und maschinenlesbare Korpora. *Germanistische Linguistik*. Niemeyer 168. Tübingen.
Lehrer A. 2003. Understanding trendy neologisms. *Italian Journal of Linguistics 15*(2). 369–382.
Lin J.W. 1994. Lexical government and tone group formation in Xiamen Chinese. *Phonology 11*. 237–275.
Lin, Yuri, et al. "Syntactic annotations for the google books ngram corpus." Proceedings of the ACL 2012 system demonstrations. Association for Computational Linguistics, 2012.
Lipka L. 1977. Lexikalisierung, Idiomatisierung und Hypostasierung als Probleme einer synchronen Wortbildungslehre. In K. Dieter & E. Herbert, *Perspektiven der Wortbildungsforschung Beitrage zum Wuppertaler Wortbildungskolloquium vom 9. – 10*. 155–164. Brekle. Bonn: Bouvier.
Lipka, Leonard. 1990. *An Outline of English Lexicology: Lexical Structure, Word Semantics, and Word-Formation*. Tübingen: Niemeyer.
Liu, T.-J. 2014. *PTT Corpus: Construction and Applications*. University of National Taiwan University MA thesis.
Love N. 2006. *Language and history: Integrationist perspectives*. Routledge.
Lyons J. 1981. *Language,Meaning,and Context*. London:Fontana.
Masini F. & Huang, h.-q. 1997. *Xiandai hanyu cihui de xingcheng: Shijiu shiji hanyu wailai ci yanjiu* [The Formation of Modern Chinese Vocabulary: Loan Words in the Nineteenth Century]. Foreign Chinese Dictionary.
McQueen, James M., and Anne Cutler. Morphology in word recognition. Blackwell, 1998.
Metcalf A. 2002. *Success, Predicting New Words: the Mystery of Their Success*. Boston New York: HoughtonMifflin Company.
Metcalf A. 2007. The enigma of 9/11. *Dictionaries 28*. 160–162.
Michel, Jean-Baptiste, et al. "Quantitative analysis of culture using millions of digitized books. science, 331 (6014): 176–182, 2011." URL: https://books.google.com/ngrams.
Miller G. A. 1990. Nouns in WordNet: A lexical inheritance system. *International Journal of Lexicography 3*. 245–264.
Miller, George A., and Christiane Fellbaum. "Semantic networks of English." *Cognition* 41.1-3 (1991): 197–229.
Milroy L. & Gordon M. 2008. *Sociolinguistics: Method and interpretation 13*.
Moon R. 2013. Braving Synonymy: From Data to Dictionary. *International Journal of Lexicography 26*(3). 260–278.
Murphy G. & Andrew J. 1993. The conceptual basis of antonymy and synonymy in adjectives. *Journal of Memory and Language 32*. 301–319.
Murphy M. 2013. What We Talk about When We Talk about Synonyms (And What it can tell us About Thesauruses). *International Journal of Lexicography*.

National Languages Committee. 1998. *xin ci yu liao hui bian I* [Collection of Neologismsl]. Taipei: Ministry of Education.
Norde M. 2002. The final stages of grammaticalization: Affixhood and beyond. In W. Diewald, *Typological Studies in Language*. 45–81.
Petrov, Slav, Dipanjan Das, and Ryan McDonald. "A universal part-of-speech tagset." arXiv preprint arXiv:1104.2086 (2011).
Plag I. 2006. Productivity. In *The handbook of English linguistics*. 537–556.
Plag, Ingo. "Productivity." The handbook of English linguistics (2006): 537–556.
Polguere A. 2014. From Writing Dictionaries to Weaving Lexical Networks. *International Journal of Lexicography*.
Renouf A. 2013. A finer definition of neology in English: the life-cycle of a word. *Corpus perspectives on patterns of lexis*. 177–207.
Renouf, Antoinette (2013) A finer definition of neology in English: The life-cycle of a word. In: Corpus Perspectives on Patterns of Lexis. Studies in Corpus Linguistics, 57. John Benjamins Publishing Company, pp. 177–208. ISBN 9789027203632
Rey A. 1995. The Concept of neologism and the evolution of terminologies in individual languages. In *In Essays on Terminology*. Amsterdam: John Benjamins.
Romagnoli C. 2013. The Lexicographic Approach to Modern Chinese Synonyms. *International Journal of Lexicography* 26(4). 407–423.
Rosch E. 1973. On the internal structure of perceptual and semantic categories. In T. E. Moore, *Cognitive Development and the Acquisition of Language*. 111–144. New York: Academic Press.
Sabino R. 2005. Survey Says... Gameday. *American Speech* 80. 61–77.
Schmid H. J. 2005. *Englische Morphologie und Wortbildung: Eine Einführung*.
Schmid H.-J. 2008. New words in the mind: Concept-formation and entrenchment of neologisms. In *Anglia-Zeitschrift für englische Philologie*. 1–36.
Sheidlower. 1995. Principles for the inclusion of new words in college dictionaries. *Dictionaries* 16. 33–44.
Sinclair John. 1991. Corpus, Concordance, Collocation. Oxford: Oxford University Press.
Speer, R. & Havasi C. 2012. Representing General Relational Knowledge in ConceptNet 5. *LREC*. 3679–3686.
Starreveld, P. A. 2004. Phonological facilitation of grammatical gender retrieval. *Language and Cognitive Processes* 6. 677–711.
Tang, T.-C. 1989. *Hanyu ci fa jufa xuji* [Chinese Semantic and Syntax].
Talmy, Givón. "Syntax: a functional-typological introduction." Benjamins: Amsterdam (1984).
Thomason, S. & Kaufman, T. 1988. *Language contact, creolization, and genetic*. Berkeley: University of California Press.
Traugot E. 2004. Exaptation and grammaticalization. In *Linguistic Studies Based on Corpora*. 133–156. Tokyo: Hituzi Syobo Publishing Co.
Traugott E. & Bernd, H. 1991. *Approaches to Grammaticalization*. Amsterdam: Benjamins.
Traugott Elizabeth C & Richard B. Dasher. 2005. *Regularity in Semantic Change*. Cambridge: CambridgeUniversity Press.
Ulrike O. 2010. Using Corpus Methodology for Semantic and Pragmatic Analysis: What Can Corpora tell Us About the Linguistic Expression of Emotions? *Cognitive Linguistics* 21(4). 727–763.
Vincent N. 1995. Exaptation and grammaticalization. In *Andersen, Amstertam studies in the theory and history of linguistic science series*. 433–448.

Wang Z.-m. 2010. *Jiyu shijian kuadu de hanyu jiaoxue changyong ci biao tongji yanjiu*[Statistic Information for Chinese Teaching Wordlists based on Temporal Information]. *huawen jiaoxue yu yanjiu*(4). 49–55.
Wang W. S., Ke, J. & Minett, J. W. 2004. Computational studies of language evolution. In *Monograph Series B*. 65–108).
Warren, P. 2012. *Introducing Psycholinguistics*. Cambridge: Cambridge University Press.
Weinreich, U. 1953. *Languages in contact: findings and problems*. The Hague: Mouton.
Williams, G. 2003. Les collocations et l'école contextualiste britannique. In F. Grossmann & A. Tutin, *Les Collocations: analyse et traitement*. 33–44. Amsterdam: De Werelt.
Wischer, I. & Diewald, G. 2002. *New reflections on grammaticalization 49*. John Benjamins Publishing.
Yip, M. 1980. *The tonal phonology of Chinese*. Ph D Dissertation, MIT. Published.
Yip, M. 1994. Isolated Uses of Prosodic Categories. In J. Cole & C. Kisseberth. Stanford,California: Center for the Study of Language and Information.
Yip, M. 2003. What Phonology has Learnt from Chinese.
Yip, M. 2007. Tone. *The Cambridge Handbook of Phonology*. 229–252.
Yip, P. 2000. *The Chinese lexicon: a comprehensive survey*. Psychology Press.
Yu, N. 1998. *The Contemporary Theory of Metaphor: A Perspective from Chinese*. Amsterdam: Benjamins.
Yu, N. 2002. Body and Emotion: BodyParts in Chinese Expression of Emotion. *Pragmatics & Cognition*10. 341–367.
Zhu, J.-n. 2000. Taiwan xiaoyuan xin ci de fazhan he dua jiaoxue de yingxiong [Influence of Neologisms from Taiwan Campus on Teaching]. *6th Global Chinese Teaching Conference*. Taipei.

Satoko Imaizumi
2 Typological study on expressions of possibility and their related meanings in English, Chinese and Japanese – How modality and voice intersect

Abstract: The purpose of this study is to visualize a conceptual space of "possibility" and its related meanings in English, Chinese,[1] and Japanese, and discuss what scales are necessary to define the concept. The visualization is performed by statistical semantic maps constructed by multi-dimensional scaling based on quantitative data of distance values between parallel clauses collected from a novel and its translations. Through an observation of the distributions on the three-dimensional maps, the three dimensions are interpreted as the scales of "event/speaker-orientation", "controllability by an agent", and "immediacy", respectively. The distribution of the marked forms in each language on the maps shows that in English and Chinese, the dimension of speaker-orientation seems to be important to their semantic continuity, whereas in Japanese, the dimension of controllability is more essential to the semantic continuity.

Keywords: semantic map, multi-dimensional scaling, event/speaker-orientation, controllability

1 Cross-linguistic diversity on possibility

1.1 Meaning of possibility

The first two definitions of "possibility" in the Oxford English Dictionary are the following:

(1) a. The fact of something (expressed or implied) being possible to one, whether through circumstance or power; capacity, capability, power, ability; (also) pecuniary ability, means.

---

[1] Mandarin Chinese. The text data of Chinese used in this study is in standard Mandarin as spoken in China.

Satoko Imaizumi, Hokkaido University, Hokkaido, Japan, satoko.nyt@gmail.com

https://doi.org/10.1515/9783110610895-003

b. in possibility (also later, in a possibility): in such a position that something (expressed or implied) is possible; having a prospect, expectation, or chance (of something or to do something).

The former concerns what is called dynamic possibility and deontic (or root) possibility. The latter is epistemic possibility, which concerns the degree of the speaker's certainty. These meanings seem not to be culturally specific concepts but universal concepts shared by speakers of different languages around the world. Wierzbicka (1996) includes *Can* as one of the "semantic primes", which is a universal set of innate concepts. However, she also mentions that *Can* is particularly difficult to identify, partly because it is often involved in complex patterns of polysemy and partly because its exponents often appear to be bound morphemes rather than distinct words (Wierzbicka 1996: 67).

There are several semantic origins of possibility in the world's languages. Heine and Kuteva (2002) list four types as sources of "ABILITY": "ARRIVE", "GET", "KNOW", and "SUITABLE". The English *Can*, for example, originally derived from a verb "to know". One of the Chinese auxiliaries, *De*, belongs to the "GET" type, and most of the Japanese potential suffixes are said to belong to the "ARRIVE" type. It is not unusual that different constructions which derive from different sources coexist within a language.

According to van der Auwera and Amman (2013), there are three types of languages distinguished by their strategy to mark situational possibility.[2] The first type includes languages that express situational possibility with verbal affixes. The second type uses verbal constructions including auxiliary and serial verb construction, and the third group uses other kinds of markers. Among the 234 languages surveyed in van der Auwera and Amman (2013), the second type is the most frequent, while the third type is the least. The strategy to mark epistemic possibility is also divided into the three types, although the most dominant type is the third type. English and Chinese belong to the second type, while Japanese belongs the first type. The verbal constructions that express possibility in English and Chinese are mainly studied in the field of modality, while the potential suffixes in Japanese have to do with voice. As is commonly known, modality and voice are different fields of linguistics; one is a semantic category, and the other concerns grammatical relations. Although the study of each field has developed in its own way, little attention has been paid to their mutual relationship (except Narrog (2010)). This study tries to seek a way to integrate the two categories through a semantic analysis of possibility and its related meanings.

---

[2] In van der Auwera and Amman (2013), the term "situational possibility" is used to include participant-internal/external possibility, as they all describe a possibility that exists in a given situation.

1.2 Possibility in English, Chinese, and Japanese

In English and Chinese, as well as many languages of the Indo-European family especially, possibility is an important concept in defining modality. Modality, which is often stated to express a speaker's (subjective) attitudes and opinion, has plenty of definitions presented in the literature. Among the huge number of studies on modality, van der Auwera and Plungian (1998: 80) define modality as "semantic domains that involve possibility and necessity as paradigmatic variants". They classify modality into four types as presented in Table 1.[3] Although this definition of modality is rather restricted, it is useful to show the polysemy of modal auxiliaries in English and Chinese.

Table 1: Modality type (extracted from van der Auwera and Plungian (1998: 82)).

Possibility			
Non-epistemic possibility			Epistemic possibility (Uncertainty)
Participant-internal possibility (Dynamic possibility, Ability, Capacity)	Participant-external possibility		
	(Non-deontic possibility)	Deontic possibility (Permission)	

1.2.1 Expressions of possibility in English

The English auxiliary *Can* was originally derived from the Old English verb *cunnan* which means 'know how to' (Goossens 1992). The meaning of this mental ability has extended to express physical ability and is further generalized to the use of ability in general. Participant-internal possibility including ability refers to a kind of possibility internal to a participant engaged in the state of affairs, as in (2).

(2) *I can lift this stone.*

Participant-external possibility, which is also called "situational possibility", refers to circumstances that are external to the participant and make the state of affairs possible, as in (3). Deontic possibility is a subdomain of participant-external possibility, in which case the enabling or compelling circumstances are some person(s) or some social or ethical norm(s) (van der Auwera and Plungian 1998: 81). Permission expressed by *May* in (4a) is an example. *May* was originally

---

[3] The original table includes the paradigm of "necessity", which is omitted here.

derived from the Old English verb *mæg*, which means 'have power to'. It started from physical ability and went through a similar development as *Can* did (Bybee et al. 1994: 193). Epistemic possibility refers to a judgment of the speaker, as (4b) indicates that John's arrival is judged as possible by the speaker.

(3) *To get to the station, you* can *take bus 66.* (van der Auwera and Plungian (1998: 80))

(4) a. *John **may** leave now.*
    b. *John* may *have arrived.* (van der Auwera and Plungian (1998: 81))

Bybee et al. (1994) present the path of semantic change of *Can* as Figure 1 shows. Table 2 summarizes the meanings that each auxiliary covers.

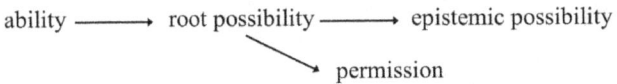

ability ⟶ root possibility ⟶ epistemic possibility
                         ↘ permission

Figure 1: A path to epistemic possibility (Bybee et al. 1994: 199).

Table 2: Distribution of *Can, Could, May, Might* (based on Li (2003: 64), modified by the author).

	Possibility			
	Non-epistemic			Epistemic
	Participant-internal	Participant-external		
		Non-deontic	Deontic	
Can	■	■	▨	▨
Could	■	■	▨	□
May	□	▨	■	■
Might	□	□	■	■

■ prominent marker   ▨ often used, but not a prominent marker   ▨ not a prominent marker   □ not used

1.2.2 Expressions of possibility in Chinese

Li (2003) studied Chinese modal auxiliaries based on the study by van der Auwera and Plungian (1998). According to Li (2003), auxiliaries *Neng, Nenggou Hui, Ke*, and *Keyi* that express ability/possibility cover the meanings as in Table 3.[4]

---

4 Li (2003) studies more auxiliaries, but here I chose these three which are more frequently used.

Table 3: Distribution of *Neng, Nenggou, Hui, Ke,* and *Keyi* (based on Li (2003:176), modified by the author).

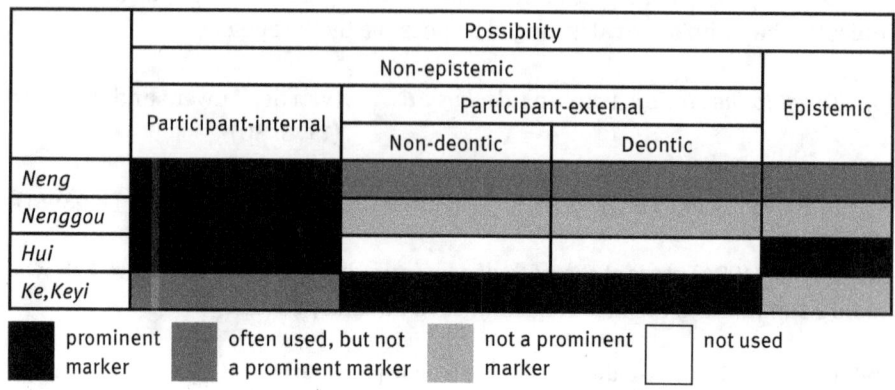

As we can see from Table 2 and Table 3, the paradigm of possibility is useful to systematically show how each auxiliary covers different meanings of possibility.

Chinese also has the potential complement constructions *V-de-C* and *V-bu-C*, which express participant internal/external possibility. According to Wu and He (2015), employing complement construction for situational possibility is rarely seen in other languages of the world, and is thus a unique phenomenon to Chinese.

1.2.3 Expressions of possibility in Japanese

Japanese uses the verbal suffix *-eru, -(r)areru, -dekiru*[5] to express participant-internal possibility and participant-external possibility. Among these markers, *-(r)areru* is also used to mark passive, spontaneous and honorific.[6] There is also a compound construction *V-kotogadekiru*, which includes a nominalization of the event by *koto* 'thing, event'. This can be attached to any verbs regardless of their inflectional pattern. Contrary to the common continuity presented in Figure 1, These Japanese markers rarely express epistemic possibility. On the other hand,

---

[5] Japanese verbs are divided into three groups concerning their inflectional patterns. *-eru* is attached to the Group 1 verbs (category of inflectional type), *-rareru* to the Group 2 verbs, and *-dekiru* to the Group 3 verbs.

[6] For passive, spontaneous, and honorific use, *-areru* is attached to the Group I verbs, and *-rareru* is attached to the Group 2 verbs.

they are continuous to spontaneous, passive and honorific. In (5b) below, the object of the verb is marked with the nominative case, the same as the passive construction in (5c),[7] as well as spontaneous (5d), and honorific in (5e). Spontaneous is defined in Shibatani (1985: 827) as "an event automatically occurs, or a state that spontaneously obtains without the intervention of an agent". In other words, as Narrog (2010: 75) says, "it indicates a lack of volition or control on part of the subject". In (5d), the subject who experiences the mental state is not (or cannot be) explicitly expressed. Instead, the object of mental activity ("the past") is marked with the nominative case. Thus, the agent (or in this case, experiencer) is deleted. This is parallel to the demotion of an agent in passive construction comparing to the active sentence in (5a). The honorific use can be considered to have developed through a pragmatic effect: it is preferred to avoid directly mentioning the respectful subject. Shibatani (1985) discusses that this correlation among potential, passive, spontaneous and honorific is based on "agent-defocusing".

(5) a. *Mary **ga** niku o taberu.*
    Mary NOM meat ACC eat
    'Mary eats meat'.
  b. *Mary wa niku **ga** tabe-**rareru**.*
    Mary TOP meat NOM eat-POT
    'Mary can eat meat'.
  c. *Sekaijuu de niku **ga** tabe-**rareru**.*
    All over the world in meat NOM eat-PASS
    'Meat is eaten all over the world'.
  d. *Mukashi no koto **ga** omoidas-**areru**.*
    past of thing NOM remember-SPO
    'It reminds me of the past'.
  e. *Tanaka sensei **ga** niku o tabe-**rareru**.*
    Tanaka teacher NOM meat ACC eat-HON
    'Professor Tanaka eats meat'.

There is no documented evidence that allows us to trace back the diachronic relationship of these four usages. However, not a few prior studies suggest that the potential use of the suffix -*(r)areru* is historically derived from the spontaneous use (e.g., Shibatani 1985, Narrog 2010). Although it might be hard for the speakers

---

[7] In passive sentences, patients are compulsorily marked with nominals, but in potential sentences patients can be marked either with the accusative or the nominative.

of Indo-European languages as well as Chinese to understand that passive and potential are semantically related, it is not a special trait of Japanese but rather a cross-linguistically observed polysemy. For example, the Indonesian potential suffix is polysemous among potential, passive, spontaneous and coincidentally occurring events (Shibatani 1985).

Although there have been only three languages introduced briefly above, you may notice that each language employs quite different manners to express the meaning of *Can*. However, this cross-linguistic variability poses a problem, as Cysouw (2007: 226) mentions: "what should be compared with what, when everything is different?" As a solution to this problem, a number of typological studies use semantic maps, whose goal is to sketch out the relations between various "*tertium comparisons*" as established by the cross-linguistic variability of their structural encoding among the world's languages (Cysouw 2007: 226).

2 Semantic map

2.1 What is a semantic map?

A semantic map is "a method for describing and illuminating the patterns of multifunctionality[8] of grammatical morphemes" (Haspelmath 2003: 213). It describes distributional variation for a grammatical form onto a conceptual space representing the situations conventionally encoded by the form, and allows one to capture the universals underlying the diversity (Croft and Poole 2008: 2).

2.2 "Connectivity map" and "statistical map"

There are two types of semantic maps: one is called a "connectivity map" or "implicational map", and the other is a "statistical map" or "similarity map". The former is a traditional way of constructing a map by depicting the connections between meanings with lines. As they are constructed based on

---

8 Haspelmath (2003: 212) prefers the terms "function" and "multifunctionality" instead of "sense" and "polysemy", avoiding the confusion between conventional meanings and contextual meanings.

semantic analysis complemented by knowledge of cross-linguistic data, the maps are implicational. The examples of previous studies presented using connectivity maps are Haspelmath's (1997) study on indefinite pronouns, van der Auwera and Plungian's (1998) study on modality, Haspelmath's (1999) study on datives, and so on. While the connectivity map is constructed manually by researchers, the statistical map is constructed automatically by statistical data and represents a similarity between meanings by spatial adjacency. Previous studies that use statistical maps include Cysouw (2007) on personal pronouns, Croft and Poole (2008) on tense and aspect, and Wälchli (2010) on positional phrases.

2.3 Modality's semantic map

Among the typological studies using semantic maps, van der Auwera and Plungian (1998) and Li (2003) worked on modality. van der Auwera and Plungian (1998) presented a connectivity map of possibility, as Figure 2 shows.

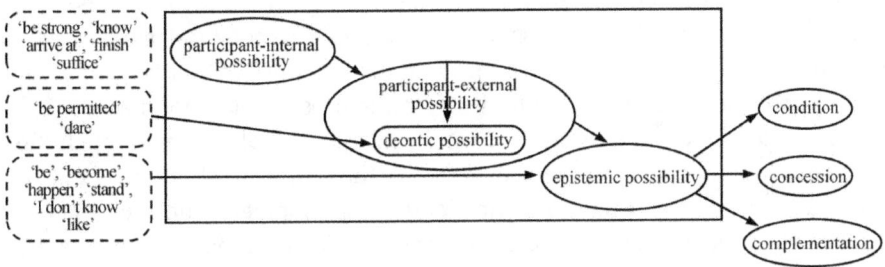

Figure 2: To possibility and beyond (van der Auwera and Plungian 1998: 91).

In this map, the relationships between the meanings are indicated by the arrows to show that the development of semantic changes of modals goes hand in hand with grammaticalization. However, the constellation is arbitrary and each axis does not imply any variable. On the other hand, the semantic map of modality presented by Narrog (2005) consists of two dimensions: one is "volitive" vs. "non-volitive" and the other is "speaker-orientated" vs. "event-oriented". The former concerns the "element of will"; while epistemic and dynamic modalities are non-volitive, deontic modalities are volitive (Narrog 2005: 684). The latter concerns subjectivity; speaker-oriented modality is directly linked to the speaker's own modal judgment at the time of speech, while event-oriented modality concerns the described situations and conditions on the participants of the event (Narrog 2005: 685). The different meanings of the English *Can* are fitted in, as Figure 3 shows.

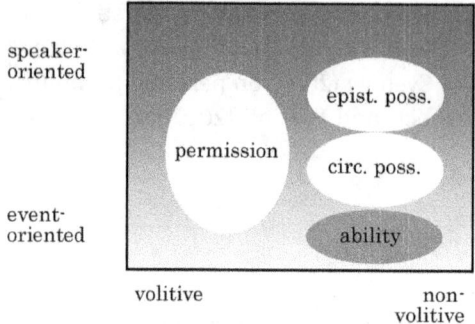

Figure 3: Fitting in *Can* (Narrog 2005: 695).

These two maps nicely capture the polysemy and development of modals in English and Chinese. It is also possible to fit the Japanese potential markers in this map, though the map itself cannot represent the full range of functions of *-rareru* since it is basically constructed to describe the uses of modality markers only. It could also be possible to draw an implicational map of possibility including passive, spontaneous and honorific based on the polysemy of *-rareru*; however, we lack the evidence of their historical path of development: the extant materials do not supply enough information to track back which meaning was derived from which meaning. The only way left to know their relationships is to infer diachronic developments from their synchronic distribution patterns. For this latter purpose, a parallel corpus can provide us with quantitative data for usage-based analysis. A number of implicational maps for modality have been proposed in the literature, but to my knowledge, no one has worked out a statistical map based on quantitative data.

Therefore, this study employs a statistical semantic map to conduct a bottom-up and usage-based survey based on corpus data. Although the survey should ideally include data from a larger sampling of languages, here we have chosen to focus on three languages for technical feasibility. However, these are suitable for this survey since each language has a distinctive marking system and polysemy concerning possibility. Moreover, each belongs to a different language family, which is a desirable sampling for a typological study.

3 Survey

3.1 Data and target

The data for this survey is parallel text data that were collected from the Japanese novel "*Kitchen*" and its translations in English and Chinese. This survey targets the following constructions: Japanese *-eru, -(r)areru, -dekiru, -kotogadekiru*; Chinese[9] *Neng, Nenggou, Ke, Keyi, Hui,* and potential complement construction (*V-de-C, V-bu-C*); and English *Can, Could, May,* and *Might.* Although there are many other constructions that express possibility, here we did not include lexical items (content words) that have a meaning of possibility, but only chose functional words that belong to the closed classes.

3.2 Method

This survey followed the procedure conducted in Wälchli (2010) using a statistical semantic map. Examples collected from parallel texts were automatically mapped onto a graph by multi-dimensional scaling using the R program (R Core Team 2016).

3.2.1 Data collection

First, clauses in which the target forms are used were collected from the texts in each language. In the next step, corresponding translations of each context in other languages were collected. Table 4 shows the total numbers of collected clauses in each language. Let us remember that the semantic map method is based on the principal that if one certain form is used to express two or more different meanings, those meanings are related. Semantic maps try to depict the relationships of the meanings based on the observation of forms as variables. Thus, collection of data is based on the forms, not on the meanings.[10]

---

9 Although Chinese has a more diverse set of auxiliaries, here I chose those with more frequency to restrain the number of variables.

10 Sentences in different languages are not always "parallel" since the data is literary works. There were actually a larger number of clauses in which the target constructions were used in the text. However, if any of the corresponding clauses in other languages did not use the same verb, they were excluded from the data. Therefore, the numbers of clauses in Table 4 are much less than the numbers of actual appearance of each construction in the text.

Table 4: Numbers of collected clauses in which target constructions are used.

	English		Chinese		Japanese	
Numbers of clauses	Can	26	Neng	34	-eru	42
	Could	55	Nenggou	2	-(r)areru	61
	May	5	Keyi	25	-dekiru	13
	Might	9	Ke	1	-kotogadekiru	8
			Hui	81		
			V-de-C	8		
			V-bu-C	17		
total		95		168		124

Note: The examples of Chinese *Ke* used as contrastive conjunction have been excluded, since they do not function as auxiliaries but function on the clause level. The development of *Ke* to contrastive use is an important factor when we discuss the polysemy of *Ke*; however, I limited the scope of investigation to verbal constructions here. Chinese *V-bu-C* and *V-de-C* were recognized as different constructions since their forms are not identical; while semantically they both are categorized as potential complement constructions. In this survey I did not distinguish negative constructions from their affirmative counterparts except *V-bu-C/V-de-C*. However, semantics of possibility/potential has a lot to do with affirmative/negative polarity, which needs to be taken into further consideration but this study could not afford to.

In this sense, this study tried to use a more bottom-up or usage-based method on semantic analysis. The data includes examples of *-(r)areru* used as passive constructions. Considering the semantic category of "possibility", it may seem inappropriate to include the examples of passive use. However, they were not excluded since the form is identical to potential suffixes and it is one of the goals of this study to depict the continuity among different usages of *-(r)areru*, as I discussed in 2.3.

As a result, 274 contexts were collected, deleting overlaps from all the collected clauses in Table 4. This means that each of the 274 contexts has three parallel clauses in English, Chinese and Japanese. (6)–(8) are examples of parallel clauses. In (6), all of the three languages use the target constructions, namely, *Can*, *Neng* and *-eru*. In (7), English and Chinese use target constructions, while Japanese does not. In (8), only Chinese uses the target construction *Hui*, while English uses *Will* and Japanese leaves the verb unmarked.

(6) a. Do you think you **can** handle a knife, half-asleep?
 b. Kan   ni   shui   de   yunyunhuhu de,   **neng**   na   caidao   ma?
    Look you sleep SUB half-asleep SUB can   hold knife   PRT
 c. Sonnani   nebokete-te   houchou mot-**eru**?
    like this half-sleep-PROG   knife   hold-POT

(7) a. *You **can** go pick it up if you like.*
    b. *Ni **keyi** xian qu ti   wo na yixia a.*
       you can first go instead I   pick a little PRT
    c. *Tori-ni itte-kure-<u>temoii</u>-wayo*
       pick-for go-for me-can-PRT

(8) a. *Naturally, <u>I'll</u> pay rent and everything.*
    b. *Fangzu, wo yiding **hui** jiao de.*
       rent   I surely will pay SUB
    c. *Chanto heyadai ire<u>masu</u>.*
       Surely rent   pay

3.2.2 Calculation of distance matrix

Next, the distance matrix of 274 contexts was calculated using Hamming distance as a distance measure. If two clauses use the same construction in a language, they are judged to have the same meaning. If they use different constructions, they are judged to have different meanings. The Hamming distance value was calculated as the number of differences in the constructions in each language. For example, in contexts 27 and 29 in Table 5, all three languages use different markers, which means that the number of difference is 3. Therefore, the distance value between the two results is 3. As for 43 and 78, Chinese uses the same construction but English and Japanese do not, which means that the distance value is 2. As for 27 and 37, only English uses different markers, so the distance value is 1. The difference is zero if all of the languages use the same form, as in 40 and 193; these two contexts are then judged to express the same meaning. The calculation was applied to every pair of contexts,[11] resulting in a distance matrix of 274×274 cells, of which half have identical values, as presented in Table 6.

Table 5: Extract from the 274 parallel texts data.

NO.	English	Chinese	Japanese
1	conditional	Keyi	-toii
⋮	⋮	⋮	⋮
27	Could	Neng	-eru
29	be+pp	Bei	-(r)areru

(continued)

---

11 The calculation of distance values was conducted using Excel.

Table 5 (continued)

NO.	English	Chinese	Japanese
37	Can	Neng	-eru
40	Can	Neng	-dekiru
43	Will	Hui	V
78	Might	Hui	kamoshirenai
193	Can	Neng	-dekiru
⋮	⋮	⋮	⋮
274	Could	V	imperative

* "V"=Verbs which are unmarked.

Table 6: The structure of the distance matrix.

	1	2	3	4	...	271	272	273	274
1	0								
2		0							
3			0						
4				0					
⋮					0				
271						0			
272							0		
273								0	
274									0

3.2.3 Visualization by MDS

Based on the distance values calculated above, the 274 contexts are plotted onto a graph using the Multi-Dimensional Scaling (MDS) procedure by the R function *cmdscale()*. MDS is "a method that represents measurements of similarity (or dissimilarity) among pairs of objects as distances between points of a low-dimensional multidimensional space" (Borg and Groenen 2005: 3). In other words, "two objects that are similar are placed close to each other, and objects that are less similar are placed further away from each other" (Cysouw 2007: 236). In this survey, it means that two contexts whose distance value is small are plotted closely, while two contexts whose distance value is large are plotted far away from each other. As the entire number of data sets is 274, there should be a maximum of 273 dimensions in terms of dissimilarity. MDS reduces the number of dimensions, maintaining the relationship as much as possible. According to the Mardia fit measure test[12] presented in Table 7, the appropriate number of dimensions was judged to be more than 5. In this survey, the number of dimensions was decided to be 3, which is the limit of human visual ability, since the main goal of this study is to visualize the distributions of the target forms.

Table 7: The result of Mardia fit measure test.

	Mardia fit measure 1	Mardia fit measure 2
2	0.25	0.60
3	0.31	0.69
4	0.38	0.76
5	0.43	0.82

3.3 Result

The result of MDS calculation is visualized using the R function *scatterplot3d()*, as Figure 4 shows. Each dot represents each context of the data set.[13] This represents a "conceptual space" (Croft 2001) of what the target constructions in three languages express, constructed from the 274 parallel clauses in "*Kitchen*".

Next, in order to compare cross-linguistic variation, the plots are marked based on the constructions in each language. Figures 5 to 7 show how each language categorizes and marks the contexts. Figure 5 represents the distribution of target constructions in English: *Can, Could, May,* and *Might*; in addition, *Will, Would,* and the potential suffix *-(a)ble* are added. Figure 6 represents the distribution of Chinese *Neng, Nengou, Hui, Ke, Keyi* and potential complement construction. Figure 7 represents the distribution of Japanese *-eru, -(r)areru, -dekiru* and *kotogadekiru*. The cross marks (+) represent that verbs are unmarked or used with other constructions. The x marks in Figure 7 represent Japanese potential verbs *mieru* 'can be seen', *kikoeru* 'can be heard' and *wakaru* 'can understand', which originally have a potential meaning and the object of the perception is marked with the nominative case.

---

[12] If the result of any measurement test 1 or 2 is more than 0.8, the graph is guaranteed as maintaining the relative constellation of the original well. Setting the number of dimensions as 2 and 3 did not pass the test, which means that the result constellation is rather skewed because of the reduction of the dimension.

[13] There is supposed to be 274 dots in the constellation; however, there appears to be fewer on the graph. This is because some contexts which are judged identical (i.e., the distances are calculated as 0) are plotted on exactly the same places.

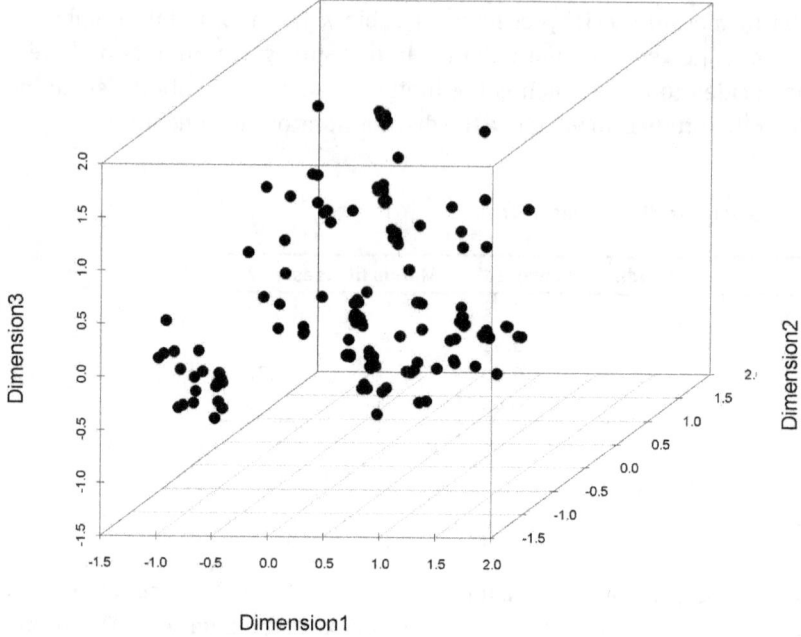

Figure 4: MDS calculation result.

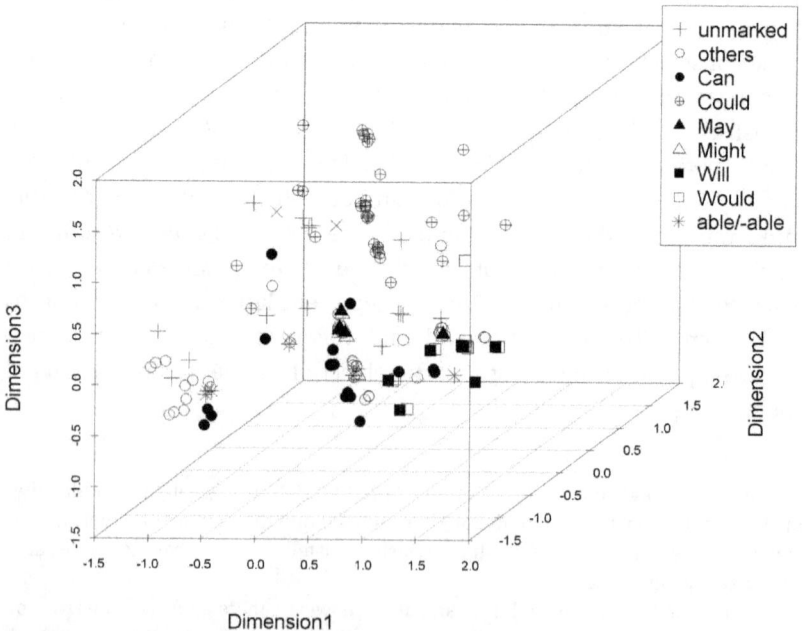

Figure 5: Distribution of English target constructions.

Typological study on expressions — 71

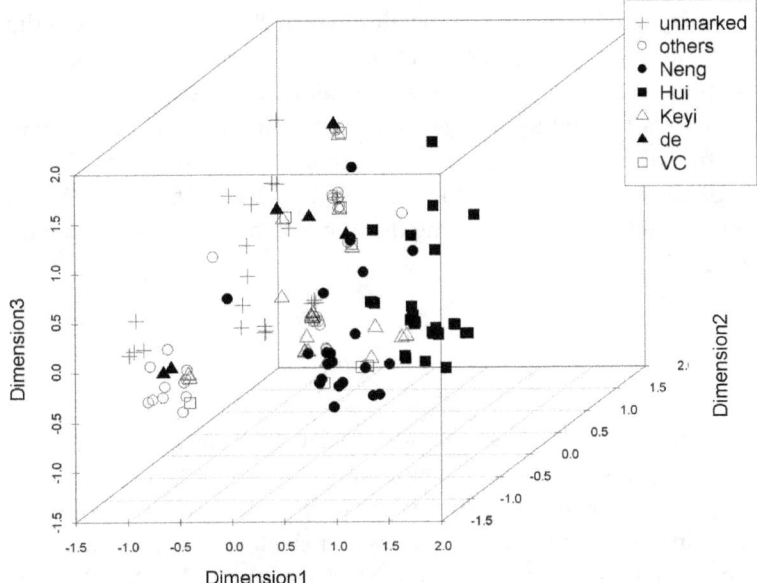

Figure 6: Distribution of Chinese target constructions Chinese.
Note: Examples of *Nenggou* and *Ke* were integrated into the examples of *Neng* and *Keyi*, respectively, since only a few examples were collected.

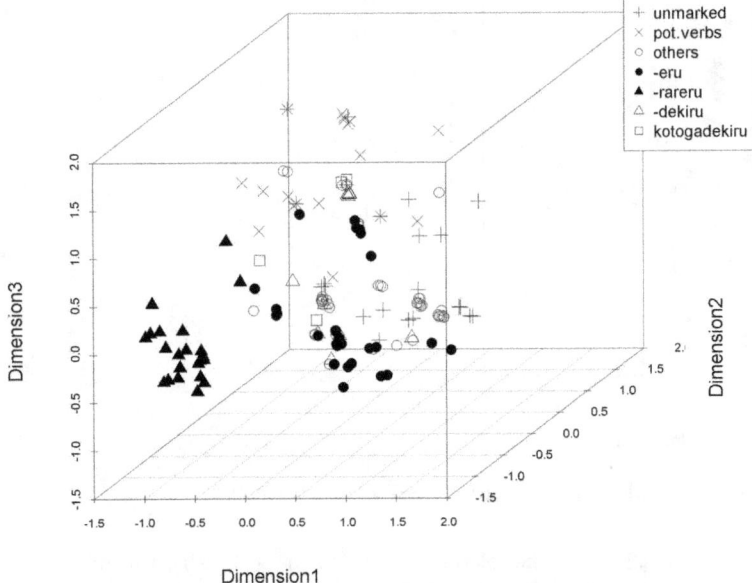

Figure 7: Distribution of Japanese target constructions Japanese.

The scales on each dimension are automatically given by R. The magnitude of the scales does not mean a lot for this survey. Even the positive-negative polarity is arbitrary; the importance here is the relative constellation of the distribution.[14]

Each dimension is labeled as "Dimension1" (the horizontal axis), "Dimension2" (the axis from the front to the back) and "Dimension3" (the vertical axis) for now. These dimensions are also automatically given by R. The researcher is left with the job of labeling and interpreting the dimensions, and this is taken up in the following section.

3.4 Analysis

The following sections examine distributional patterns in each language and compare how each language categorizes the meanings. Based on this observation, we will discuss interpretations of the three dimensions of the conceptual space which is showed as Figure 4 in the previous section. However, three-dimensional maps are not suitable to observe the constellation, especially along Dimension2. Therefore, here we use the two-dimensional maps presented in Figures 8 to 10 to observe the constellation in the D1-D2 plane. In these two-dimensional maps, Dimension3 in the three-dimensional map has been removed, while Dimension1 and Dimension2 remain.

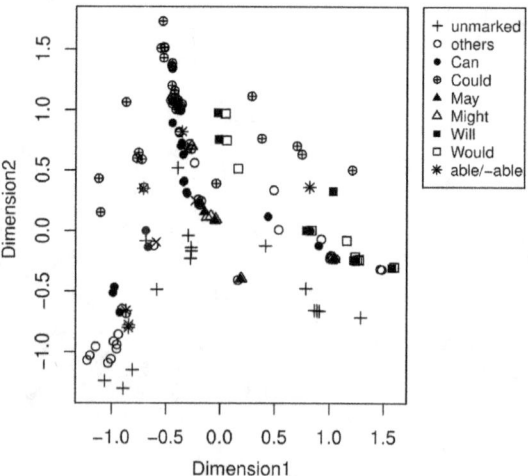

Figure 8: Distribution of English target constructions (Two-dimensional).

---

14 In the following section, I will use the polarity ("negative" and "positive") just to indicate the orientation in the graph. They do not mean that they are actually minus or plus concerning the variables that the dimensions imply.

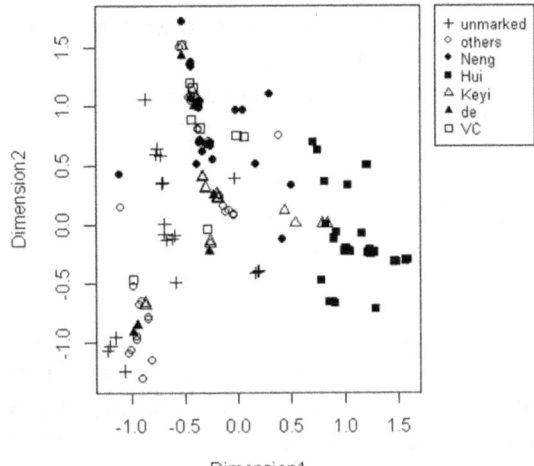

Figure 9: Distribution of Chinese target constructions (Two-dimensional).

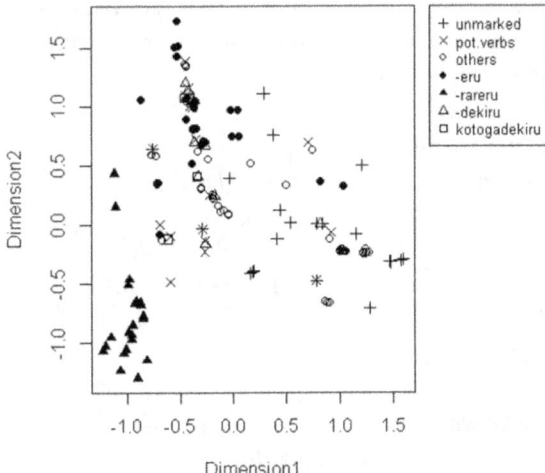

Figure 10: Distribution of Japanese target constructions (Two-dimensional).

3.4.1 Dimension1

In the maps of English and Chinese, the distribution of an auxiliary tends to spread along the D1 (Dimension 1) axis. In Figures 8 and 9, the distributions of the English *Can, Could* and Chinese *Neng* spread from the minus (the left) edge of D1 to the middle part, while the English *May, Might, Will, Would,* and Chinese *Keyi, Hui* spread from the middle part of D1 to the positive side (the right). The examples plotted on the upper left part are the examples of participant internal/external possibility, such as (6). The examples of the English *Can*, *May* and Chinese *Keyi* which express permission ((7) and (9)) are situated in the middle part.

(9) a. ***May*** *I come in?*
    b. ***Keyi*** *jinqu ma?*
       can   enter PRT
    c. *Hait-<u>temoii</u>-n-desho?*
       enter-may-NMLZ-isn't it

On the other hand, examples plotted on the right side of the map are the ones that express the speaker's epistemic attitudes. The English *Will* and *Would* in Figure 8 and Chinese *Hui* in Figure 9 are plotted on the right edge of D1. *Can* in (10), which is used to express epistemic possibility, is also plotted on the right side compared to the examples (6) and (7). In the same way, some examples of *May* and *Might* such as (11)[15] are also plotted on the right. Japanese tends to use other expressions of speculation such as *darou* in (8c) and *kamoshirenai* in (11) or chooses to leave the verb unmarked, which can be observed in the distribution of "others" and "ummarked" on the right side of Figure 10.

(10) a. *[...], and **can't** get any worse.*
    b. *Wo quexin tongku **bu** **hui** zai jiasheng le.*
       I believe pain NEG can again get deeper PFT
    c. *Kore ijou rokudemonai koto wa nai <u>darou</u> to*
       this more than bad   thing TOP NEG will   QUOT
       kakushinshi-tei-ta noni.
       believe-PROG-PST though

(11) a. *I **might** end up falling in love with him.*
    b. *Huoxu wo **hui** zai moyitian xihuan shang ta.*
       maybe I can in someday like   up   him
    c. *Sukini-naru <u>kamoshirenai</u>*
       like-become may

---

[15] However, some of the epistemic examples also remain in the middle. Actually, all the examples of *Might* should be on the right side if it follows the sequence in (12), but there was no difference observed concerning the distribution of *May* and *Might* in the map. The reason for this may be that the number of examples of *May* and *Might* are too small to depict the underlying tendency.

Considering the observation above, the sequence of the meanings from the negative side to the positive side of the D1 axis can be summarized as follows:

(12) Participant-internal possibility
　　　Participant-external possibility (situational possibility)
　　　　> Participant-external possibility (permission)
　　　　　> epistemic possibility

This sequence corresponds to the dimension of "event-oriented" vs. "speaker-oriented" presented in Figure 3. The term "event/speaker-oriented" should be more appropriate as a label of the scale than "participant-internal/external", since the map also includes passive and the epistemic usage in its realm. The examples of passive, which concern propositional property of the sentences, are plotted on the very left of the map. It is also difficult to clarify the regions of internal/external possibility in the map, since the examples of these meanings are often unclear if the enabling condition is internal or external to the participant. However, we can infer that participant-external possibility would be situated more to the right, since permission is a subpart of external possibility. Therefore, we can interpret the D1 axis as presented in Figure 11.

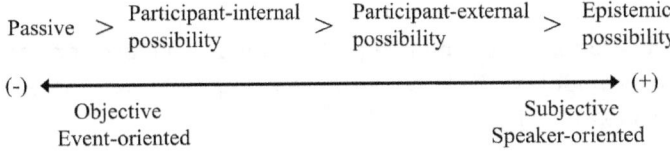

Figure 11: Interpretation of dimension1.

English and Chinese auxiliaries tend to spread along the D1 axis, while Japanese target constructions are concentrated on the left side, which means that Japanese target constructions are more event-oriented. Chinese potential complement constructions, which express participant internal/external possibility as in (13), are also distributed on the left side.

(13)　a.　*I **can't** carry it all in one trip.*
　　　b.　*Yigeren　genben **na**　**bu**　shanglai.*
　　　　　one person　at all　take　NEG　come up
　　　c.　*Hitori de motteko-**rare-nai**-no.*
　　　　　alone　by　bring-can-NEG-PART

3.4.2 Dimension2

When we observe the distribution along the D2 (Dimension 2) axis, the examples of participant-internal/external possibility distribute on the positive side (the upper part of the two-dimensional maps), while the negative side (lower part of the two-dimensional maps) gathers the examples of passive and spontaneous as (14) and (15),[16] respectively.

(14) a. *I was crying for having <u>been left</u> behind in the night.*
    b. Ziji   gulingling de   <u>bei</u>   paoqi zai le zhe jimo   de
       myself   alone   SUB PASS abandon in PFT this lonely SUB
       jiaoren mamu   de   shenye   li.
       paralyzing   SUB   midnight in.
    c. Hitori   okizarinis-**are**-ta-kara-da.
       alone   leave-PASS-PST-because-be

(15) a. *I <u>had felt</u> as if Yuichi were in some other world.*
    b. <u>Ganjue</u> ye   xiang zai dianhua ling   yibian de   shijie li.
       feel   too   like   in   telephone other   side   SUB   world in
    c. Denwa   no   mukou no   sekai ni iru youni kanji-**rare**-ta.
       telephone GEN over   GEN world to be like   feel-SPO-PST

The examples of permission lie in the middle part, and epistemic uses on the right side spread from the middle to the lower part. Therefore, along D2, different meanings sequence as presented in (16).

(16) Participant-internal/external possibility
       > Permission/Epistemic possibility
           > Spontaneous/Passive

This sequence does not correspond to Narrog's (2005) scale of "volitional" vs. "non-volitional" which is shown on the vertical axis in Figure 3. According to the map shown in Figure 3, all the meanings except permission are non-volitional. Participant-internal possibility, as defined earlier, expresses that the power that causes the event is innate to the agent of the event. Participant-external possibility still leaves a possibility for the agent to have some effect on the realization of the event, but the controllability by the agent is not very high. As for permission, the

---

[16] There was no example of honorific use of -*(r)areru* found in the data for this study.

enabling entity is not attributed to the subject of the sentence, but to the authority other than the subject, which results in the lower controllability by the agent. Epistemic possibility merely concerns a speculation about an event to happen; therefore, the controllability also gets lower. In a passive sentence, the subject of the sentence is a patient of the event, which receives a certain kind of effect from the action happening in the event, but which cannot control the realization of the event by itself. Although the occurrence of the event or the obtainment of the state is attributed to the agent (more precisely, the "experiencer"), they cannot be controlled by the agent itself. From the above, D2 can be interpreted as a scale of controllability by an agent.

As mentioned in 1.2.3, the subjects of Japanese potential constructions are not a typical agent. An object of a potential sentence can be marked with nominative, and the agent sometimes can be marked with the dative. It is called "atypical agent" in Shibatani (1985). Therefore, semantic roles of the subjects of the sentences are aligned as "agent < experiencer < patient" along the D2 axis and their controllability of the action decreases as D2 proceeds from the positive side to the negative side as presented in Figure 12.

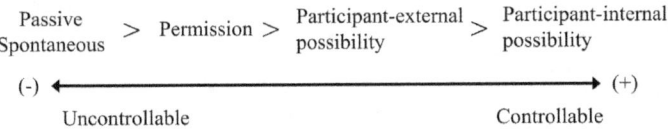

Figure 12: Interpretation of dimension2.

3.4.3 Dimension3

In Figure 5, *Can* is situated on the negative side (the lower part of the three-dimensional maps) of the D3 (Dimension 3) axis while *Could* lies on the positive side (the upper part of the three-dimensional maps). The D3 axis seems not very relevant to the categorization in the other two languages. Only *Can* and *Could* are differentiated on the D3 axis. According to Langacker (2009: 242), the difference between *Can* and *Could* resides in their "immediacy": *Can* is immediate while *Could* is non-immediate. In other words, their variable is a distance from the reality. In our data, some examples of *Could* are a matter of tense, such as (17) which represent the past tense. Also, *Could* is used to express counterfactual, as in (18).

(17) a. *I **couldn't** meet his eyes*
    b. <u>*Wufa*</u>   *zhishi* *ta* *de*   *yanjin.*
       no way stare he SUB eye

c. *Kare no me o miru-**kotogadeki**-nakat-ta.*
   he GEN eye ACC look-can-NEG-PST

(18) a. *I'm sure it **could** have been prevented.*
   b. *Wo jue **bu** **hui** rang na zhong shiqing fasheng*
      I definitely NEG can let that kind incident happen
   c. *Zettaini anna koto s-ase-nakat-ta.*
      definitely like that thing do-CAUS-NEG-PST

I employ the label "immediate" vs. "non-immediate" for D3 as presented in Figure 13 for now; however, this interpretation needs more consideration because the distributions of *May/Might* and *Will/Would* do not display the immediate/non-immediate contrast.

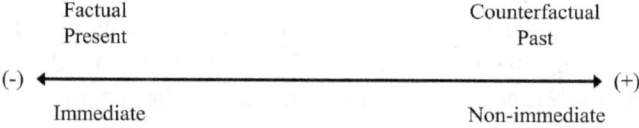

Figure 13: Interpretation of dimension3.

4 Conclusion

Figure 14 integrates the interpretations of the three dimensions discussed in section 3.4. Figure 15 shows how the different meanings related to possibility are distributed in the D1-D2 plane of the conceptual space.

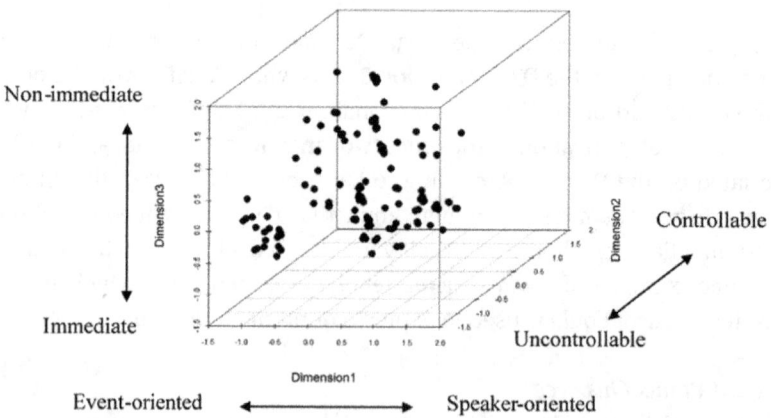

Figure 14: Three-dimensional conceptual space of the target constructions in *"Kitchen"*.

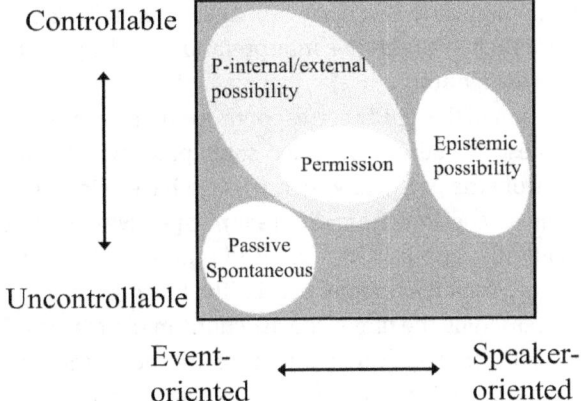

Figure 15. Two-dimensional conceptual space.

These maps show that modality and voice intersect as the dimension of controllability by an agent and the dimension of speaker-orientation. The semantic maps constructed in this survey show not a few correspondences to what has been proposed in the literature, especially to the two semantic maps of modality by van der Auwera and Plungian (1998) and Narrog (2005), as well as the path of semantic change presented in Bybee et al. (1994). The other dimension that constitutes the modality's semantic map presented by Narrog (2005) is the scale of "volitionality"; however, this study concludes that the scale of "controllability" is more appropriate as a semantic map of possibility, not of modality, which includes the continuity to the passive and spontaneous in its realm. For English and Chinese, the dimension of speaker-orientation seems to be important to their semantic continuity, and there are more marked forms on more speaker-oriented meanings. In contrast, the dimension of controllability is more essential to the semantic continuity in Japanese. There are more marked form distributions on the event-oriented side, contrary to the distributions of English and Chinese.

This difference in the tendencies of distribution seems to have a correlation with the preferences on construal styles that each language has. Ikegami (2015: 3–4) proposes two types of construal and argues that the speakers of Japanese prefer "subjective construal", while the speakers of English (and also of Chinese) tend to prefer "objective construal". Ikegami (2015: 6) also mentions as follows: "English, [however,] is a language whose speakers definitely prefer objective construal. Consequently, subjective construal as an alternative is generally viewed as something patently 'marked', something exceptional which the speaker has recourse to only on certain special occasions". This discussion corresponds to the distributions of the semantic maps constructed in our survey: the marked forms in English and Chinese are distributed on more "speaker-oriented" side in Figures 5, 8 and 6, 9. However, this is just a tentative interpretation for the present and needs more evidence and investigation.

Although most of the conclusion of this study corresponds to what has already been proposed in previous studies, this survey provided some proof which supports the preceding discussions from the perspective of the usage-based statistical method, and considered how the discussions from different perspectives interact and can be integrated on a semantic map.It is important to note that the maps presented here cannot be called *the* semantic map of possibility; these are just the semantic maps of meanings expressed by the target constructions in the restricted data for this survey. If more data or examples of other languages are added, the constellation of the map will be changed. However, this is also the nature of semantic maps; as Wälchli (2010: 341) states, semantic space is dynamic rather than static.

However, there are still some methodological problems left. First, the identification of the constructions is problematic. A judgment if two sentences use the same construction is not always objectively determined; it is subjective to the researcher. Although in this method we do not need to directly compare constructions in different languages since distance values are calculated by the (dis)similarity of constructions used in different contexts within a language, it is not always clear what property of the sentence should be compared. Second, it is still questionable if the reduction of variables by MDS really can depict the extremely complex entity of semantics created by human cognitive processes. We should note that the three dimensions discussed in this study are merely one subset of the variables that form the complex concept of possibility. As we had a problem in interpreting D3, how we should interpret the reduction of dimensions is a crucial matter in this method. Third, as the semantic map is dynamic, it is susceptible to sampling and quantity and quality of data. This survey used the parallel texts of which the original is in Japanese, so it should be fair to include the data of which the originals are in other languages, too. Moreover, the amount of data employed here was too small to collect enough examples for all the different meanings. The map will be improved with the larger amount and the wider variety of parallel clause data. If we can solve the problems mentioned above, statistical semantic maps would be a powerful tool to deduce the diachronic path of semantic change from the synchronic cross-linguistic variability.

Acknowledgement: This paper is based on the oral presentation "Typological study on expressions of ability and possibility in English, Chinese and Japanese" at CLDC 2016. I wish to thank all the audiences and wish to give special thanks to those who gave me instructive comments and suggestions. I also wish to thank all the committee members and staff who gave me an opportunity to make a presentation. I am also grateful to the anonymous reviewers for the precious comments and suggestions which improved this paper greatly. This work was supported by JSPS KAKENHI Grant Number JP15H03221.

Abbreviations: NOM nominative; ACC accusative; CAUS causative; GEN genitive; HON honorific; NEG negative; NMLZ; nominalizer; PASS passive; PFV perfective; POT potential; PRF perfect; PROG progressive; PRT sentence final particle; PST past; QUOT; quotative; SPO spontaneous; SUB; subordinator; TOP topic

References

Borg, Ingwer & Patrick J.F. Groenen. 2005. *Modern multidimensional scaling: Theory and applications*, 2nd edn. New York: Springer Science & Business Media, Inc.
Bybee, Joan L., Revere Dale Perkins & William Pagliuca. 1994. *The evolution of grammar*. Chicago, London: The University of Chicago Press.
Croft, William. 2001. *Radical construction grammar*. New York: Oxford University Press.
Croft, William & Keith T. Poole. 2008. Inferring universals from grammatical variation: Multidimensional scaling for typological analysis. *Theoretical Linguistics* 34(1). 1–37.
Cysouw, Michael. 2007. Building Semantic Maps: The case of person marking. In Miestamo Matti & Bernhard Wälchli (eds.), *New challenges in typology: broadening the horizons and redefining the foundations (Trends in linguistics studies and monographs 189)*. 225–247: Walter de Gruyter.
Goossens, Louise. 1992. CUNNAN, CONNE(N), CAN: The development of a radial category. In Kellermann, Günter & Michael D. Morrissey (eds.), *Diachrony within synchrony-language history and cognition: Papers from the international symposium at the university of duisburg*. 377–394: Peter Lang Pub Inc.
Haspelmath, Martin. 1997. *Indefinite pronouns*. Oxford: Clarendon Press.
Haspelmath, Martin. 1999. External possession in a european areal perspective. In Payne Doris L. & Immanuel Barshi (eds.), *External possession*. 109–135. Amsterdam & Philadelphia: John Benjamins Publishing.
Haspelmath, Martin. 2003. The geometry of grammatical meaning: Semantic maps and cross-linguistic comparison. In Michael, Tomasello (ed.), *The new psychology of language vol.2*. 211–242. New York, London: Psychology Press.
Heine, Bernd & Tania Kuteva. 2002. *World lexicon of grammaticalization*. Cambridge: Cambridge University Press.
Ikegami, Yohihiko. 2015. 'Subjective Construal' and 'Objective Construal': A typology of how the speaker of language behaves differently. *Journal of Cognitive Linguistics* 1. 1–21.
Langacker, Ronald W. 2009. *Investigations in cognitive grammar*. Berlin, New York: Walter de Gruyter.
Li, Renzhi. 2003. *Modality in english and chinese: A typological perspective*. Dissertation.com.
Narrog, Heiko. 2005. Modality, mood, and change of modal meanings: A new perspective, *Cognitive Linguistics* 16(4). 677–731.

Narrog, Heiko. 2010. Voice and non-canonical case marking in the expression of event-oriented modality. *Linguistic Typology* 14(1). 71–126.
Oxford English Dictionary, 3rd edn. 2006. Oxford: Oxford University Press.
R Core Team (2016). R: A Language and Environment for Statistical Computing. R Foundation for Statistical Computing. Vienna, Austria. https://www.R-project.org/(accessed May 24 2018)
Shibatani, Masayoshi. 1985. Passives and related constructions: A prototype analysis. *Language* 61(4). 821–848.
van der Auwera, Johan & Vladimir A. Plungian. 1998. Modality's semantic map. *Linguistic Typology* 2. 79–124.
van der Auwera, Johan & Andreas Amman. 2013. Situational possibility. In Dryer, Matthew S. & Martin Haspelmath (eds.), *The World atlas of language structures online*. Leipzig: Max Planck Institute for Evolutionary Anthropology. http://wals.info/chapter/74 (accessed May 24 2018)
Wierzbicka, Anna. 1996. *Semantics: Primes and universals*. New York: Oxford University Press.
Wu, Fuxiang & Yancheng He. 2015. Some typological characteristics of mandarin chinese syntax. In Wang, William S-Y. & Chaofen Sun (eds.), *The Oxford handbook of chinese linguistics*. 380–392. New York: Oxford University Press.
Wälchli, Bernhard. 2010. Similarity semantics and building probabilistic semantic maps from parallel text. *Linguistic Discovery* 8(1). 331–371.

Corpus Data Sources

Japanese: Yoshimoto, Banana. 1991. *Kicchin*. Tsunokawabunko.
English: Translated by Backus, Megan. 1993. *KITCHEN*. faber and faber.
Chinese: Translated by Li, Ping. 2004. *Chufang*. Shanghai Yiwen Chubanshe.

Li-chiung Yang
3 Rhythmic synchrony in conversation

Abstract: A key goal for participants in language communication is to bring about a mutually shared experience of ideas, event narratives, and emotional responses. This goal is achieved not only through the exchange of lexical meaning, but also through interactive signaling to coordinate information status. In this study, we aim at studying convergence in the prosody of natural conversation, explore the link between convergence and the structure of conversations, and show how interactive response and feedback link to the changing convergence patterns in conversation.

Results of our study show that prosodic synchrony and dyssynchrony both occur in conversation, and that synchrony is achieved gradually as participants cooperate to build up a shared information and involvement state. Our analysis further indicates that feedback functions rhythmically in cooperative adaptation to new information and is a critical element in bringing about convergent speaker states. Our findings suggest that feedback and prosodic synchrony phenomena occur as a mirror of topically and emotionally synchronized participant states and also act as organizational indicators providing key information on the degree of understanding, emotional synchrony, and perceived status of a mutually fulfilling topic flow.

Keywords: synchrony, entrainment, rhythm, prosody, feedback, emotion, cognition, interaction

1 Introduction

Human language provides an especially cogent platform for studying the phenomenon of imitative and convergent behaviors in human communication, as speech communication integrates a complex mix of cognitive, emotional, and interactive social processes that are expressed in a number of different forms: the language specific choice of lexical items to communicate meaning, visually-based information exchange of gestures and facial expressions, and the shaping of the oral and aural environment through variations in prosodic flow. Scientific studies have shown convergent behaviors in body movements and gesturing in

---

Li-chiung Yang, Tunghai University, Faculty of Arts, Taichung, Taiwan, lichiung.yang@gmail.com

https://doi.org/10.1515/9783110610895-004

conversation (Condon and Sander, 1974; Nagaoka et al., 2007, 2008; Paxton and Dale, 2013) and in speech (Giles and Smith, 1979; Pardo, 2006; Campbell, 2009, 2010; Lelong and Bailly, 2011; Gill, 2012), and focused on their role in creating harmony and rapport between conversational participants through the use of feedback markers, and through timing and frequency of non-verbal facial and movement gesturing (Gratch et al., 2007; Heylen et al., 2011; Buschmeier et al., 2011; Huang and Gratch, 2012).

Spontaneous conversation is multi-functional in both its goals and processes: the most evident goal of transmitting information simultaneously carries a social goal of building rapport and the sharing of attitudes and emotions towards the information transmitted (Chafe, 2001). In the conversational process, speakers provide propositional and emotional information through prosody, gesturing, and feedback, and engage in interactional probing to build a shared knowledge state and guide topic in a mutually desired direction. Prosody plays a key role in this process, as it provides a powerful and informative resource to communicate multiple levels of coherence and meaning by providing a direct and immediate link to fundamental expressive states.

In this paper, we focus on the integration of two aspects of synchrony: synchrony as facilitator and indicator of rapport, and synchrony as an active component of information exchange. In conversational speech, two contemporaneous information and cognitively related flows occur, one signaling the ever-changing attitudinal and pragmatic relationships between the speakers, and one signaling the ongoing development of the topic themes. Our approach is that the information exchanged in synchronous speech behavior is actively used as an evaluative signal towards the other participant and towards the specific information communicated as topic. In this view, convergence and divergence are both considered as information-rich patterns that speakers use to monitor comprehension, communicate disinterest or encouragement, and signal different levels of agreement and judgment on topic. Synchrony and divergence thus act as key guiding streams of information for participants to achieve both interpersonal and information goals in a mutually fulfilling way.

1.1 Convergence, synchrony, and entrainment

Synchrony refers to behavior that is matched in time, while the term convergence is suggestive of the process by which synchrony is achieved. Other researchers have used different terms such as accommodation, coordination, entrainment, mimicry, imitation, rapport, and alignment, depending upon the field, perspective, or emphasis.[1] Synchrony is at times distinguished from entrainment, with synchrony designating activity aligned rhythmically in time, but not necessarily mutually coupled together, while entrainment is distinguished as both simultaneously occurring and coupled or mutually adapted to the other participants' behavior or speech, or to the temporal structure of external events (Gill, 2012; Fusaroli et al., 2015). Entrainment has also been described as a process in which two independent rhythmic streams interact and mutually adjust to a common phase (Clayton et al., 2004). For this paper, we primarily use the terms synchrony or entrainment, emphasizing either the temporal dimension alignment or the mutually adaptive relationship.

2 Goal, data, and methodology

The current study presents our results on prosodic convergence and divergence in spoken dialogues, drawing from extended conversational data in Mandarin Chinese. Because of the multi-dimensional goals at work in language, synchrony is approached as both building social interactional harmony, and also reflecting informational, organizational and expressive processes in conversations. The coherence achieved in a successful dialog is a shared coherence, one that is constructed through interactions of participants to discover and overcome respective inadequacies of information state.

For this study, our data corpora consist of two extended spontaneous conversations in Mandarin Chinese, each approximately one hour in length. Both conversations selected were mixed-gender pairs, with 1 male and 1 female participant. The speech data are a subset of Academia Sinica's Mandarin Conversational Dialogue Corpus (MCDC)[2] of natural conversations between newly-met participants, created by Dr. Shu-Chuan Tseng (Tseng, 2004). The corpus consists of 8 fully annotated and transcribed spontaneous dialogues. Subjects were selected through a random sampling process to achieve balance across a spectrum of different demographic characteristics, including gender, social status, age, and pronunciation. The conversations were recorded in stereo in a quiet room. For these conversations, there were no preset topics and the speakers were free to

---

[1] For a detailed account of terms, see Gill, 2012.
[2] The MCDC corpus is publicly distributed via the Association for Computational Linguistics and Chinese Language Processing (ACLCLP). Website: http://www.aclclp.org.tw

talk about anything that arises naturally from the communication process.[3] To facilitate annotation, as well as for efficiency in processing, each hour-long dialogue was segmented into 20 subsections of approximately 3 minutes each (see Tseng, 2004 for a detailed account of the recording and processing procedures).

For the current study, the conversational data were further segmented to the phrase level, i.e. phrase-size chunks, based on a combination of lexical, syntactic, semantic, as well as acoustical criteria, similar to intonation unit, prosodic unit, or intonational phrase, commonly adopted by researchers working on spoken language processing, conversational analysis, and discourse prosody (Chafe, 1994, 2001; Tseng, 2008). An intonation unit or prosodic unit is a segment of speech with a single coherent prosodic contour, delineated by pitch reset, final lengthening, pauses, changes in tempo or voice quality, and operationally tied to changing focal points in the flow of ideas (Chafe, 1994). A larger unit consisting of a short series of intonation units with overall fall in pitch is called a declination unit. While work on the specific criteria is on-going, evidence for the validity of such a prosodic unit construct has been accumulated through recent work on discourse and spoken language such as boundary-marking features and tempo variability.

Specific target tokens of interest, including feedback markers analyzed for this study, were annotated and extracted. Measurements of fundamental frequency (f_0) and amplitude were automatically computed, and normalized to each speaker's pitch mean and range. For each speaker and each phrase, low, average, and high values for both f_0 and amplitude were extracted as a means to show global pitch and amplitude movement variation. The acoustic measurements were then examined and correlated with incidence of feedback response and speaker interactions. Altogether there were 1,246 phrases for the female speaker and 2,273 phrases for the male speaker in mcdc01, and 2,256 for the female speaker and 2,014 for the male speaker in mcdc05, resulting in 3,519 phrases for mcdc01 and 4,280 for mcdc05 with a total of 7,799 phrases.

Table 1: Frequency counts of phrases and feedback markers *dui*, *oh* and *umhum* for 2 conversations, mcdc01 and mcdc05.

Data	Phrases	Dui	Oh	Umhum	Time (min)
mcdc01	3519	308	106	566	~60
mcdc05	4280	491	216	734	~62
Total	7799	799	322	1300	~122

---

[3] Topics covered included job, leisure activities, economics, and hobbies for mcdc01, and job, family, social status, insurance, history, ethnicity, and neighborhood for mcdc05. Full topic analysis is left to future studies.

To provide a measure of overall pitch movement at different scales, moving averages of phrase maximum f_0 values were calculated to capture more dynamic patterns of f_0 change and f_0 synchrony in our data. By use of locally averaged values of peak f_0 points from our data, a moving average sublimates higher frequency f_0 variation by acting as a low pass filter to preserve more global quasi-cyclical behavior and overall trends in general pitch level and change. Thus, moving averages facilitate focus on the underlying determinants of overall pitch level change through the mechanisms of the gradual development in topic, interest, emotions, and level of interaction that characterize normal conversational speech.

3 Results I

In this section we present our results on prosodic convergence and divergence in spontaneous conversational dialogues in Mandarin. Our goal is to study convergence in the prosody of natural conversation, explore the link between convergence and the structure of conversations, and show how interactive response and feedback link to the changing convergence patterns in conversation.

3.1 Conversational structure and prosodic convergence

The goals of participants in spontaneous discourse are linked to the fundamentally communicative nature of spoken conversation both in the signaling and sharing of cognitive and emotional representations, and in the relationship speakers seek to build with each other during the course of a conversation. A key ingredient for successful communication is that speakers have an understanding of the other participant's changing cognitive and attitudinal receptivity to the information exchanged. Thus, signals are sent and monitored by both participants so that a continual updating of this additional dimension of information on the interactive status of the communication is achieved. Prosody constitutes a concurrent signal on the underlying state that is simultaneously transmitted with the intended propositional content, and provides an especially powerful interactive signal that is based on fundamental ties between underlying cognitive states and their expression in physiological form.

The degree of prosodic synchrony in a conversation is itself a guide to the adequacy of information exchange and emotional unity. In conversations, *prosodic convergence* occurs when participants match corresponding movements in pitch ranges of an utterance to indicate support of the topic development hierarchy, and to signal enthusiasm and sympathetic agreement with the other speaker's point of view. *Prosodic divergence* occurs when speakers use opposite pitch movement patterns under conflicting discourse goals or to indicate an acknowledgement and understanding of the topic organizational hierarchy presented by the main speaker. Thus, prosodic convergence acts as one useful measure of the overall success of a conversation.

Our results demonstrate that prosodic convergence and divergence occur in conversations, and are globally expressed in pitch level movements of phrases as topics develop. Figure 1 (top and middle) shows the non-normalized pitch peaks of individual phrases for the male and female speaker of one conversation from MCDC (N=4280, M=2024, F=2256), and the global pitch movement of phrases for each speaker independently. This pattern is captured clearly in Figure 1 (bottom), which shows the normalized global phrase movement for the two speakers in the dialogue.

Because each plot condenses the hour-long conversation substantially, to achieve a fine-grain moment-to-moment analysis, we further break the conversation into three 20-minute sections, as presented in Figures 2–4, to illustrate how the prosody of a conversation, and the interrelated patterns of prosody between speakers, reflect the structure of a conversation, on both the topic and interactive levels. The breakout brings to light detailed focus on three well-established stages of development for real-world events: warm-up or introduction, progression to a peak or climax, and gradual fade to a close (Fusaroli et al., 2015). Each individual subsection highlights significant patterns in phrase-to-phrase movement as topics develop over time.

In Figures 2–4, we can see the global pitch movements of the two speakers of the mcdc05 conversation across the three 20-minute sections. Each point represents the smoothed pitch peak f_0 of a phrase for a given speaker, and the points are normalized to each speaker's mean and variation of phrase peak f_0, and calculated as 51-period moving averages to obtain a clearer representation of global pitch height movement over the time course of the conversation.

3.2 Orientation, negotiation, and topic development

Spoken dialogues commonly progress through different phases that encapsulate the evolving relations between participants and the development of topics. At the beginning of the conversation, a mutually satisfying topic has yet to be determined, and speakers engage in frequent give-and-take to orient or re-orient to each other. During this period, new topics are frequently introduced by both

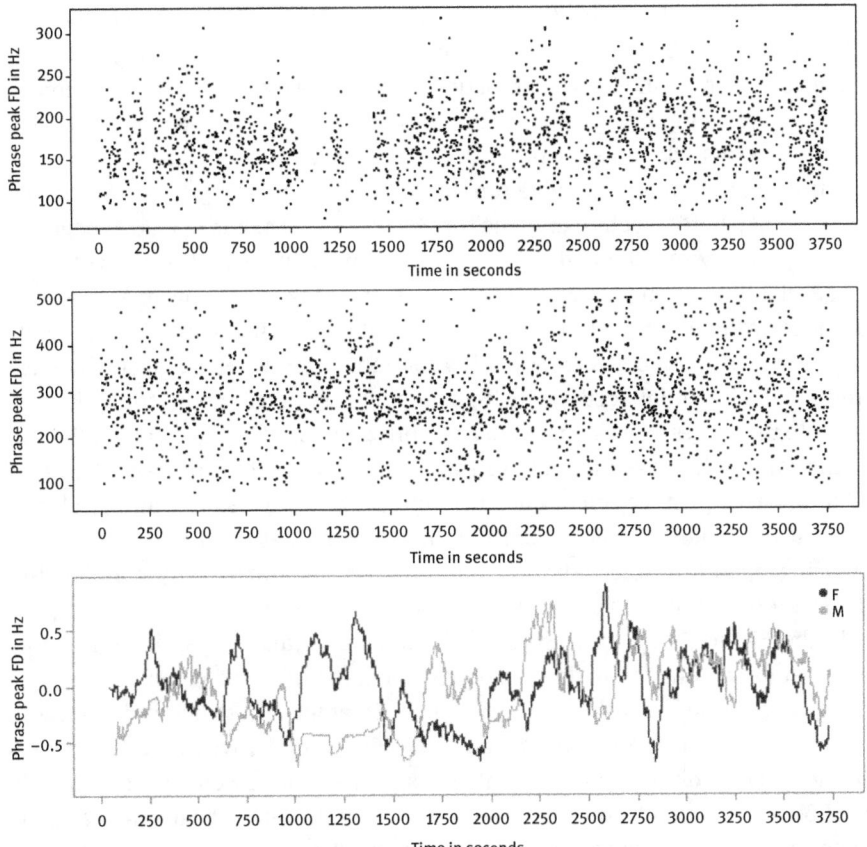

Figure 1: Time series of phrase peak f_0 in Hz for the male speaker (top), female speaker (middle), and normalized phrase peak f_0 with 51-period moving averages for both speakers (bottom) in a 62-minute long conversation. Each dot represents the peak pitch value of one phrase. The horizontal axis is time in seconds and the vertical axis is pitch in Hz.

participants, and speakers interactively probe for responses that would guide the optimum topic direction (Yang, 2006).

The mixed prosodic patterns between the participants seen in Figure 2 in the beginning sections (0–1200 seconds, equivalent to episodes[4] 1–7) of the conversation reflect the initial mutually non-coordinated topic direction, as well as the

---

[4] We use the term episode to refer to each of the 20 contiguous subsections of the full dialogues to distinguish from larger subsections of dialogues without the presumption of a complete narrative substructure.

efforts taken by both parties to resolve this gap. The pitch movements of both speakers from 0–1200 seconds exhibit a mix of convergent and divergent patterns between speakers as the conversation develops. At the start, from 0–180 seconds, the falling vs. rising divergence in pitch movement trends between the speakers indicates the unsettled topic instability as speakers engaged in frequent overlap, rapid turn-taking, and interactive probing to find a common ground. At the 180 second point, there is a change in the turn-taking pattern, and speakers began to alternate with more extended stretches of primarily one-sided narratives, with rising and falling pitch patterns reflecting the on-going topic movement.

The subsequent progression of the conversation is indicative of the ultimately cooperative nature of conversational interactions, even when speakers diverged Throughout this initial section, the female speaker contributed frequently with agreeable responses, raises questions, and provides clarifications and additional information, with active attempts to establish rapport. This constant stream of feedback has a positive effect on the shape of the conversation and is clearly shown in the male speaker's increasing involvement, as seen by his gradually increasing pitch level throughout, captured in the predominantly parallel rise-fall arcs for both speakers in the 300–650 seconds section here.

In the 650 to 750 seconds section, the female speaker expanded on a topic of interest to her, and the male speaker's responses and involvement in the topic gradually increased and this led to the more interactively structured and more level convergent prosodic pattern from 750–900 seconds, where both speakers were actively involved with frequent turns and greater intensity of feedback. From 900 to 975 seconds, the male speaker took on the main speaker role and the female speaker responded with interested feedback, resulting in the short convergent falling pitch levels in that section.

Divergence often occurs when speakers have conflicting goals or when the involvement levels or mutual interactivity between speakers is mismatched. In the 975–1200 seconds section into the conversation, the female speaker took the main speaker role in another extended narrative, sharing her viewpoint on a topic on which the male speaker had great reservations and a high degree of uncertainty. This divergent cognitive state is indicated in the rise-fall prosodic pattern of the female, and the male's flat pitch shape, as well as the sparse feedback he provided.

Our results show that the interactive nature of conversation and speaker roles taken on by participants are important elements in the prosodic structure of conversations and the degree of synchrony exhibited. The mixed global prosodic movements seen in Figure 2 in the beginning sections of the conversation result from the initial interactive uncertainty and the give-and-take probing to move the topic in a mutually satisfactory direction. Both convergence and divergence

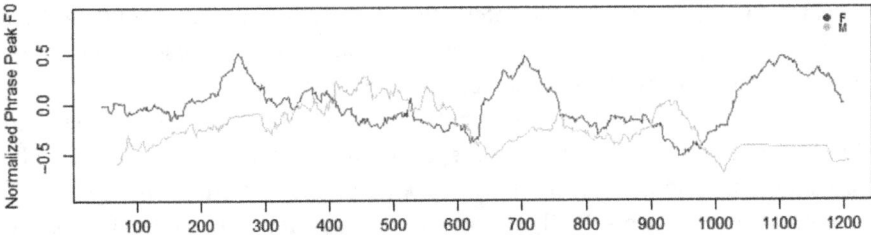

Figure 2: 51-period moving averages of phrase peak f_0 for both speakers in the initial 20-minute section, comprising the first 7 episodes. In this section, both convergence and divergence in pitch patterns occurred frequently, as speakers first worked to establish a common relationship basis, and began to explore different topics. For example, convergence occurred in the 300–650 and 800–900 periods, while divergence occurred in 0–150, 650–750 and 1000–1200.

provide key information to guide topic flow and lay the groundwork for greater cohesiveness and convergent goals in subsequent phases.

3.3 Components of convergent language processes: Cooperation, interaction, and rapport

The communication of information is interlinked with the relationship between speakers, the existing knowledge status of each speaker, and the differing desired topic directions which speakers wish to pursue. Each of these elements is initially not fully known, or entails different degrees of uncertainty. Conversations therefore can be viewed as progressive resolution of uncertainty at increasingly more local scopes. Conversations frequently progress from accommodation to a speaker's personality and character, to a cooperative implicit agreement on topic, and finally to resolving differences and uncertainties that relate to a more specific local topic.

Analysis of our results shows that prosody of a discourse mirrors this process, and that prosodic synchrony increases gradually as the rapport and cognitive cohesiveness of participants increases, and becomes more complete as the conversation progresses. This process is seen in Figure 3, which shows the global pitch movements of the second major phase of the conversation, from approximately 1200 to 2400 seconds in the conversation, equivalent to episodes 8 to 13.

The gradual increase in convergence is seen in the second 20-minute phase of the conversation here. By this section of the conversation, the systematic empathetic and encouraging feedback of the female speaker in the initial phase of the conversation had brought about a corresponding greater involvement by the male speaker. This sense of shared grounding and trust was supported by his increased responsiveness in feedback and interactions, starting from about 1600 seconds on, as well as by his active participation in the on-going topic discussion and by his providing further details on the topics in an open manner.

Our data show that pitch movements also vary according to overall patterns of topic development and intensity of speaker involvement. This is shown in the corresponding gradual increase in convergence in this section, as speakers' pitch movements move from initially divergent pitch development to greater convergence in pitch movements in this second phase. In the current section, both speakers began an exchange on a topic of high interest to both, and the male speaker became the predominant main speaker, with very high emotional involvement in the topics introduced, in the 1650 to 1950 seconds section and the 2150 to 2350 seconds section respectively.

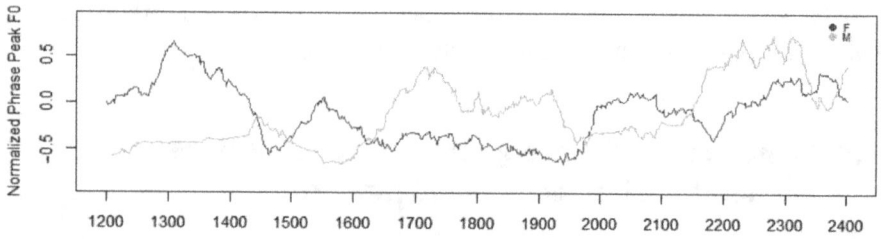

Figure 3: 51-period moving averages of phrase peak f_0 for both speakers in the second 20-minute section, comprising episodes 8–13. In the initial period of this section, the speakers alternated in providing extended sub-narratives, providing greater information on which to draw out a common ground and status. Divergence is seen in 1200–1500 and 1500–1650, and convergence occurs in 1750–1850, and 2180–2320.

Taking a closer view of our data shows that convergence occurs as participants mutually develop and reach climatic high points in topic, and global pitch level for each speaker rises in synchrony. Analysis of the conversation shows that the two convergent rise-fall arcs seen in Figure 3 also coincide with the development of a major subtopic theme that both speakers actively contributed to. This involvement is signaled by the increasing pitch heights of both speakers. The pitch levels for both speakers follow parallel rising trends during this period, as both speakers openly and actively shared their viewpoints. Both speakers' involvement reached a peak of excitement roughly at the 2100 to 2350 section, and the topic reached a climatic point at about 2293 seconds into the conversation, as the male speaker started to describe an emotionally moving experience that he encountered, at which point the highest pitch point also occurred. The pitch level then gradually descends as the main speaker gave more specific details in concluding the topic.

The pitch levels of both speakers also converge and follow the same rise-fall pattern as interest in the topic increases and then is cooperatively resolved. This shows that there exists an overall systematic prosodic structure that integrates topic progression and speaker involvement through a process of shared conversational goals, cooperation to increase rapport, and matching degrees of prosodic synchrony.

3.4 Convergence as a shared goal of conversational participants

Once reached, convergence is often sustained over extended time periods of the conversation, mirroring the rapport that participants achieve in pursuing a topic of high interest to both. This is seen in the final phase of the conversation in Figure 4, starting at about 2750 seconds and continuing to the conversation end. As occurred in the second phase of the conversation, points of mutually shared emotional climax can act as trigger points for high involvement and convergence. In this conversation, a second emotional climax point occurs at about 2546 seconds (42.4 minutes) into the conversation. At that point, both speakers were suddenly surprised to discover that they shared a strong unifying connection, and the high intensity of involvement is echoed by both speakers reaching their highest pitch points in the conversation. Both speakers then begin to respond in a very enthusiastic way, initiating a pattern of very high and sustained pitch level synchrony that extends to the very end of the conversation. The rapport between the speakers had increased greatly because of this newfound solidarity and alignment, and from about 2725 seconds on, the involvement and intensity level of both speakers becomes very high, and turn-taking is rapid but mutually reinforcing on topic. The global pitch movements show that prosodic convergence is remarkably high throughout, as pitch level rises and falls in waves as both speakers actively and enthusiastically contributed to the conversation.

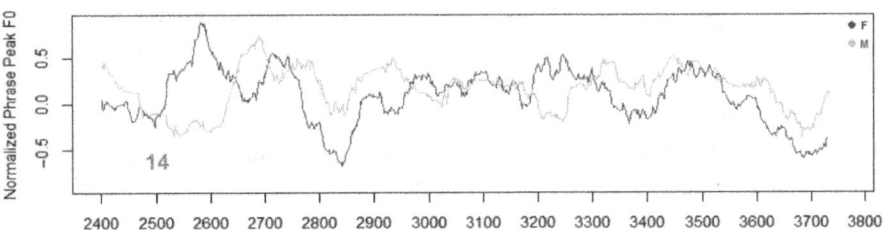

Figure 4: 51-period moving averages of phrase peak f_0 for both speakers in the final 22-minute section, comprising episodes 14–20. After a climactic turning point, both speakers became mutually attuned to a common topic path, and very high degree of pitch synchrony occured almost continuously from 2750 to the end.

The final phase of the conversation illustrates how increased rapport and social cohesion is expressed in a high degree of prosodic synchrony in communication. The high synchrony achieved resulted from the active cooperation of both speakers to this point. In this conversation, an initial imbalance in social relations between speakers and a relatively high level of reserve by the male speaker was transformed through the encouraging responses of the female speaker.

Our data also show that when both speakers are highly involved and presenting substantial information on a topic, alternating and emotionally-matching contributions by both speakers may result in lagged convergence in pitch. This can be seen in this conversation at the turning point at about 2560 seconds where the female speaker arrived at a topic climatic peak, with the male speaker's matching rising sequence arriving at a peak about 90 seconds later. The pitch sequence representations indicate that lags, from a single speaker's perspective, may be positive or negative, as speaker roles change and new topics are brought up.

Viewing the structure of the conversation as a whole, both speakers progressed from initial introductions and probing for topics, through more one-sided narratives, and finally to very lively and active give-and-take on topics of high interest to both speakers. This resulted in the achievement of a strong convergence pattern seen in the last section of the conversation. Once the participants in this conversation had reached this high level of rapport and mutual topic cohesion, prosodic synchrony *persisted* through the completion of the conversation. Figure 4 (2750 seconds to end) shows the parallel synchronous movement as participants matched descending pitch patterns in a shared recognition of the coming conclusion.

3.5 An integrated view of synchrony

In this section, we have shown that synchrony between speakers in a conversation occurs in prosody and feedback, and is closely linked to interactive rapport and intensity of involvement. Changing speaker roles and the evolution of topic development in a conversation give rise to varying degrees of synchrony over the course of a conversation. Figure 5 shows 51-period moving average time series for the entire conversation for both speakers, and the changing global and more local prosodic pitch movements reflect topic development decisions negotiated by participants.

The degree of convergence is highest in the final section of the conversation, and correlates with intensity of involvement in topic. The overall pitch levels seen for both speakers in Figure 5 exhibit a gradual rise over most of the conversation, especially the latter half, indicating the rising intensity level of speaker participation. Comparison of the three phases (0–1200, 1200–2400, 2400–3762) in Figure 5 shows that the final section has the highest degree of convergence at both global and localized extents. By the final phase, the process of probing and negotiation towards a suitable topic had produced a unified agreement on topic direction, and the mutual understanding and interest level of participants were high. Rapport was further strengthened through the shared topic goal, and synchronous behavior was reinforced and continued at a high level, as is reflected clearly in the remarkably high level of synchrony seen in the latter third of Figure 5.

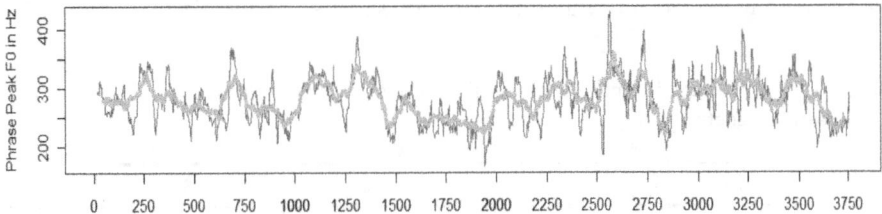

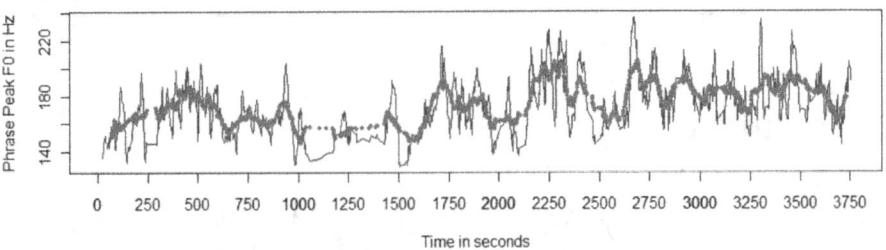

Figure 5: Time series comparison of prosodic structure for both speakers, showing short (13-period) and long term (51-period) moving averages of phrase peaks, in thin and thick lines respectively. The top panel shows the female speaker's pitch movement and the bottom panel shows the male speaker's. These representations allow us to visualize both local and global patterns of speaker involvement and interaction.

3.6 Statistical evidence

Further evidence for progressive increase in synchrony is shown in Table 2. Conversation mcdc05 was divided into four timewise equal quarters, and nonparametric Kendall rank correlation tests were run separately on each quarter. Table 2 shows the Kendall coefficients, which measure the strength of association between the pitch values of the male and female speakers, and the associated p values. At the start of the conversation (quarter 1), there was little or no correlation between the two speakers. The second quarter coefficient 0.53 was much stronger, but with a negative correlation between the two speakers' pitch values, reflecting the frequent but systematic divergence in pitch between the speakers in this area of the conversation. The correlation became strongly positive and strengthened even more in the third and fourth quarters, at high levels of significance. The coefficients demonstrate the increasingly strong mutual coordination of pitch level signaling, and the increasing pitch convergence movements between the speakers across the span of the conversation. This increasing convergence in prosody through a conversation mirrors results found by Nagaoka and Komori (2008) for growing body movement synchrony in conversations.

Table 2: Correlation coefficients and significance levels by conversation quarter, conversation mcdc05.

Quarter	1	2	3	4
Kendall Coefficient	0.04579458	0.53683435	0.79442905	0.74131774
p-level	2.909350e-04	2.358596e-36	6.780196e-10	5.701031e-04
Statistic	−3.623241	−12.591266	6.171134	3.445453

4 Results II

4.1 Feedback and prosodic convergence: The building of interactivity and rapport through feedback

The existence of patterns of convergence and divergence in discourse highlights the interactive nature of discourse. The contribution of convergence and divergence patterns to the direction of topic is critical because speakers negotiate topic flow by mutually monitoring and influencing each other through the system of pitch height signals. The interactional functions of convergence and divergence are expressions of relationships which participants have towards the topic and towards each other, and are reflections of evolving underlying cognitive and emotional states.

Feedback or "backchannels" is closely related to convergence and divergence. Researchers in various fields have been interested in studying both verbal and nonverbal feedback (Schegloff, 1982; Allwood et al., 1992; Drummond and Hopper, 1993; Clark, 1996; Ward and Tsukahara, 2000; Gratch et al., 2007; Buschmeier et al., 2011; Heylen et al., 2011; Huang and Gratch, 2012; Beňuš, 2016; Włodarczak and Heldner, 2017) and their role in communication. Feedback in general represents an on-going and non-disruptive commentary on the hearer's responses and involvement in the conversation. Feedback utterances are used to express support and understanding of the speaker, and to signal the interest level and degree of agreement with on-going topic development. Such utterances can indicate that the speaker is not interested in the topic, or conversely, signal to the speaker that "I'm following you". Even when there is no feedback, it can be revealing of the discourse process, i.e. inferences can be drawn from the non-responsive behavior. Feedback, therefore, is often the crucial element in interaction and plays an essential role in convergence and divergence. In the following section, we illustrate how feedback is intricately linked to the phenomena of convergence and divergence in our data.

4.2 Variability across speaker and conversation

Figure 6 presents all the incidences of the markers *oh* and *dui* for both conversations by speaker and episode. The data clearly show that there are great variations in the overall frequency and distribution of these two markers across 20 continuous 3-minute episodes of conversations mcdc01 and mcdc05. *Dui* 'right' and *oh* 'oh' are among the highest frequency feedback markers in Mandarin conversations (Tseng, 2004; Yang, 2006) and they play key roles in interactive response and accommodation to information exchange between participants.

As seen in Figure 6 and Tables 3 and 4, the frequency of feedback for conversation mcdc01 is less than half of that for conversation mcdc05: for mcdc01, the male and female speakers' *oh* and *dui* feedback over all episodes totals 305, or 43.1% of mcdc05's total feedback frequency of 707. The use of feedback by the female speaker in mcdc01 is especially low for both *oh* and *dui*, with only 111 instances total. This indicates that the differing use of feedback among speakers is closely related to speaker style characteristics (Huang and Gratch, 2012) and degree of expressivity, as well as discourse-related factors such as the degree of familiarity and involvement with topic.

Another interesting pattern emerges when we compare the usage of feedback markers *dui* and *oh* across speaker gender. In these two conversations, both female speakers' use of *oh* is relatively greater than *dui*: 82 vs. 29 in mcdc01, and 207 vs. 169 in mcdc05. Conversely, the male speakers' use of *dui* in both conversations is *much* greater than their use of *oh*: 171 vs. 23 in 01 and 322 vs. 9 in 05. Both males have a striking near exclusion of the use of *oh* in both conversations. These patterns are consistent across our data and this indicates that there is a gender preference among different markers used that may be conditioned on social and discourse relationship.

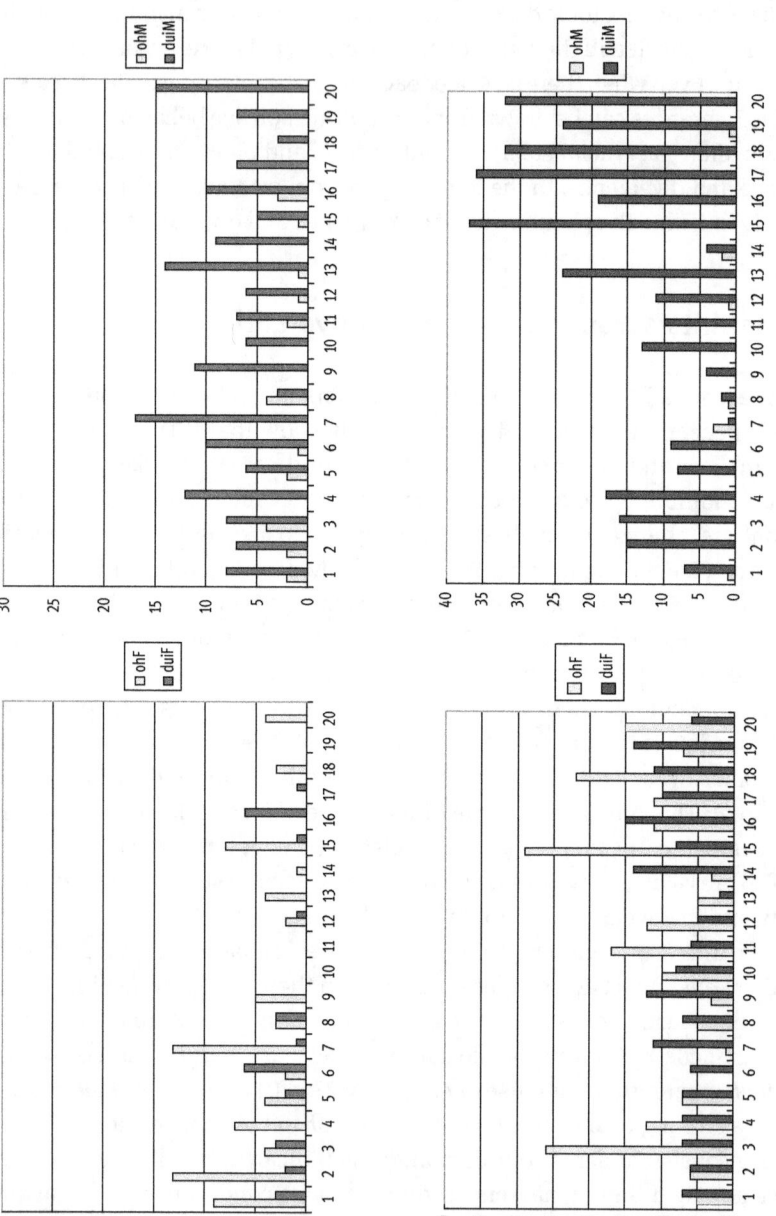

Figure 6: Frequency counts of feedback markers *oh* and *dui* by episode and by speaker for mcdc01, female speaker on the top left and male speaker on the top right; bottom charts show frequency counts of *oh*, and *dui* for mcdc05, female on the left and male on the right.

Table 3: Counts of feedback markers *oh* and *dui* by speaker for 2 conversations, mcdc01 and mcdc05.

Gender	mcdc01				mcdc05			
	Female		Male		Female		Male	
Token	oh	dui	oh	dui	oh	dui	oh	dui
Counts	82	29	23	171	207	169	9	322
Subtotal	111		194		376		331	
Total		305				707		

Table 4: Mean counts of feedback markers *oh* and *dui* by speaker for 2 conversations, mcdc01 and mcdc05.

Gender	mcdc01				mcdc05			
	Female		Male		Female		Male	
Token	oh	dui	oh	dui	oh	dui	oh	dui
Mean ct. per ep.	4.05	1.45	1.15	8.55	10.35	8.45	0.45	16.10
stdev	3.99	1.86	1.31	3.67	7.84	3.32	0.80	11.11

The temporal distribution of feedback within conversations also varies greatly by speaker and conversation. In mcdc01, the female speaker had a higher concentration of feedback responses in the first 7 episodes of the conversation, and gradually reduced her feedback in the latter half of the conversation, while the male speaker's feedback distribution was more uniform across the conversation. By contrast, the feedback for both speakers in mcdc05 occurred with higher frequency across the conversation, and also exhibited cyclical behavior, concentrating on three distinct wave structures for each speaker. This indicates that there are higher level cognitive and discourse factors governing the flow of conversation.

4.3 Patterns of feedback distribution in conversations

Feedback markers are key interactive signals that communicate the adequacy of information exchange, and the distribution of specific markers is closely linked to their specific functions and to the emotional and involvement states of speakers, as well as the interactivity level of the conversation. Imbalances in participant state commonly give rise to different degrees of cognitive certainty or uncertainty, and feedback provides immediate signals to speakers that adjustment or restatement of information may be necessary.

For example, *oh, dui,* and *umhum* are three of the most frequent feedback markers in Mandarin (Tseng, 2004; Yang, 2006), and each signals different degrees of cognitive uncertainty and receptivity towards communicated information. While *oh* functions as a response to information, marking surprise, unexpectedness or newness, and necessitating a cognitive adjustment or reorientation, *dui* acts as confirmation and agreement to information received and implied as already known or accepted. The predominant function of *umhum (uhhuh)*, on the other hand, is as expression of acknowledgment or encouragement. Thus, *oh, dui,* and *umhum* each has its unique different functions and occurs under different informational environments. The specific functions of these markers have great significance for their frequency and distribution in a given conversation.

Taking a closer look at the following figures and tables, Figure 7 and Tables 5–6, where we tabulated and plotted the occurrences of these three feedback markers through time in mcdc05 by speaker, a clearer pattern emerged that reinforces our point above: there is a clear gender difference and preference for the use of these markers. In this conversation, the male speaker has a mean of 7.6 instances of *umhum* per episode, just 26% of the female's mean frequency of 29.1 for the same marker. A similar large gap exists for *oh*, with the female speaker having about *20 times* as many *oh*'s as the male speaker. Conversely, the male speaker used *dui* about twice as often as the female speaker, with mean episode counts of 16.1 for the male speaker vs. 8.45 for the female.

The relationships for *oh* and *dui* in mcdc05 are consistent with the results for mcdc01, with female *oh* and male *dui* having higher relative frequencies, as presented earlier. The much greater use of *oh* and *umhum* by the female and greater use of *dui* by the male speaker presented here suggest that there exist some social-cultural expectations of greater male authority (dominance) and greater female supportiveness in male-female social interactions, and this feature might be especially marked in conversations where politeness and role-conformity could be expected to exert greater force. This point is consistent with Tseng (2006).[5]

---

[5] In analyzing the distribution patterns across three different corpora collected for the study of spoken Mandarin, Tseng (2006) found that feedback and backchannels comprised a significant proportion, about 1/5 of all discourse items in the corpora, and exhibited a strong male-female imbalance in frequency. Over all three corpora, females used feedback such as *umhum* nearly twice as frequently as males, while for newly-met participants (MCDC), females used feedback even more – more than twice as often as males. The higher imbalance was attributed to greater politeness appropriate to the social setting between strangers. Our results above are consistent with their findings.

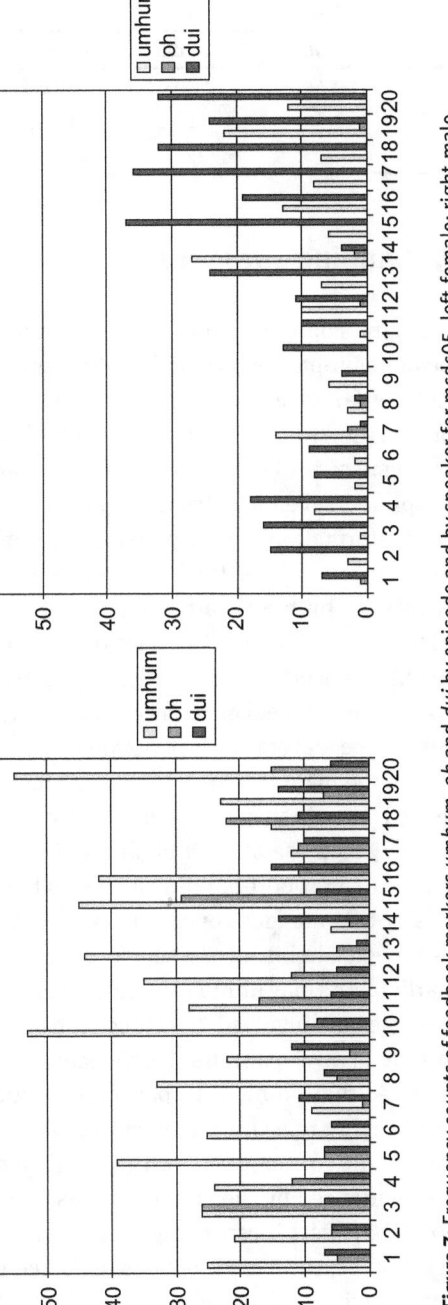

Figure 7: Frequency counts of feedback markers *umhum*, *oh* and *dui* by episode and by speaker for mcdc05, left-female; right-male.

Table 5: Mean frequency of feedback markers *umhum*, *oh*, and *dui* by speaker for mcdc05.

Feedback	Male			Female		
	umhum	oh	dui	umhum	oh	dui
Mean	7.60	0.45	16.10	29.10	10.35	8.45
Stdev	7.05	0.80	11.11	13.57	7.84	3.32
Counts	152	9	322	582	207	169

4.4 Feedback, changing speaker state, and turning points

As indicators of changing cognitive states, the temporal distribution of specific feedback varies locally as topics evolve and participants take on different roles and undergo cognitive challenges to new information. The progression of feedback use in this conversation followed the activities of each speaker as they interacted to bring about a successful conversation. At the start of this conversation, both participants explored several topics in sequence, with the female speaker more open in sharing information and responsive to the male speaker in the first half of the conversation. The initial topics served as self-introductions and as search activity to arrive at a mutually satisfying topic.

As shown in Figure 7 and Table 6, the relatively low feedback activity of the male speaker in the initial episodes is matched by a high frequency of encouraging *umhum* feedback by the female speaker, to provide support for the male speaker. In episodes 7–9, the female speaker started an extended narration to tie her own experience and viewpoint to the male speaker's account, which was an essential cohesion-building strategy. The male speaker stayed relatively silent during this period, and this resulted in very low use of both *oh* and *dui* for both speakers in those episodes. After the repeated rapport-building activities by the female speaker, the male speaker gradually became more open and emotionally expressive, and this transformation was reflected in his increased use of feedback from that point on.

In discourse, participants may unintentionally hit an area of high interest, and participants may become very involved. In this conversation the topic hits a major turning point in episode 14 at 42.4 minutes (2546 seconds), which is marked in the waveform in Figure 8. At that point, both participants suddenly discover something unexpected but highly relevant and meaningful to both of them, and this transforms the nature of the conversation, with a high intensity of involvement by both participants, as evidenced by the greatly increased use of feedback markers from that episode on. This effect is especially dramatic for the male speaker.

As can be seen in Table 7, the male speaker's use of feedback increased greatly after the turning point, with *umhum* increasing to over 3 times its pre-turning

Rhythmic synchrony in conversation — 103

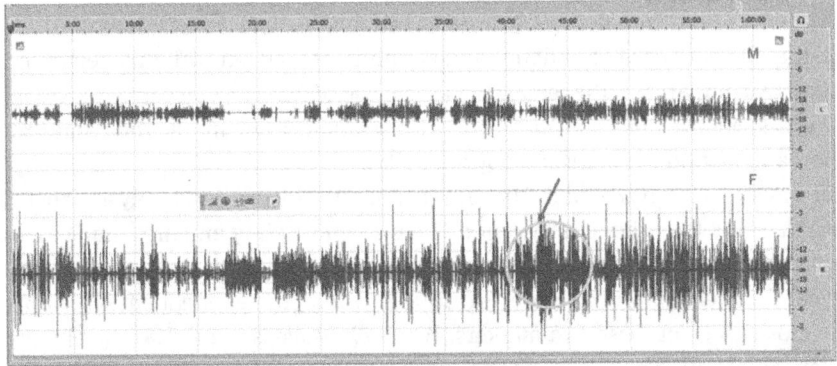

Figure 8: Waveform of the total conversation of mcdc05, with the climactic turning point marked. Comparison of waveforms for the pre- and post-climax periods shows clearly the increased intensity of both speakers after this point.

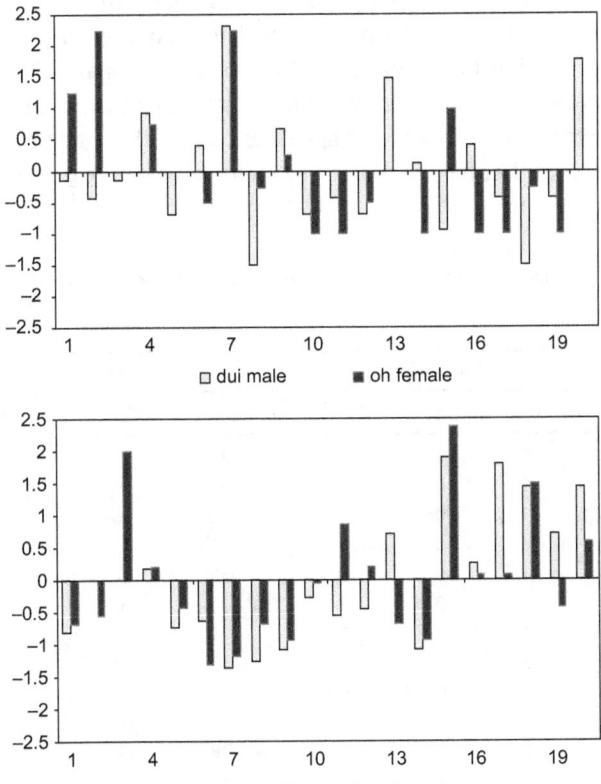

Figure 9: Comparison of normalized frequencies of female oh to male dui by episode, for mcdc01 (top) and mcdc05 (bottom), showing cross-feedback synchronous distribution patterns.

point average, and *dui* about 2.5 times, while his use of *oh* decreased slightly, indicating his increased confidence and certainty associated with this newfound identity. By comparison, the female speaker's use of feedback also increased and was consistent over the conversation, with *umhum* occurring at the same frequency, and *oh* and *dui* increasing by about 2/3.

The markers *oh* and *dui* 'right' have special significance in synchrony and rhythmic behavior as they signal divergent degrees of uncertainty and are complementary in function. Figure 9 compares the normalized counts of female *oh* frequency with male *dui* frequency by episode. Figure 9 shows that there is frequent synchrony of the cross-usage of these two markers. When *oh* usage is high, *dui* usage by the other speaker is often high, and when *oh* frequency is low, *dui* frequency tends to be low, as seen in mcdc05 (left). The cross-marker congruence in counts started early in the conversation, suggesting that these markers are entrained and have an active rhythmic role in bringing about overall convergence in speaker involvement and pitch synchrony. Figure 9 (right) shows a similar pattern exists for mcdc01.

The results of our study suggest that the use of feedback to encourage rapport can consist of a feedback loop that increases rapport between participants and leads to more synchronous feedback patterns over time. Our finding further provides evidence that convergent patterns occur as speakers cooperatively achieve a shared common ground, and that feedback is a key element of how speakers reach this goal in communication.

Table 6: Distribution counts of feedback markers *umhum*, *oh* and *dui* for each speaker by episode for mcdc05.

Episode	Time	Male			Female		
		Umhum	*Oh*	*Dui*	*Umhum*	*Oh*	*Dui*
1	189031	0	1	7	25	5	7
2	380205	3	0	15	21	6	6
3	566749	1	0	16	26	26	7
4	755074	8	0	18	24	12	7
5	949614	2	0	8	39	7	7
6	1136998	2	0	9	25	0	6
7	1326995	14	3	1	9	1	11
8	1515444	3	1	2	33	5	7
9	1703272	6	0	4	22	3	12
10	1892292	0	0	13	53	10	8
11	2080149	1	0	10	28	17	6
12	2267807	10	1	11	35	12	5
13	2450108	7	0	24	44	5	2

(Continued)

Table 6 (continued)

		Male			Female		
Episode	Time	Umhum	Oh	Dui	Umhum	Oh	Dui
14	2631258	27	2	4	6	3	14
15	2822970	6	0	37	45	29	8
16	3014206	13	0	19	42	11	15
17	3204482	8	0	36	12	11	10
18	3392224	7	0	32	15	22	11
19	3583697	22	1	24	23	7	14
20	3770367	12	0	32	55	15	6
Totals	62.83945	152	9	322	582	207	169
Total by speaker				483			958
Grand total							1441

Table 7: Counts and mean use per episode of feedback, pre- and post-turning point by speaker, ratio calculation based on 1-13:14-20.

	Male			Female		
	umhum	oh	dui	umhum	oh	dui
Pre TP	57.0	6.0	138.0	384.0	109.0	91.0
Post TP	95.0	3.0	184.0	198.0	98.0	78.0
Pre mean	4.4	0.5	10.6	29.5	8.4	7.0
Post mean	13.6	0.4	26.3	28.3	14.0	11.1
Ratio	3.1	0.9	2.5	1	1.7	1.6

*TP stands for turning point

4.5 Feedback, convergence, and meaning

In this section, we examined the relationships among feedback frequency, feedback distribution, and prosodic convergence. Our data indicate that prosodic convergence is high in episodes with a high level of interactive give-and-take and participant rapport. Consistent with other researchers' findings (Huang and Gratch, 2012), speakers can differ greatly in their overall use of feedback. For the current data, the female speaker used feedback twice as often as the male, with even greater variation for the different markers. Comparing standard deviations, the male speaker's feedback use varied greatly over the different episodes, and his feedback markers increased greatly as he became more confident, open, and involved after a key emotional turning point, while the female speaker's use was more consistent over the episodes. There is high prosodic convergence between speakers when both speakers' use of feedback is high, because the frequency of specific markers is linked to the emotional and involvement states of the two speakers. Our data and analysis support the view that shared emotion is an essential component of rapport.

Our findings also show that speaker role plays a significant role in the incidence and location of feedback markers with respect to the prosodic patterns. Feedback markers of high interest or surprise such as *oh*, and encouraging markers such as *um* or *umhum* occurred more frequently in areas of high pitch and convergence, and less frequently in divergent prosodic sections. The marker *dui* 'right' occurred more frequently in areas of convergence and stretches of extended rise as the hearer provided added encouragement or confirmation, respectively. Thus, feedback markers often provide explicit marking of the same underlying relational states that are provided by synchrony phenomena. Figure 10 provides an illustration of how meaning is effectively encoded in such short feedback utterances for spoken communication. As an example, *oh* can indicate a multitude of different degrees of uncertainty, surprise, and reaction to new information, and the particular prosodic shapes of *oh* function to distinguish the many possible interpretations. It is the specific nature of the judgment which determines the particular variants of a given marker within the overall prosodic shape.

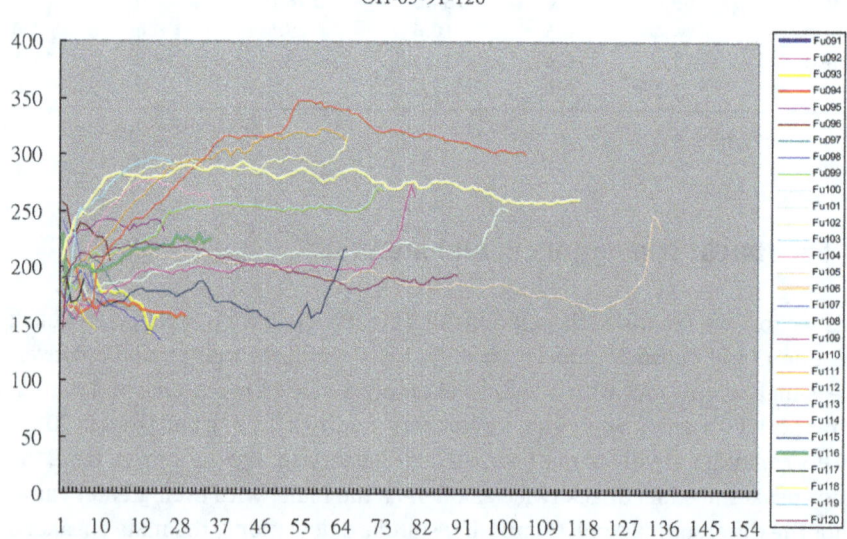

Figure 10: 30 instances of the female speaker's *oh*s in mcdc05, numbered sequentially, approximately occurring from episode 11 to the beginning of episode 14, showing different forms relating to different states and functions in spontaneous conversation.

5 Discussion: Domains of influence on synchrony

The importance of participant cohesion and rapport and the multimodal nature of human communication provide the basis for the consistency of our results on feedback as compared to research across similar sociological and discourse environments. Studies on both verbal and non-verbal feedback have identified gender-linked differences comparable to those we found for verbal feedback. In their research on phonetic convergence, Lelong and Bailly (2011) found that same-sex pairs show a strong tendency for convergence, with female-female pairs showing the strongest convergence. By contrast, in investigating entrainment in task-oriented game scenario dialogues, Levitan (2014) found that while female-female pairs entrained more than male-male pairs, entrainment is the strongest and most prevalent for male-female pairs, and this held for both English and Mandarin Chinese.

The strong effect of speaker role is especially characteristic of feedback. Participants change between main speaker and listener roles, and also in their relative status and involvement with the current topic. Sadler et al. (2009) found a similarly strong effect for speaker role in cyclical patterns of dominance and affiliation. Sadler and her colleagues were interested to determine in which direction adaptation occurs, and found, somewhat surprisingly, that participants judged to be at a more dominant position are more likely to adapt to the other person, rather than the reverse. In our own data, a change in main speaker role created both positive and negative lags in synchrony. These results point to the role of the underlying cognitive environment in giving rise to synchrony phenomena. The determinants of synchronous behavior have their roots in the cognitive and emotional states of participants, individual character, and mood, and this highlights the importance of individual variation in interactive behavior (Huang and Gratch, 2012).

The pattern we found of progressively higher synchrony of prosody and cohesion of feedback responses are also consistent with Levitan's findings (2014) of increased entrainment over time and its importance for successful conversations, as well as Nagaoka and Komori's (2008) similar finding of increasing synchrony in client-counselor dialogue in high rapport cases. The remarkably similar results that have been found to occur across distinctly different physiological modes of communication point to powerful parallel paths for the expression of interpersonal relationships and cognitive states.

6 Conclusion: A global view of synchrony

Results of the current study show that synchrony between speakers in a conversation occurs in two separate modes of expressive communication: *prosody* and *feedback frequency*. The multimodal synchrony seen in conversations both reflects and guides the interactive conversational structure, which frequently occurs in three major phases. In the initial phase, orientation and non-cohesion on topic direction are reflected in prosodic divergence and less-integrated feedback. In the second developmental stage, participants begin to explore certain topics in greater depth and gradually work towards a greater mutual understanding, and both prosody and feedback frequency gradually become more synchronized. In the final phase, the gradual establishment of convergent states is accomplished, and synchronous communication behavior is at its peak. Once achieved, the rapport and cohesiveness established between participants persist, and are reflected in a continued high level of synchrony.

In our view, it is the expressiveness and multimodal nature of language communication that is key to the synchronic phenomena in spoken language. Both aural memory and empathetic convergence of speaker states provide the foundation for progressively greater convergence seen in conversational speech. In communicating underlying cognitive and emotional states, participants seek not just a unidirectional transmission of information, but a confirmatory reflective loop that substantiates the cognitive states recognized and matched by the recipient, and this acts to mirror and increase cohesion and rapport between participants. Because of the close link between a cognitive state and its physiological expression, the mirrored expression of state in prosody and feedback provides a powerful and efficient method for this confirmatory loop, giving synchrony in language its great significance as a communicator and measure of a fundamental goal of language – the convergence of underlying cognitive and emotional states.

Acknowledgments: This work was initiated while I was a visiting scholar at the Linguistic Institute of Academia Sinica during 2012. I would like to express my sincere thanks to Dr. Shu-Chuan Tseng and Dr. Chiu-yu Tseng of Academia Sinica for their generous support, and to Dr. Janice Fon of the Graduate Institute of Linguistics at National Taiwan University for her encouragement. Finally, I am grateful to Professor Wallace Chafe for his inspiration and interest in this work. This research was supported in part by National Science Council of Taiwan under Grant No. NSC97-2410-H-029-026. The views expressed herein are those of the author and do not necessarily represent the views of the funding agency.

References

Allwood, J., Nivre, J. and Ahlsén, E. (1992). On the semantics and pragmatics of linguistic feedback. *J. Sem.*, 9:1–26.

Beňuš, Š. (2016). The prosody of backchannels in Slovak. *Proceedings of 8th International Conference on Speech Prosody, pp. 75–79*.

Brennan, S. E., and Clark, H. H. (1996). Conceptual pacts and lexical choice in conversation. *J. of Exp. Psychol.: Learning, Memory, and Cognition*, 22(6), 1482–1493.

Buschmeier, H., Z. Malisz, M. Włodarczak, S. Kopp, and P. Wagner. (2011). 'Are you sure you're paying attention?' – 'Uh-huh'. Communicating understanding as a marker of attentiveness. *Proceedings of INTERSPEECH 2011*, Florence, Italy, 2057–2060.

Campbell, N. (2009). An audio-visual approach to measuring discourse synchrony in multimodal conversation data, in *Proceedings of Interspeech 2009*, 2159–2162.

Campbell, N., and Scherer, S. (2010). Comparing measures of synchrony and alignment in dialogue speech timing with respect to turn-taking activity. *Proceedings of Interspeech2010*, 2546–2549.

Chafe, W. (1994). *Discourse, consciousness, and time: The flow and displacement of conscious experience in speaking and writing*. Chicago: University of Chicago Press, 53–70.

Chafe, W. (2001). "The analysis of discourse flow," in *The Handbook of Discourse Analysis* eds. Deborah Schiffrin, D. Tannen, and H. Hamilton, Oxford: Blackwell, 673–687.

Clark, H. (1996). *Using language*. Cambridge: Cambridge University Press.

Clayton, M., Sager, R., and Will, L. (2004). In time with the music: the concept of entrainment and its significance for ethnomusicology. *ESEM CounterPoint*, Vol. 1, 1–45.

Condon, W. S., and Sander, L. W. (1974). Neonate movement is synchronized with adult speech, interactional participation and language acquisition. *Science*, Vol.183, 99–101.

De Looze, C., Scherer, S., Vaughan, B., Campbell, N. (2014). Investigating automatic measurements of prosodic accommodation and its dynamics in social interaction. *Speech Communication* 58: 11–34.

Drummond, K. and Hopper, R. (1993). Back channels revisited: acknowledgment tokens and speakership incipiency. *Res. on Lang. and Soc. Int.* 26 (2):157–177.

Fusaroli R., Perlman M., Mislove A., Paxton A., Matlock T., Dale R. (2015). Timescales of massive human entrainment. *PLoS ONE* 10(4): e0122742.

Giles, H., and Smith, P. (1979). Accommodation theory: Optimal levels of convergence. In H. Giles & R. St. Clair (Eds.), *Language and social psychology* (pp. 45–65). Oxford: Blackwell.

Gill, S. P. (2012). Rhythmic synchrony and mediated interaction: towards a framework of rhythm in embodied interaction. *AI & Soc.* 27, 111–127.

Gratch, J., Wang, N., Gerten, J., Fast, E., and Duffy, R. "Creating rapport with virtual agents". 2007. *The 7th International Conference on Intelligent Virtual Agents*. Paris, France, 125–138.

Heylen, D., Bevacqua, E., Pelachaud, C., Isabella Poggi, Gratch, J., and Schröder, M. (2011). "Generating Listening Behaviour," in *Emotion-Oriented Systems*, eds. P. Petta et al. (Springer-Verlag Berlin Heidelberg), Cognitive Technologies, 321–347.

Huang, L., Morency, L., and Gratch, J. (2010). Learning backchannel prediction model from parasocial consensus sampling: A subjective evaluation. *The 10th International Conference on Intelligent Virtual Agents (IVA 2010)*, Philadelphia, PA, USA.

Huang, L. and Gratch, J. (2012). Crowdsourcing backchannel feedback: understanding the individual variability from the crowds. *The Interdisciplinary Workshop on Feedback Behaviors in Dialog*, Portland, Oregon.

Jonsdottir, G., Gratch, J., Fast, E., and Thórisson, K. (2007). Fluid semantic back-channel feedback in dialogue: challenges and progress. In *IVA 2007*, eds. C. Pelachaud et al. (Springer-Verlag Berlin, Heidelberg), LNAI 4722, 154–160.

Kuhlena, A., Brennan, S. (2010). Anticipating distracted addressees: how speakers' expectations and addressees' feedback influence storytelling. *Discourse Processes*, 47:567–587.

Levitan, R. 2014. *Acoustic-Prosodic Entrainment in Human-Human and Human-Computer Dialogue*. PhD thesis, Columbia University, New York.

Levitan, R., Beňuš, Š., Gravano, A., Hirschberg, J. (2015). Acoustic-prosodic entrainment in Slovak, Spanish, English and Chinese: a cross-linguistic comparison. *Proceedings of 16th Annual Meeting of the Special Interest Group on Discourse and Dialogue*, pp. 325–334.

Lelong, A. and Bailly, G. (2011). "Study of the phenomenon of phonetic convergence thanks to speech dominoes," in *Analysis of Verbal and Nonverbal Communication and Enactment: The Processing Issue*, eds. A. Vinciarelli, K. Vicsi, C. Pelachaud and A. Nijholt (Springer-Verlag), 280–293.

Menenti, L., Pickering, M. J., and Garrod, S.C. (2012). Toward a neural basis of interactive alignment in conversation. *Frontiers in Human Neuroscience*, 2012; 6: 185.

Nagaoka, C., Komori, M., and Yoshikawa, S. (2007). "Embodied synchrony in conversation," in *Conversational informatics: an engineering approach*, ed. T. Nishida (Wiley Series in Agent Technology. John Wiley & Sons), 331–352.

Nagaoka, C., Komori, M. (2008). Body movement synchrony in psychotherapeutic counseling: a study using the video-based quantification method. *IEICE Transactions on Information and Systems*, E91-D(6), 1634–1640.

Pardo, J. 2006. On phonetic convergence during conversational interaction. *J. of the Acous. Soc. Am.* 119(4): 2382–93.

Paxton, A., and Dale, R. (2013). Frame-differencing methods for measuring bodily synchrony in conversation. *Behavior Research Methods*, 45(2),329–343.

Sadler, P., Ethier, N., Gunn, G.R., Duong, D., and Woody, E. (2009). Are we on the same wavelength? Interpersonal complementarity as shared cyclical patterns during interactions. *J. of Person. & Soc. Psychol.* 97(6):1005–20.

Schegloff, E. (1982). "Discourse as an interactional achievement: some uses of *uh huh* and other things that come between sentences," *GURT 1981 Analyzing Discourse: Text and Talk*, ed. D. Tannen (Georgetown University Press), 71-93.

Tollefsen, D., Dale, R., and Paxton, A. (2013). Alignment, transactive memory, and collective cognitive systems. *Review of Philosophy and Psychology*, 4(1), 49–64.

Tseng, S.-C. (2004). Processing Spoken Mandarin Corpora. *Traitement automatique des langues. Special Issue: Spoken Corpus Processing*, 45(2): 89–108.

Tseng, S.-C. (2006). A study of discourse items and prosody. *Technical Report*, National Science Council of Taiwan.

Tseng, S.-C. (2008). Spoken corpora and analysis of natural speech. *Taiwan J. Ling*, vol. 6.2, 1–26.

Ward, N. and Tsukahara, W. (2000). Prosodic features which cue back-channel responses in English and Japanese. *J. Prag*, 23, 1177–1207.

Ward, N. (2006). Non-lexical conversational sounds in American English. Prag. & Cog., 14:129–182.

Włodarczak, M., and Heldner, M. (2015). "Respiratory properties of backchannels in spontaneous multiparty conversation," in *Proceedings of the 18 International Congress of Phonetic Sciences (ICPhS 2015)* (Glasgow).

Włodarczak M and Heldner M (2017). Respiratory Constraints in Verbal and Non-verbal Communication. Front. Psychol. 8:708.doi: 10.3389/fpsyg.2017.00708

Yang, L-C. (2006). "Integrating prosodic and contextual cues in the interpretation of discourse markers," in *Approaches to Discourse Particles*, ed. K. Fischer (Elsevier), 265–297.

Part II: **Language variation from a nonlinguistic perspective**
   A Variation in speakers' cognitive capability

Karlien Franco and Dirk Geeraerts
1 Botany meets lexicology: The relationship between experiential salience and lexical diversity

Abstract: In this paper, we explore the relationship between the experiential salience of natural concepts (i.e. the degree to which the concepts are well-known to language users, because they occur frequently in the everyday environment of the speakers) and the structure of the lexicon. More specifically, we focus on whether the amount of lexical dialect variation found in names for naturally occurring plants in ecologically consistent geographical regions in the northern part of Belgium, is influenced by the frequency of these plants in these regions. In contrast with previous research in linguistics, which has mostly focused on the relationship between the (textual) frequency of constructions in language use and language variation and change, we confront non-linguistic referential data with linguistic dialect data.

In practice, we use the distribution of naturally occurring plants in the language area, as described in the standard reference work on plant distribution in the northern part of Belgium (Van Landuyt et al. 2006), to determine whether more frequent plants show less variation. The linguistic data come from the digitized databases of the Dictionaries of the Brabantic, Limburgish and Flemish dialects (WBD, WLD, WVD). We consider several measures that quantify the amount of lexical variation per plant. First, we take into account the number of unique lexemes per plant per (ecologically consistent) region. Second, we use the type-token ratio per plant per region, with the number of types equal to the number of unique lexemes per plant and the number of tokens calculated as the total number of records per plant. Third, we use a measure of internal uniformity per plant per region, which quantifies the degree of lexical standardization in the names for each plant.

The results for the three measures per plant per region diverge. Overall, they show that, although plant frequency alone does not cause complete lexical standardization in a particular region, more frequent plants do show a smaller amount of lexical variation.

Keywords: lexical variation, dialectology, Dutch, cognitive sociolinguistics, onomasiology

---

Karlien Franco, KU Leuven, Belgium, karlien.franco@kuleuven.be
Dirk Geeraerts, KU Leuven, Belgium, dirk.geeraerts@kuleuven.be

https://doi.org/10.1515/9783110610895-005

1 Background

This paper focuses on variation in the names given to plants that occur naturally in the northern part of Belgium where Brabantic, Limburgish and Flemish dialects of Dutch are spoken (i.e. Flanders and Brussels). While a variety of work on plant name variation exists about these dialects (see Brok 2003), most of this research focuses on a small set of plants, the names that occur for these plants in particular locations and an etymological interpretation of the name (see for instance Pauwels 1933, Brok 1991, 2006). In this paper, we take a different approach. More specifically, we use the semantic field of plant names as a case study to investigate whether lexical diversity, i.e. variation in the number of names that exist for a particular plant, correlates with the degree of salience of the plant for language users.

Two contrasting hypotheses can be envisaged concerning the influence of concept salience on lexical diversity. On the one hand, previous research concerning the influence of semantic features on lexical geographical variation across the Limburgish dialects indicates that more salient concepts show a smaller amount of lexical diversity (Geeraerts & Speelman 2010, Speelman & Geeraerts 2008). For example, the concept KNOKKELKUILTJES 'the little dents between the knuckles of the hand' shows more lexical heterogeneity than the more salient concept KEEL 'throat'. While these studies focused on concepts from the semantic field of the human body, Franco, Geeraerts & Speelman (2015) showed that the influence of salience on lexical geographical variation also holds in other semantic fields.

Further evidence for this hypothesis comes from Swanenberg (2000), who relies on notions identified in the Cognitive Linguistics research paradigm to analyze variation in the naming and classification of birds. He shows, for instance, that the degree of preponderance of a particular type of bird in comparison to related bird types has an influence on the names that are used for the bird. Types of birds that are more familiar for the language users (like VELDLEEUWERIK 'skylark', Galerida cristata) are, for instance, named more frequently with hyperonymous names that actually refer to the category as a whole (like *leeuwerik* 'lark', Alaudidae), than less salient ones.

On the other hand, more salient concepts can sometimes also show more lexical variability. The degree of familiarity of a concept has been shown to influence differences in categorization between languages or dialects (for a recent study, see Bromhead 2011). As a result, naming differences occur as well. According to Goossens (1964), for instance, the global applicability of a lexeme[1] correlates with

---

[1] The global applicability of a lexeme ('globaliteitstoepasselijkheid', Goossens 1964:8) refers to the usage of one lexeme for a concept in a particular region, while the concept is conceptualized in a more detailed way in other areas. This contrasts with the local applicability of lexemes

the lack of familiarity of the concept. He argues, for instance, that one reason for the survival of two different names for the two handles of a scythe in the dialects spoken in the central part of Limburg in Belgium, is the high frequency of usage of the instrument in this region. As a result, language users categorize the different parts of the instrument in a more detailed way, by discerning the upper from the lower handle. In the rest of the south-eastern part of the Dutch language area, his dialect map only shows one name to refer to both the upper and lower handle. In this region, the less familiar concept SCYTHE shows less lexical diversity.

Overall, even though these two diverging hypotheses concerning the relationship between salience and lexical diversity can be distinguished, a positive correlation between salience and the amount of lexical diversity (i.e. more salient concepts show more lexical variation) seems to apply primarily to cases like the example of the scythe mentioned above, in which differences of categorization are involved. As the linguistic data that we use were collected at the level of the concept (viz. by the use of questionnaires in which the dialect name for a particular concept is elicited), categorization differences are diminished. For this reason, we expect to find a negative correlation between salience and lexical diversity (i.e. more salient concepts show less lexical variation).

To test this hypothesis, we operationalize local plant salience as the frequency of the plant in the geographical area of the language user, under the assumption that plants that naturally occur more frequently in a specific region are more familiar for the people living in that region. Additionally, the fact that some plants that are infrequent in a particular region but relatively frequent across the entire language area (i.e. locally infrequent, but globally frequent) are probably better known than plants that are infrequent everywhere, may result in a higher degree of salience for the first group of plants. For this reason, we also take into account the global frequency of the plant in the northern part of Belgium.

Interestingly, research in linguistics on the relationship between language variation and frequency has mostly focused on the (textual) frequency of constructions in language use (Divjak & Caldwell-Harris 2015: 54). Schmid (2007:119), for instance, argues that "the frequency of occurrence of concepts or constructions in a speech community has an effect on the frequency with which its members are exposed to them." Rather than relying on corpus data to determine the frequency or entrenchment of plant names or plant concepts in the speech community, in this paper, we aim to determine whether the referential frequency of the plants in everyday life affects language variation as well.

('fragmatoepasselijkheid'), which entails that in some regions conceptual and, thus, lexical differentiation occurs for a concept that is conceptualized as a whole in other regions.

Consequently, we rely on what we will refer to as the degree of *experiential salience* of a plant: the likelihood of language users encountering a particular plant in their everyday environment. To gauge experiential salience, we rely on measures of the referential frequency of the plants. However, other factors that affect experiential salience, like whether or not a plant has medicinal applications, or whether or not a plant is poisonous and to be avoided, can be envisaged as well (see Discussion).

We assume that experiential salience is related to the degree of onomasiological salience of a plant, in the sense that language users probably refer more frequently to concepts they often come into contact with. As a result, experiential salience may affect variation in the names that are given to plants: experientially more salient plants are expected to show less lexical diversity. For example, salient plants, like the common aspen (Populus tremula), which grows frequently throughout the language area under scrutiny, has fewer dialectal variants in the dictionaries that we use (viz. 40) than less frequent plants like the common cowslip, which occurs with 217 different names. The geographical distribution of these plants is shown in Figure 1 and 2. The magnitude of the dots is proportionate with the frequency of the plant in that location (i.e. in that so called hour square, see below) in the period 1972–2004. The squares reflect the distribution of the plant for the period 1939–1971 (also in hour squares).

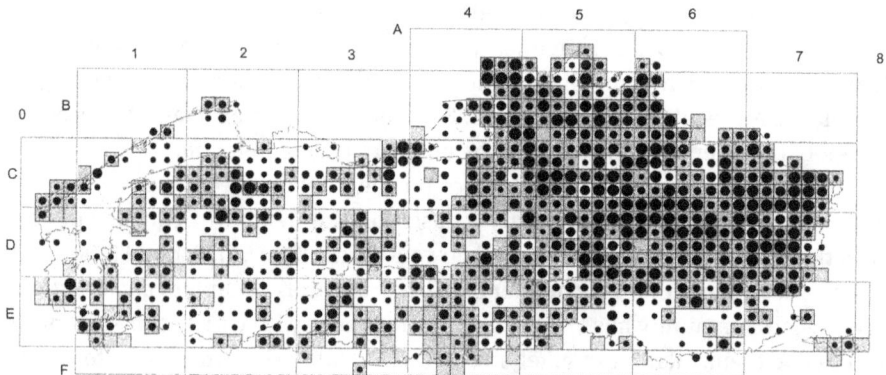

Figure 1: Geographical distribution of the common aspen (Populus tremula), a very frequent plant (Van Landuyt et al. 2006: 688).

This paper is structured as follows. Section 2 elaborates on the referential plant frequency data and on the linguistic data that are used in this study. In section 3, the results concerning the correlation between local and global plant

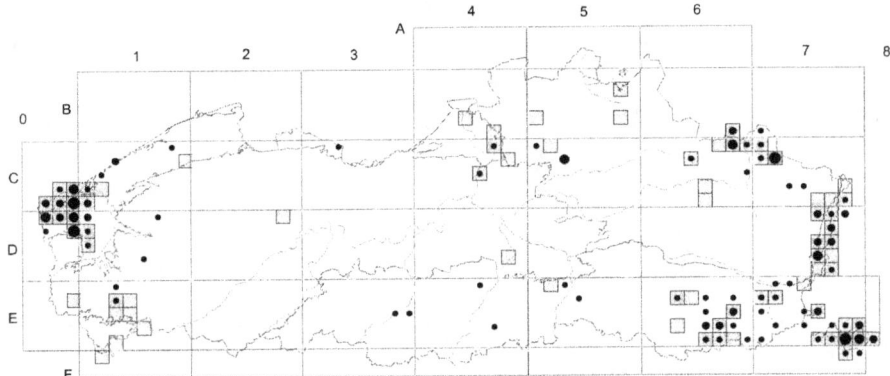

Figure 2: Geographical distribution of the common cowslip (Primula veris), a very infrequent plant (Van Landuyt et al. 2006: 712).

frequency and lexical diversity are provided. Section 4 provides a discussion of these results, followed by an overview of the restrictions on the present study and some suggestions for future research. Section 5 ties it all together in a conclusion.

2 Data

2.1 Referential and linguistic data

2.1.1 Referential data

As explained in section 1, we use frequency data of naturally occurring plants to gauge the familiarity of the plant in the language area under investigation. These referential data come from the *Atlas van de flora van Vlaanderen en het Brussels Gewest* (Van Landuyt et al. 2006), the standard reference work concerning the distribution of plants in the northern part of Belgium. The data are also available online (http://flora.inbo.be/).

The frequency of plants in the atlas is calculated as follows. The focus area of the atlas (i.e. the northern part of Belgium) is divided into kilometer squares of 1x1 kilometer. These kilometer squares are grouped into hour squares of 4x4 kilometers (see Figure 3). For each hour square, trained field workers investigated at least one quarter of the kilometer squares. The field workers were

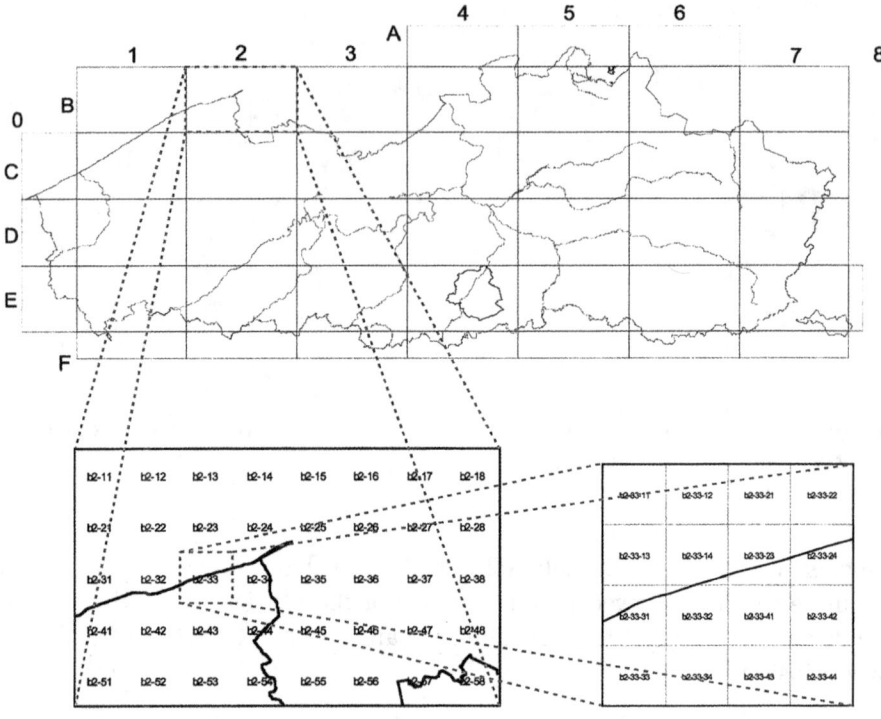

Figure 3: Hour and kilometer squares in the northern part of Belgium (Van Landuyt et al. 2006: 34).

asked to record which plants they encountered while walking through the kilometer square.[2]

We adopt two types of measures of plant frequency that are available in the atlas. On the one hand, we take into account the global frequency of a plant in the northern part of Belgium, expressed as the absolute number of hour and kilometer squares where the plant was encountered. On the other hand, we also use the relative number of investigated kilometer squares in which the plant was found per ecological region to gauge the local salience of a plant. The division of the northern part of Belgium into ecological regions is based on a simplified version of the ecologically coherent districts described in Sevenant et al. (2002). In the atlas, six ecological regions are distinguished: the

---

[2] Some of the data in the atlas also come from secondary sources. However, for the most part, the frequency data relies on the information provided by the field workers (Van Landuyt et al. 2006: 34–37).

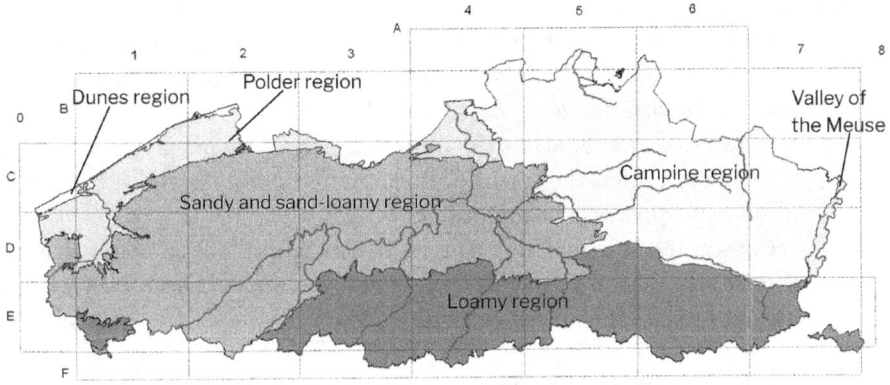

Figure 4: Ecological regions in the northern part of Belgium (Van Landuyt et al. 2006: 87).

Dunes region, the Campine region, the Loamy region, the region of the valley of the river Meuse, the Polder region and the Sandy and sand-loamy region (see Figure 4).

Because the atlas not only contains different measures of plant frequency (viz. local and global plant frequency), but also data from different periods,[3] we use four measures of plant frequency in total: one measure of local plant frequency and three measures of global plant frequency. The measure of local plant frequency is provided as a proportion in the atlas, i.e. the number of kilometer squares in which a plant was encountered divided by the total number of reliably investigated kilometer squares in a particular ecological region (Van Landuyt et al. 2006: 99). The measures of global frequency, however, are supplied as absolute values, i.e. the total number of kilometer or hour squares in which a plant was found in the northern part of Belgium.

1. local plant frequency:
    the relative number of investigated kilometer squares in which a plant was encountered per ecological region between 1972 and 2004 (*local relative frequency km squares 1972–2004*)

---

3 Due to historical developments, the atlas contains data from two different periods (1939–1971 and 1972–2004; see Van Landuyt et al. 2006: 9–31, 35). As the data collection process has remained the same since 1939 and as we have no obvious theoretical reasons to only rely on data from one period, we include data from both periods in the analysis.

2. global plant frequency:
   a. the absolute number of kilometer squares in which the plant was encountered throughout the northern part of Belgium between 1972 and 2004 (*global absolute frequency km squares 1972–2004*)
   b. the absolute number of hour squares in which the plant was encountered throughout the northern part of Belgium between 1939 and 1971 (*global absolute frequency hour squares 1939–1971*)
   c. the absolute number of hour squares in which the plant was encountered throughout the northern part of Belgium between 1972 and 2004 (*global absolute frequency hour squares 1972–2004*)

As the amount of kilometer squares in the northern part of Belgium is very large and as not all kilometer squares were investigated by the fieldworkers, most plants seem to be relatively infrequent when kilometer square calculations are used (although some plants are locally very frequent, see Van Landuyt et al. 2006: 69–80). As a result, global frequency per hour square is probably a better measure of plant frequency. However, all four plant frequency measures are highly correlated in the data set ($.85 \leq r \leq .98$; $p < 0.001$).

2.1.2 Linguistic data

The linguistic data used in this study come from three related sources. We use the digitized databases of the *Flora* chapter of the Dictionaries of the Brabantic, Limburgish and Flemish dialects (WBD, WLD, WVD). These onomasiological dictionaries contain the lexemes that are used in a large number of locations throughout the three dialect areas (N = 1033 locations). We focus on the data from locations in the Belgian part of the Dutch language area and exclude data from The Netherlands, because the referential plant frequency data only contain information about plants in the northern part of Belgium.

Furthermore, we only include data from these databases that were elicited through large-scale questionnaires that were distributed systematically in every location of each dialect area (i.e. in the Brabantic, Limburgish and Flemish dialect areas), and exclude data from small-scale local dictionaries or other sources with a limited scope.[4] In practice, for the Brabantic and Limburgish

---

4 The databases, which serve as the source material for the dictionaries, also contain data from other sources, such as local dictionaries or questionnaires with a smaller geographical range. The Brabantic and Limburgish questionnaires were distributed between 1960 and 1982. The Flemish questionnaire data were elicited later: between 1998 and 2000.

data, we only use data that were collected on the basis of the questionnaires of the *Nijmeegse Centrale voor Dialect- en Naamkunde* (Nijmegen Centre for Dialectology and Onomastics). For the Flemish data, we also limit the dataset to only include data collected through the questionnaires that were sent out systematically throughout the dialect area by the lexicographers. Even though these Flemish questionnaires are not identical to the Brabantic and Limburgish ones, they are equivalent. The Flemish questionnaires include, for instance, questionnaires on plants in general (number 104, distributed in 1998), on grass (number 112, distributed in 1999) and on trees and shrubbery (number 115, distributed in 1999). The Limburgish and Brabantic data mostly come from questionnaire N 82 (1981; plants in general and trees and shrubbery), and from questionnaire N 92 (1982; names for plants and herbs). We restrict our attention to plants that occur in all three databases.

As the three dictionaries have been collaborating since 1990 (Kruijsen 1996) to achieve consistency and alignment of the databases, we believe that restricting our attention to the data that were collected through the large-scale questionnaires and that occur in all three dictionaries, ensures maximal comparability between the sources. Moreover, the analysis requires that the data were collected in a systematic way, because counting the number of different lexemes per plant concept is only feasible if the data were collected in the same locations for each concept. By only relying on the questionnaire data, we ensure that the geographical scope of the data that we use is as systematic as possible.[5]

Table 1: Number of concepts and number of records per ecological region.

ecological region	number of concepts	number of records
Dunes region	84	1887
Polder region	101	9636
Sandy and sand-loamy region	114	22755
Loamy region	132	5738
Campine region	118	692
Valley of the river Meuse	65	99

---

[5] However, as the analysis will show, the amount of data is still relatively small for a number of plants and can differ between plants. Two explanations can be envisaged. First, it is possible that the questionnaires were not distributed as systematically as expected throughout the language area. However, another explanation may be that the small amount of data also reflects a lack of familiarity of the plant concepts (see Geeraerts & Speelman 2010 and Speelman & Geeraerts 2008): perhaps the respondents did not reply to questions of the questionnaire about plants that they were unfamiliar with, because they did not know the name for the plant in their local dialect.

Overall, the data set contains 137 different concepts. The number of concepts and the total number of records per ecological region is shown in Table 1. This table reveals large differences between ecological regions. On the one hand, this can be explained by the fact that the surface area of the ecological regions differs. The Dunes region, for example, is a rather narrow strip of land in the west of the northern part of Belgium. As a result, the number of locations in this region is relatively small. On the other hand, differences in the number of concepts and records per ecological region can also be explained by the fact that, overall, a large proportion of the data come from the WVD. This dictionary contains 30 666 records for the plant concepts under scrutiny, while the WLD and WBD combined only contain 10 203 records. As the data from the WVD mostly span the Dunes region, the Polder region and parts of the Loamy region and of the Sandy and sand-loamy region (see Figure 5), it is not surprising that the number of records is the largest in these regions.

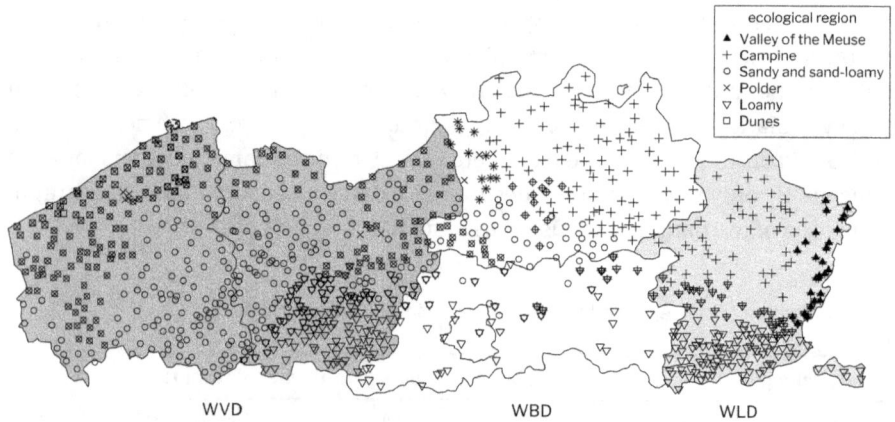

Figure 5: Dialect boundaries as represented by the WBD (white), WLD (light grey) and WVD (dark grey) and ecological regions in the northern part of Belgium.

Figure 5 further shows that the data is relatively sparse in the south of the center of the northern part of Belgium, which is covered by the WBD. It also indicates that some locations belong to more than one ecological region. This has to do with the fact that the ecological regions are defined at the level of the municipality in Sevenant et al. (2002), even though the borders of ecological regions sometimes run through a municipality. For example, the municipality of Bruges belongs to three different ecological regions: the western part of Bruges belongs to the Dunes region; the central, largest part of this municipality is part of the

Polder region; the eastern part of Bruges is included in the Sandy and sand-loamy region.

2.2 Calculating lexical diversity per concept

To operationalize the amount of lexical diversity that is found for the plant concepts in the dataset, we compare the influence of plant frequency on three measures of lexical richness. Each measure is calculated per plant per ecological region.

The first measure, *number of different lexemes*, is computed by counting the number of lexemes that occur per plant per ecological region. The number of different lexemes ranges from 1 to 92, but most concepts have a relatively low value for this variable (mean = 8.14, sd = 11.49). We include this simple calculation of lexical diversity because it is also used in other studies that were mentioned in section 1 on the relationship between concept salience and lexical heterogeneity in the WLD (Franco, Geeraerts & Speelman 2015, Geeraerts & Speelman 2010, Speelman & Geeraerts 2008).

However, a strong positive correlation between the number of different lexemes and the number of records that occur in the data set per concept exists (see Figure 6; r = 0.91, p < 0.001). As noted before, we only use data from the

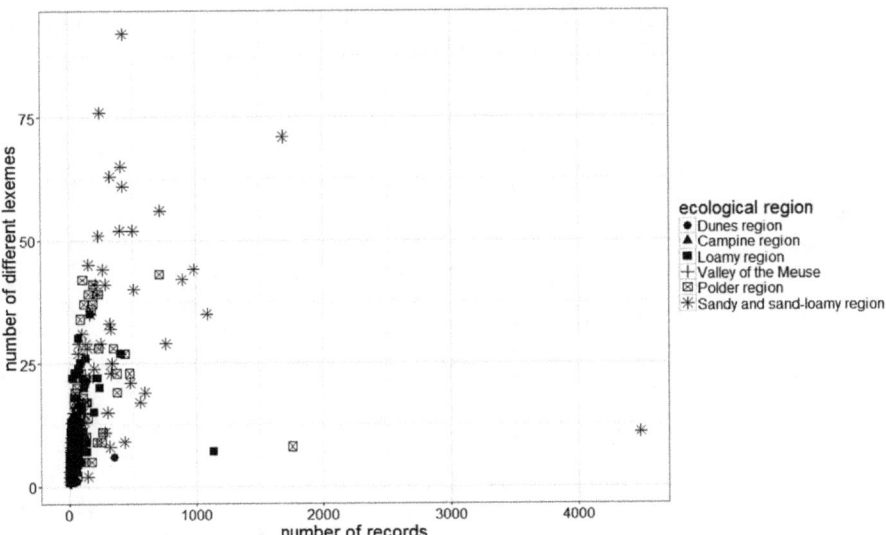

Figure 6: Correlation between number of records and number of different lexemes.

questionnaires in the dictionary to ensure that the data was collected as systematically as possible. As Figure 6 indicates, however, the number of records per concept differs strongly: the number of records ranges from 1 to 4487, with mean 66.46 and standard deviation 240. Most of the concepts with a large number of records come from the Sandy and sand-loamy region (indicated with *). The concepts on the bottom right side of the plot represent the concept OAK in three different regions. From left to right, they are based on data from the Loamy region, from the Polder region and from the Sandy and sand-loamy region.

A second measure of lexical diversity that is included in the analysis, is the type-token ratio (TTR) per plant per ecological region (see for example Tweedie & Baayen 1998). We use it to account for differences in the number of records (i.e. the number of tokens) that are available per concept, which can affect the number of different lexemes (i.e. the number of types) that are found for each concept per region. The type-token ratio approaches 0 when a small number of types is available, given the number of tokens. It is equal to 1 when the number of types is equal to the number of tokens.

TTR decreases when more tokens for the same number of types occur per concept, with values close to 1 expressing a large amount of lexical variation and figures close to 0 indicating that the concept shows a small amount of lexical diversity (left panel of Figure 7). For example, the ratio is close to 0 when for a total of 1000 tokens, only 90 different lexical items are found (.09), while it is close to 1 when the same number of unique lexical items occurs for 100 tokens

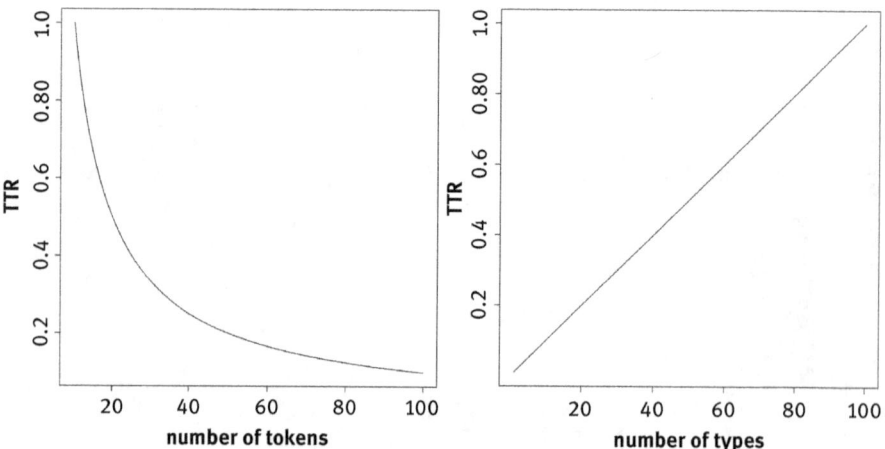

Figure 7: Type-token ratio for increasing numbers of tokens (left panel) and increasing numbers of types (right panel).

(.9). TTR is also smaller when fewer types for the same number of tokens occur per concept (right panel of Figure 7), again with low values for a small amount of lexical diversity and with values close to 1 demonstrating a large amount of lexical variation for the concept. For instance, TTR is high (.9) when 90 unique lexical items occur for a total of 100 observations (i.e. a lot of lexical diversity: almost one new lexeme for every additional observation), while it is low (.1) when 10 unique lexical items occur for the same amount of tokens (i.e. little lexical variation).

However, TTR is also sensitive to the amount of observations per concept ($r = -0.87$, $p < 0.001$), probably because the dataset contains a relatively large proportion of concepts that have the same number of types and tokens (viz. 28.2%). For all these concepts, a limited number of records is available in the data. For example, the aspen (Populus tremula) occurs only once in the data from the Campine region; the forget-me-not (Myosotis arvensis) occurs once in the data from the Meuse valley. The plant with the largest number of types and tokens and TTR = 1 is the common corn-cockle (Agrostemma githago) in the Loamy region (11 types, 11 tokens).

A third measure we use is the measure of internal uniformity, which was first used in Geeraerts, Grondelaers & Speelman (1999; also see Speelman et al. 2003) to determine the degree of uniformity in the usage of lexical variants in a speech community. Maximal uniformity (or standardization) occurs when everyone uses a single variant to describe a particular concept in the same situation. In our dataset, a complete lack of uniformity in an ecological region would occur when a different lexical item is used for every observation for the plant in that ecological region. In this paper, we calculate this measure to determine whether plants that are more frequent in a particular region also show a higher degree of lexical standardization, in the sense that one lexical variant takes precedence over its competing heteronyms. However, since the ecological regions often span more than one dialect area, other factors, like dialect boundaries, probably influence the degree of standardization as well. (Note that, in this paper, we are interested in a descriptive form of lexical standardization, whereby one lexical item becomes the preferred variant to refer to a particular concept, resulting in highly homogeneous (and, thus, standardized and uniform) language use. We are not concerned with a normative reading of the term 'standardization', which assumes that the preferred variant is prescriptively imposed upon a community of language users.)

The quantification of uniformity takes into account both the number of alternatives that occur in the data to express a certain concept (uniformity is smaller if more alternatives for the same concept exist) and the relative frequency of each of these variants (uniformity is higher if there is a clearly dominant term for a concept). For concept Z in data set Y, internal uniformity $I_Z(y)$ is calculated as follows:

$$I_Z(Y) = \sum_{i=1}^{n} F_{Z,Y}(x_i)^2$$

In this formula, x_1 to x_i are the lexemes that are used to express concept Z in data set Y and $F_{z,y}$ is the relative frequency of lexeme x in data set Y for concept Z. The measure of internal uniformity ranges from 0 to 1, with 0 indicating a complete lack of uniformity (i.e. a lot of lexical diversity) and 1 indicating complete uniformity (i.e. a lack of lexical diversity). The correlation between this operationalization and the number of records per concept is lower, but still significant (r = -0.665, p < 0.001): concepts with more records in the dataset show a smaller amount of uniformity.

To match the linguistic and the referential data, we restrict our attention to plant concepts that are available in the questionnaires from all three dictionaries (see above). We exclude plant concepts that do not refer to actual plants, like BLOEMKNOP 'bud', or that are too general, in the sense that they do not refer to a particular type of plant, like MOS 'moss'. Then, we assign each location in the dictionary data to the ecological regions that were distinguished in the atlas. For this procedure, we rely on Sevenant et al. (2002), which contains an overview of the municipalities in Belgium per ecological region. However, we make some adaptations to the description of Sevenant et al. (2002) to obtain the simplified version of the ecological regions that is used in the atlas. In a next step, we add both the global plant frequency information and local plant frequency per plant per ecological region to the dataset, on the basis of the scientific names of the plants that are provided in the Dictionary of the Limburgish Dialects (WLD: 25–30). Finally, we calculate the number of different lexemes, the type-token ratio and internal uniformity per plant per ecological region.

For example, the dataset contains the three measures of lexical diversity (columns 5–7 in Table 2) for the wood anemone (Anemone nemorosa) in five ecological regions (viz. the Campine, Dunes, Loamy, Polder and Sandy and sand-loamy region; column 3).[6] It also includes the local frequency of this plant in these five regions, expressed in percentages (column 8), and the global frequency of the plant (measured in three ways in columns 9–11, see above) in the northern part of Belgium. In contrast with the measure of local frequency (i.e. per ecological region), global plant frequency is the same in each ecological region, as it is a measure of the frequency of the plant in the northern part of Belgium. In the

---

6 Note that we have no information about the wood anemone in the ecological region of the valley of the Meuse, because no linguistic data is available for this plant from locations belonging to this ecological region.

Table 2: Wood anemone (Anemone nemorosa) in the final dataset.

1	2	3	4	5	6	7	8	9	10	11
plant	scientific name	ecological region	number of records	number of diff. lexemes	TTR	internal uniformity	local rel. freq. kmsq. '72–04	global abs. freq. kmsq. '72–'04	global abs. freq. hoursq. '39–71	global abs. freq. hoursq. '72–04
wood anemone	Anemone nemorosa	Campine	1	1	1	1	9.80	2031	409	507
wood anemone	Anemone nemorosa	Dunes	12	5	0.417	0.222	0.00	2031	409	507
wood anemone	Anemone nemorosa	Loamy	90	25	0.278	0.117	48.60	2031	409	507
wood anemone	Anemone nemorosa	Polder	72	23	0.319	0.118	0.40	2031	409	507
wood anemone	Anemone nemorosa	Sandy- & sandloamy	206	41	0.199	0.199	23.90	2031	409	507

analysis, we aggregate over all the regions and over all the plants (N = 614). We test whether the measures of lexical diversity (columns 5–7) correlate with the measures of plant frequency (columns 8–11).

2.3 Correlating plant frequency and lexical diversity

To test whether plant frequency has a significant influence on the diversity in the names for plants in the data set, we use Spearman's rank correlation tests. More specifically, we test whether the plant frequency measures (*local relative frequency km squares 1972–2004, global absolute frequency km squares 1972–2004, global absolute frequency hour squares 1939–1971* and *global absolute frequency hour squares 1972–2004*) correlate significantly with each of the three operationalizations of lexical diversity (*number of different lexemes, type-token ratio* and *internal uniformity*). We also calculate the correlation coefficient. This coefficient ranges from -1 to 1, with negative values representing a negative correlation between the variables and positive values indicating a positive correlation. When the coefficient is 0, no correlation between the variables is found.

Note that the interpretation of the correlation coefficient differs for the number of different lexemes per concept and TTR on the one hand, and for internal uniformity on the other hand. A positive correlation coefficient for plant frequency and the former measures indicates that more frequent plants show *more* lexical diversity. However, a positive correlation coefficient for plant frequency and the latter measure shows that internal uniformity correlates positively with plant frequency and, thus, that more frequent plants show *less* lexical diversity.

3 Results

This section presents the results of the analysis. All the analyses were carried out with R 3.2.4 (R Core Team 2016). In 3.1, we correlate the four measures of plant frequency from the atlas with the three measures of lexical diversity, calculated per plant per ecological region. In 3.2, the relationship between global and local plant frequency is scrutinized. Although we expect to find negative correlations between number of different lexemes and TTR and the plant frequency measures, and a positive correlation between these measures and internal uniformity, we consistently find the opposite effect for number of different lexemes and for the measure of internal uniformity. An explanation for these findings is provided in the discussion (Section 4).

3.1 The relationship between plant frequency and lexical diversity

Table 3 provides an overview of the p-value and Spearman's rank correlation coefficient for each combination of the measures of plant frequency and of lexical diversity per plant. The table indicates that a significant correlation (alpha = 0.05) exists between plant frequency and lexical diversity in all the cells. However, as the absolute values of the coefficients are never larger than 0.261, the correlation between plant frequency and lexical diversity is not very strong. Furthermore, plant frequency does not always correlate with lexical diversity in the way that was expected. More specifically, for number of different lexemes, which is shown in the second column of the table, positive correlations are found, while internal uniformity, in the fourth column, shows significant negative correlations. This means that more variation is found for plants that are more frequent, both locally and globally.

Table 3: Correlation between measures of plant frequency and measures of lexical diversity per plant.

	number of different lexemes	type-token ratio (TTR)	internal uniformity
local relative frequency km squares 1972–2004	0.261 $p < 0.001$	−0.256 $p < 0.001$	−0.191 $p < 0.001$
global absolute frequency km squares 1972–2004	0.241 $p < 0.001$	−0.261 $p < 0.001$	−0.156 $p < 0.001$
global absolute frequency hour squares 1939–1971	0.233 $p < 0.001$	−0.223 $p < 0.001$	−0.155 $p < 0.001$
global absolute frequency hour squares 1972–2004	0.240 $p < 0.001$	−0.256 $p < 0.001$	−0.158 $p < 0.001$

For the third column in the table, which provides the results for TTR, all the measures of plant frequency show a negative correlation with lexical diversity. This is in accordance with what was expected: more frequent plants show a smaller amount of lexical diversity. However, as suggested in section 2.2, TTR is sensitive to the number of tokens per concept, in the sense that TTR is high for concepts with the same number of types and tokens, even when only a small number of records is available for these concepts. As about one third of the concepts in the data set have a TTR value of 1, inspecting whether the negative correlation persists when only plants with a TTR value lower than 1 are included in the analysis may offer some more insight into the relation between plant frequency and

TTR. Table 4 shows Spearman's rank correlation coefficients and the p-values for this subset of the data. Even though the correlation coefficients are slightly lower than in Table 3, the significant negative correlations persist: more frequent plants show a smaller amount of lexical diversity.[7]

Table 4: Correlation between four measures of plant frequency and TTR per plant for concepts with TTR smaller than 1.

	correlation coefficient and p-value for Spearman's rank correlation
local relative frequency km squares 1972–2004	−0.220 $p < 0.001$
global absolute frequency km squares 1972–2004	−0.261 $p < 0.001$
global absolute frequency hour squares 1939–1971	−0.206 $p < 0.001$
global absolute frequency hour squares 1972–2004	−0.255 $p < 0.001$

3.2 The relationship between the global and local frequency of a plant

Concerning the relationship between the four measures of plant frequency that were used, Tables 3 and 4 show that both the local and global frequency of a plant correlate with lexical diversity. By solely relying on these measures, we cannot determine whether local and global frequency have the same effect on lexical diversity. As explained in section 1, we assume that plants that are only infrequent in a particular region are still more salient overall than globally infrequent

---

[7] Additionally, we checked whether significant correlations are also found for plant concepts with at least 50 records. This data set is smaller (N = 137) and, probably as a result, some of the plant frequency measures lose their significance. A significant correlation is still found between TTR and global absolute frequency hour squares 1972–2004 ($p < 0.05$, r = -0.18). Near-significant negative correlations, which would probably reach significance in a larger data set, still occur between TTR and global absolute frequency km squares 1972–2004 ($p < 0.1$, r = -0.16), and between internal uniformity and local relative frequency km squares 1972–2004 ($p < 0.1$, r = -0.15). All the correlation coefficients have the same sign as in the larger data set, but the absolute values are lower. Overall, these results suggest that the relationship between plant frequency and lexical diversity is not solely dependent on the amount of data per concept.

plants and, thus, show less lexical diversity.[8] In sum, we expect to find that lexical diversity follows the following pattern:

(1) globally and locally frequent plant	(2) locally infrequent, globally frequent plant	(3) globally and locally infrequent plant

⟶

less *more*
lexical diversity *lexical diversity*

To determine whether this relationship holds, we build three mixed-effects linear regression models with as a response variable the number of different lexemes (model 1), TTR (model 2) and internal uniformity (model 3) per plant per ecological region. Since the dataset contains multiple observations for each ecological region and for most of the plants, we use these factors as random effects in the models. We include frequency category per plant as a fixed-effects predictor in each of these models (N = 336).[9] This variable has three possible levels, depending on the global and local frequency of the plant:

1. very frequent plants, i.e. plants that occur in at least 2/3 of the hour squares that were investigated between 1939 and 1971 and that are available in at least 70% of the kilometer squares of the region under scrutiny (N = 106), e.g. the common nettle (Urtica dioica) in all ecological regions;
2. plants that are globally frequent, but infrequent in a particular region, i.e. plants that occur in at least 2/3 of the hour squares that were investigated between 1939 and 1971, but that are only available in less than half of the km squares in a particular region (N = 51), e.g. the common bent (Agrostis capillaris) in the Polder region;
3. plants that are globally and locally infrequent, i.e. plants that occur in less than 1/3 of the hour squares that were investigated between 1939 and 1971 and that are only available in less than half of the km squares in a particular region (N = 179), e.g. the sweetscented bedstraw (Galium odoratum) in all ecological regions.

---

8 As an anonymous reviewer points out, differences in experiential salience may also be found when a plant is locally frequent but globally infrequent. However, as only two plants in our dataset would belong to this category (viz. the wild privet (Ligustrum vulgare) and the goldmoss stonecrop (Sedum acre), two plants that are typically found near the sea and, thus, grow frequently in the Dunes area, but only rarely occur naturally in the rest of the northern part of Belgium), we did not take this category into account.

9 Because we are mostly interested in the extreme cases in this part of the analysis, we do not include all the plants in the models. More specifically, plants that are relatively 'neutral' regarding global or local frequency, i.e. plants that are neither locally, nor globally very frequent or infrequent, are not assigned to any of the frequency categories.

Table 5 shows the output of the three regression models. At the top of the Table, the random effects (all adjustments to the intercept) are shown with their corresponding standard deviation, and the residual error. Each model has the same random effects structure, with a random intercept for plant and a random intercept for ecological region. In each of the models, this random structure was statistically validated before including the fixed-effects predictor.[10] The bottom of the page shows the model diagnostics. Marginal and conditional R^2 show the proportion of variance explained by the fixed effects alone, and the proportion explained by the combination of the fixed and random factors, respectively.[11]

The middle part of Table 5 shows the estimate and p value for the fixed-effects predictor *frequency category*. In models 1 and 2, a higher value for the response variable indicates a larger amount of lexical variation per plant (operationalized as number of different lexemes and TTR, respectively). In these models, we would therefore expect positive estimates for the locally and globally infrequent plants, in comparison to the reference level (globally and locally frequent plants), which is captured in the intercept. However, the results are not completely in line with this expectation. For number of different lexemes, the amount of variation decreases for less frequent plants. However, this unexpected negative trend is probably connected to the fact that for less frequent plants, a smaller amount of records is available per plant. In fact, there is a significant positive correlation between the number of responses per plant and the three plant frequency categories (H = 31.645, $p < 0.001$). The globally frequent plants have 160 records on average (sd = 497); for locally infrequent plants, the mean number of records per plant is 93 (sd = 259); for globally infrequent plants, the average number of records is only 26 (sd = 60). As the number of lexemes and the number of records per plant per region are highly correlated (see 2.2), it is not surprising that for the less frequent plants, a smaller number of different lexemes is found.

In model 3, higher values for the response variable signify a smaller amount of variability. We therefore expect negative estimates for the locally and globally infrequent plants. However, in this model, we find the opposite effect as well: less frequent plants show a significantly higher amount of internal uniformity. In sum, only the results for TTR are as expected: both locally and globally infrequent

---

10 Ideally, we would have liked to use a random intercept for each plant per ecological region. However, the data do not support models with a random structure this complex. Instead, we use a separate random intercept for plant and ecological region and verify that intercept-only models with this random structure perform better than models without one or both of these random intercepts.
11 Marginal and conditional R^2 were calculated using sem.model.fits() from the piecewise-SEM-package (see https://jonlefcheck.net/2013/03/13/r2-for-linear-mixed-effects-models/, accessed 05.05.2017).

Table 5: Output for the random and fixed effects for mixed-effects linear regression models with as response variables the number of different lexemes per plant (model 1), TTR per plant (model 2) and internal uniformity per plant (model 3) per plant frequency category (reference level: globally frequent plants). Marginal R2 shows the proportion of variance explained by the fixed effects alone. Conditional R^2 depicts the proportion of variance explained by the fixed and random factors.

	model 1 nr. of different lexemes			model 2 TTR				model 3 internal uniformity			
random effects		std. dev			std. dev				std. dev		
plant	intercept	6.240		intercept	0.210			intercept	0.133		
ecological region	intercept	6.131		intercept	0.204			intercept	0.188		
residual		8.593			0.201				0.250		
fixed effects	estimate	std. error	p value	estimate	std. error	p value		estimate	std. error	p value	
intercept (glob. freq.)	11.004	2.875	< 0.01	0.434	0.093	< 0.01		0.4701	0.0842	< 0.01	
locally infrequent	−1.549	2.158	NS	0.111	0.058	< 0.1		0.1183	0.0564	< 0.05	
globally infrequent	−7.035	1.808	< 0.001	0.243	0.054	< 0.001		0.1617	0.0443	< 0.001	
model diagnostics											
marginal R^2	0.068			0.087				0.043			
conditional R^2	0.542			0.707				0.481			

plants have a significantly higher estimate than the frequent plants. This means that the less frequent a plant is, the higher its TTR value and, thus, higher the amount of variation in the names for the plant.

4 Discussion

Overall, the results of our analyses show that a correlation exists between plant frequency and lexical diversity. Although we aimed to show that experientially more familiar plants show less lexical diversity, the results are not completely in line with this expectation. One explanation for this finding is that the correlation between the measures of lexical diversity and the number of records that are available per plant influences the results to a certain extent (see 2.2). Although for TTR and internal uniformity, some (near-)significant correlations are still found when only plants with a relatively high number of records are included in the analysis, this is not the case for different number of lexemes (see section 3.1 and footnote 7). Consequently, the correlation between lexical diversity and number of records especially affects the results for the measure of number of different lexemes per concept: obtaining a higher number of different lexemes when more data is collected, is expected (although this number is likely to stabilize when enough tokens are available).

Interestingly, the results for TTR and internal uniformity differ, even though both of these measures take the number of tokens per concept into account. Before identifying some suggestions for future research in 4.2, section 4.1 will outline two explanations for these diverging results. On the one hand, TTR and internal uniformity can be different because they measure conceptually different phenomena. On the other hand, the measures were calculated per ecological region, but an ecological region may include different dialect regions.

4.1 TTR versus internal uniformity

The results for the TTR measure are as expected (less lexical diversity is found for more frequent plants and locally infrequent plants show less lexical variation than globally infrequent plants). Furthermore, the correlation persists even when only concepts are included in the analysis for which TTR is smaller than 1 (see Table 4). The results for internal uniformity show the opposite trend. Because the measures of lexical diversity are calculated at the level of the ecological region, the relationship between internal uniformity and TTR can probably be explained in terms of the degree of standardization per ecological region.

Table 6 shows the difference between the two measures. The number of tokens is comparable for the four plants, great mullein (Verbascum Thapsus) in the Loamy region, bitter dock (Rumex obtusifolius) in the Polder region, black locust (Robinia pseudoacacia) in the Sandy and sand-loamy region and forget-me-not (Myosotis arvensis) in the Dunes region. The number of different lexemes decreases from top to bottom (see Appendix 1 for an overview of the lexical items used per plant). Table 6 confirms that while the TTR measure cannot distinguish row 2 from the third one, the measure of internal uniformity can. The latter is sensitive to the number of lexemes that occur per concept *and* to the number of tokens per lexeme (i.e. type). It is low for concepts which show a smaller amount of standardization (i.e. one lexical item takes precedence over its competing dialectal heteronyms), like the bitter dock in the Polder region, and higher for plants with a larger degree of standardization, like the black locust in the Sandy and sand-loamy region.

As a consequence, even though plant frequency has an influence on the number of lexemes per concept, as indicated by the results for TTR, it does not necessarily ensure that one lexeme becomes the preferred lexeme over its competing synonyms throughout the ecological region. While for more frequent plants, the number of different variants decreases for the same amount of tokens,

Table 6: A comparison of number of different lexemes, TTR and internal uniformity.

	plant name, ecological region	number of records	distribution of types	number of different lexemes	TTR	internal uniformity
1	great mullein (Verbascum Thapsus), Loamy region	26	lexeme$_{1...18}$ occur once lexeme$_{19...22}$ occur once	22	0.846	0.050
2	bitter dock (Rumex obtusifolius), Polder region	38	lexeme$_{1,2}$ occur once lexeme$_3$ occurs 3 times lexeme$_4$ occurs 4 times lexeme$_5$ occurs 10 times lexeme$_6$ occurs 19 times	6	0.158	0.338
3	black locust (Robinia pseudoacacia), Sandy and sand-loamy region	26	lexeme$_{1,2,3}$ occur once lexeme$_4$ occurs 23 times	4	0.154	0.787
4	forget-me-not (Myosotis arvensis), Dunes region	52	lexeme$_1$ occurs 52 times	1	0.019	1

this does not mean that every language user chooses the same name in the same situation (i.e. ecological region). Geographical variation within an ecological region, for example, is not neutralized by the high natural frequency of a plant. In fact, if a plant has both a low value for TTR and for internal uniformity, this means that, while the plant does not have a large number of different lexemes given the number of available tokens, the number of records per lexeme per plant per region does not differ a lot and the tokens are distributed over the different lexemes in a relatively homogeneous way.

By inspecting the frequency of the lexemes for globally frequent plants with both a low value for TTR and for internal uniformity, we can confirm whether this explanation holds. Table 7 shows the five plants with the lowest value for internal uniformity and TTR < 0.2.[12] Tables 8 and 9 show the frequency of the lexical items that are used for the lesser burdock and the broadleaf plantain in the Sandy and sand-loamy region, (row 1–2 in Table 7) which will be discussed in more detail below. The distribution of the lexemes for the other plants in Table 7 is comparable to these plants (see Appendix 2): all five plants have about 3–5 lexemes that are very frequent in comparison to the other words for the concept.

Table 7: Overview of the five plants with the lowest value for internal uniformity and TTR < .2.

plant	ecological region	number of records	number of different lexemes	TTR	internal uniformity
broadleaf plantain (Plantago major)	Sandy and sand-loamy	218	39	0.179	0.079
lesser burdock (Arctium minus)	Sandy and sand-loamy	420	61	0.145	0.100
blackberry bush (Rubus fruticosus)	Sandy and sand-loamy	500	52	0.104	0.106
English plantain (Plantago lanceolate)	Sandy and sand-loamy	141	28	0.199	0.111
lesser burdock (Arctium minus)	Polder	226	39	0.173	0.112

---

12 The five plants in Table 6 come from the Sandy and sand-loamy or Polder region. Most of the data for the plants come from the same dictionary (WVD). They were all counted in at least 76% of the hour squares in the entire region of the atlas between 1972 and 2004, which confirms that they are globally frequent.

Table 8: Frequency of lexical items for the lesser burdock in the Sandy- and sand-loamy region (N = 420).

lexical item	N	lexical item	N	lexical item	N
kleef	2	plakkerbollen	2	plakbollen	4
klitkruid	2	plakkersbezetjes	2	plakdistel	4
wier	2	plakkerstruik	2	plakkers-, plakkertjeskruid	4
bommetjes	2	plakmadammetje	2	plakmadammetjes	4
bot	2	plakt-de-baard	2	distel	6
distelknoop	2	reit	2	klit	6
distelstekker	2	smijtdodde	2	distels	6
distelvinken	2	smijters	2	plakker	6
doppers	2	speenkruid	2	klis(se)bol	8
dotsjes	2	stekelharen	2	soldate-, soldatenknop(je)	8
everzwijnkruid	2	stekeltjes	2	klis(se)kruid	10
haakbloemen	2	stekers, stekertjes	2	stekkers, stekkertjes	12
klauwkruid	2	stekker	2	plakkruid	14
kleeftebollen	2	stekkertjeskruid	2	plakkers, plakkertjes	14
klissenstok	2	sterkerbol	2	kleefte	20
klister	2	toorvel	2	klissen	26
knopkruid	2	weerhaakjes	2	soldate(n)knoppen	28
mottebollen	2	zoete distel	2	kleef-, klevekruid	34
mouwenkruipers	2	grote klis	4	klis	116
pieker	2	kleefbollen	4		
piekertjes	2	klissebollen	4		

For the lesser burdock in the Sandy and sand-loamy region (N = 420), for example, *klis* occurs 116 times (see Table 8). Four other lexemes occur more than 15 times (*kleefte*; *klissen*; *soldate(n)knoppen* and *kleef-*, *klevekruid*). The other lexemes are less frequent. Overall, the tokens of these plants are distributed in a relatively homogeneous way over the different lexemes. Plotting the geographical distribution of the lexemes on a map indicates that more than one lexeme occurs in some locations: the language users know more than one local dialect word to refer to the concept (Figure 8). *Klis* is used throughout the ecological region. Other variants sometimes occur in locations where *klis* was found as well, or in locations close to towns with *klis*. Interestingly, these other variants also have a more limited geographical distribution than *klis*.

Furthermore, other factors can be envisaged that determine which lexeme is used in which location. For example, it may be the case that the geographical distribution of the variants within the ecological regions reflects dialect boundaries and, thus, does show some degree of standardization, albeit on a different level than per ecological region. In this case, one would be able to find a number of relatively small geographical areas where a particular variant is used. An example of this can be found if the variants for the broadleaf plantain that occur more than

Figure 8: Geographical distribution of lexemes with N ≥ 15 for lesser burdock in the Sandy and sand-loamy region.

Figure 9: Distribution of lexemes with N ≥ 15 for broadleaf plantain in the Sandy and sand-loamy region.

15 times in the data are plotted on a map (Figure 9, also see Table 9). Even though these variants are relatively frequent in comparison to the other lexemes for this concept, they all seem to only be used in a particular geographical area of the Sandy and sand-loamy region.[13]

---

[13] The distribution of the lexemes also seems to reflect the traditional dialect borders that have been distinguished in the Flemish dialects, as for instance, presented on the traditional map of Daan (1969).

Table 9: Frequency of lexical items for the broadleaf plantain in the Sandy- and sand-loamy region (N = 218).

lexical item	N	lexical item	N	lexical item	N
bree	2	varkensblad	2	zwijnegras	2
zwijnsoren	2	varkensblaren	2	grote weegbree	4
boterblad	2	varkensgras	2	kattestaart	4
breedblad	2	weegiebladen	2	weeg-, wege(s)bladen, -blaren	4
breedbladige weegbree	2	weegweeblad	2	wegaard(s)blad	4
breedbladweegbree	2	weewaarsblad	2	wegbree	6
dokke	2	weeweeblad	2	weewaarsbladen	8
dokkeblaren	2	weeweegbree	2	honde-, hondsrib	10
grote smart	2	wegaardsblaren	2	brede weegbree	14
honderibben, hondsribberen	2	wemel	2	rib	18
keunoren	2	weversbloemen	2	wever(s)bladeren, -blaren	26
papbladen	2	wilgebladen	2	weversblad	30
platen	2	zevenblaren	2	weeg-, wegebree	36

The diverging results for the models for TTR and internal uniformity per plant frequency group (Section 3.2) can be interpreted in a similar way. The analysis showed that the predicted value for TTR and for internal uniformity is smaller for the very frequent plants than for the locally and globally infrequent plants. The smaller values for TTR are in line with what was expected: a high value for global frequency can reduce the amount of diversity in the names for locally infrequent plants. The results for internal uniformity seem to contradict this finding. However, it is possible that the unexpected higher degree of uniformity of frequent plants is again related to the fact that there is no uniformity within the ecological region: the tokens for these plants may be distributed among the different lexemes that occur for the plants in a relatively homogeneous way. Additionally, since the number of records per plant also correlates with the frequency of the plant, a smaller number of tokens (and, thus, types) is available for the infrequent plants. This results in a seemingly more homogeneous distribution of the variants in the ecological regions (high degree of internal uniformity) and in a higher value for TTR.

4.2 Suggestions for future research

The analysis also showed that the absolute value of the correlation coefficients is relatively low (it is never higher than 0.261). This indicates that other factors than referential plant frequency probably influence the amount of lexical diversity found in names for plants. For example, the poisonousness, usefulness or folkloric salience of a plant also influence how familiar the plant is. Furthermore, the number of tokens per plant may serve as an operationalization of familiarity of a plant as well (see Geeraerts & Speelman 2010, Speelman & Geeraerts 2008).

However, an additional explanation for the low correlation coefficients in the analysis is that the plants that are included in the dictionary data are overall relatively frequent. For example, the mean value for relative frequency per ecological region per plant for all the plants in the online database of the atlas is 12.46%. The mean value for this measure in the data set that was used for this paper is 37.78%. Of course, it is not surprising that only dialect data for relatively frequent plants are at our disposal. On the one hand, some of the plants in the atlas are probably so infrequent that they are not known to laymen. As a result, it may be the case that the lexicographers are not aware that these plants exist. On the other hand, if they are aware of the plants, it is possible that they are not interested in the names for these plants in local dialects, because they expect that asking for the names for these plants will not provide them with enough data. As was shown above, even for the relatively frequent plants that are available in our dataset, some plants are not represented by a large number of records in the linguistic data, which may have to do with the fact that these plants are unfamiliar for language users.

Aside from the fact that collecting dialect data for less frequent plants could corroborate the findings of this paper further, there are some restrictions on the present study that should be addressed in follow-up research. First, for the analysis, we lumped together all the data from the three dictionaries that were used. Although these data were not collected in exactly the same period, we did not control for diachronic differences between the sources: because most of the data come from the dictionary of Flemish dialects and because we aggregate over all the plants and ecological regions, we expect that this diachronic noise does not bias the analysis to a large degree.[14] Further, since the editors of the three dictionaries probably did not always make the same decisions about how to group different phonological variants into one lexeme, the data set may contain false heteronyms, lexemes that are treated as separate headwords in one dictionary, while they are treated as the same word in another one. For example, in the WLD, the phonological variant *bosbessen* 'bilberry' is grouped under the lexeme *bosbes*, while in the WBD, related phonological variants like *bosbeize*, *bosbeze* and *bosbieseme* are grouped under *bosbezen*, *bosbezen* and *bosbezem*, respectively. To cope with this difficulty, it would be necessary to compare the grouping of the

---

[14] We also executed the analysis on the Flemish data alone and obtained very similar results.

phonological variants in all the dictionaries. However, as this paper aimed to take a more aggregated approach towards variation in plant naming, we assumed that the dictionaries are similar enough to be compared and that this kind of noise would be filtered out due to the aggregative approach that we employed. Therefore, an interesting addition to this study would be to extend the scope to other dialect or language areas to investigate whether the findings are stable in other datasets and outside the region of the northern part of Belgium.

Third, other lines of investigation can be envisaged as well. The response variable, lexical diversity, can be operationalized in other ways than was done in this paper. For example, we could consider Guiraud's score, a transformation of the type-token ratio that is less dependent on the number of tokens per observation, as an alternative operationalization of lexical diversity. Additionally, although we only briefly mentioned how the geographical spread of the variants can differ, including this as a measure of diversity may offer further insight into the structure of the variation.

Extensions of the predictor variable, experiential frequency, are possible as well. For instance, a valuable addition to this study would be to further investigate the relationship between the experiential salience of naturally occurring plants and the number of records that are available in the data. Furthermore, additional explanatory variables, like geographic features or dialect boundaries within the Flemish, Brabantic and Limburgish dialects, or operationalizations of plant frequency based on folkloric information (e.g. usefulness or poisonousness of plants) could be included in the analysis. Moreover, comparing lexical data across different time periods can reveal whether the degree of lexical diversity decreases for plant names over time, and whether this is influenced by plant frequency.

Finally, in this paper we aimed to investigate whether experiential salience, in the form of referential frequency, influences lexical diversity. Other semantic fields can be envisaged in which this correlation can be tested. For example, rather than focusing on flora (or fauna), it would be interesting to expand the scope to a semantic field that is more prone to cultural differences, like the field of artifacts. Using other semantic fields will also allow for a comparison between concepts that occur naturally or that are conceived in a social environment.

5 Conclusion

In this paper we linked referential data to linguistic data to test whether the referential frequency of a plant, which was used to gauge experiential salience, correlates with the amount of lexical variation that is found in the names for the plant. The analysis showed that some significant correlations exist: overall, plants that occur more frequently in a particular area seem to show a smaller degree of lexical diversity. However, the correlation is not strong enough for plant frequency to cause complete lexical uniformity within an ecological region and other factors play a role as well. Furthermore, a small-scale investigation of locally infrequent, but globally frequent plants revealed that the global frequency of a plant can cause a decrease in naming variation. However, more data is necessary to corroborate this finding. Overall, we were able to show that the everyday environment of a language user can influence the amount of lexical variation for a concept and that using referential data to study lexical variation can provide further insight into factors that influence language variation in a speech community.

Appendix 1: Lexical items for plants in Table 6

Appendix 1.1: Distribution of lexemes for the great mullein (Verbascum Thapsus) in the Loamy region

lexical item	N	lexical item	N	lexical item	N
gele kaars	1	toorts	1	zoklappen	1
gele thee	1	toppen	1	kalverwortel	1
kattenkop	1	wilde zokken	1	kaars	2
koningskaars	1	wolplant	1	paaskaars	2
lammetjesblaren	1	wolvenstaart	1	wilde tabak	2
lammetjesoren	1	zokjes	1	wolharen	2
maagdenkaars	1	zokken	1		
stalkaars	1	zokkenblaren	1		

Appendix 1.2: Distribution of lexemes for the bitter dock (Rumex obtusifolius) in the Polder region

lexical item	N	lexical item	N
wilde zuring	1	schape-, schaap(s)zurkel	4
Dokke	1	wilde zurkel	10
Paardezurkel	3	zurkel	19

Botany meets lexicology — 145

Appendix 1.3: Distribution of lexemes for the black locust (Robinia pseudoacacia) in the Sandy and sand-loamy region

lexical item	N
acajou	1
robinia	1
valse acacia	1
acacia	23

Appendix 1.4: Distribution of lexemes for the forget-me-not (Myosotis arvensis) in the Dunes region

lexical item	N
vergeet-mij-niet(je)	52

Appendix 2: Frequency of lexemes for plants with lowest value for internal uniformity and TTR < .2

Appendix 2.1: Distribution of lexemes for the blackberry bush (Rubus fruticosus) in the Sandy and sand-loamy region

lexical item	N	lexical item	N	lexical item	N
braambeien	1	hut bramen	1	braambeierstruik	3
braamberen	1	karrebezen	1	braambes(se)struik	4
braambezie	1	karrelbezie'nstruik	1	braambezi'n, -bezies	4
bramel	1	kattebeierboom	1	braambeier	5
kruip	1	moerbezen	1	braambeiers-, braambeier(en)hut	6
barstebeier	1	mondebeiers	1	bramers	6
bezenstruik	1	paters	1	braambees	7
braambeeshut	1	stekelbraam	1	braambeziestruik	12
braambeinen	1	struik braambezen	1	braambezelaar	16
braambessentronk	1	wilde frambozen	1	braamhut	20
braambezenbos	1	braam-, bramenhul	2	braambeiers	33
braambezenhul	1	braambees-, braambezetronk	2	braambees-, braambeze(n)struik	49
braambezietronk	1	braambessen	2	braam	58
braambreien	1	braambezebeier	2	braambezen	58
braamgewas	1	braambrei(en)struik	2	braam-, brame(n)struik	80
bramels	1	bramelhut	2	bramen	94
doorntakken	1	bramerstruik	2		
hul bramen	1	braambes	3		

Appendix 2.2: Distribution of lexemes for the English plantain (Plantago lanceolate) in the Sandy and sand-loamy region

lexical item	N	lexical item	N	lexical item	N
bagweeblad	1	wever(s)kruid	1	honde-, hondstong	4
dokken	1	hondsribberen	2	wegaard(s)bladen, -blaren	5
kattestaart	1	konijneneten	2	wegbree	5
keuneblad	1	weeg-, wegeblad	2	wever(s)blaren	7
kleine wegbree	1	weewaarsbladen, -blaren	2	smalle weegbree	14
papbladen	1	wegaard(s)blad	2	weeg-, wegebree	18
ribbeplaten	1	keunoren	3	honde-, hondsrib	27
stokjes	1	smalle rib	3	rib	28
vettekerte?	1	weegbladen, -blaren, wegebladen, -blaren	3		
weeweeblad	1	weversblad	3		

Appendix 2.3: Distribution of lexemes for the lesser burdock (Arctium minus) in the Polder region

lexical item	N	lexical item	N	lexical item	N
distel	2	plakdistel	2	klevers	4
kleef	2	plakker	2	klis(se)bol	4
klitkruid	2	plakpotten	2	klis(se)kruid	4
wier	2	reit	2	klissebollen	4
bommetjes	2	smijtbollen	2	plakbollen	4
distelvinken	2	smijtdodde	2	stekkers, stekkertjes	4
doppers	2	soldate-, soldatenknop(je)	2	distels	6
dotsjes	2	stekers, stekertjes	2	kleef-, klevekruid	10
kleeftebollen	2	stekmadammetjes	2	plakkers, plakkertjes	10
klissebloem	2	sterkerbol	2	soldate(n)knoppen	10
klister	2	zoete distel	2	klissen	22
pieker	2	grote klis	4	kleefte	24
piekertjes	2	kleefbollen	4	klis	64

References

Brok, Har. 1991. *Enkele bloemnamen in de Nederlandse dialekten: Etnobotanische nomenclatuur in het Nederlandse taalgebied (Publikaties van het P. J. Meertens-instituut voor dialectologie, volkskunde en naamkunde van de Koninklijke Nederlandse akademie van wetenschappen 18)*. Amsterdam: Meertens Instituut

Brok, Har. 2003. *Publicaties over plantennamen in Nederland, Nederlandstalig België en Frans-Vlaanderen (Werken van de Koninklijke commissie voor toponymie en dialectologie. Vlaamse afdeling 24)*. Tongeren: Michiels.

Brok, Har. 2006. *Stinkend-juffertje en duivelskruid: Volksnamen van planten*. Amsterdam: Salome.

Bromhead, Helen. 2011. Ethnogeographical categories in English and Pitjantjatjara/Yankunytjatjara. *Language Sciences* 33(1). 58–75.

Daan, Jo. 1969. Dialecten. In Jo Daan & Dirk P. Blok, *Van randstad tot landrand. Toelichting bij de kaart: Dialecten en naamkunde (Bijdragen en mededelingen der Dialectencommissie van de Koninklijke Nederlandse akademie van wetenschappen te Amsterdam 37)*, 7–43. Amsterdam: Noord-Hollandsche uitgeversmaatschappij.

Divjak, Dagmar & Catherine L. Caldwell-Harris. 2015. Frequency and entrenchment. In Ewa Dąbrowksa & Dagmar Divjak (eds.), *Handbook of Cognitive Linguistics (Handbooks of Linguistics and Communication Science = Handbücher zur Sprach- und Kommunikationswissenschaft 39)*, 53–74. Berlin: De Gruyter Mouton.

Franco, Karlien, Dirk Geeraerts & Dirk Speelman. 2015. The influence of semantic features on lexical geographical variation. In Johannes Wahle, Marisa Köllner, Harald R. Baayen, Gerhard Jäger & Tineke Baayen-Oudshoorn (eds.), *Proceedings of the 6th Conference on Quantitative Investigations in Theoretical Linguistics. Quantitative Investigations in Theoretical Linguistics (QITL). Tübingen, Germany, 4–6 November 2015*. art.nr. 11.

Geeraerts, Dirk, Stefan Grondelaers & Dirk Speelman. 1999. *Convergentie en divergentie in de Nederlandse woordenschat: een onderzoek naar kleding- en voetbaltermen*. Amsterdam: Meertens Instituut

Geeraerts, Dirk & Dirk Speelman. 2010. Heterodox concept features and onomasiological heterogeneity in dialects. In Dirk Geeraerts, Gitte Kristiansen & Yves Peirsman (eds.), *Advances in Cognitive Sociolinguistics*, 23–40. Berlin/New York: De Gruyter Mouton.

Goossens, Jan. 1964. Enkel- en veeltoepasselijkheid van betekenaars op de taalkaart. In *Taalgeografie en semantiek. Lezingen gehouden voor de dialectencommissie der koninklijke Nederlandse academie van wetenschappen op 27 december 1962 door dr. J. Goossens en dr. Jan van Bakel. (Bijdragen en mededelingen der dialectencommissie van de koninklijke Nederlandse akademie van wetenschappen ter Amsterdam XXVIII)*, 3–27. Amsterdam: Noord-Hollandse uitgevers maatschappij.

Kruijsen, Joep. 1996. De Nijmeegse dialectlexicografische projecten. *Trefwoord* 11. 93–107.

Pauwels, Jan. 1933. *Enkele bloemnamen in de Zuidnederlandsche dialecten (Noord- en Zuid-Nederlandsche dialectbibliotheek 5)*. The Hague: Nijhoff.

Pickl, Simon. 2013. Lexical meaning and spatial distribution: evidence from geostatistical dialectometry. *Literary and Linguistic Computing: Journal of the Association for Literary and Linguistic Computing and The Association for Computers and the Humanities* 28(1),63–81.

R Core Team. 2016. *R: A language and environment for statistical computing*. R Foundation for Statistical Computing, Vienna, Austria. URL: https://www.R-project.org/.

Schmid, Hans Jörg. 2007. Entrenchment, salience and basic levels. In Dirk Geeraerts & Hubert Cuyckens. *The Oxford Handbook of Cognitive Linguistics*, 117–138. Oxford: Oxford university press.

Sevenant, Marjanne, Jan Menschaert, Martine Couvreur, Anne Ronse, Moira Heyn, Joks Janssen, Marc Antrop, Maarten Geypens, Martin Hermy & Geert De Blust. 2002. *Ecodistricten: ruimtelijke eenheden voor gebiedsgericht milieubeleid in Vlaanderen. Studieopdracht in het kader van actie 134 van het Vlaams Milieubeleidsplan 1997–2001*. Commissioned by the Ministry of the Flemish Community. Administration of the Environment, Nature and Land Use.

Speelman, Dirk, Stefan Grondelaers & Dirk Geeraerts. 2003. Profile-based linguistic uniformity as a generic method for comparing language varieties. *Computers and the Humanities* 37(3). 317–37.

Speelman, Dirk & Dirk Geeraerts. 2008. The role of concept characteristics in lexical dialectometry. *International Journal of Humanities and Arts Computing* 2. 221–242.

Swanenberg, Jos. 2000. *Lexicale variatie cognitief-semantisch benaderd: over het benoemen van vogels in Zuid-Nederlandse dialecten*. Doctoral dissertation. Nijmegen: Radboud University.

Tweedie, Fiona J. & Harald R. Baayen. 1998. How variable may a constant be? Measures of lexical richness in perspective. *Computers and the Humanities* 32. 323–352.

Van Landuyt, Wouter, Ivan Hoste, Leo Vanhecke, Paul van den Bremt, Ward Vercruysse & Dirk de Beer. 2006. *Atlas van de Flora van Vlaanderen en het Brussels Gewest*. Brussels: Research Institute for Nature and Forest, National Botanic Garden of Belgium & Flo.Wer.

WBD = Swanenberg, Jos & Har Brok. 2002. *Woordenboek van de Brabantse Dialecten. Deel III, 4.3, Flora*. Assen: Van Gorcum.

WLD = Kruijsen, Joep & Har Brok. 2002. *Woordenboek van de Limburgse dialecten. Deel III, 4.3, Flora*. Assen: Van Gorcum.WVD = De Pauw, Tineke, Jacques Van Keymeulen & Har Brok. 2002. *Woordenboek van de Vlaamse dialecten. Deel III, 3: Flora*. Tongeren: Michiels.

Ching Chu Sun, Peter Hendrix, Harald Baayen and Michael Ramscar
2 The price of knowledge: A bilingual paired associate learning study

Abstract: Age effects in experimental psychology are typically interpreted as evidence for cognitive decline. Alternatively, age-related decreases in performance on cognitive tasks could be a result of increased linguistic experience (Ramscar et al. 2014). We present the results of a paired associate learning experiment in which we tested old and young German monolinguals and Chinese-German bilinguals. Younger participants performed similarly in L1 and L2. Older participants performed better in L2 than in L1. The current findings cannot be accounted for by cognitive decline, but follow straightforwardly from basic principles of learning.

Keywords: paired associate learning, aging, bilingual, NDL, discrimination learning

1 Introduction

As adults age, their performance on various measures of cognition – such as those testing reasoning, memory, and response speeds – changes, with scores on many tests declining. Two obvious explanations suggest themselves for this. The first takes these changes as evidence of a loss of cognitive function over time (Naveh-Benjamin and Old 2008; Deary et al. 2009; Salthouse 2009; Singh-Manoux et al. 2012) advocating the view that, "the sad truth is that even normal aging has a devastating effect on our ability to learn and remember, on the speed with which we process information, and on our ability to reason" (Epstein 2012). The other posits that these changes reflect the increased information processing demands that accompany greater learning from experience and the failure of cognitive measures to control for this (Ramscar et al. 2013; Ramscar et al. 2014).

It is clearly important to understand whether or how much cognitive abilities decline in adulthood. Attempts to discern which account is correct, however, are forced to struggle with a seemingly inevitable confound: older adults have more experience than younger adults in almost any cognitive domain. In what follows, we de-confound the association between age and experience by testing the

---
Ching Chu Sun, University of Tübingen, ching-chu.sun@uni-tuebingen.de
Peter Hendrix, Harald Baayen and Michael Ramscar, University of Tübingen

https://doi.org/10.1515/9783110610895-006

same cognitive ability (Paired Associate Learning; henceforth PAL) in native (L1) speakers of German and Chinese and second-language (L2) speakers of German. Whereas native speakers' experience is confounded with age, this is much less the case for L2 speakers' experience. If the cognitive abilities underlying PAL performance decline with age, then we ought to expect to see the same patterns of performance differences between older and younger participants in both L1 and L2. However, if PAL performance simply reflects experience with a language, we ought to see better performance for older speakers in L2 than in L1.

1.1 Paired associate learning

Paired Associate Learning is a common psychometric measure of people's ability to learn and recall new information. In standard verbal versions of the test such as the PAL subtest of Wechsler's Memory Scale (WMS) (des Rosiers and Ivison 1986), participants hear pairings between words that act as cue items (e.g., *baby*; *jury*) and words that are response items (*cries*; *eagle*). Participants listen to lists of the pairings, and then supply the response to each cue at test. Although performance on the individual pairs in the test varies, performance becomes progressively slower and less accurate as age increases.

These changes in PAL test performance can only be interpreted as evidence of declining cognitive performance if one assumes that the functioning of the cognitive processes engaged by the PAL task can be estimated from exposure to a uniform association rate for each test item (i.e., participants hear each w_1-w_2 pair the same number of times). However, convergent results from a huge body of empirical work (Miller et al. 1995; Siegel and Allan 1996; Ramscar et al. 2010), as well as human neuroscience findings (McDannald et al. 2014, d'Acremont et al. 2009; Schultz 2006; Schultz et al. 1997), animal studies (Yin and Knowlton 2006; Tremblay et al. 1998; Kamin 1969; Rescorla 1968) and computational and mathematical models (Dayan and Berridge 2014; Daw et al. 2008; Sutton and Barto 1981; Pearce and Hall 1980; Rescorla and Wagner 1972) show that association rates (the rate at which PAL items are encountered together) are insufficient to explain the patterns of behavior produced by associative learning.

Rather, what is traditionally called associative learning has been shown to be a discriminative process that detunes uninformative and reinforces informative dimensions within a system of inputs in order to minimize future prediction error (see Ramscar et al. 2010 for a review). As such, apart from association rates, at least two other quantitative factors must be taken into account in predicting and assessing the performance of this system. First, the background rates of cue words (see Rescorla 1968; Ramscar, Dye, and Klein 2013) co-determine the predictability of response words. The background rate of the cue word is the frequency with which it appears in the absence of a response word. When association rates are held constant, cue words with higher background rates are less informative for response words than cue words with lower background rates. The greater the frequency of the cue word, therefore, the harder it is to learn the association with the response word (Ramscar, Dye, and McCauley 2013). A second factor that needs to be taken into account is blocking (see Kamin 1969; Arnon and Ramscar 2012). Blocking refers to the principle that once a learner is able to accurately predict an outcome, the need to learn associations between additional cues and that outcome no longer exists (see Rescorla 1968; Ramscar, Dye, and Klein 2013). In the context of paired associate learning, greater predictability of an outcome word given a cue word based on prior learning thus makes it harder to learn a cue-outcome pair in the PAL task.

Moreover, the skewed distribution of language implies that the relative influence of these factors will inevitably change with experience (Ramscar et al. 2013; Ramscar et al. 2014). To demonstrate how this can be expected to influence PAL performance over time, Figure 1 simulates the development of associations between items in a very simple model lexicon comprising two easy (*North - South*; *Cat - Dog*) and two hard (*Banana - Dog*; *North - Dog*) PAL pairs using the Danks equilibrium equations (Danks 2003) for the Rescorla-Wagner model (Wagner & Rescorla 1972), as implemented in the ndl package for R (Arppe et al. 2014). To show that learnability cannot be predicted from a fixed association rate, the association rates of the hard items were held constant while those for the easy items were varied. As can be seen in Figure 1, as the frequencies of the easy phrases and the words that comprise them increases, the expected association between *North* and *Dog* after 1 exposure declines as the frequency of the easy items increases (see Ramscar et al. 2013).

One straightforward consequence of the nature of learning and the long tail of linguistic distributions is evident in even this very simple model: linguistic experience will tend to increase background rates relative to association rates, making PAL learning harder. It will also tend to disfavor the learning of PAL pairs comprising words that co-occur infrequently in language more as compared to those that co-occur frequently. Interestingly, this pattern is actually evident in empirical studies of PAL learning.

Figure 2 plots the mean performance by item for 100 older (age 40–49) and 100 younger (20–29) adults (50% females in each group) tested in a normative study of the WMS-PAL subtest (desRosiers and Ivison 1986). As can clearly be seen, the decline in the performance of the 40-something adults is far greater on the hard (low co-occurrence) items than on the easy (high co-occurrence) items. This is a direct result of increased discrimination between the uninformative hard pairings and the informative easy pairings, and occurs as a result of the actual function of the associative learning system, as opposed to a decline in its functionality.

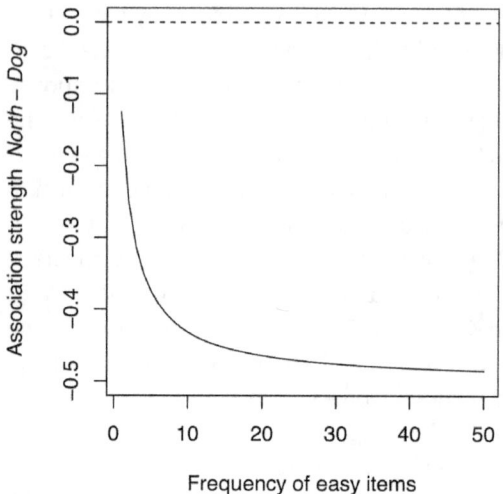

Figure 1: The association strength for *North* to *Dog* given one trial of training as a function of the frequency of two easy (common) associations *North - South* and *Cat - Dog*. The frequency of the two hard (uncommon) pairings *Banana - Dog* and *North - Dog* is always 1. When learning is simulated using the (Danks 2003) equilibrium equations for the (Wagner and Rescorla 1972) model, the association weight between *North* and *Dog* declines as the easy pairs' frequencies increase, even though both the structure of the lexicon and the association rate of *North - Dog* remain unchanged (adapted from Ramscar et al. 2013).

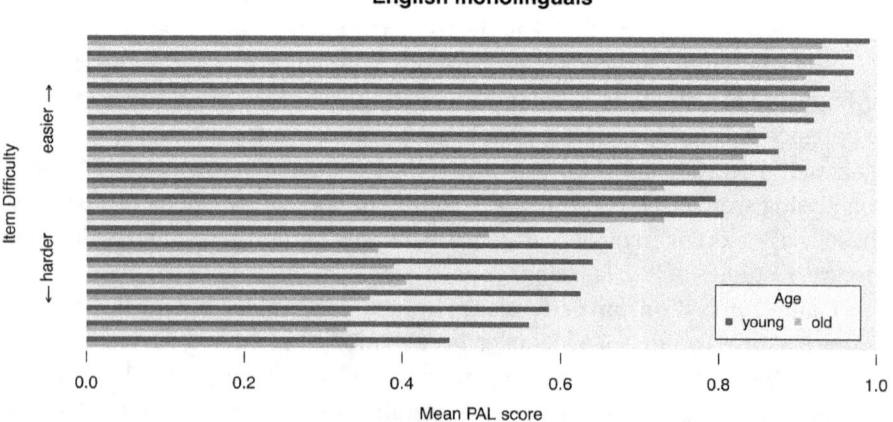

Figure 2: By-item performance on forms 1 and 2 of the WMS-PAL subtest for 100 younger (20–29) and 100 older (age 40–49) participants (desRosiers and Ivison 1986). The younger adults outperform older adults on all items, and performance differences are greater for the hard items than for the easy items.

A re-analysis of the full desRosiers and Ivison (1986) data set with 20–29, 30–39, 40–49, 50–59 and 60–69 year-old adults using a (beta regression) generalized additive mixed-effect model yields not only a random effect for Item (χ^2 = 470.577, $p < 0.001$) and a main effect of Gender (females perform better than males, $z = -4.952$, $p < 0.001$), but also significant interactions of Age by Co-occurrence Frequency (i.e., association rate: the number of times w_1 and w_2 appear next to each other in Google documents, $\chi^2 = 88.716$, $p < 0.001$) and Age by Cue Frequency (i.e., the frequency of the cue word, $\chi^2 = 44.027$, $p < 0.001$). These effects are presented in Figure 3.

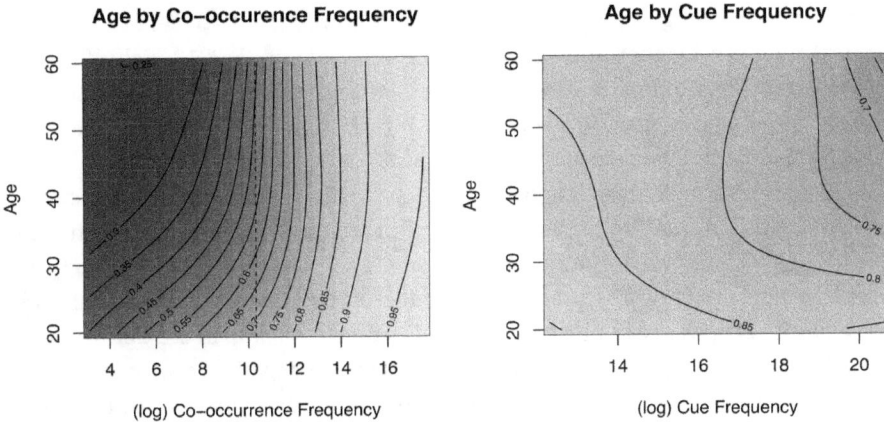

Figure 3: Effects of the (log-transformed) Co-occurrence Frequency by Age (left panel) and the (log-transformed) Cue Frequency by Age (right panel) on the Paired Associate Learning performance for English monolinguals. Color coding indicates proportion of correct responses in the paired associate learning test. The dotted line in the left panel indicates the mid-point of the (log) Co-occurrence Frequency range.

The left panel of Figure 3 shows the Age by Co-occurrence Frequency interaction. Consistent with the predictions of discrimination learning, lower co-occurrence frequencies lead to decreased performance in the PAL task. Furthermore, the sensitivity to the association rate between w_1 and w_2 increases as a function of age. Whereas the difference in performance for items with high co-occurrence frequencies is small, at the midpoint of the Co-occurrence Frequency range the predicted performance for the youngest participants is 72%, whereas the predicted performance for the oldest participants is 49% only (difference: 23%, see dotted line in the left panel of Figure 3).

The effect of Age by Cue Frequency (right panel of Figure 3) is more subtle in nature. Nonetheless, it is clear that PAL performance decreases as a function of the frequency of the cue word and does so to a greater extent for older participants than for younger participants. The re-analysis of the desRosiers and Ivison (1986) data therefore indicates that adults' PAL performance becomes ever more closely aligned with the informativity of w_1 and w_2 in their native language (i.e., the distributional information determining w_1-w_2 learnability) as their age increases.

1.2 Paired associate learning in L1 versus L2

Attempts to separate the effects of age and learning run into an obvious confound in that age and experience are highly correlated. Moreover, the nature of human and animal learning systems (in which, as we emphasized above, error plays a critical role; see Wagner and Rescorla 1972; Ramscar et al. 2010; Schultz 2006) means that this problem cannot be solved by designing novel tasks and stimuli, simply because it is impossible to design a task or stimulus that engages only novel sensory and behavioral dimensions.

PAL tests suggest an alternative approach to this problem because languages are structured, quantifiable systems that afford their speakers training in some of their aspects in ways that are very predictable. For example, although two English speakers of different ages with similar experience of German will differ in semantic experience (while both may have equal exposure to the German word *Brief* ('letter'), an older speaker will likely have more experience with letters and the word *letter*; see Arnon and Ramscar 2012), their experience with the distributional structure of the L2 (how often *Brief* occurs with other German words) will be very similar. More importantly, 45-year-old native English speakers with 10 years experience of German will have had less experience of the word *Brief* than the word *letter*, and their experience of the associative properties of the German lexicon will have resulted in them learning to dissociate the word *Brief* from *Herbst* less than their experience of the English lexicon will have resulted in them learning to dissociate the word *letter* from *autumn*. Accordingly, because there is less prior learning to overcome, we might expect that all other things being equal, learning the L2 PAL pair *Brief - Herbst* ought to be easier than learning the L1 pair *letter - autumn*.

However, all other things are not equal: underlining the point we made earlier about background rates in apparently novel items, because German and English are related languages, they share phonetic, orthographic, lexical and other features at various levels of systematic abstraction. Most obviously, *brief* is also a word in English (and similarly, although *Herbst* is not an English word, *herbs* is). Further, while *brief* and *letter* do not have a common orthography, *Butter* and *butter* do. And while *Milch* and *milk* are orthographically distinct, they barely differ phonetically and semantically.

It follows that our predictions about PAL learnability in L1 and L2 can better be tested in two languages in which the degrees of phonetic, orthographic, and lexical overlap between L1 and L2, and any systematicity therein, can be minimized. To this end, in the following experiment, we contrasted German (a non-tonal, West Germanic language that derives most of its lexicon from the Germanic branch of the Indo-European family of languages) with Mandarin Chinese (a tonal language that is a member of the Sino-Tibetan language family).

If PAL tests are a straightforward measure of learning and memory capacity (or, more opaquely, 'cognition', see Lindenberger 2014), either PAL performance for older participants should be similar in L1 and L2, or else we might find better performance in L1 than in L2 due to greater experience with the language. By contrast, basic principles of learning theory predict that older participants should perform better in L2 than in L1.

2 Methods

2.1 Participants

Four groups of participants took part in the experiment: young Chinese-German bilinguals, old Chinese-German bilinguals, young German monolinguals and old German monolinguals. Young participants were 18 to 28 years old, while old participants were 38 to 53 years old.[1] The age range for the older participants was set to 38 to 53 years old for two reasons. First, as can be seen in the left panel of Figure 3, the strongest age-related decline in performance in the normative PAL data desRosiers and Ivison (1986) takes place between the ages of 20 and 45. After the age of 45, the decline in performance is minimal. The age of the older participants in our study, therefore, is high enough to show the typical age effects observed in the PAL task. Second, increasing the age of the older participants in our study would increase the probability of including participants with undiagnosed mental diseases, such as dementia. While the effects of such diseases on cognitive functioning are interesting, they are outside the scope of the current study, which focuses on normal, healthy aging. After excluding participants with insufficient vocabularies in their second language (see below) and otherwise non-useable participants from the data,

---

[1] Note that our use of the terms "old" and "older" deviates from the typical use of these words in the aging literature, which typically defines older adults as 65+ years old. The use of these terms throughout this paper refers to the relative age of the 38 to 53 years old participants as compared to the 18 to 28 year old participants, and is used for ease of reference.

Table 1: By-group age and vocabulary scores for each of the 4 groups of participants. Standard deviations are provided in brackets.

		Age	German Vocabulary	Chinese Vocabulary
Chinese-German bilinguals	young	24.55 (2.27)	31.75 (5.35)	67.65 (6.46)
	old	43.60 (4.66)	40.25 (7.86)	64.65 (7.09)
German monolinguals	young	23.45 (3.06)	81.95 (6.25)	– (–)
	old	44.90 (4.36)	84.10 (4.38)	– (–)

20 participants remained for each group. The mean age and the average vocabulary score in both languages for the 20 participants in each group is shown in Table 1.

The harder items in the PAL task contained relatively infrequent words. To ensure that participants knew all the words used in the test, we conducted vocabulary tests prior to the PAL task in both languages to assess the linguistic competence of participants in each language. For a more detailed description of these vocabulary tests, see the Materials section.

The performance on the vocabulary test in German was highly variable, particularly for the young Chinese-German bilinguals. Participants in this group were typically graduate students at the University of Tübingen. While some of these students were highly competent in their L2, others had considerably less experience. A number of these less experienced L2 learners explicitly stated that they did not know some of the words in the German PAL test.

To minimize the risk of young Chinese-German bilingual participants not knowing words in the PAL test, we selected from the group of 34 young Chinese-German bilinguals we were able to recruit in the Tübingen area the 20 participants with the best performance on the vocabulary pretest in German. Vocabulary test performance was calculated as a weighted sum of the number of correct answers, with item weights being the proportion of correct answers for the items across the young and old bilingual participants. This procedure has the added advantage that the difference in German vocabulary scores between old and young bilingual participants is smaller than it would otherwise be.[2]

On average, old Chinese-German bilinguals had somewhat more experience in their second language than did young Chinese-German bilinguals. The problem of insufficient L2 proficiency therefore proved much less prominent for old

---

[2] The German PAL performance of the Chinese-German bilinguals with the worst vocabulary scores was worse than that of the 20 participants included in the analysis below (proportion correct: 0.64 versus 0.78). This suggests that at least some participants with poor vocabulary scores indeed did not know some of the items in the German PAL test.

Chinese-German bilinguals than for young Chinese-German bilinguals. Nonetheless, for consistency with the selection criterion used for young Chinese-German bilinguals, we excluded from the old Chinese-German bilinguals those participants with vocabulary scores lower than that of the 20th best young Chinese-German bilingual. This resulted in the exclusion of 4 old Chinese-German bilinguals.

Apart from insufficient proficiency in the second language, a total of 5 participants across the 4 groups were excluded for not meeting the requirements outlined in the experiment advertisement (4 participants did not attend university, 1 "German monolingual" was not a native speaker of German). Due to a shortage of old German participants that met the requirements outlined in the experiment advertisement, the final set of 20 old German participants contains one participant who did not attend university.

2.2 Materials

For both languages we administered a paired associate learning test as well as a vocabulary test. The vocabulary tests for both German and Chinese consisted of 100 multiple choice questions with 4 possible answers. The 3 incorrect answers were chosen from the same part-of-speech category as the correct answer. An example item for German, for instance, is the test word *Hemd* ('shirt'), with the four possible answers *Shirt* ('shirt'), *Jacke* ('jacket'), *Pullover* ('sweater') and *Weste* ('vest'). An example item for Chinese is 暮色 ('twilight'), with the four possible answers 浓雾 ('thick fog'), 黄昏 ('dusk'), 清晨 ('morning') and 月亮 ('moon').

The word frequency distributions for the German and Chinese vocabulary tests were matched. Test words on the German vocabulary test ranged in frequency from 10 to 0.001 per million in a 9 billion word corpus of German web pages. For Chinese, we did not have a similarly large corpus at our disposal. We therefore first selected words with a frequency ranging from 10 to 0.2 per million from the 5 million word Taiwan Sinica Corpus (CKIP 2014). For these words we also obtained Google search frequencies. We then used the median Google-to-Sinica frequency ratio and a list of Google frequencies for low frequency words in Chinese to complete the list of test items for the Chinese vocabulary test.

The PAL test in both languages consisted of three groups of 10 pairs. Pairs ranged in difficulty from easy (e.g., *Nord - Süd* ('north' - 'south') or 学校 - 读书 ('school' - 'study')) to hard (e.g., *Schiff - Puppe* ('ship' - 'doll') or 洋葱 - 手指 ('onion' - 'finger')). The anticipated difficulty of an item was gauged through the co-occurrence frequency of the words in a pair (see below for details). The first group contained the easiest items, the second group contained items with medium difficulty, and the third group contained the most difficult items. Words occurred no more than once in each of the paired associate learning tests. None of the words used in the paired associate learning tests were used as test words or answer alternatives in the vocabulary tests. The full list of the items used in the PAL tests in German and Chinese is presented in Table 2 (German) and Table 3 (Chinese) in Appendix 1.[3]

For each of the 30 pairs, we obtained the Co-occurrence Frequency of the words in that pair through the number of Google documents in which these words occurred together. Furthermore, we extracted the Google search unigram frequencies for all words in the PAL test as a measure of the background rates of both words. PAL items were designed such that the Cue Frequency, Response Frequency and Co-occurrence Frequency distributions for each language were approximately normal. An exact matching of the item difficulty in the German and Chinese PAL tests was impossible, given the fact that the exact size of Google in Chinese and German is hard to determine (or, more generally speaking, the unavailability of a sufficiently large corpus with a known corpus size for Chinese). Nonetheless, we matched items in the German and Chinese PAL tests for item difficulty as well as possible using average frequency conversion ratio's based on Google frequency counts for sample words in both languages. All frequency measures were log-transformed prior to analysis to remove a rightward skew from the frequency distributions.

2.3 Design

The vocabulary pre-test for each language consisted of 100 multiple-choice questions with 4 possible answers. The order of the answers was randomized for each question, but consistent between participants. The paired associate learning task for each language consisted of three blocks of 10 pairs. The order of the blocks was held constant between participants, with the block of easy items being administered first and the block of hard items being administered last. Similarly, the order of the items was held constant between participants. The items appeared in the same order in the training phrase and in the test phase. Vocabulary pre-tests were administered prior to the paired associate learning test in each language. For the Chinese-German bilinguals the vocabulary pre-test and the paired associate learning test in Chinese preceded both tests in German.

---

[3] Three semantic concepts, "dog", "city" and "to swim", occurred in both the Chinese PAL test and the German PAL test. These concepts appeared in different pairs in both languages, which should make pairs including these concepts somewhat harder the second time around. Given that for Chinese-German bilinguals the PAL test in Chinese preceded the PAL test in German, the repetition of these three semantic concepts therefore biases against our hypothesis that participants should perform better in the second language.

The dependent variable is the correctness of the response in the paired associate learning task. Paired associate responses were scored as correct when the response was either the target word or a member of the target word's morphological paradigm. For the target word *Blume* ('flower'), for instance, the plural form *Blumen* ('flowers') was considered a correct response. Similarly, for the target word *Wärme* ('warmth'), the response *warm* ('warm') was scored as correct. Furthermore, because of the differences between the phonology of Mandarin Chinese and German, some pronunciations for German target words by bilingual participants resembled phonological neighbors of the target word in German. For the item *Tanz - Feld*, for instance, it was hard to distinguish the target response/fɛlt/from pronunciations such as/fɛrt/or/fert/(pronunciation of *Pferd* ('horse') for native speakers of German in northern and central Germany) and/felt/(pronunciation of *fehlt* (3rd person singular of 'to lack')). For these types of phonologically ambivalent responses we followed the original scoring by a Chinese-German bilingual at the time of acquisition (i.e., the test phase of the experiment). We corrected the scoring at the time of acquisition from correct to incorrect for two responses to the word pair *Tanz - Feld* (one young bilingual, one old bilingual). In these cases the initial "pf" cluster in the pronunciation/*pfert*/indicated that a participant intended to pronounce *Pferd* rather than *Feld*.[4]

A number of predictors were included as independent variables in the design. For each participant the Age (numerical), Gender (categorical: male, female) and Education (categorical: non-PhD, PhD), as well as the result of the vocabulary pre-test in each language (numerical, 0–100) was included as a predictor. We also included a binary variable, In Second Language, which was set to 0 if an item was administered in the native language and to 1 if the item was administered in the second language. In addition, the Cue Frequency, the Response Frequency and the Co-occurrence Frequency as described in the materials section above were included as predictors. Finally, we included the order of an item in a list (i.e., in a block of 10 pairs) and the order of an item within the experiment as a whole as experimental control variables.[5]

---

[4] Note that one could argue that even if a participant pronounces *Pferd* this is indicative of successful learning, because it suggests that a participant misperceived *Feld* as *Pferd*, but correctly remembered the perceived pair *Tanz - Pferd*. The difficulty of this pair is similar to that of *Tanz - Feld* (log co-occurrence frequency: 8.23 versus 7.04). Nonetheless, we decided to be conservative and score as incorrect the two responses mentioned above for which the initial "pf" cluster in the pronunciation indicated that the intended pronunciation was *Pferd* rather than *Feld*.

[5] The correlation between the order of an item in a list and the order of the item in an experiment is $r = 0.33$, and is therefore unlikely to result in suppression in statistical models (see Wurm and Fisicaro 2014).

2.4 Procedure

The experiment was presented through a web page interface on a 15 inch MacBook Pro laptop. Items in both the vocabulary pretest and the paired associate learning test were presented auditorily through the laptop speakers. The items for the vocabulary and paired associate learning tests in both languages were recorded from native female speakers of Mandarin Chinese and German in a sound booth using professional recording equipment.

For each item in the vocabulary pre-test, participants were auditorally presented with the test word and the 4 possible answers. Participants were asked to select the answer that was most similar in meaning to the test word by clicking one of four buttons labelled 1 through 4 on the screen. Participants were asked to guess if they did not know the correct answer to a question.

In the paired associate learning task each block of 10 pairs consisted of a training phase and a test phase. Participants were asked to memorize the pairs of words presented in the training phase. In the test phase, participants were asked to produce the word that formed a pair with the auditorily presented word. The order of the words in a pair was consistent between the training and the test phase, such that the first word of a pair that was presented during the training phase was the auditorily presented "cue" word during the test phase. The test phase was self-paced: participants were asked to press the next button on the screen to move on to the next test word after verbally responding to a test word.

The average time required to complete the vocabulary pre-test for each language was about 30 minutes. The 3 blocks of paired associate learning took about 25 minutes per participant in each language, including a short break between each block. Including instructions and breaks, the duration of the experiment was about 1 hour for German monolinguals and 2 hours for Chinese-German bilinguals.

3 Analysis

The performance in the paired associate learning test was evaluated using a logistic generalized additive mixed-effect model (GAMM), as implemented in version 1.8–3 of the mgcv package for R (Wood 2006). The use of GAMMs allowed us to model non-linear predictor effects while also accounting for random effects.

We included a random intercept for Item, as well as random by-participant smooths for the order of an item in a list and in the experiment as a whole in the model to control for subject-, item- and task-related variance (cf., Baayen et al. 2015). The effects of categorical predictors were modeled through simple parametric terms, whereas the effects of numerical predictors were modeled through predictor smooths to allow for non-linear effects. R code for the reported GAMM is presented in Appendix 2.

4 Results

The GAMM analysis of the data revealed a significant random effect of Item (χ^2 = 310.673, p < 0.001), as well as significant by-participant smooths for the Item Position in a list (χ^2 = 47.584, p < 0.001) and the Item Position in the experiment as a whole (χ^2 = 138.523, p < 0.001). The by-participant smooths for the Item Position in a list (left panel) and in the experiment (right panel) are presented in Figure 4.

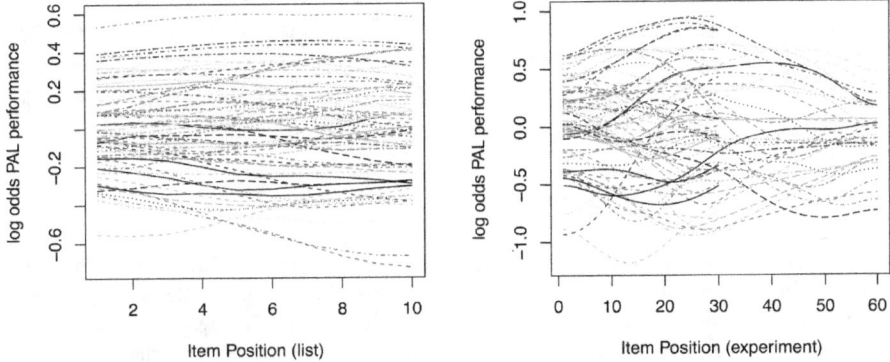

Figure 4: Penalized participant factor smooths for the position of an item in a block (left panel) and in the experiment as a whole (right panel). The effects of item position within a list and within the experiment show considerable variation between participants.

The left panel of Figure 4 demonstrates there is some between-participant variance for the effect of the order of an item in a list, with primacy effects for some participants and recency effects for others. The by-participant smooths for the position of an item within the experiment show more substantial variation. Some participants improve over the course of the experiment, whereas others become worse.

In addition, the GAMM analysis revealed a marginally significant main effect of Education (z = –1.758, p = 0.079), with PhDs performing somewhat worse than non-PhDs. This main effect of Education Level was significant in a post-hoc analysis in which we included the data for the old participants only ($z = -2.073$, $p = 0.038$). The poor performance of highly educated older participants follows straightforwardly from the principles of discrimination learning: the greater the experience of a person with the language, the worse that person should be at learning arbitrary associations in the paired associate learning task.

Finally, while the main effect of InSecondLanguage was not significant ($z = -0.483$, $p = 0.629$), we observed a significant interaction (as modelled through a te() smooth) between Age and Co-occurrence Frequency ($\chi^2 = 38.687$, $p < 0.001$). This interaction was significantly different between the First Language and the Second Language ($\chi^2 = 9.122$, $p = 0.028$).[6]

The contrast surface for InSecondLanguage for the tensor product interaction between Age and Co-occurrence Frequency is presented in Figure 5. Figure 5 shows that performance on the paired associate learning task is highly similar in L1 and L2 for the young participants. A post-hoc analysis in which we included the data for the young participants only showed an Age by Co-occurrence Frequency interaction that was significant ($\chi^2 = 19.658$, $p = 0.001$), but that did not differ between the First Language and the Second Language ($\chi^2 = 1.357$, $p = 0.961$). Furthermore, this post-hoc analysis revealed no main effect of InSecondLanguage ($z = 0.250$, $p = 0.803$).

---

[6] Note that we used (log-transformed) unaltered Google co-occurrence frequencies for both German and Chinese, in spite of the fact that the size of Google in Chinese and German is different. We decided not to further calibrate the scales of the Co-occurrence Frequencies in German and Chinese for two reasons. First, the (log-transformed) Co-occurrence Frequency distribution was relatively similar for German and Chinese without any further adjustments (German: mean = 9.54; sd = 2.77, Chinese: mean = 11.45; sd = 2.88). Second, given the fact that the size of Google in German and Chinese is hard to determine it would be unclear how exactly to calibrate the Co-occurrence Frequency ranges in German and Chinese (see Materials section).

To verify that potential scale differences between Co-occurrence Frequency in German and Chinese did not influence our interpretation of the results, however, we carried out a post-hoc analysis in which the Co-occurrence Frequency of all items in Chinese was divided by the ratio of the mean Co-occurrence Frequency in Chinese and the mean Co-occurrence Frequency in German prior to the log-transformation (correlation with the original logged Co-occurrence Frequency measure: $r = 0.984$). In this analysis the tensor product interaction between Age and Co-occurrence Frequency remained significant ($\chi^2 = 43.458$, $p < 0.0001$) and this tensor product interaction remained significantly different between the First Language and the Second Language ($\chi^2 = 8.220$, $p = 0.042$). In addition, the main effect of InSecondLanguage reached significance: ($z = 2.354$, $p = 0.019$), with a better overall performance in the second language than in the first language.

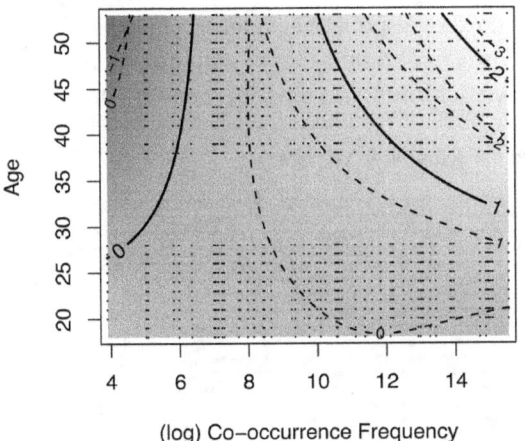

Figure 5: Effect of the (log-transformed) Co-occurrence Frequency and Age on the Paired Associate Learning performance: contrast between First Language and Second Language. The z-axis represents performance in the paired associate learning test on the logit scale. While young participants perform similarly in L1 and L2, old participants show an advantage of performing the PAL task in their L2 for most of the Co-occurrence Frequency range.

Older participants, however, show an advantage of performing the paired associate learning task in L2. As can be seen in Figure 5, older participants perform better in the second language for all but the pairs with the lowest co-occurrence frequencies, showing improved performance in L2 for co-occurrence frequencies of 6.5 or higher (i.e., for 90% of the word pairs). The better performance of older participants in the second language was confirmed by a post-hoc analysis on the data for the old participants only, which showed an Age by Co-occurrence Frequency interaction ($\chi^2 = 36.335$, $p < 0.001$) that was significantly different between the First Language and the Second Language ($\chi^2 = 14.959$, $p = 0.002$). In addition, this post-hoc analysis showed a main effect of InSecondLanguage ($z = 2.113$, $p = 0.035$), with a better performance in the second language than in the first language.

Figure 6 presents the by-item averages for the older monolinguals and the older bilinguals in German. Items are ranked from easy to hard. We re-defined item difficulty as the mean paired associate learning performance across the old and the young participants (as opposed to our a priori estimation of item difficulty on the basis of the co-occurrence frequency of the words in a pair that was used to construct the materials for this study). Consistent with the results from the GAMM, the performance of the Chinese-German bilinguals in their L2 is much better than that of the German monolinguals in their L1 for most of the item difficulty range.

In total, the older bilinguals outperformed the older monolinguals on 19 of the 30 items, while the older monolinguals performed better for 7 items only. For 13 items the German proportion of correct responses is at least 0.15 lower for the monolinguals than for the bilinguals (versus 5 items for which the proportion of correct responses is at least 0.15 lower for bilinguals than for monolinguals).

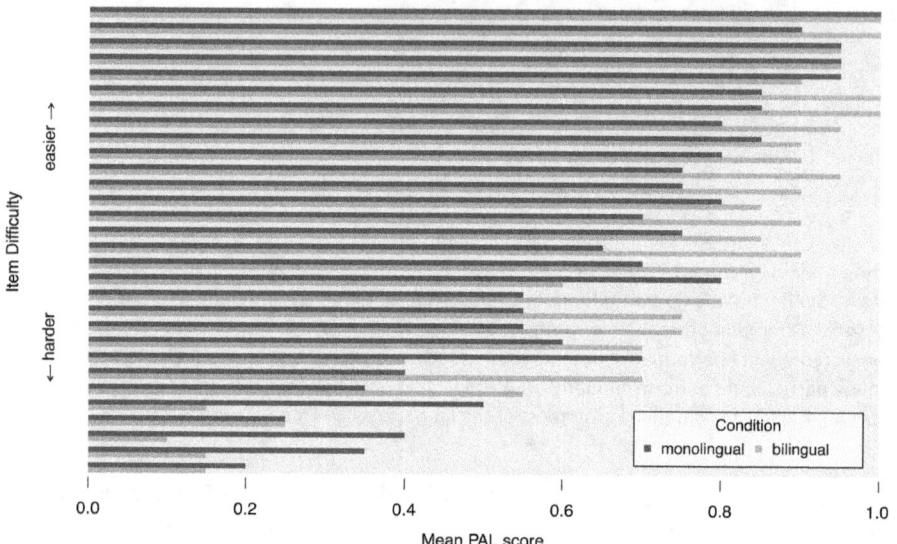

Figure 6: By-item performance in the Paird Associate Learning task for old monolinguals and bilinguals in German. For all but the hardest items, old Chinese-German bilinguals perform better in German than do age-matched German monolinguals.

The difference between the monolinguals and the bilinguals in German presented in Figure 6 was confirmed in an additional post-hoc analysis of older participants in German only, which once more showed an Age by Co-occurrence Frequency interaction ($\chi^2 = 24.828$, $p < 0.001$) that was significantly different between the First Language and the Second Language ($\chi^2 = 10.244$, $p = 0.017$).[7]

As can be seen at the bottom of Figure 6, the performance of older participants in their second language is particularly poor for the hardest pairs. This decrease in performance is substantially reduced for younger participants (see Figure 5). The experience of older bilingual participants in their first language is much greater

---

[7] Note that the main effect of InSecondLanguage did not reach significance for this subset of the data ($z = 0.246$, $p = 0.806$).

than that of young bilinguals. Not only were the old bilinguals older than the young bilinguals, they also moved to Germany at a later age (mean age of learning the second language for old bilinguals: 27.45, young bilinguals: 19.90). Participants in the paired associate learning task are not restricted to thinking in the language the task is presented in. One potential explanation for the poor performance of older adults on the hardest items in their second language, therefore, is that older bilinguals may have recruited their native language when asked to learn arbitrary associations between relatively infrequent words in their second language.

In addition to the improved performance of older participants in the second language, we observed an attenuation of the Age effect in the second language. Figure 7 shows the predicted performance (Proportion Correct) in the First Language and in the Second Language as a function of Age and Co-occurrence Frequency. As can be seen in Figure 7, there is a clear age effect in the first language, which is qualitatively similar to the age effects reported in monolingual paired associate learning studies (see the GAMM for the English PAL data reported above). Throughout the left panel of Figure 7, the performance of the old participants is worse than that of the young participants. The difference is small for items with high association rates, but increases as Co-occurrence Frequency decreases. At the mid-point of the co-occurrence frequency range (as indicated by the dashed lines in Figure 7), for instance, the estimated performance of the oldest participants is 59% correct, whereas the performance of the youngest participants is 76% correct (difference: 17%). In the second language this age effect is substantially reduced. A clear age effect in the second language is present for the hardest pairs only, albeit for different reasons than in the first language (see above). At the mid-point of the co-occurrence frequency range the estimated performance is between 73% and 76% across the age range. For the easiest pairs old participants even perform somewhat better than young participants, although the performance of both groups is close to ceiling.

An inspection of the by-item averages for the German monolinguals in German, the Chinese-German bilinguals in Chinese and the Chinese-German bilinguals in German sheds further light on the reduced age effect for bilinguals in their second language. First, consider Figure 8, which shows the by-item performance of young and old German monolinguals in German. Young monolingual German participants performed better than old monolingual German participants across the item difficulty range. In total, the young monolingual German participants outperformed the old monolingual German participants on 23 of the 30 items, while the older participants performed better for 3 items only. For no less than 14 of the 30 items in the German paired associate learning test the mean item score (i.e., proportion correct) is at least 0.15 lower for the old participants than for the young participants.

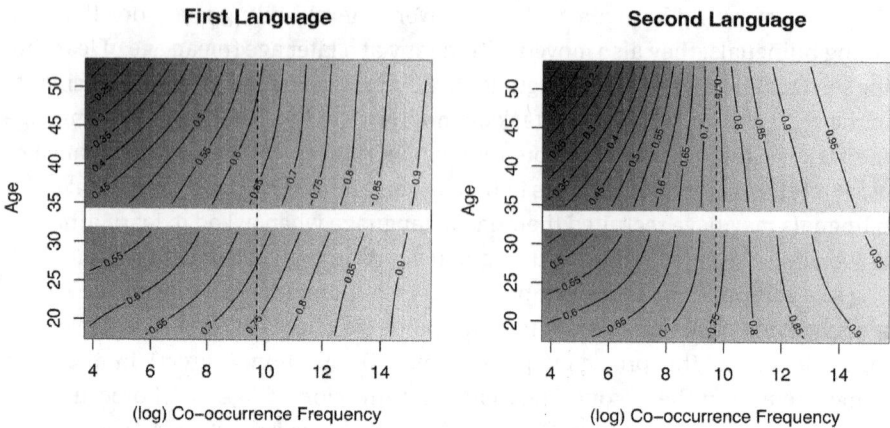

Figure 7: Effect of the (log-transformed) Co-occurrence Frequency and Age on the Paired Associate Learning performance in the first and second language. The z-axis represents proportion correct in the paired associate learning test. Dotted lines indicate the mid-point of the (log) Co-occurrence Frequency range. Older participants, but not younger participants show improved performance in their second language. The typical age effect for monolinguals is present in L1; this age effect is substantially reduced in L2.

Figure 8: By-item performance in the Paired Associate Learning task for German monolinguals in German. Young participants perform better than old participants across the Item Difficulty range.

Figure 9 shows the by-item performance of the Chinese-German bilinguals in Chinese. For the easiest one third of the items the difference between old and young participants is negligible. For the hardest two thirds of the items, however, clear age differences are present. The young bilinguals outperformed the old bilinguals for 18 of the 30 items, while the old bilinguals did better for 4 items. For 9 out of the 30 items in the Chinese paired associate learning test the mean item score is at least 0.15 lower for the old participants than for the young participants. For 2 items the older Chinese-German bilinguals have an item score that is 0.15 higher than that of the young Chinese-German bilinguals for 2 items. Interestingly, these two items consist of pairs of words that may well be more associated for older participants than for younger participants: 喝水 - 吃药 ('drink water' - 'take medicine') and 房子 - 漏水 ('house' - 'water leakage').

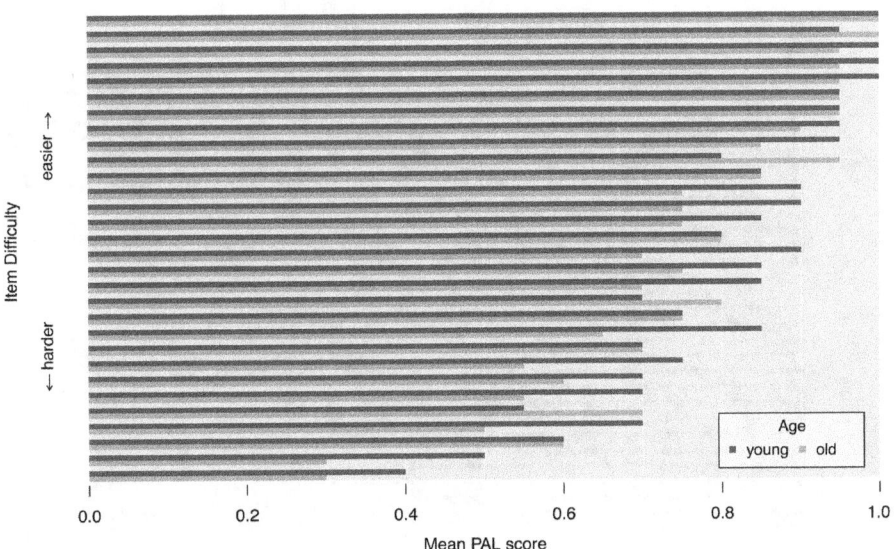

Figure 9: By-item performance in the Paired Associate Learning task for Chinese-German bilinguals in Chinese. As a result of less divergent experience with the language, the age effect is reduced as compared to German monolinguals in German. Nonetheless young participants still perform substantially better than old participants.

Similarly, the fact that the age effect is reduced for Chinese-German bilinguals as compared to German monolinguals follows from the reduced experience of Chinese-German bilinguals in their native language as compared to German monolinguals. German monolinguals typically lived in Germany for the entire duration of their life. The experience of young and old German monolinguals in German, therefore, is more-or-less a linear function of their age. By contrast, many of the old Chinese-German bilinguals have lived and worked in a German speaking environment for years and communicate in their first language less frequently. As a result, the difference in linguistic experience between young and old Chinese-German bilinguals in Chinese is much smaller than that between young and old German monolinguals in German – which results in a reduced age effect.

Despite the fact that the old Chinese-German bilinguals typically have somewhat more linguistic experience in German than the young Chinese-German bilinguals, the experience of young and old Chinese-German bilinguals in German should be more similar than that of young and old Chinese-German bilinguals in Chinese and that of young and old German monolinguals in German. We therefore expected to see a further reduction of the age effect for Chinese-German bilinguals in German. As can be seen in Figure 10 this prediction is borne out.

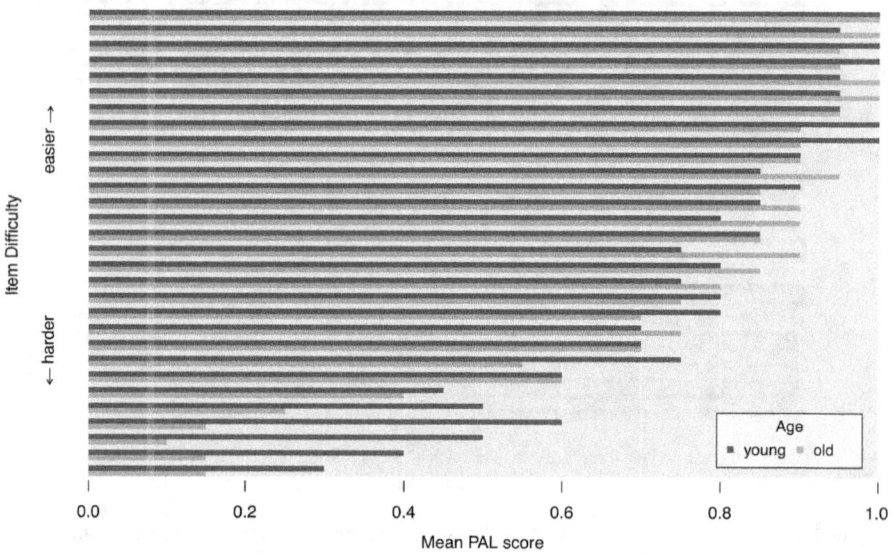

Figure 10: By-item performance in the Paired Associate Learning task for Chinese-German bilinguals in German. Young and old participants perform comparably for most of the items. Old participants are outperformed by young participants on a few of the hardest items only (see discussion in the text).

The difference between the old and young participants is negligible for most of the item difficulty range. In total, the young participants performed better than the old participants at 14 items, whereas the old participants outperformed the young participants on 10 items. A difference of at least 0.15 between the mean item scores for young and old participants is present for 6 of the hardest items only.[8]

For 1 item, older participants performed substantially better than younger participants: *waschen - Seife* ('to wash' - 'bar soap'). Although this effect may be due to variance, it could also be the case that the advantage for older participants may reflect an interesting aspect of discrimination learning: the association between a cue word and a response word is determined not only by the co-occurrence frequency of the cue word and the target word, but also by the co-occurrence frequency of the cue word with other words. The more words the cue occurs with and the higher the co-occurrence frequencies with other words, the weaker the association strength between the cue word and the target word.

Figure 11 illustrates this point for the item 'to wash' - 'bar soap', by showing the frequency for the word *bar soap*, as well as the frequency of two other words that are expected to frequently co-occur with *to wash*: *shower gel* and *body wash* in the Google n-gram viewer from 1988 to 2008. The frequency of *bar soap* remained fairly constant over the last 20 years. Simultaneously, however, the frequency of other words that are expected to co-occur with *to wash* substantially increased. By 2008, words like *shower gel* and *body wash* were more frequent than *bar soap*.

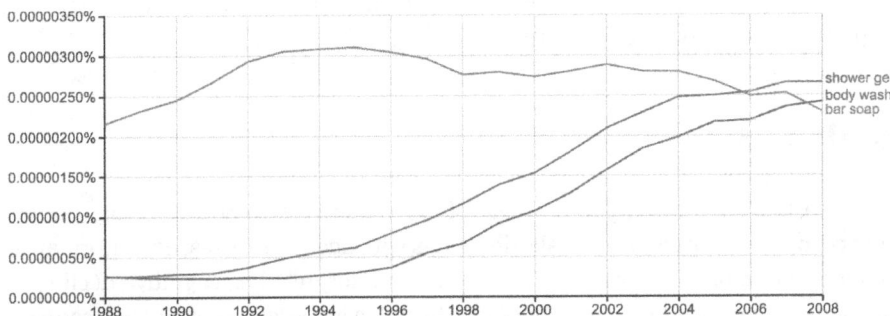

Figure 11: Frequency of *bar soap*, *shower gel* and *body wash* in the Google n-gram viewer from 1988 to 2008. The frequency of *bar soap* remains fairly constant, whereas the frequency of *shower gel* and *body wash* increases over time. As a result, the association strength between *to wash* and *bar soap* is weaker for recent L2 learns of German, which makes the PAL item 'to wash' - 'bar soap' harder for young Chinese-German bilinguals than for old Chinese-German bilinguals.

---

8 As mentioned above, this difference may be due to older participants recruiting their first language for the hardest pairs.

The old bilingual participants in our study have been in Germany for an average duration of 16.15 years, whereas the young bilinguals have been in Germany for an average duration of 4.65 years. When it comes to words that frequently co-occur with *to wash*, therefore, old participants have years of experience teaching them to almost exclusively expect *bar soap*, while young participants have a much more diverse experience that includes words like *shower gel* and *body wash*. From this perspective, the fact that old bilingual participants outperform young bilingual participants for the item 'to wash' - 'bar soap' is unsurprising.

While the advantage for the item 'to wash' - 'bar soap' for older bilingual participants as compared to younger bilingual participants is a non-significant effect for a single item only, it illustrates an important point with regard to discrimination learning in the context of paired associate learning. The expected performance in the paired associate learning test is determined not only by the association rates of the words in a pair, but by the distributional properties of the language as a whole, as well as by the linguistic experience of each individual participant.

The plots of the by-item performance in the paired associate learning test presented in Figures 8 through 10 demonstrate that the differences in performance on the paired associate learning test between old and young participants are most pronounced when the difference in linguistic experience is the greatest. By contrast, the differences between old and young participants are limited when the difference in experience is limited as well. More simply put: greater linguistic experience leads to worse performance.

5 Discussion

A well-established finding in the field of experimental psychology is that performance in a range of cognitive tasks decreases with age. The decreased performance of older participants in these tasks is typically interpreted as cognitive decline: a general and inevitable decline in cognitive function in the later stages of life (see e.g., Naveh-Benjamin and Old 2008; Deary et al. 2009; Salthouse 2009; Singh-Manoux et al. 2012). Recently, however, we have argued that age-related changes in the performance on cognitive tasks may be a result of increased experience with the stimuli used in these tasks (see Ramscar et al. 2013; Ramscar et al. 2014).

Paired associate learning is a classic example of a task in which older participants perform worse than younger participants (see e.g., desRosiers and Ivison 1986). The age effect in paired associate learning is small for "easy" word pairs (i.e., *north - south*) and large for "hard" word pairs (i.e., *jury - eagle*). This interaction between age and item difficulty does not readily fit with a view in which age-related changes in performance are due to a general decline in cognitive function.

Instead, from such a perspective, we would expect a main effect of age that is independent of item difficulty.

By contrast, from a discrimination learning perspective, the interaction between age and item difficulty is a natural consequence of experience. Under this view, the crucial distinction between hard and easy items in the paired associate learning task is the association between the cue word and the response word. The words *north* and *south* often occur together and therefore are highly associated. The words *jury* and *eagle* rarely co-occur and thus are weakly associated. Due to increased experience with the language, older participants are more sensitive to the association rates of words in the language. A lifetime of learning has taught them that *jury* and *eagle* do not occur together, and makes it hard to learn to respond *eagle* when presented with the word *jury*.

Despite the fact that the age by item difficulty interaction fits better with a discrimination learning approach than with cognitive decline, it is not straightforward to provide compelling evidence against the idea of cognitive decline. Experience with linguistic stimuli and age are highly correlated. Indeed, it is impossible to separate the effects of age and linguistic experience for paired associate learning when testing monolinguals.

Comparing the performance of monolinguals with the performance of bilinguals, however, allows us to tease apart the effects of age and linguistic experience. Experience in L1 is much greater for older participants than for younger participants. Experience in L2, however, varies as a function of the time spent learning L2, rather than as a function of age per se. The "cognitive decline" perspective on age-related changes in cognitive behavior predicts that older participants should show similar performance in L1 and L2, or better performance in L1 than in L2. Discrimination learning, however, predicts that older participants should perform better in L2 than in L1.

Here, we reported the results of a paired associate learning task for monolingual speakers of German, as well as for Chinese-German bilinguals. The results are consistent with the predictions of the discrimination learning perspective on the decreased performance of older participants in paired associate learning. Overall, older participants performed better in L2 than in L1, whereas younger participants showed similar performance in L1 and L2. For L2 word pairs with medium-to-high association rates older participants performed equally well or slightly better than younger participants. It was only for the items with the lowest association rates that we found an adverse age effect in L2. Possibly, this age effect is due to older participants recruiting their first language for the hardest L2 items (see our discussion above).

Interestingly, we furthermore found an effect of education level. Older participants with a PhD degree performed significantly worse than older participants without a PhD degree. Under the assumption that participants with a PhD degree have increased experience with the language, this is another example of a counter-intuitive effect that readily fits with the predictions of discrimination learning: the greater the experience with a language, the harder it is to learn new associations.

The results reported here are in line with findings from a number of recent studies that have documented the influence of linguistic experience on the performance in cognitive tasks (see Ramscar et al. 2013; Ramscar et al. 2014). Collectively, these studies suggest that a careful re-evaluation of experimental findings results in a more balanced view on age-related decreases in performance, in which surprisingly little evidence for a decline in cognitive function at an older age remains once the behavioral consequences of learning are accounted for.

Appendix 1

Table 2: Items for the German PAL test.

	Cue	Response	Cue (English)	Response (English)
Group 1	Stadt	Köln	'city'	'Cologne'
	Nord	Süd	'north'	'south'
	Reise	Urlaub	'travel'	'holiday'
	Liebe	Herz	'love'	'heart'
	Vater	Sohn	'father'	'son'
	Katze	Hund	'cat'	'dog'
	Spielzeug	Kinder	'toys'	'kids'
	Metall	Eisen	'metal'	'iron'
	Nacht	Sterne	'night'	'stars'
	schlafen	träumen	'to sleep'	'to dream'
Group 2	Schnee	Ski	'snow'	'ski'
	Sonne	Wärme	'sun'	'warmth'
	Bett	Kissen	'bed'	'pillow'
	Garten	Blume	'garden'	'flowers'
	waschen	Seife	'to wash'	'soap'
	Strom	Lampe	'power'	'light'
	Auto	Ziel	'car'	'destination'
	Schrank	Hose	'cabinet'	'pants'
	schwimmen	Insel	'to swim'	'island'
	Fuß	Stein	'foot'	'stone'
Group 3	Kerze	Teller	'candle'	'plate'
	denken	malen	'to think'	'to paint'
	Mauer	Student	'wall'	'student'
	Brief	Herbst	'letter'	'autumn'
	Salz	Pflanze	'salt'	"plant"

Table 2: (Continued)

	Cue	Response	Cue (English)	Response (English)
	Mensch	Flasche	'person'	'bottle'
	Tanz	Feld	'dance'	'field'
	Schiff	Puppe	'ship'	'puppet'
	Banane	See	'banana'	'lake'
	Schlüssel	Zigarette	'key'	'cigarette'

Table 3: Items for the Chinese PAL test. For many words parts-of-speech tagging out of context is ambivalent between noun and verb. For these words the translation to English is listed as '(to) [word]'.

	Cue	Response	Cue (English)	Response (English)
Group 1	运动	健康	'exercise'	'health'
	日本	国家	'Japan'	'country'
	医生	疾病	'doctor'	'disease'
	吃饭	旅行	'to eat'	'(to) travel'
	股票	买卖	'stock'	'(to) trade'
	妈妈	家庭	'mother'	'family'
	朋友	帮助	'friend'	'(to) help'
	杀人	犯罪	'to murder'	'to commit a crime'
	学校	读书	'school'	'(to) study'
	美丽	眼睛	'beautiful'	'eyes'
Group 2	赚钱	银行	'to make money'	'bank'
	房子	漏水	'house'	'to leak / leakage'
	天空	飞机	'sky'	'airplane'
	喝水	吃药	'to drink water'	'to take medicine'
	头发	乌黑	'hair'	'black'
	城市	拥挤	'city'	'crowded'
	小狗	咬人	'dog'	'to bite'
	金钱	工作	'money'	'job'
	小鸟	鸣叫	'bird'	'(to) chirp'
	马路	冬天	'road'	'winter'
Group 3	车祸	黑暗	'car accident'	'darkness'
	桌子	树木	'table'	'tree'
	公园	气球	'park'	'balloon'
	眼镜	走路	'glasses'	'(to) walk'
	游泳	天气	'(to) swim'	'weather'
	糖果	胡椒	'candy'	'pepper'
	铅笔	书包	'pencil'	'backpack'
	领带	饼干	'necktie'	'cookie'
	法官	老鹰	'judge'	'eagle'
	洋葱	手指	'onion'	'finger'

Appendix 2

```
# Load library (version 1.8-3)
library(mgcv)

# Load data
load("data.rda")
# Model
model = bam(Correct ~ s(Item, bs="re") +
                      s(PositionExperiment, Participant,
                      bs="fs",m=1) +
                      s(PositionList, Participant,
                      bs="fs", m=1) +
                      PhD + InSecondLanguage +
                      te(CooccurrenceFrequency, Age) +
                      te(CooccurrenceFrequency, Age,
                      by=InSecondLanguage),
            data=data, family="binomial")
```

References

Arnon, Inbal & Michael Ramscar. 2012. Granularity and the acquisition of grammatical gender: How order of acquisition affects what gets learned. *Cognition*, 122 (3), 292–305.

Arppe, Antti, Peter Hendrix, Petar Milin, Rolf Harald Baayen & Cyrus Shaoul. 2014. ndl: Naive discriminative learning [Computer software manual]. Retrieved from http://CRAN.R-project.org/package=ndl (R package version 0.2.16)

Baayen, Rolf Harald, Shravan Vasishth, Douglas Bates & Reinhold Kliegl. 2015. Out of the Cage of Shadows. arXiv: 0707.3168.

CKIP. 2014. Academia Sinica balanced corpus. Published at http://asbc.iis.sinica.edu.tw. Taipei: Chinese Knowledge Information Processing Group, Academia Sinica.

d'Acremont, Mathieu, Zhong-Li Lu., Xiangrui Li, Martial van der Linden & Antoine Bechara. 2009. Neural correlates of risk prediction error during reinforcement learning in humans. *NeuroImage*, 47 (4), 1929–1939.

Danks, David. 2003. Equilibria of the Rescorla-Wagner model. *Journal of Mathematical Psychology*, 47 (2), 109–121.

Daw, Nathaniel D., Aaron Courville & Peter Dayan. 2008. Semi-rational models of conditioning: The case of trial order. In Nick Chater & Mike Oaksford (eds.), *The probabilistic mind*. Oxford: Oxford University Press.

Dayan, Peter & Kent C. Berridge. 2014. Model-based and model-free pavlovian reward learning: Revaluation, revision, and revelation. *Cognitive, Affective, & Behavioral Neuroscience*, 1–20.

Deary, Ian J., Janie Corley, Alan J. Gow, Sarah E. Harris, Lorna M. Houlihan, Riccardo E. Marioni, Lars Penke, Snorri B. Rafnsson & John M. Starr. 2009. Age-associated cognitive decline. *British Medical Bulletin*, 92, 135–152.

desRosiers, Gabriel & David Ivison. 1986. Paired-associate learning: normative data for differences between high and low associate word pairs. *Journal of Clinical Experimental Neuropsychology*, 8, 637–642.

Epstein, Robert. 2012. Brutal truths about the aging brain. *Discover*, 33, 48–50.

Kamin, Leon J. 1969. Predictability, surprise, attention, and conditioning. In Byron A. Campbell & Russell M. Church (eds.), *Punishment and aversive behavior*, 279–296. New York: Appleton-Century-Crofts.

Lindenberger, Ulman. 2014. Human cognitive aging: Corriger la fortune? *Science*, 346, 572–578.

McDannald, Michael A., Joshua L. Jones, Yuji Takahashi & Geoffrey Schoenbaum. 2014. Learning theory: A driving force in understanding orbitofrontal function. *Neurobiology of Learning and Memory*, 108, 22–27.

Miller, Ralph R., Robert C. Barnet, & Nicholas J. Grahame. 1995. Assessment of the Rescorla-Wagner model. *Psychological Bulletin*, 117 (3), 363–386.

Naveh-Benjamin, Moshe, & Old, Susan R. 2008. Aging and memory. In John H. Byrne, H. Eichenbaum, Randolf Menzel, Henry L. Roediger, & David Sweatt (eds.), *Learning and memory: A comprehensive reference*, 787–808. Oxford: Elsevier.

Pearce, John M., & Geoffrey Hall. 1980. A model for pavlovian learning: variations in the effectiveness of conditioned but not of unconditioned stimuli. *Psychological Review*, 87, 532–552.

Ramscar, Michael, Melody Dye & Joseph Klein. 2013. Children value informativity over logic in word learning. *Psychological Science*, 24 (6), 1017–1023.

Ramscar, Michael, Melody Dye & Stewart McCauley. 2013. Error and expectation in language learning: The curious absence of 'mouses' in adult speech. *Language*, 89 (4), 760–793.

Ramscar, Michael, Peter Hendrix., Bradley Love, & Harald Baayen. 2013. Learning is not decline: The mental lexicon as a window into cognition across the lifespan. *Mental Lexicon*, 8 (3), 450–481.

Ramscar, Michael, Peter Hendrix, Cyrus Shaoul, Petar Milin & Rolf Harald Baayen. 2014. The myth of cognitive decline: Non-linear dynamics of lifelong learning. *Topics in Cognitive Science*, 6, 5–42.

Ramscar, Michael, Daniel Yarlett, Melody Dye, Katie Denny & Kirsten Thorpe. 2010. The effects of feature-label-order and their implications for symbolic learning. *Cognitive Science*, 34 (6), 909–957.

Rescorla, Robert. 1968. Probability of shock in the presence and absence of CS in fear conditioning. *Journal of Comparative and Phsyiological Psychology*, 66 (1), 1–5.

Rescorla, Robert. 1988. Pavlovian conditioning: It's not what you think it is. *American Psychologist*, 43, 151–160.

Salthouse, Timothy. 2009. When does age-related cognitive decline begin? *Neurobiology of Aging*, 30, 507–514.

Schultz, Wolfram. 2006. Behavioral theories and the neurophysiology of reward. *Annual Review of Psychology*, 57, 87–115.

Schultz, Wolfram, Peter Dayan, & P. Read Montague. 1997. A neural substrate of prediction and reward. *Science*, 275, 1593–1599.

Siegel, Shepard, & Lorraine G. Allan. 1996. The widespread influence of the rescorla-wagner model. *Psychonomic Bulletin & Review*, 3 (3), 314–321.

Singh-Manoux, Archana, Mika Kivimaki, M. Maria Glymour, Alexis Elbaz, Claudine Berr, Klaus P. Ebmeier, Jane E. Ferrie & Aline Dugravot. 2012. Timing of onset of cognitive decline: results from whitehall ii prospective cohort study. *British Medical Journal*, 344.

Sutton, Richard S., & Andrew G. Barto. 1981. Toward a modern theory of adaptive networks: Expectation and prediction. *Psychological Review*, 88, 135–170.

Tremblay, Léon, Jeffrey R. Hollerman & Wolfram Schultz. 1998. Modifications of reward expectation-related neuronal activity during learning in primate striatum. *Journal of Neurophysiology*, 80 (2), 964–977.

Wagner, Allan & Robert Rescorla. 1972. A theory of Pavlovian conditioning: Variations in the effectiveness of reinforcement and nonreinforcement. In Abraham H. Black & William F. Prokasy (eds.), *Classical conditioning II*, 64–99. New York: Appleton-Century-Crofts.

Wood, Simon N. 2006. *Generalized additive models*. New York: Chapman & Hall/CRC.

Wurm, Lee H., & Sebastiano A. Fisicaro. 2014. What residualizing predictors in regression analysis does (and what it does not do). *Journal of Memory and Language*, 72, 37–48.

Yin, Henry H., & Barbara J. Knowlton. 2006. The role of the basal ganglia in habit formation. *Nature Reviews Neuroscience*, 7 (6), 464–476.

Cheung Hin Tat
3 The use of cognitive state verbs in narratives of school-age Cantonese-speaking children with and without language impairment

Abstract: The present study examined the use of complement-taking cognitive state verbs by Cantonese-speaking children. A total of 105 language samples archived in a completed normative study were used. Forty-five samples were from children with language impairment and 60 from age-matched controls. Two types of complement-taking cognitive state verb, (1) mental state verb, such as 'consider' and (2) perception verb, such as 'see', were analyzed. The results showed that children with language impairment were less capable in using cognitive state verbs when compared with their age-matched peers. Between mental state verb and perception verb, the language impaired group showed more difficulties with the former. Besides, lexical substitutions were frequently found, with mental state verbs replaced by perception verbs, which could be caused by a different interpretation when processing the input script. Together these findings pointed to a possible specific deficit in verbal expressions of mental constructs in children with language impairment that could further be associated to their development of Theory of Mind.

Key words: cognitive state verb, narrative development, Cantonese, language impairment

1 Introduction

There is a growing interest in understanding the causal relation between Theory of Mind (ToM), our mental representation and interpretation of other minds, and the development of child language. Of particular concern is the chicken-egg issue on the acquisition of mental state verbs for expressing mental constructs such as intention, desire, belief, and knowledge. deVilliers and her colleagues argued that the verb complement structure provides a representational structure for embedded propositions and offers the child a new representational capacity for describing mental events (De Villiers and De Villiers,

---

Cheung Hin Tat, The Education University of Hong Kong

https://doi.org/10.1515/9783110610895-007

2000; de Villiersand Pyiers 2002) . Empirical evidence demonstrated that an exposure to mental state verbs can facilitate children's understanding of epistemic states, which is an important element in Theory of Mind (Hale and Tager-Flusberg, 2003; Lohmann and Tomasello, 2003). Gamannossi and Pinto (2014) also showed that narrative competence in using mental state terms is related to the comprehension of deception in children. Besides, Cantonese-speaking children as young as 20 months old started using mental state verbs such as *jiu4* 'want' and *zi1* 'know' (Tardiff and Wellman 2000) but the contribution of using complement-taking mental state verbs to Theory-of-Mind development is not unique when the general language ability of the child is taken into the picture (Cheung at al. 2004).

Specific language impairment (SLI) is a language disorder that delays the mastery of language skills in children who have no hearing loss or other developmental delays. Children with SLI should be intact in their cognitive and social domains and there is little concern on their ToM. However, as a deficit in verb is one of the characteristics of children with SLI, their verbal expressions on their own and other party's mental states could very likely be affected. Several studies have shown that children with specific language impairment were less productive in their lexical choice and used more semantic substitutions such as "make" and "do". They were weak in the use of complement-taking mental state verbs, such as "know" and "want" (Johnston, Miller and Tallal, 2001; Owen, 2010). As pointed out by Owen and Lin (2011) cognitive state verbs carry rich semantic information, sometimes abstract, on mental states of perception, emotion, thought and, desire, many of which would be beyond the reach of young children. These verbs are also complex at the syntactic level, not only for their co-occurrence with complement clause but also for the involvement of alternative syntactic frames, a verb plus a direct object as in 'know something' and a verb plus a complement clause, in 'know that something happens". Lee and Rescorla (2008) found that late talkers used significantly fewer mental state verbs than the controls between age 3 to age 5. Owen (2010) reported that children with SLI have more problems in using mental state verbs in finite complement clauses than with clauses that use action verbs. Besides, patients with High Functioning Autism produced fewer mental state terms (Bang, Burns and Nadig, 2013). While there are reports on the use of complement-taking mental state verbs by typically-developing Cantonese-speaking children (Tardiff and Wellman, 2000; Cheung et al., 2004), only one related study is found in the literature, which showed that Cantonese-speaking children SLI children scored significantly lower than the control groups in the measure of syntactic complexity (To, Stokes, Cheung, and T'sou 2010).

2 Language samples and target Verbs

To examine the use of complement-taking cognitive state verbs in Cantonese-speaking children, language samples that were archived in a normative study of a standardized test (Tsou et al. 2006) were retrieved and analyzed. The language samples were elicited by a story-retelling task. The child was tested individually in a quiet room, and was asked to retell a story of a rescue attempt after he/she was orally presented with a model story, aided by a 24-frame wordless picture book. Elicited narratives were then scored in four major dimensions, story content, syntactic complexity, connectivity, and referencing. For the purpose of examining the use of complement-taking cognitive state verbs, six pictures, in two types, were selected from the original test stimuli for re-analysis. Three pictures came with input scripts containing mental state verbs, *jing6 wai4* 'consider', *hang2ding6* 'sure' and *faat3gok3* 'realize' and three pictures with the perception verb *kin3* 'see', as shown in Table 1.

Table 1: Input scripts used in the storytelling task.

Pic#	Input script with perception verb
8	喺欄杆上面嗰兩個男仔見到佢哋游到筋疲力盡 Two boys who are standing on the railing <u>saw</u> that they are already exhausted
9	就即刻救佢哋上岸，其他嘅小朋友見到浸親嘅男仔上到嚟面青青，本來都好擔心 so they pull them up immediately; the other kids are worried in the beginning when they saw the drowned boys look pale
10	但係當見到佢哋兩個面色好番啲之後，大家先至鬆一口氣 However they finally felt a sense of relief after they <u>see</u> they are getting better

Pic#	Input script with mental state verb
5	有一個好高嘅男仔同埋一個攣頭髮嘅男仔認為自己好似游泳選手咁叻 A tall boy and a boy with curly hair <u>think</u> they are as good as swimming athletes
13	好大力咁吹咗幾吓口哨，因為佢好肯定如果佢吹口哨嘅話就可以吸引到啲海豚嚟幫佢哋 she blew the whistles hardly, because she is so <u>sure</u> that she can attract the dolphins to help them if she blow the whistle
16	上到岸之後，佢哋發覺原來隻貓俾啲樹枝夾實咗 When they arrived, they <u>realize</u> that the cat is being stuck up by the tree

These complement-taking perception verbs and mental state verbs were selected because they express cognitive states at different levels. According to Nicolopoulou and Richner (2007), the portrait of characters as having belief and desire at the "Person" level, is one level higher than characters presented as having physical actions and perceptual capacities, at the Agent level. In other words, the perception verb *kin3* 'see', used in Picture 8, 9, and 10, are describing characters as having a simple psychological capacity while mental state verbs used in Picture 5 'consider', Picture 13 'sure' and Picture 15 'realize' depict characters as entities with more complex mental representations, such as belief and desires.

Furthermore, these six complement-taking cognitive state verbs provide causal interpretation of events in the absence of causal connectives, contributing to the overall textual organization of the story. For example, in the input script of Picture 9 (Table 1), the perception verb *kin3* 'see' links up causally the event of the drowning of two boys and the mental states "being worried" of the by-standers. The causal link is expressed through the perspective of the by-standers, not the narrator. If the perception verb 'see' is not used, the mental states of being worried will be presented from the narrators' perspective and the agent role of the characters in this part of the story will disappear.

According to an earlier report that Cantonese-speaking children with SLI were weak in complex syntax (To et al. 2013), it was predicted that the SLI group would have more difficulties in using both types of cognitive state verbs when compared with age-matched controls. It was further predicted that children with SLI would be less capable in using mental state verbs than perception verbs, following the character representation framework of Nicolopoulou and Richner (2007). These predictions were examined by a two-step analysis, as illustrated in Table 2. First, children's coverage of the target event was computed. Then the use of cognitive state verb in verb complement structure was tabulated and compared. Finally, lexical choices were analyzed.

A total of 105 language samples were extracted and analyzed, with one sample contributed by one child. Of these 105 children, 45 of them were children with specific language impairment (SLI) and they were equally subdivided in three age groups (age 6, age 7 and age 8). Sixty typically developing children, in three age-groups, formed the age-matched control group (TD). The SLI children were recruited by a local public child assessment center for the normative study. They were diagnosed by speech therapists and their language impairment was not directly resulted from sensory, emotional, intellectual or physical impairments. Their non-verb IQ scores, as measured by Wechsler Intelligence Scale for Children-III (WISC-HK), were all higher than 85. While the initial diagnosis was a clinical one, their status of being language impaired was confirmed by their performance in HKCOLAS (T'sou et al., 2006). Performance of both groups of participant in the original four narrative domains can be found in Appendix 2.

Table 2: Examples of event coverage and use of verb complement (VCL).

Picture 8 Target event in the input script ...見到佢哋游到筋疲力盡 ...see that they are already exhausted	Target event covered	Target event expressed with CP*
8a. ...兩個男仔就即刻救嗰兩個男仔 ...two boys immediately save these two boys	No	No
8b. ...跟住兩個男仔游唔到, ...and two boys cannot swim across	Yes	No
8c ...佢哋見到佢哋用晒啲氣力, 都唔得, ...they see that they have used up their energy and failed	Yes	Yes
Picture16 Target event in the input script 佢哋發覺原來隻貓俾啲樹枝夾實咗 **They realiz that the cat has been stuck up by twigs**	**Target event covered**	**Target event expressed with CP**
16a. 跟住個男仔想爬上去救隻貓 And the boy wants to climb up to save the cat	No	No
16b. 跟住個貓個腳仲係鬆唔到 ...and the cat's foot still cannot be released	Yes	No
16c 跟住見到個貓係俾樹枝夾住咗 ...and (they) see the cat was stuck by twigs	Yes	Yes

*CP – complement clause structure

3 Result and discussion

Overall speaking, target events encoded with mental state verbs were mentioned more often than that of perception verbs (mental state = 2.04 (68%); perception = 1.62 (54%)). Between the two language groups, the SLI group mentioned the target events less than 50% of the time, much lower than their age-matched peers, which was around 70% of all target events (see Table 3). A 2 x 2 x 3 ANOVA, with two input verb types (mental state verbs vs perception state verbs) as the within-subject repeated measure, two between-subject factors, i.e. 2 levels of language group (typically developing vs SLI) and 3 levels of age groups (age 6, age 7 and age 8), was conducted. The input verb type main effect was found significant, i.e. more events encoded by mental state verbs were mentioned in the task ($F(1, 104)$, = 26.078, $p < 0.01$.) The language group main effect ($F(1, 104) = 12.154$, $p < 0.01$) and the age group main effect were also found significant (age 6 = 2.94 (49%); age 7 = 3.75 (63%); age 8 = 4.29 (72%); $F(2, 103) = 5.31$, $p < 0.01$). Post-doc analyses for the age group effect revealed that the age 6 group mentioned fewer target events than the age 8 group did. One interaction effect was found significant, i.e. input verb type by language group interaction effect (F (1, 101) = 13.07, $p < 0.01$). The TD group was found to have a higher coverage in mental state verbs (mental state = 81% vs perception state = 61%), while such difference is not found significant in the SLI group (mental state = 67%; perception = 53%).

Table 3: Average number of target events reproduced.

	TD (n = 20)			SLI (n = 15)		
	(1) Mental state	(2) Perception	(1)+(2)	(1) Mental state	(2) Perception	(1)+(2)
age 6	2.20* (73%)	1.40 (53%)	3.60 (67%)	1.40 (40%)	0.87 (24%)	2.07 (32%)
age 7	2.55 (85%)	1.80 (60%)	4.35 (78%)	1.80 (47%)	1.53 (51%)	2.93 (49%)
age 8	2.50 (83%)	2.10 (70%)	4.60 (72%)	2.10 (67%)	1.83 (62%)	3.87 (64%)
Overall	2.42 (81%)	1.77 (61%)	4.18 (70%)	1.77 (67%)	1.42 (53%)	2.95 (49%)

*max score = 3

Events encoded with mental state verbs in the input seem to draw more attention from both groups of children. On the functional side, a mental state verb can also work as a logical operator that can change the truth value of the proposition stated in the complement clause. For example, in "I thought Mary will come", the mental state verb 'thought' highlights that it is just a belief of the speaker that "Mary will come" and the belief is false. Given this crucial role in the comprehension process, it is quite reasonable that more attention will be paid to the sentence and it is more likely to be retold later. On the other hand, the surface meaning of a perception verb might only direct children's attention to its role of portraying a character as an agent, with perceptual capacities in making observations. The use of a perception verb will only bring an additional tier of subjectivity in indicating that the event is an observation made by the character. These perception verbs would not bear the same kind of weight as mental state verbs did in the comprehension stage of the story-retelling task.

When using mental state verbs for encoding targeting events, children in the TD showed a developmental growth in using complement clauses, with a major growth from age 7 to age 8 (age 6 = 30%; age 7 =33%; age 8 = 76%). A growth trend is also found in the TD group in using perception verbs (age 6 = 38%; age 7 =81%; age 8 = 76%) with a big jump from age 6 to age 7 (see Figure 1 and Figure 2). By age 8, most typically developing Cantonese-speaking children have developed the capacity in presenting characters as individuals with mental states. On the other hand, children with SLI were less capable in using complement-taking mental state verbs but their use of perception verb was at a level very close to that of the TD group. SLI children at age 6 and age 7 often reported the target event directly without using mental state verbs and a better performance was found with the age 8 SLI group.

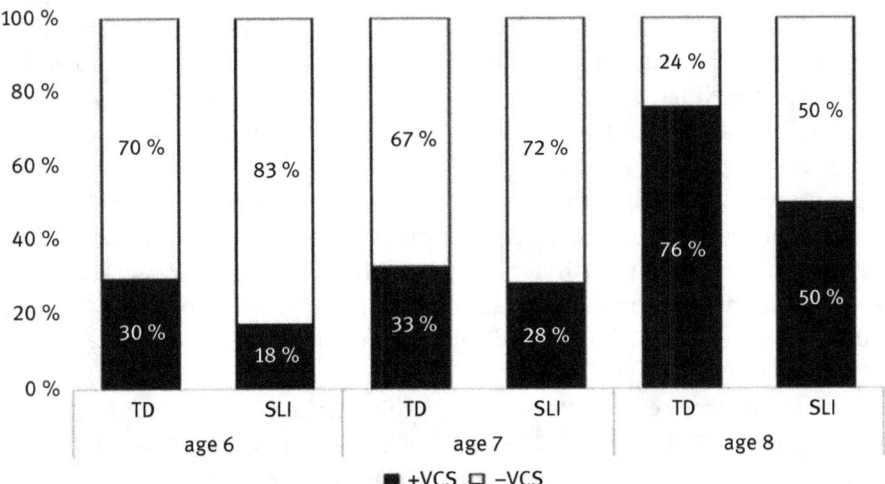

Figure 1: Using mental state verb with/without complement clause structure (VCS).

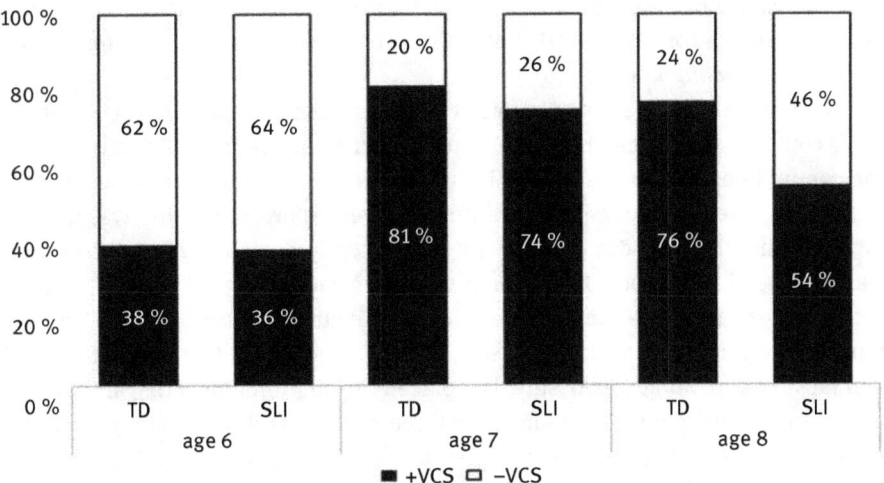

Figure 2: Using perception verb with/without complement clause structure (VCS).

A 2 x 2 x 3 ANOVA, with two verb types (mental state verbs vs perception state verbs) as a within-subject repeated measure, two between-subject factors, language group (typically developing vs SLI) and age groups (age 6, age 7 and age 8) was conducted. The verb type main effect was found significant, i.e. more complement clause structure were used with perception verbs than that of mental state verbs ($F(1, 104)$, = 8.707, $p < 0.01$.) The language group main effect ($F(1, 104)$ = 7.466, $p < 0.01$) and the age group main effect were also found significant ($F(2, 103) = 8.657$, $p < 0.01$). Post-doc analyses for the age group main effect revealed that the age 6 group mentioned fewer target events than the age 7 and the age 8 group did. The difference between the age 7 and the age 8 group was not significant. One interaction effect was found significant, i.e. input verb type by age group ($F (2, 99) = 17.776$, $p < 0.01$). Post-hoc analyses revealed that the two verb types came with two different growth patterns. For the use of perception verbs with complement clause structure, a big gain was found between the age 6 with the age 7 group but the growth stopped at age 8 (age 6 = 15%; age 7 = 44% and age 8 =45%). On the other hand, the use of mental state verb showed an insignificant gain from age 6 to age 7 but a significant increase at age 8 (age 6 = 15%; age 7 = 22%; age 8 = 50%).

Two factors may contribute to the predominant use of perception verbs by TD and SLI groups. First, the lexical meaning of perception verb *kin3* 'see' is simpler than that of the three mental state verbs. It refers to the basic sensory function of human body and therefore variation in interpreting the lexical meaning of *kin3* 'see' in the input script would be minimal. As shown in Table 3 below, the verb *kin3* 'see' is used 85% of the time in the TD group and 50% in the SLI group and only two other verbs being used as substitutions in all 105 language samples, *tai2* 'look'(17) and *mong6*, 'watch'(6).

Greater lexical variations are found with the three mental state verbs as they carry complex lexical meanings and are subject to individual interpretations in the comprehension process, which in turn will lead to a different choice of verb in the story retelling process. For example, the verb *yi3wei3* 'thought' was used to highlight that the two boys were having misconception when *jing6wai4* 'consider' was provided in the input. The other mental state verb *faat3gok3* 'realize', used in describing the mental states of the children in Picture 16, has been consistently replaced by perception verbs, *kin3* 'see', *mong6* 'watch', and *tai2* 'look'. The third mental state verb *hang2ding6* 'sure' is replaced by four different verbs. in the adult group. In fact, TD children replaced the three mental state verbs with perception verbs 67% (41/61) of the time and the replacement is 87% (20/23) in SLI children. In the context of the present study, the substitution of perception verb for mental state verb is made to present the character at a lower level, from a person to an agent, withholding their belief and desire. It could be resulted from a different interpretation of the episode and/or a failure in understand the precise meaning of these mental state verbs by the children. When there is a different understanding of the story, the projection of characters will also be different. It is quite obvious that these children could only present characters at a lower level of agent, just with physical actions and perceptual capacities without a higher level of thinking and desire.

Table 3: Lexical variations in using cognitive state verbs.

Pic #	Input -	Verb Produced	TD (60*)	SLI (45)
Perception verb				
8,	kin3 'see'	kin3 'see' 見	30	8
		tai2 'look' 睇	6	9
		mong6 'watch' 望	5	1
9	kin3 'see'	kin3 'see' 見	7	3
		tai2 'look' 睇	0	1
10	kin3 'see'	kin3 'see' 見	24	2
		tai2 'look' 睇	0	2
Mental state verb				
5	jing6wai4 'consider'	gok3dak1 'feel' 覺得	2	0
		yi3wei3 'thought' 以為	5	1
		waa6 'said' 話	7	7
		lam2 'think' 諗	1	0
13	hang2ding6 'sure'	hang2 ding6 'sure' 肯定	3	0
		zi1dou3 'know' 知道	2	1
		gok3dak1 'feel' 覺得	2	0
		lam2 'think' 諗	2	1
		waa6 'say' 話	0	2
16	faat3 gok3 'realize'	faat3 gok3 發覺	2	0
		faat3jin6 'discover' 發現	1	0
		kin3 'see' 見	33	9
		mong6 'look' 望	1	1
		waa6 'say' 話	0	1

* total number of language samples

Although the present study did not examine directly the chicken-egg issue on the acquisition of mental state verb for expressing belief and other mental constructs, some new observations were made from the differences in using complement taking perception verbs and mental state verbs. Since both typically developing and language impaired groups showed a better use of perception verb, syntactic complexity in using complement clause structure might not be a factor contributing to the difficulty in using mental state verbs. Lexical substitutions of mental state verbs by perception verbs also suggested that even though these children were able to use complement clause, a required means for holding an additional tier of mental representation, they were still constrained in expressing their belief and intention explicitly. In other words, the results here suggested a causal direction from the development of Theory of Mind to the restricted use of mental state verbs, not vice versa.

4 Conclusion

This study examined the use of cognitive state verb in Cantonese-speaking children with specific language impairment by analyzing language samples collected in the normative study of HKCOLAS. When retelling a story, children with SLI did not mention as many target event as their age-peers did. They omitted more target events that were encoded with mental state verbs. When these target events were mentioned, they were often presented as direct observations of the narrator, without using complement-taking cognitive state verbs. Yet, age 7 and age 8 SLI children used perception verbs for encoding target events at the same level as their age-matched peers. Only the age 6 SLI group had problems in capturing the role of perception verbs when listening to the input script, resulting in a higher percentage of omission of target events. Between the two types of cognitive state verbs examined in this study, the use of perception verb *kin3* 'see' in a complementation form was found to be mastered by children first. In some situations, auditory perception verb *waa6* 'say' and visual perception verb 'see' were used as substitutions for mental state verbs. This lexical substitution can be seen as a general constrain in presenting characters at a lower level. Together these results suggested a causal direction from the development of Theory of Mind to the use of mental state verbs.

Since this study is a re-analysis of language samples collected earlier, many factors were not controlled, such as the target verbs, the number and the variety of verb types, the distribution of target events in terms of their relative position in the story and the syntactic complexity of the input script. As memory capacity is taxed in the story-retelling task, the inferior performance of the SLI group could also be a consequence of memory limitation. These issues should be considered when designing a new narrative task for examining the use of cognitive state verbs in children in future study. With all these limitations, findings in the present study remain tentative and interpretations and generalizations should be made with great care.

Appendix I

Appendix 1: Input scripts used in HKCOLAS

Pic1	有一日，有一班男仔同埋女仔好開心咁喺沙灘度玩 Jau5 jat1 jat6, jau5 jat1 baan1 naam4 zai2 tung4 maai4 neoi5 zai2 hou2 hoi1 sam1 gam2 hei2 saa1 taan1 dou6 waan4 One day, a group of boys and girls are playing happily on a beach
Pic2	其中一個戴帽嘅女仔聽到有一啲聲音喎 kei4 zung1 jat1 go3 daai3 mou6 ge1 neoi5 zai2 teng1 dou3 jau5 jat1 dik1 seng1 jam1 wo3 A girl wearing a hat heard some noise
Pic3	於是佢就用望遠鏡睇吓，原來對面岸有隻貓喺樹上面就嚟跌落嚟 jyu1 si6 keoi5 zau6 jung6 mong6 jyun5 geng3 tai2 haak3, jyun4 loi4 deoi3 min6 ngon6 jau5 zek3 maau1 hei2 syu6 soeng6 min6 zau6 lai4 dit3 lok6 lai4 So she looks around with a telescope, it turns out there is a cat almost falls off from a tree.
Pic4	佢就叫其他小朋友諗辦法去救隻貓 keoi5 zau6 giu3 kei4 taa1 siu2 pang4 jau5 lam2 baan6 faat3 heoi2 gau3 zek3 maau1 She asks other kids to come up with a plan to rescue the cat
Pic5	有一個好高嘅男仔同埋一個孿頭髮嘅男仔認為自己好似游泳選手咁叻 jau5 jat1 go3 hou2 gou1 ge1 naam4 zai2 tung4 maai4 jat1 go3 lyun4 tau4 faat3 ge1 naam4 zai2 jing6 wai4 zi6 gei2 hou2 ci5 jau4 wing6 syun2 sau2 gam3 lek1 A tall boy and a boy with curly hair thought they are as good as swimming athletes
Pic6	就自告奮勇咁第一時間去救隻貓，淨低嘅小朋友就爬上去啲欄杆度同佢哋打氣 zau6 zi6 gou3 fan5 jung5 gam2 dai6 jat1 si4 gaan3 heoi2 gau3 zek3 maau1, zeng6 dai1 ge1 siu2 pang4 jau5 zau6 paa4 soeng5 heoi2 dik1 laan4 gon1 dou6 tung4 keoi5 dei6 daa2 hei3 so they volunteer themselves to rescue the cat immediately, the rest of the kids climb on the railing to cheer up for them.
Pic7	但係因為水流好急，所以游緊水嗰兩個男仔點搏命游都游唔到過去 daan6 hai6 jan1 wai6 seoi2 lau4 hou2 gap1, so2 ji5 jau4 gan2 seoi2 go3 loeng5 go3 naam4 zai2 dim2 bok3 meng6 jau4 dou1 jau4 ng4 dou3 gwo3 heoi2 But because of the strong water current, that two boy who are swimming cannot get through no matter how hard they try
Pic8	喺欄杆上面嗰兩個男仔見到佢哋游到筋疲力盡 hei2 laan4 gon1 soeng6 min6 go3 loeng5 go3 naam4 zai2 gin3 dou3 heoi5 dei6 jau4 dou3 gan1 pei4 lik6 zeon6 Two boys who are standing on the railing can see they are already exhausted

Pic9	就即刻救佢哋上岸，其他嘅小朋友見到浸親嘅男仔上到嚟面青青，本來都好擔心 zau6 zik1 haak1 gau3 keoi5 dei6 soeng5 ngon6, kei4 taa1 ge1 siu2 pang4 jau5 gin3 dou3 zam3 can1 ge1 naam4 zai2 soeng6 dou3 lai4 min6 ceng1 ceng1, bun2 loi4 dou1 hou2 daam1 sam1 so pull them up immediately, other kids are worried when they saw they look pale after drowning
Pic10	但係當見到佢哋兩個面色好番啲之後，大家先至鬆一口氣 daan6 hai6 dong1 gin3 dou3 keoi5 dei6 loeng5 go3 min6 sik1 hou2 faan1 dik1 zi1 hau6, daai6 gaa1 sin1 zi3 sung1 jat1 hau2 hei3 However they finally felt a sense of relief after they saw they are getting better
Pic11	有一個紮孖辮嘅女仔就講喇，水流太急喇，就算好似游泳選手咁好身手嘅人都無可能游到過去啦 jau5 jat1 go3 zaat3 maa1 bin1 ge1 neoi5 zai2 zau6 gong2 la1, seoi2 lau4 taai3 gap1 la1, zau6 syun3 hou2 ci5 jau4 wing6 syun2 sau2 gam3 hou2 san1 sau2 ge1 jan4 dou1 mou4 ho2 nang4 jau4 dou3 gwo1 heoi3 laa1 One girl with double ponytail says, the current is too strong, no one can pass through it even though one swims as good as swimming athlete.
Pic12	忽然之間，佢靈機一觸 fat1 jin4 zi1 gaan1, keoi5 ling4 gei1 jat1 zuk1 Suddenly, she gets an idea
Pic13	好大力咁吹咗幾吓口哨，因為佢好肯定如果佢吹口哨嘅話就可以吸引到啲海豚嚟幫佢哋 hou2 daai6 lik6 gam3 ceoi1 zo2 gei2 haa5 hau2 saau3, jan1 wai6 keoi5 hou2 hang2 ding6 jyu4 gwo2 keoi5 ceoi1 hau2 saau3 ge1 waa6 zau6 ho2 ji5 kap1 jan5 dou3 dik1 hoi2 tyun4 lai4 bong1 keoi5 dei6 she blows the whistles hardly, because she is so sure that she could attract the dolphins to help them if she blow the whistle
Pic14	冇幾耐，真係有一群海豚喺岸邊好有秩序咁排成一條直線 mou5 gei2 noi6, zan1 hai6 jau5 jat1 kwan4 hoi2 tyun4 hei2 ngon6 bin1 hou2 jau5 dit6 zeoi6 gam2 paai4 sing4 jat1 tiu4 zik6 sin3 A moment later, there are a bunch of dolphins queueing up orderly at the seaside
Pic15	跟住啲小朋友就小心翼翼咁騎上啲海豚度過去對面岸嘞 gan1 zyu6 dik1 siu2 pang4 jau5 zau6 siu2 sam1 jik6 jik6 gam2 ke4 soeng5 dik1 hoi2 tyun4 dou6 gwo1 heoi3 deoi3 min6 ngon6 la1 then the kids ride on the dolphins carefully and go to the opposite side
Pic16	上到岸之後，佢哋發覺原來隻貓俾啲樹枝夾實咗 soeng5 dou3 ngon6 zi1 hau6, keoi5 dei6 faat3 gok3 jyun4 loi4 zek3 maau1 bei2 dik1 syu6 zi1 gep6 sat6 zo2 After they arrived, they find out that the cat is being stuck up the tree

Pic17	無論隻貓點掙扎，都搵唔到隻腳出嚟，仲越叫越大聲添 mou4 leon4 zek3 maau1 dim2 zang1 zaat3, dou1 man1 ng4 dou3 zek3 goek3 ceot1 lai4, zung6 jyut6 giu3 jyut6 daai6 seng1 tim1 No matter how hard the cat struggle to free, she couldn't pull her leg out, so she screams louder and louder
Pic18	於是高嗰個男仔就懶叻咁話，等佢爬上棵樹度去救隻貓 jyu6 si6 gou1 go2 go3 naam4 zai2 zau6 laan5 lek1 gam3 waa6, dang2 keoi5 paa4 soeng5 po1 syu6 dou6 heoi3 gau3 zek3 maau1 Therefore the tall guy says with over confidence, let him climbs on the tree in order to rescue the cat
Pic19	但係因為棵樹太高，所以佢爬爬吓，就pʊm4一聲跌咗落地下，仲跌到個phɛt7 phɛt7好痛添 daan6 hai6 jan1 wai6 po1 syu6 taai3 gou1, so2 ji5 keoi5 paa4 paa4 haa5, zau6 pʊm4 jat1 seng1 dit3 zo2 lok6 dei6 haa6, zung6 dit3 dou3 go3 phɛt7 phɛt7 hou2 tung3 tim1 However, the tree is too high that he fell on his butt hardly while climbing
Pic20	戴帽嗰個女仔哩就提議不如用騎膊馬呢個方法去救隻貓 daai3 mou6 go2 go3 neoi5 zai2 le1 zau6 tai4 ji3 bat1 jyu4 jung6 ke4 bok3 maa5 nei1 go3 fong1 faat3 heoi3 gau3 zek3 maau1 That girl wearing a hat suggests that what if they build a castell to rescue the cat
Pic21	首先由最肥嗰個男仔企喺下面做支撐，然後其他男仔就一個一個咁疊上去，最後等佢自己爬上去 sau2 sin1 jau4 zeoi3 fei4 go2 go3 naam4 zai2 kei2 hei2 haa6 min6 zou6 zi1 caang1, jin4 hau6 kei4 taa1 naam4 zai2 zau6 jat1 go3 jat1 go3 gam2 daap6 soeng5 heoi3, zeoi3 hau6 dang2 keoi5 zi6 gei2 paa4 soeng5 heoi3 Firstly, the fattest boy stays at the bottom as support, then other boys lifted up one by one, lastly, she will climb to the top
Pic22	啲男仔準備好之後，戴帽嗰個女仔就好輕而易舉咁將隻貓救落嚟 dik1 naam4 zai2 zeon2 bei6 hou2 zi1 hau6, daai3 mou6 go2 go3 neoi5 zai2 zau6 hou2 heng1 ji4 ji6 geoi2 gam2 zoeng1 zek3 maau1 gau3 lok6 lai4 After everyone is ready, the girl wearing a hat rescues the cat from the tree effortlessly
Pic23	跟住紮孖辮嗰個女仔同隻貓包紮傷口 gan1 zyu6 zaat3 maa1 bin1 go2 go3 neoi5 zai2 tung4 zek3 maau1 baau1 zaat3 soeng1 hau2 Then the girl with double ponytail helps the cat to bandage the wound
Pic24	之後，成班小朋友就騎番啲海豚返去喇 zi1 hau6, seng4 baan1 siu2 pang4 jau5 zau6 ke4 faan1 dik1 hoi2 tyun4 faan1 heoi3 laa1 After all, the group of kids ride on the dolphin and go back

Appendix 2

Appendix 2: Background information of participants and their scores in the narrative test of HKCOLAS

	TD-6	TD-7	TD-8	SLI-6	SLI-7	SLI-8
Gender (M/F)	(10/10)	(10/10)	(10/10)	(/9/6)	(10/5)	(10/5)
Mean age	5;7	7;2	8;11	5;8	7;1	8;11
HKCOLAS Narrative Test score	90.5	96.6	106	30.42	46	56.53
Sub-score						
Content	44	46.5	51.2	21.95	29.67	37.26
Connective	9.5	10.2	11.4	1.89	3.39	4.11
Referential expression	17.5	19.6	20.7	4.68	9.56	11.05
Syntactic complexity	19.5	20.3	22.7	1.89	3.39	4.11
Language sample						
Average length in words	362	395	402	180	207	391
Average verb type	41	44	46	24	37	40

References

Bang, Janet, Burns, Jesse and Nadig, Aparna. 2013. Conveying subjective experience in conversation: Production of mental state terms and personal narratives in individuals with high functioning autism. *Journal of Autism Developmental Disorders* 43. 1732–1740.

Cheung, Him, Chen, Hsuan-Chih, Creed, Nikki, Lisa, Ng, Wang, Sui Ping and Lei, Mo. 2004. Relative roles of general and complementation language in Theory-of-Mind development: Evidence from Cantonese and English. *Child Development* 75. 1150–1170.

De Villiers, Jill G and Pyers, Jennie E. 2002. Complements to cognition: A longitudinal study of the relationship between complex syntax and false-belief-understanding. *Cognitive Development* 17. 1037–1060.

De Villiers, Jill G and De Villiers, Peter A.. 2000. Linguistic determinism and the understanding of false beliefs. In: Peter. Mitchell and Kevin, Riggs (ed.), *Children's reasoning and the mind*, 189–226. Hove, UK: Psychology Press.

Gamannossi, Beatrice, Accorti, and Pinto, Giuliana. 2014. Theory of mind and language of mind in narratives: Developmental trends from kindergarten to primary school. *First Language* 34. 262–272.

Hale, Courtney, Melinda, and Tager-Flusberg, Helen. 2003. The influence of language on Theory of Mind: A training study. *Developmental Science* 6. 346–359.

Johnston, Judith R., Miller, Jon F and Tallal, Paula J. 2001. Use of cognitive state predicates by language-impaired children. *International Journal of Language & Communication Disorders* 36. 349–370.

Lee, Eliza, Carlson, and Rescorla, Leslie. 2008. The use of psychological state words by late talkers at ages 3, 4, and 5 years. *Applied Psycholinguistics* 29. 21–39.

Lohmann, Heidemarie and Tomasello, Michael. 2003. The role of language in the development of false belief understanding: A training study. *Child Development* 74. 1130–1144.

Nicolopoulou, Ageliki and Richner, Elizabeth S. 2007. From actors to agents to persons: The development of character representation in young children's narratives. *Child Development* 78(2). 412–429.

Owen, Van, Horne Amanda, J. and Lin, Shanju. 2011. Cognitive state verbs and complement clauses in children with SLI and their typically developing peers. *Clinical Linguistics & Phonetics* 25. 881–898.

Owen, Van and Horne Amanda, J. 2010. Factors affecting accuracy of past tense production in children with specific language impairment and their typically-developing peers: The influence of verb transitivity, clause location, and sentence type. *Journal of Speech, Language, and Hearing Research* 53. 993–1014.

T'sou, Benjamin, K., Lee, Thomas, Tung, Peter Chi-sun, Chan, Amy, Man, Yonnie and Kit-Sum, Carol To. 2006. *Hong Kong Cantonese Oral Language Assessment Scale*. Hong Kong: City University of Hong Kong Press.

Tardif, Twila and Wellman, Henry M. 2000. Acquisition of mental state language in Mandarin- and Cantonese-speaking children. *Developmental Psychology* 36. 25–43.

To, Carol Kit-sum, Stokes, Stephanie Fay, Cheung, Hin-Tat and T'sou, Benjamin K. 2010. Narrative assessment for Cantonese-speaking children. *Journal of Speech, Language, and Hearing Research* 53. 648–669.

B Variation in the general context

Thomas Van Hoey and Chiarung Lu

1 Lexical variation of ideophones in Chinese classics: Their implications in embodiment and migration

Abstract: This paper is an innovative attempt to combine as well as explore some issues related to language variation, embodied cognition, language diffusion, human migration, and geographical distribution of lexicon. These seemingly different issues converge at one research target, i.e., ideophones in Classical Chinese. Due to the depictive imaginative nature of ideophones, their emergence and use imply some embodied cognition between language and environment. Since we trace the usages of the same ideophones diachronically, the results provide some insights into language variation and language diffusion in part of the Chinese history. Such an approach relies on the authorships of some particular ideophones, which can be related to migration and geographical distribution. This paper adopts a corpus linguistic approach that fully utilizes the abundant resources of historical materials, i.e., the Scripta Sinica constructed by the Academia Sinica, Taiwan, with a focus on the Chinese ideophone *mangmang* and its related variants. Finally, this paper utilizes GIS maps to represent our findings.

Keywords: ideophones, language variation, diffusion, semantics, reduplication, corpus linguistics, GIS

1 Introduction

It is a well-known fact that, in general, language changes diachronically. Even in one particular language, it varies slightly or tremendously according to age group, area, gender, occasion, and social status when studied synchronically. To grasp the nature of language, both in its structure and use, language variation is

---

Thomas Van Hoey, Graduate Institute of Linguistics, National Taiwan University, d04142001@ntu.edu.tw https://orcid.org/0000-0002-5226-9752
Chiarung Lu, Graduate Institute of Linguistics, National Taiwan University, chiarung@ntu.edu.tw
https://orcid.org/0000-0002-9275-7371

an intriguing topic to linguists. In this field, most of the studies focus on observing language use in natural social settings and categorizing the linguistic variants according to their social distribution. This paper probes into language variation from a different perspective, i.e., we try to combine the approaches of historical linguistics and embodiment theory, by using historical corpora and examining the use and distribution of a highly environment sensitive linguistic genre, ideophones.

Ideophones, by definition, are iconic in nature. They are pervasive in our real-time daily lives; however, they are difficult to trace in historical data. This is the challenge of this paper. Since ideophones are often overlooked in the studies of language variation, this paper aims to explore the possibility and the role that ideophones can play in this steady but dynamic field.

This paper is structured as follows. Section 2 gives some literature review. Section 3 provides detailed account of the methodology and materials used in this study. Section 4 presents our results and discussion on the analysis and findings. Section 5 gives the concluding remarks.

2 Literature review

This section gives reviews of some key literature related to our topic. The focuses are mainly on lexical variation, the introduction to ideophones, and the nature of written data used in language variation.

2.1 Lexical variation

Variationist approaches studying modern linguistic usage tend to focus on sociolinguistic factors (Tagliamonte 2006) and often involve fieldwork. From their fieldwork data, their targets usually would be divided into types such as phonetic variation, morphological variation, or syntactic variation discussing on the accents and dialects. In the abovementioned categories, this paper focuses on the lexical level, in an attempt to explore the functions and distribution of variants of ideophones from a diachronical view. Our targets involve environment related ideophones *mangmang* and its variants: 芒芒 *mangmang$_G$*, 茫茫 *mangmang$_{GW}$*, 蒼茫 *cangmang*, etc., to see their distribution in the history and in the geography. To test the hypothesis of the relation between ideophone and environment, we include one set of ideophones to serve as a control group: 蒼蒼 *cangcang*, 崢嶸 *zhengrong*, and 徘徊 *paihuai*. Section 3.4 will provide more details of these ideophones.

2.2 Ideophone and embodied cognition

The term "embodiment" has many definitions in the literature. According to Krois et al. (2007), in the widest sense, "embodiment" can simply mean the instantiation or materialization of a kind of process, dated from Aristotle. In the 20th century, in an attempt to present an alternative view from intellectualism or idealism, Maurice Merleau-Ponty has approached the world from a phenomenological and embodied perspective, i.e., body as the medium to experiencing the world, arguing that the properties of things that we think to be "real" and "objective" also tacitly assume a reference to the body's norms and its adoption of levels. In Johnson's (1987) work on metaphor, he emphasized on this embodied cognition, maintaining that our body "influences the attainment of knowledge," and "the specific character of knowledge is a function of the knower's particular embodiment" (Krois et al., 2007: xv).

Why do ideophones relate to embodied cognition? In this paper, we discuss embodied cognition mainly at two levels. At one level they relate to the strategy of word formation; at the other level they relate to the environment. At the word formation level, in the system of a particular language, ideophones by definition are highly sound symbolic in nature. The link between the environment and the coding of language is stronger than other types of words, that is, humans intend to imitate the sounds or movement of the environment to form the shape of language. In other words, our perception system receives as well as screens the information from the outer world, and then we use our articulatory muscles to encode the meaning. Behind ideophones lurks the embodied cognition.

In addition, one of the major innovations of Cognitive-Functional linguistics is a renewed interest for iconicity in language (Van Langendonck 2007). Driven by the basic cognitive notion of markedness, iconicity is argued to play a key role in all different levels of language: from the phonic to the syntactic. However, even before this resurgence of this kind of research, two areas in which iconicity has played a continuously important role are those of onomatopoeia and sound symbolism. It is not strange that these two have also received new attention in the last thirty years, as two volumes on the two phenomena show: Hinton, Nichols, and Ohala (1994) is a seminal volume on international research concerning sound symbolism, while Voeltz and Kilian-Hatz (2001) discusses the theme of ideophones in a cross-linguistic context.

Ideophones, defined by Dingemanse (2011; 2012) as "marked words that depict sensory image" seem to be situated at the intersection of different layers of language: "phonology, prosody, morphosyntax, discourse usage and even extra-linguistic factors such as iconic gesture" (Jacques 2013:256). Obviously, the area of lexical semantics is also of prime interest when one researches ideophones.

To clarify the issue of this paper, the following gives more examples of ideophones. Most linguists ought to be familiar with the term 'onomatopoeia', i.e., a set of words that depict the sound of a certain construal. English examples include tick tock (sound of a clock ticking), click clack (sound of a woman's heels), bam! pow! (sound of somebody getting punched as is frequently seen in comics), or woof woof (sound of a dog barking). Using the definition outlined above, we can conceive of these words as 'marked words that depict sound'. They are marked by their iconicity, which often depends on sound symbolism or mechanisms like reduplication.

However, ideophones as a category cover more than the depiction of sound. As English examples like *bling bling*, *criss-cross*, or *hip-hop* show, vision and movement can also be depicted in a similar fashion. Because these kinds of words cross-linguistically constitute a much larger class of words in East Asian languages, there have been many studies on the same phenomena in e.g., Japanese (e.g., Kita 1993; Lu Chiarung 呂佳蓉 2006; Akita 2009; 2012; 2013) and Korean (e.g., Shin 2012). Notable Japanese examples include e.g., *korokoro* 'small object rolling' vs. *gorogoro* 'big object rolling', *pikapika* 'bright', *fuwafuwa* 'fluffy' etc. That their iconicity boosts novel word learning has been successfully shown in cross-linguistic experiments (Lockwood, Dingemanse, and Hagoort 2016).

Since the target of this paper is Chinese ideophones, more introduction is given below. The field of Chinese linguistics has long paid attention to similar phenomena, focusing mostly on onomatopoeia, for which a good survey can be found in Zhao Aiwu 赵爱武 (2008). He notes the influence Japanese research has had on its Chinese counterparts, especially in terms of terminology (1)–(4). While earlier Chinese studies focused mostly on onomatopoeia (1) (e.g., Lu Ping 卢平 2001; Zhao Aiwu 赵爱武 2005; Li Jing'er 李镜儿 2007; Liu Guodong 柳国栋 2008; Man Fang 滿芳 2009; Wang Xiuli 王秀丽 2010; Lu Yan 陆燕 2011), there has been an increase in Western studies on the Chinese phenomena that adopt the terminology in (2–4) (e.g., Mok 2001; Bodomo 2006; De Sousa 2008; De Sousa 2011; Lu Chiarung 呂佳蓉 2006; Lu Chiarung 呂佳蓉 2011; Meng 2012; Wu 2014; Van Hoey 2015).

(1)　　*xiang-sheng-ci*　　象-聲-詞　'resemble-sound-word; onomatopoeia'

(2)　　*ni-sheng-ci*　　　擬-聲-詞　'mimic-sound-word; phonomime'[1]< Jap. *giongo* 擬音語

---

[1] Corresponding to Akita's (2009) terminology phonomimes come closest to what is traditionally understood as onomatopoeia in the West; phenomimes depict states, and psychomimes express feelings.

(3) ni-tai-ci   擬-態-詞 'mimic-state-word; phenomime' < Jap. *gitaigo* 擬態語

(4) ni-qing-ci   擬-情-詞 'mimic-feeling-word; psychomime' < Jap. *gijōgo* 擬情語

In (5)–(7) we list some examples of Mandarin Chinese ideophones to show that they also adhere to the definition proposed by Dingemanse (2011; 2012) that was given above: '*marked words* that *depict sensory imagery*' [emphasis mine]. This definition can be dissected into a formal requirement ('marked words') and a semantic requirement ('depiction of sensory images'). The formal markedness of Chinese ideophonic words is mainly derived from (partial) reduplication and sound symbolism, cf. examples (5)–(7) with translations by Kroll (2015):

(5)   *meng~meng*[2] 濛~濛 'steaming mistily, drizzly-mizzly'

(6)   *pai~huai*   徘~徊 'go round and about, back and forth; loiter and linger'

(7)   *ling~long*   玲~瓏 'goffered, honeycombed, tintling tinkle of gems'

However, not all forms that show reduplication (in traditional terms *die-zi* 疊-字 'reduplicated-characters', *die-yun* 疊-韻 'reduplicated-rhyme' and *shuang-sheng* 雙-聲 'double-sounds [alliteration]') can be understood as ideophones – the latter, semantic requirement of Dingemanse's definition prohibits forms with a purely referential[3] (usually distributive) function to be subsumed in the same category, e.g., *ri~ri* 日~日 'every day', *ye~ye* 夜~夜 'every night'.

The perception of most in-depth studies on ideophones in different languages seems to be semasiological (Geeraerts 2010:23) in nature. This tendency to focus on the different meanings of a given form follows from the descriptive nature of most of these studies. However, we argue in this paper that the converse, onomasiological picture – studying different forms that map onto a similar meaning – can adopt a more variationist[4] approach to the study of ideophones in Chinese and will yield very interesting implications for the fields of lexical semantics and ideophones, which will provide a model for future studies.

---

2 In the examples, full and partial reduplication will be marked with a tilde between morphemes, as stipulated in the Leipzig Glossing Rules (Bickel, Comrie & Haspelmath 2008). However, in the six ideophones studied below this tilde will generally be left out.
3 In the sense of Croft's (2001) discussion on prototypical parts-of-speech.
4 'Variation' being the theme of the 2016 edition of the Conference on Language, Discourse and Cognition (CLDC 8) held at National Taiwan University, Taipei.

How can we study ideophones in the onomasiological vein? A good way to handle this is to use diachronic data (cf. sections 2.3 and 3), since "the variationist enterprise is essentially, and foremost, the study of the interplay between variation, social meaning and the evolution and development of the linguistic system itself" (Tagliamonte 2006). The results of our study will be discussed in section 4, which will be followed by a discussion and conclusion.

2.3 Written documents as sources

As Schneider (2002) has pointed out, the study of language variation and change usually relies on performance data and thus mainly uses spoken records such as sociolinguistic interviews, tape recordings, acoustic analysis, etc. However, due to the absence of native speakers, historical linguistic studies have to adopt an empiricist approach that relies on corpus research. Usually some types of written documents are taken to be appropriate for this kind of research. For instance, they are texts close to speech, texts of different origins, texts that display variability of the phenomenon under investigation, and texts that fulfill certain size requirements (Schneider 2002).

As to the application of corpus linguistics, an important methodological distinction that is made separates a corpus-driven approach (section 3.2) from a corpus-based approach (section 3.3). According to Biber (2015:196), corpus-driven research takes the corpus as the basis with as little theory as possible. It is more inductive and allows for the emergence of linguistic phenomenon of interest. It is used with an attempt to search for any possible candidates. Corpus-based research, on the other hand, uses the corpus to investigate a certain phenomenon, and allows for the interplay between different genres and language usage. We will come back to these issues in sections 3.2 and 3.3.

3 Methodology and materials

The general question that drives this study is how to study the historical onomasiological development of ideophones from a variationist perspective. In section 3.1 we will first briefly address the candidacy of ideophones for this study.

In section 3.2 we will map out data that can be derived from the corpus-based analysis in section 3.3 in order to visualize the historical development of the ideophones that are studied in this paper.

3.1 Ideophone as a fossilized yet productive entity

Ideophones, as introduced above, very often have a fixed construction cross-linguistically, i.e., the reduplicated form. In Chinese, the typical formal structure of an ideophone is the so-called A~A form, i.e., two reduplicated Chinese characters, although partial reduplications do occur as well. The roots of these constructions can be traced back to at least 11th century BCE, as can be seen in the famous Chinese classic *Shijing* 詩經 (*Book of Songs/Odes*), dating back to the 11th–8th centuries BCE . Those ideophones found in the *Shijing* are quite stable and most of them are still being used nowadays in mostly literary language, although their radicals might slightly change (Mok 2001). This gives us a hint to probe into the issue of variation by investigating ideophones. In this study we use the historical corpus of the *Three Hundred Tang Poems* 唐詩三百首 instead of the *Shijing* simply because the number of ideophones found in the *Three Hundred Tang Poems* is relatively greater than that in the *Shijing*. This provides a more sufficient point-of-departure to account for these issues, as well as a snapshot of their use in Middle Chinese.

3.2 Corpus-driven approach

The first step in this paper is the selection of ideophones for investigation, for which we use a corpus-driven approach. As briefly discussed above, corpus-driven approaches allow for the emergent study of linguistic phenomena, limiting a priori assumptions about the phenomena under investigation to a minimum. In the introduction we pointed out that Chinese investigations mainly focus on pure onomatopoeia, while the broader category of ideophones is only more recently being studied in predominantly Western studies. A corpus-driven approach of Middle Chinese ideophones therefore seemed a good starting point for the identification of ideophones and their historical development.

In the context of this study, this part was performed on a smaller sample of material, namely the *Three Hundred Tang Poems* 唐詩三百首, as was shown in Van Hoey (2015). This collection of poems dates back to the Tang dynasty (618–907), but the collection itself has been assembled around 1763 by Qing-dynasty scholar Sun Zhu[5] (1711–1778).

---

5 Sun Zhu's 孫洙 (1711–1778) courtesy name was Lin Xi 臨西 and he was often referred to as Hengtang tuishi 蘅塘退士 'Retired Master of Hengtang'. He compiled the collection out of dissatisfaction with the anthology *Qianjiashi* 千家詩 'Poems by a thousand masters' which was

The huge gap between the compilation and the period in which the poems were written raises questions about the representability of the corpus for Middle Chinese. However, there are no other similar corpora that can be traced back with absolute certainty.[6] Furthermore, this collection of about 300 poems holds somewhat canonical status in literary education, giving this small collection of poems a prototypical quality.

In Van Hoey (2015) it was shown that there are about 200 ideophones in the corpus of some 300 poems, which was argued to be a very high frequency. Using an adapted version of Dingemanse's (2012) cross-linguistic semantic implicational hierarchy for ideophones, the ideophones were divided over the categories: sound; movement; vision; texture and temperature; time; cognitive states, evaluation and inner feelings. This showed that Chinese ideophones cover a territory well beyond onomatopoeia which traditionally is being studied in Chinese research (cf. supra). The result corresponds with the Japanese onomatopoeia (Lu 2006). Even with the polysemy and synaesthesia that was evident in the corpus, the semantic category of vision markedly had the highest frequency. This was argued to be a genre effect of the poetry and the compilation, viz. what counts as a good poem is one that can transport the reader in the scenery it describes.

The result of the corpus-driven approach, i.e., the selection of the ideophones to be investigated and the control set, are discussed in section 3.4.

3.3 Corpus-based approach

The methodological aspects of the corpus-driven approach (section 3.2) and the operationalization of the research question (section 3.4) will be explored in a larger historical corpus, viz. we use a corpus-based approach after the corpus-driven cycle. To do so, we use a combination of a historical database and two modern ones for contrast.

The historical database we used is the Scripta Sinica database 漢籍全文資料庫計畫. It is an ongoing project that started in 1984 and aims to digitize all documents essential to research in traditional sinology as well as to establish a full-text database for academic research. Until present, it is the largest Chinese full-text database that encompasses historical materials (Academia Sinica 2015).

---

compiled by Liu Kezhuang 劉克莊 during the Southern Song (1127–1276) and was influenced by Ming dynasty (1368–1644) as well (Three Hundred Tang Poems 2016).

6 For instance, even bigger similar collections of texts (such as the *Quan Tang shi* 全唐詩 'Complete Tang Poems') can only be traced back to the 11th century (Mair 2001:278–281).

It contains more than 949 titles with a total of 655,456,171 characters at the time of writing. The database mainly follows the traditional classification method of the four categories (*si bu* 四部): the (Confucian) classics (*jing* 經); historiography (*shi* 史); masters and philosophers (*zi* 子); and anthologies (*ji* 集).

The first modern database is the Leiden Weibo Corpus, developed in 2012. It contains 5,103,566 messages posted on Sina Weibo in the period of 8 to 30 January 2012 (van Esch 2012).

The second modern database is a set of corpora that are searchable, called COPENS (LOPE lab 2015). It is a collection of corpora in different domains, such as news, social media, politics, and contains also media targeted towards children and spoken corpora. Both of these databases – the Leiden Weibo Corpus and the COPENS database – show a balanced view of contemporary language use in both Mainland China and Taiwan.

3.4 *Mangmang*, its variants, and the control set

One of our hypotheses is that an ideophone is a form of embodied cognition interacting with the environment. To test this hypothesis, we examine two sets of ideophones, aiming to explore their diachronical distributions and onomasiological performance. The experimental set strongly relates to the surroundings with some environmental features encoded within the words. To be specific, in this paper these candidates are *mangmang* 芒芒, *mangmang* 茫茫 and *cangmang* 蒼茫, all with a prominent feature of water imagery, as shown in the following paragraph. On the contrary, the control set consists of three ideophones that have no connections with water.

How were these candidates chosen? Since quantification is an important methodology of variationism, frequency is the most crucial index. Based on their high frequencies in the *Three Hundred Tang Poems*, *mangmang* 芒芒, *mangmang* 茫茫 and *cangmang* 蒼茫 are chosen for investigation. These three candidates have similar meanings for the onomasiological and variationist approach. In (8)-(10) we show the three ideophones we selected with their pronunciation in *Hanyu pinyin*, a Middle Chinese (MC) reconstruction and an Old Chinese (OC) reconstruction. The latter two are based on Baxter & Sagart's (2014) reconstruction method[7]

---

[7] Other reconstructions, such as Li Fang-Kuei's 李方桂 show similar results: mang 芒 < MC m-âng < OC m-ang; mang 茫 < MC m-âng < OC m-ang; cang 蒼 < MC tsh-âng < OC tsh-ang (National Taiwan University Chinese Department 國立臺灣大學中國文學系 & Academia Sinica 中央研究院 2011).

of Middle and Old Chinese. The reader who is familiar with Chinese notices that the radicals used in *mang* (8) is grass (⁺⁺); the ones used in *mang* (9) are grass (⁺⁺) and water (氵). We will refer to these ideophones as *mangmang*~G~ and *mangmang*~GW~ respectively.

(8) 芒芒 máng~máng~G~ < MC mang~mang < OC mˤaŋ~mˤaŋ
   1. 'pointy leaf > 'mango' [in Modern Chinese]
   2. 'extensive, vast, wide, spacious; indistinct, blurred, obscure'

(9) 茫茫 máng~máng~GW~ < MC mang~mang < OC mˤaŋ~mˤaŋ;
   'vast, expansive; boundless, undertermined; illimitable; to the limits of vision, lost to sight; vague and vast, stretching farther than eye can see, lost in the distance, measureless and indeterminate, afar and aloof'

(10) 蒼茫 cāng~máng < MC tshang~mang < OC tsʰˤaŋ~mˤaŋ;
   'distantly indistinct, faint and far-off, blurred and boundless, dimmed by distance'

All three ideophones, defying the 'one-syllable one-character' tendency of Pre-Modern Chinese (Baxter and Sagart 1998; Sun 1999), are made up of characters that share a long history: *mang*~G~ 芒 and *cang* 蒼 both occur in bronze script (Shang and Zhou dynasties), while *mang*~GW~ 茫 first occurs as seal script. As can be seen in some typical examples below (11–13), all three of them roughly mean 'vast', 'without beginning or end', and 'wide'.

(11) 浸潤　下　民，　芒芒　　　南　　土。
   jin~run　xia　min　mang~mang~G~　nan　tu
   soak　down　people　wide　　　south　earth
   '[The rain] falls down heavily on the people; wide is the southern earth.'
   (Ji Yong, *Jiuyishan mingbei* 九嶷山銘碑)

(12) 茫茫　　　江　漢　上，　日　暮　復　何　之？
   mang~mang~GW~　Jiang Han　shang　ri　mu　fu　he　zhi
   wide　　　Jiang Han　on　sun　set　again　what　go.to
   'Now, on such vastness of waters near Jiang-Han there; I wonder, with the sun setting, he will drift where!'
   (Liu Changqing, *Song Li Zhongcheng gui Hanyang bie ye* 送李中丞歸漢陽別業)

(13) 明　　月　　出　　　天山，　　　蒼茫　　　雲　　海　間。
　　　ming　yue　chu　　Tian.shan　　cang~mang　yun　hai　jian
　　　bright moon come.out Tian mountain wide　　cloud sea between
　　　'From the Mountain Tian rises the moon bright; in a vast sea of clouds it shines its light.'
　　　(Li Bai, *Guanshan yue* 關山月)

The selection of these three candidates, which have a very similar meaning, occur in similar contexts⁸ and share a similar internal make-up, will prove to be good candidates of our hypothesis. The only difference seems to be that *mangmang*$_G$ can be used to depict the vastness of both land and water, while *mangmang*$_{GW}$ and *cangmang* are originally used mainly for water.

To increase the robustness of the conclusions drawn thus far, we should perform a similar analysis for some control ideophones, viz. we use three other ideophones to contrast with the previous set to detect possible faults in our reasoning that the geographical background of authors did play a role in their possibility of using a certain ideophone.

The control set we have selected on the same corpus-driven basis as before, emergent from the *300 Tang Poems* 唐詩三百首 (Van Hoey 2015), is combined with the corpus-based study that uses the Scripta Sinica database. The three selected ideophones⁹ can be seen in examples (14)–(16).

(14)　蒼~蒼　cāng~cāng < MC tshang~tshang < OC *tsʰˤaŋ~tsʰˤaŋ
　　　　　'bluish-green: elegant variation for the blue of the sky, cerulean; silvery-grey: shadowy and faint, soft and silver, as of moonlight'

(15)　崢~嶸　zhēng~róng < MC dzreang~hjwaeng < OC *dzˤreŋ~ɢʷˤreŋ
　　　　　'precipitous masses of rock; loftily lifted; sheer steepness; high-piled; rocky heights'

---

8 An anonymous reviewer wondered whether the three ideophones were really in competition with each other. When this study was first presented at a conference, we had only looked at the referents of the ideophones in question, which seemed congruent enough, especially between *mangmang*$_G$ and *mangmang*$_{GW}$. A corpus-based investigation revealed that *mangmang*$_{GW}$ slowly overtook the function of *mangmang*$_G$, except for a set of fossilized linguistic environments.

9 An anonymous reviewer correctly remarked that it may be better to use three synonyms for the control set. While we agree with this comment in principle, we wanted to follow the same rationale as for the previously investigated trio of ideophones. Furthermore, a comparable set of near-synonyms that is semantically fit for such an investigation, i.e., depicting moving or stative visual senses, was unfortunately not identified in the corpus-driven stage.

(16) 徘~徊 pái~huái < MC bwoj~hwoj < OC *bˤrəj~ɢʷˤəj
'go round and about, back and forth; shilly-shally, aimlessly irresolute, restless but hesitant, loiter and linger, dawdle and delay'

We chose *cangcang* 蒼蒼 (14) to test the idea that *cangmang*$_{GW}$ 蒼茫 is a rhyming ideophonic construction consisting of the *cang* 蒼 in *cangcang* and the morpheme *mang*$_{GW}$ 茫 in *mangmang*$_{GW}$ 蒼茫. If this is the case, as suggested at the end of section 4.1, then this hints at a possible reanalysis, viz. the two source ideophones *cangcang* and *mangmang*$_{GW}$, whose written forms each consist of two reduplicated characters, may have blended together. This blending seems conditional: they are still formally marked by rhyme between the two syllables. A comparison between the geographical developments of *mangmang*$_{GW}$, *cangmang* and *cangcang* (Figures 3–5) shows how the former and the latter are very similar. A combination of *mangmang*$_{GW}$ and *cangcang* to form *cangmang* is therefore not unruly, and may be further supported by the lower frequency and geographical spread of *cangmang* in relation to these two other ideophones.

Zhengrong 崢嶸 (15) was chosen because we wanted to investigate another rhyming ideophone, rather than a fully reduplicated one. Besides this formal criterion, its mountain radical (山) was assumed to possibly display different results when compared to the water radical (氵) in the previous selected set of ideophones. After all, we argued that one of the factors that may explain the development of the variation studied above, is the increased saliency of the water radical for *mangmang*$_{GW}$ 茫茫, up until the point that this written variant is so ubiquitous that this written form is so entrenched and well-accepted that it plays no longer a role. Since water (氵) is a semantic antonym of mountain (山) in Chinese, it was hypothesized that the geographical spread of this ideophone may situate itself more in mountainous regions.

Paihuai 徘徊 (16), another rhyming ideophone, was included in the study because it belongs to another semantic category in the conceptual hierarchy (cf. section 2.2), i.e., movement instead of stative vision. The stepping radical (彳) suggests that, under assumption of a stronger saliency influence of radicals, it occurs more frequently in places that are more easily passable, viz. land inward, but not necessarily in mountainous regions. As Figure 7 shows, it covers the most diffuse area of all six ideophones studied here – virtually the whole Eastern Chinese plain is covered. One explanation for this may be the entrenchment of *paihuai* in vocabulary and its loss of markedness.[10]

---

10 At least in Modern Chinese, informal discussions with native speakers suggest that *paihuai* 徘徊 is (no longer) recognized as marked vocabulary (Dingemanse & Akita 2016); indeed, it

3.5 Geographic visualization

The data that is gathered from the historical corpus can be linked to the (assumed) author, which the Scripta Sinica database provides in most cases. We have to bear in mind that this kind of historical data is data by male adult speakers who belong to the literati class. It is written data, and can be loosely categorized according to the four categories (classics, historiography, masters and anthologies, cf. supra). The most important variable is that the literati data has to do with government. But where did literati first learn to write? Rawski (1979), Lee (1985) and Li and Branner (2011) all seem to agree that basic literacy – before literati took any state exam (*keju* 科舉) – was taught at home or in local schools. This is a very important step in our reasoning of this study.

Since we know from some psychological experiments that ideophones are acquired easier and earlier than other words (Imai and Kita 2014; Dingemanse et al. 2015; Lockwood, Dingemanse, and Hagoort 2016), it can be hypothesized that the background of authors influenced the authors in some way or another. Luckily, there is ample biographical data that usually mentions the place a person is from. For instance, the writer Ouyang Xun 歐陽詢 (557–641) is said to come from Linxiang district, Tanzhou 潭州臨湘縣人, which currently is called Changsha City, Hunan Province [in China] 今湖南省長沙市. In our study we thus link all ideophones that the database links to Ouyang Xun in a second step to the coordinates of Changsha City: 28° 11' 46" N, 112° 58' 20" E. Gathering enough data of this kind allows us to visualize this on a map. For this we use the open source geographical software QGIS 'Q Geographical Information System', version 2.14 Essen (QGIS Development Team 2016). The results of this workflow are shown in the next section.

4 Results and discussion

As was discussed in section 3.4, as a case study, we found three corpus-driven ideophones that fit the criterion of being comparable: *mangmang*$_G$ 芒芒, *mangmang*$_{GW}$ 茫茫, and *cangmang* 蒼茫. Below we will first discuss their frequency over time (section 4.1) which will be followed by the geographical analysis (section 4.2) as outlined above.

---

occurs mostly as a predicated in the nucleus of the clause (cf. Akita 2009). Following Van Hoey's (2017) presentation, *paihuai* might belong to a more literary stratum of ideophones, different from a colloquial stratum. This issue needs further investigation, although it could explain the greater frequencies of *mangmang*$_{GW}$ 茫茫 and *paihuai* 徘徊 in modern times.

4.1 Frequency over time

In Table 1 we show the frequency over time of the three ideophones based on data from the Scripta Sinica database. The numbers are grouped according to the categories in the database, but are roughly three-hundred-year periods.[11]

Table 1: Token frequency over time of the selected ideophones

	Pre-Qin 先秦	QinHan 秦漢	Three Kingdoms 魏晉	Sui Tang 隋唐	Song 宋	Yuan 元	Ming 明	Qing 清	Republic Modern 民國
芒芒 mangmang$_G$	15	47	84	29	51	6	74	86	11
茫茫 mangmang$_{GW}$	3	34	113	349	608	329	636	1211	3909
蒼茫 cangmang$_{GW}$	3	N/A	20	79	236	126	86	455	80
蒼芒 cangmang$_G$	1	N/A	3	2	4	N/A	1	1	0

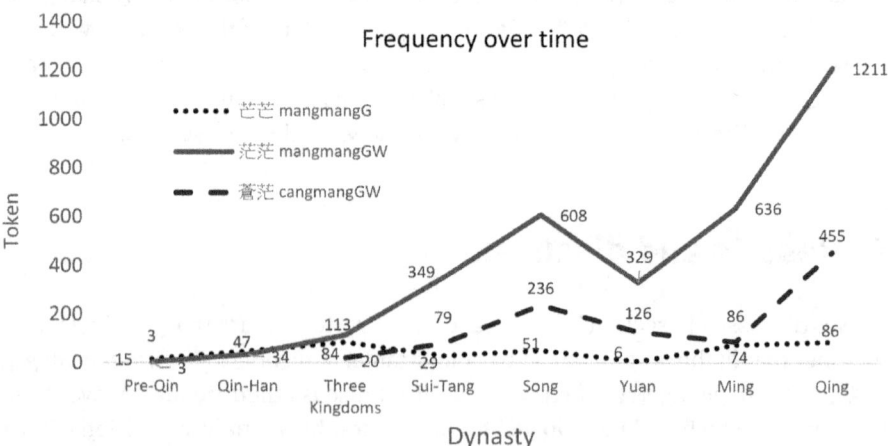

Figure 1: Frequency of *mangmang* over time (Scripta Sinica).

---

11 Pre-Qin (±1000 BC–221 BC); Qin-Han (221 BC–220 AD); Three Kingdoms (220–581); Sui-Tang (581–907); Song (907–1279); Yuan (1279–1368); Ming (1368–1644); Qing (1644–1911); Republic Modern (1911–present).

As can be seen in Table 1 and Figure 1, up until the period referred to as 'Three Kingdoms', which comprises the Three Kingdoms (220–280), Jin dynasty (265–420) and Northern and Southern dynasties (420–589), the frequency of *mangmang$_G$* 芒芒 and *mangmang$_{GW}$* 茫茫 is very similar.[12] Up until this period *mangmang$_G$* has a very broad applicability, depicting the broadness of concrete referents, such as areas, plains and surroundings, as well as metaphorical usage. *Mangmang$_{GW}$* refers more to bodies of water, but can also depict the wideness of areas. Below (17)–(18) are some examples taken from the ancient scripts.

(17) *mangmang$_G$*
       '**vast** were the traces of [the legendary] Yu, it became the nine provinces' (*mangmang$_G$ Yu ji, hua wei jiu zhou* 芒芒禹跡，畫為九州。)
       '**vast** and vague; he sees it's without edges' (*mangmang$_G$ huanghu; shi zhi wu duan* 芒芒恍惚。視之無端。)
       'He was hunting in the **vastness** of the green woods' (*lie qing lin zhi mangmang$_G$* 獵青林之芒芒。)

(18) *mangmang$_{GW}$*
       '**vast** were the traces of [the legendary] Yu' (*mangmang$_{GW}$ Yu ji* 茫茫禹迹。)
       'the southern nests are **vast**' (*nan chao mangmang$_{GW}$* 南巢茫茫。)
       '**vast** were the nine provinces' (*mangmang$_{GW}$ jiu zhou* 茫茫九州。)

From the Sui dynasty (589–618) onwards, *mangmang$_G$* decreases in usage. *Mangmang$_{GW}$*, however, spectacularly increases in frequency. It seems that *mangmang$_G$*'s functions are not very productive anymore in this period. Furthermore, a third ideophone that depicts wideness, *cangmang*,[13] is used more after the period of the Three Kingdoms, Jin dynasty and Northern and Southern dynasties. Its function at this point is mostly poetic in nature, occurring in the anthology category (*ji* 集) of traditional Chinese classification in the historical corpus rather than in other categories like historiography. Some typical examples are shown in (19)–(21).

---

12 We have not made a distinction between referential, modifying and predicative functions of these ideophones in the study, as one anonymous reviewer kindly suggested. Under the idea of 'conceptual reification' (Langacker 1987; 2008) the effects of such differentiation could foster future research.

13 *Cangmang* is almost invariably written with the grass-and-water radical (艹氵) *mang$_{GW}$* 茫. However, there exist some curious anomalies, where it is written with only a grass radical (艹) *mang$_G$*. It is provided in table 1 to display how it is virtually a hapax legomenon. For this reason, we only write *cangmang* in this paper, without explicitly referring to its radicals.

(19) mangmang$_G$
'**vast** were the traces of [the legendary] Yu, it became the nine provinces' (*mangmang$_G$ Yu ji, hua wei jiu zhou* 芒芒禹跡，畫為九州。)
'he was hunting in the **vastness** of the green woods' (*lie qing lin zhi mangmang$_G$* 獵青林之芒芒。)

(20) mangmang$_{GW}$
'the **vast** desert' (*mangmang$_{GW}$ shamo* 茫茫沙漠)
'**vast** are the four seas' (*mangmang$_{GW}$ si hai* 茫茫四海)

(21) cangmang
'the sea of clouds approaches, it's **vast**' (*yunhai jin, cangmang* 雲海近蒼茫)
'**vast** and boundless are the intentions' (*cangmang wuxian yi* 蒼茫無限意)

By the Qing dynasty, *cangmang* is used in other genre classes as well, similar to *mangmang$_G$* and *mangmang$_{GW}$*. *Cangmang* is used mainly with reference to bodies of water, focusing on their wideness as well as their greyish colour. *Mangmang$_G$* by this point is not productive anymore, occurring only in set phrases and quotes from earlier works. *Mangmang$_{GW}$*, however, is productive and has taken over most functions from the other *mangmang$_G$*, including the metaphorical extensions,[14] see (22)–(24).

(22) mangmang$_G$
'If the liver is hurt, then it causes **blurred** vision' (*gan shang ze ling mu shi mangmang$_G$* 肝傷則令目視芒芒)
'**vast** southern soil' (*mangmang$_G$ nan tu* 芒芒南土)

(23) mangmang$_{GW}$
'the **vast** universe' (*mangmang$_{GW}$ yuzhou* 茫茫宇宙)
'**vast** is the eastern sea' (*mangmang$_{GW}$ dong hai* 茫茫東海)

(24) cangmang
'the rivers and seas are **vast**' (*jiang hai cangmang* 江海蒼茫)
'the rain is **vast** as well' (*yu yi cangmang* 雨亦蒼茫)

---

14 In Modern Chinese, only *mangmang$_{GW}$* is in usage, and only occurs in metaphorical expressions. This is probably the continuation of the evolution sketched in this paper. Some examples of metaphorical usage include: *mang~mang ren-hai* 茫~茫 人-海 'vast.ideophone people-sea; boundless huge crowd'; *qian-tu mang~mang* 前-途 茫~茫 'front-way vast.ideophone; unknown future'.

From these examples (17)–(24) it can be seen that in a first stage *mangmang*$_G$ and *mangmang*$_{GW}$ were in slight variational competition. In the next stage the usage of *mangmang*$_G$ started to fossilize, probably due to the widening scope of *mangmang*$_{GW}$ and the increasing usage of *cangmang*. In the third stage it is *cangmang* and *mangmang*$_{GW}$ that are in competition rather than *mangmang*$_G$. As outlined above (section 3.4), one possible reason for this evolution may be due to the environment that the literati were brought up in. This geographical analysis is discussed in the next section.

4.2 Geographical analysis

As announced in section 3.5, presenting a geographical distribution of the target word is important for the variationist approach. Filtering the data by period enables us to track the diffusion throughout time, and project the data in Figure 1 and Table 1 on a map. For clarity, we have marked the diachronic expansion with full stripe-arrows. The different geographical profiles can be seen in Figures 2–4.

During the process of establishing these geographical profiles some ideophone data was inevitably unavailable,[15] mostly in the case where no biographical data was available or any mention of the author's background or birthplace was lacking.

As can be seen in Figures 2–4, all three profiles seem to follow the main migration streams of Han culture throughout time: first Eastward, then Southward. The linguistic consequences of migration waves in China were previously discussed in LaPolla (2006). This is of course a very logical consequence of using Han Chinese cultural data (the Scripta Sinica database) while establishing these geographical profiles. However, it is also evident that the profiles differ considerably.

Both *mangmang*$_G$ 芒芒 (Figure 2) and *mangmang*$_{GW}$ 茫茫 (Figure 3) appear first in the cradle of Chinese civilization at the Yellow River. The former is the oldest and presumably initially most prototypical, as *mang*$_G$ appears in an earlier script form, i.e., bronze script (*jinwen* 金文), compared to *mang*$_{GW}$, which first occurred in seal script (*zhuanshu* 篆書). Both, however, fit findings in sound-symbolic research: the two nasals /m/ and /ŋ/ combined with the low, open vowel /a/ in this reduplication construction all indicate largeness rather than smallness, as outlined in the theory of the Frequency Code (Hinton, Nichols, and Ohala

---

[15] For some authors, geographical references have been lost in time. This analysis rests on about 2000 useful references, of which many refer to the same place.

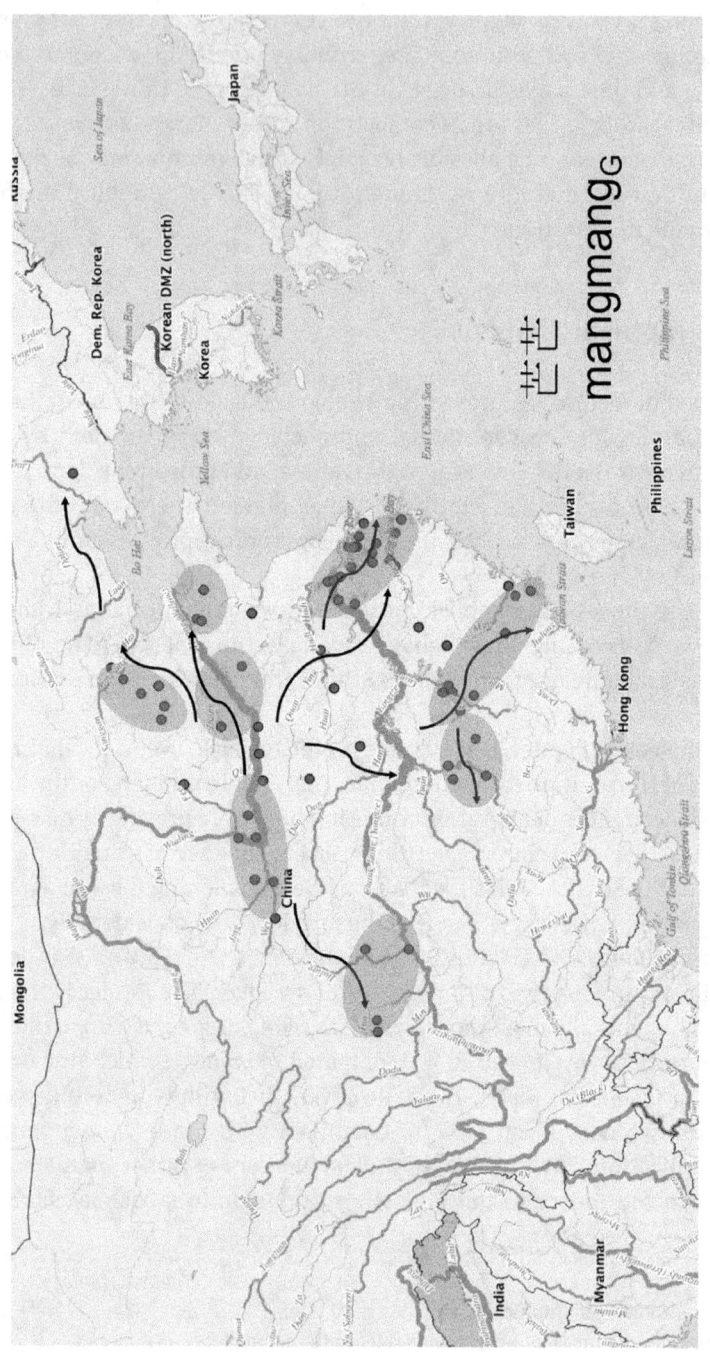

Figure 2: Geographical profile of *mangmang*$_G$.

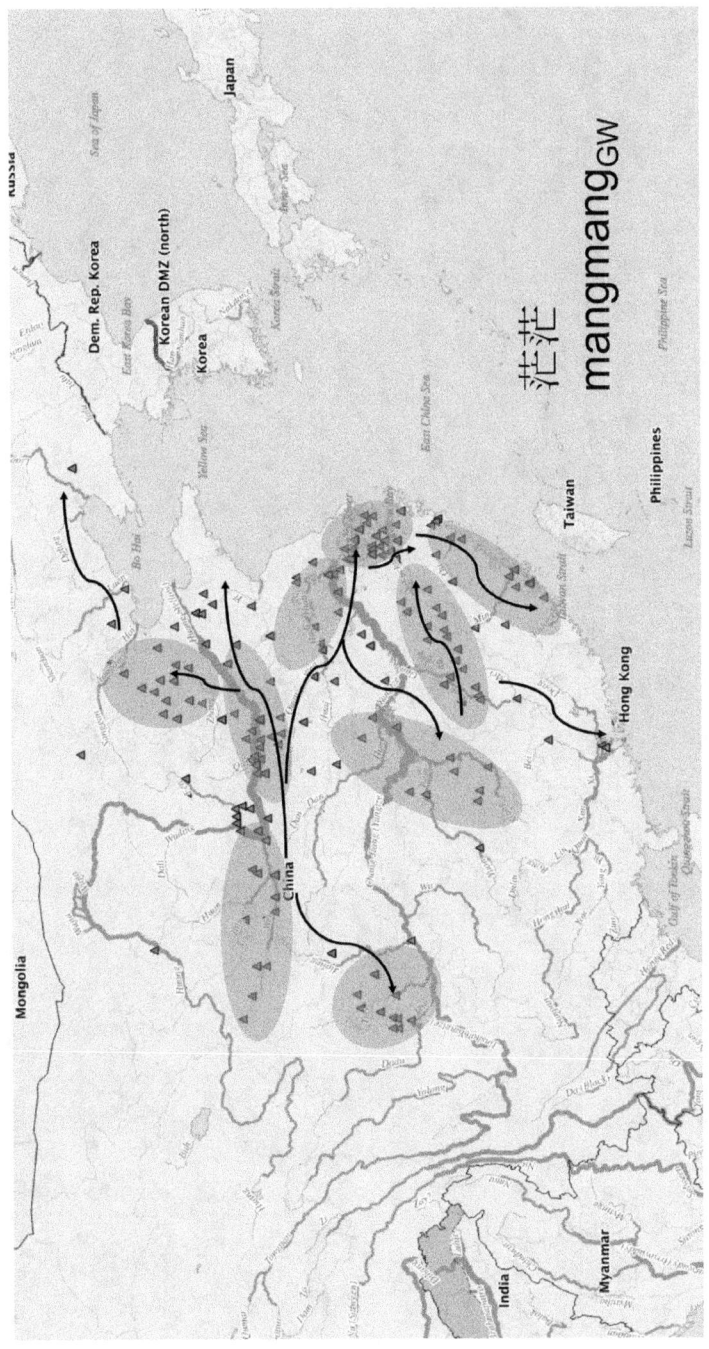

Figure 3: Geographical profile of *mangmang*$_{GW}$.

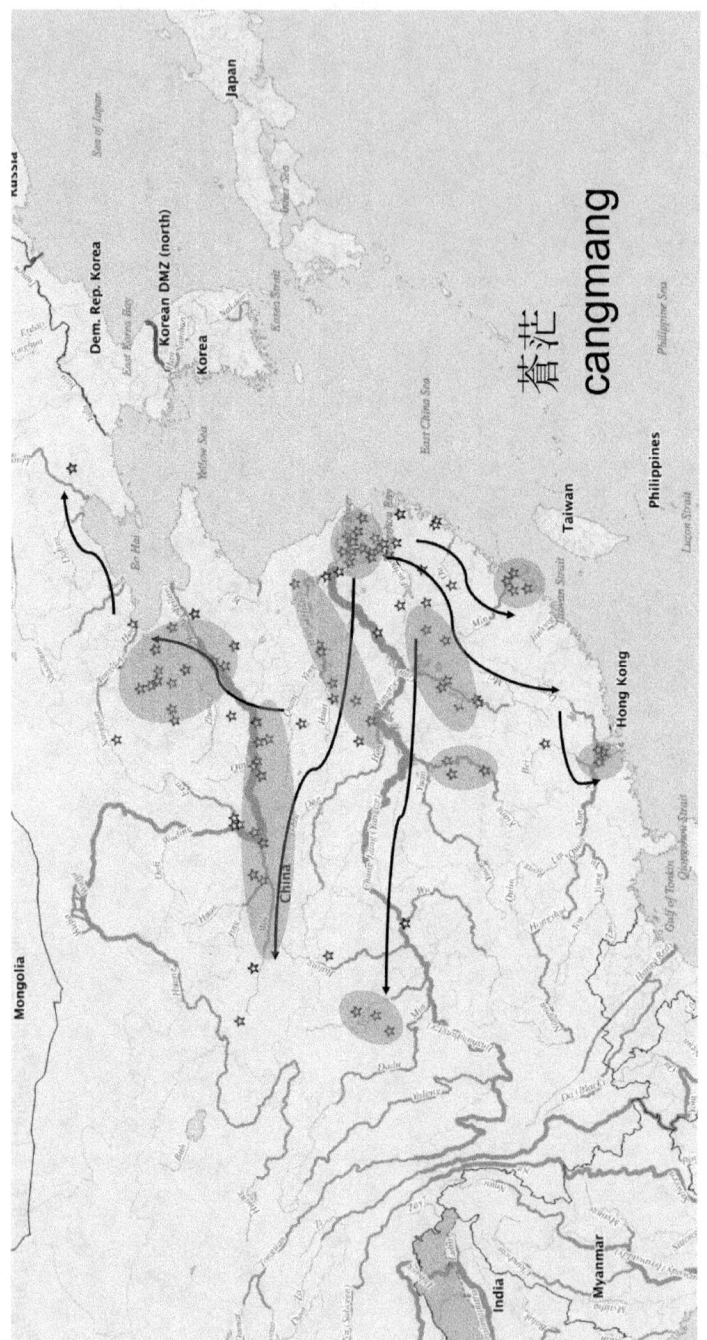

Figure 4: Geographical profile of *cangmang*.

1994:10). For this reason, it is not unlikely that both (as well as *cangmang*) depict 'vastness' as a prototypical sense.

Even though the basic migration patterns influence all of the geographical visualizations presented in this paper, there are some clear diffusional differences noticeable. For *mangmang$_G$* there is a basic alignment along the two biggest rivers of China: the Yellow River and the Yang-tze, as well as some other smaller major rivers like the Gan River. *Mangmang$_{GW}$*, additionally, has a more diffuse, encompassing pattern. We hypothesize this is first due to migration waves to the Southeast (Fujian) in the 1st–2nd centuries AD and later again in the 3rd–4th centuries. Later, increased traffic between North and South after the establishment of the North-South canal, which was well in use during the Middle Empire (Twitchett 1979; Vande Walle 2007), could be responsible for this. This increased usage of waterways may have found its way in the expression of water-related depicted vastness. The saliency of the water radical (氵) may have thus found its way in this variational competition between *mangmang$_G$* and *mangmang$_{GW}$*, as perceived by ancient Chinese literati.

Cangmang 蒼茫 (Figure 4) is the youngest of these three ideophones. Based on available data (cf. note 12), it seemed to have evolved near the mouth of the Yang-tze. The next stage shows a spread to the Yellow River as well as one toward the South. This indicates that it was either picked up fairly easily land inwards (contrary to *mangmang$_{GW}$* and *mangmang$_G$*), or was in usage before traceable records. In any case, its link to bodies of water is clear. Furthermore, something very interesting is going on with the internal composition of this ideophone. The *cang* part itself seems to stem from another ideophone *cangcang* 蒼蒼 'bluish, greyish'. When this morpheme *cang* is combined with the 'vastness + water' of *mang$_{GW}$*, one gets a rhyming ideophone to describe vast bodies of greyish, bluish water. This may also be the very reason that this ideophone was traced back to the east coast of China and presumably made its way land inwards, via waterways.[16]

4.3 Geographical profiles of the control set

In the previous section, we showed the three different geographical profiles that we could establish by using a combination of corpus-based data and geographical

---

16 As mentioned before, the occurrence of *cangmang$_G$* 蒼芒 is considered anomalous in the grand historical corpus of Chinese, making the salience of the water radical (氵) an acceptable factor in the variation between the three target words of this study.

software. We saw that the profiles followed the general tendencies of Han migration, but at the same time displayed unique properties in terms of variation and diffusion. In this section, the control set of ideophones, i.e., *cangcang* 蒼蒼, *zhengrong* 崢嶸, and *paihuai* 徘徊, is presented.

Table 2 shows how the raw frequency of these newly selected ideophones compared to the three original objects of this study. It can be seen that the number of *paihuai* grows dramatically from Three Kingdoms dynasty way down to the Republic era, compared to the other five ideophones. Since *paihuai* is a verb, it is highly possible that it is not restricted to depicting concrete scenery but also describes human movements which occur in more contexts.

Table 2: Token frequency over time of the selected ideophones and the control set

	Pre-Qin 先秦	QinHan 秦漢	Three Kingdoms 魏晉	Sui Tang 隋唐	Song 宋	Yuan 元	Ming 明	Qing 清	Republic Modern 民國
芒芒 mangmang$_G$	15	47	84	29	51	6	74	86	11
茫茫 mangmang$_{GW}$	3	34	113	349	608	329	636	1211	3909
蒼茫 cangmang$_{GW}$	3	N/A	20	79	236	126	86	455	80
蒼蒼 cangcang	19	31	69	267	665	233	386	718	144
崢嶸 zhengrong	N/A	19	70	219	476	151	240	422	41
徘徊 paihuai	11	61	404	664	1417	306	1645	1688	3495

Figure 5 shows the result of *cangcang*. The diachronical path of *cangcang* is not directly related to water.

As can be seen in Figures 6–7, *zhengrong* 崢嶸 and *paihuai* 徘徊 are difficult to arrive at a definite conclusion, but it does occur in authors associated with places that are not necessarily near rivers.

From this control set of ideophones we can see in the first place the main migration patterns of the Han culture (or sinification) throughout time, viz. migration towards the East and then towards the South. However, it does stand out that the six geographical profiles we established in this study are all different from each other in relevant ways, suggesting there really may be some influence of the surroundings, as we will explain in the discussion (section 4.4).

Lexical variation of ideophones in Chinese classics — 217

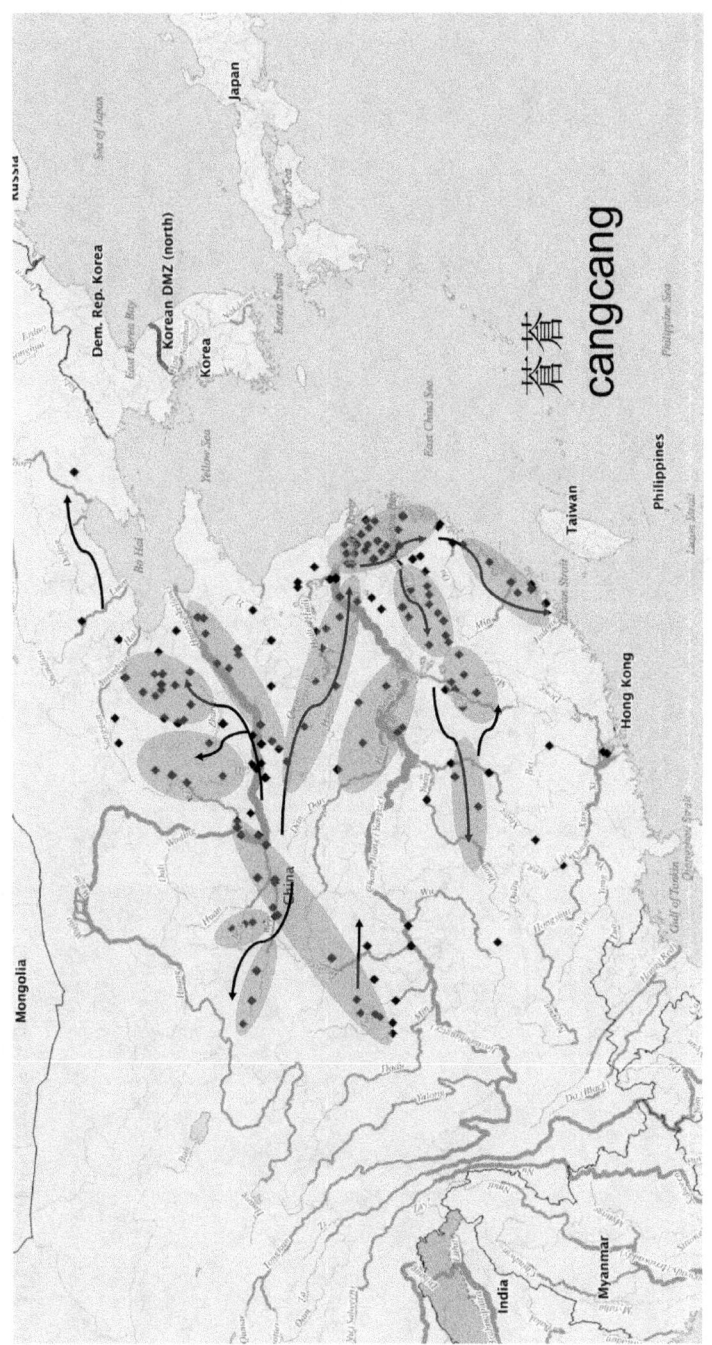

Figure 5: Geographical profile of cangcang.

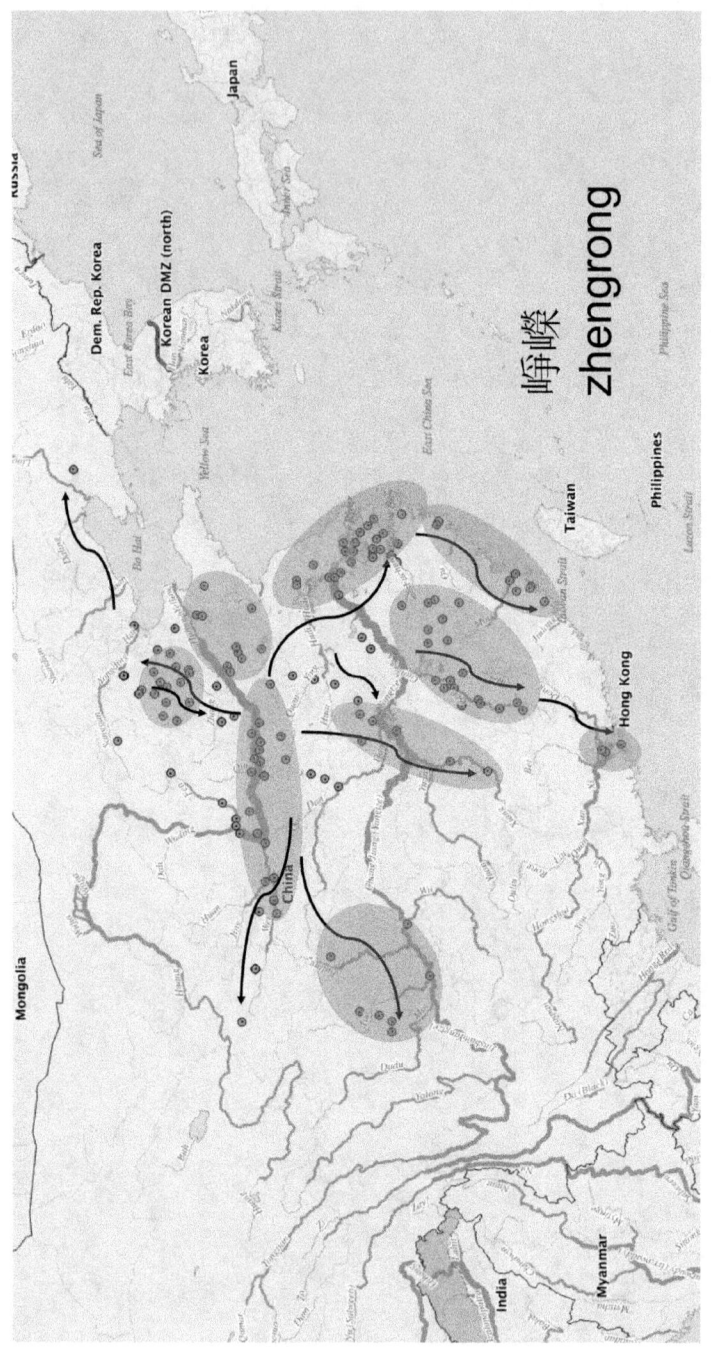

Figure 6: Geographical profile of *zhengrong*.

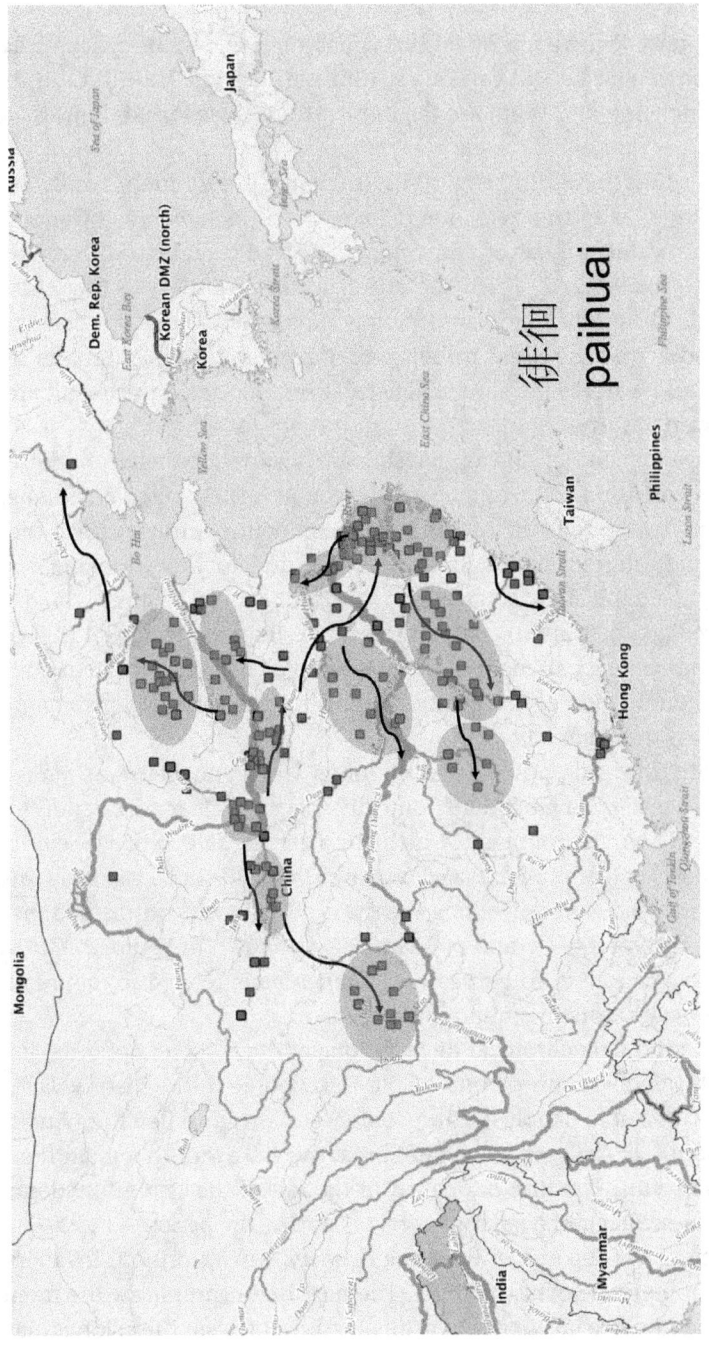

Figure 7: Geographical profile of *paihuai*.

4.4 Discussion and implications

This paper started with a few questions which then set out our research agenda. Do ideophones have lexical variants in Chinese classics? How did they distribute in the ancient texts? What are the implications if we found their traces over time?

Firstly, as discussed in section 4.1, ancient Chinese ideophones did have lexical variants, as in the case of *mangmang$_G$* and *mangmang$_{GW}$*. Generally, we saw that the water radical of *mangmang$_{GW}$* 茫茫 did make a difference when compared to *mangmang$_G$* 芒芒: the latter occurred only in a few clusters in China, while the former appeared mostly along rivers and the coastal areas and diffused across the areas in between. *Cangmang$_{GW}$* 蒼茫 then, as the ultimate "vast and water" ideophonic construction originated in coastal areas but spread inward via rivers.

The development of the onomasiological variation between these three ideophones consisted of three stages (cf. section 4.1). In stage one *mangmang$_G$* and *mangmang$_{GW}$* were in slight variational competition. In stage two the usage of *mangmang$_G$* started to fossilize, probably due to the widening scope of *mangmang$_{GW}$* and the increasing usage of *cangmang*. In stage three it is *cangmang* and *mangmang$_{GW}$* that are in competition rather than *mangmang$_G$*. The high frequency of *mangmang$_{GW}$* in modern language and its metaphorical extendibility is the current termination of this evolution in which the variant *mangmang$_{GW}$* takes over functions from *mangmang$_G$*.

Secondly, the geographical distributions we found between *mangmang$_G$*, *mangmang$_{GW}$*, and *cangmang* diachronically suggest a clear connection between language and the environment, which then serves as a piece of evidence of embodied basis of ideophone. Based on the authors' birthplaces, these three ideophones were used generally along the rivers. This result contrasts to the distributions of *zhengrong* 崢嶸, and *paihuai* 徘徊 as shown in Figure 8. *Paihuai* is a verb so that it can be used pervasively. *Zhengrong* is related to mountains and naturally appears more in mountainous areas.

Thirdly, all the diachronical distributions of these six ideophones generally accord with the migration pattern of the Han people in the history. Due to the invasions of nomadic peoples, Han people were forced to flee from Luoyang 洛陽 to the south. In the long history of China, there are three big migration waves towards the south. The first happened in the era of the Three Kingdoms (Wei, Shu, and Wu, which had overlapping reigns during the period A.D. 220–80). The second occurred at the end of the Tang dynasty, when northern invaders came down to terminate the dynasty in 907. The next half-century saw the fragmentation of China into five northern dynasties 五代 and ten southern kingdoms 十國.

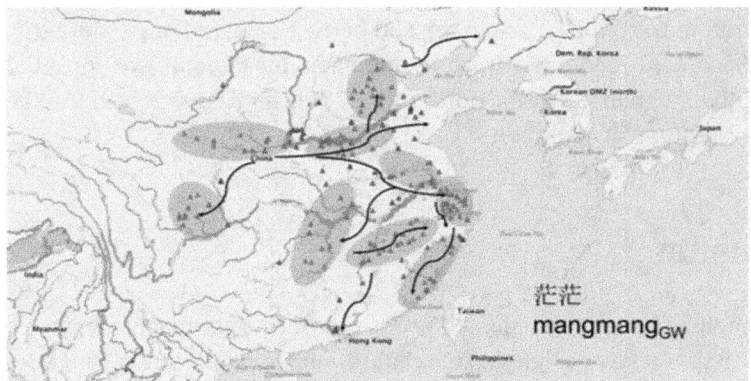

*mangmang*_{GW} 茫茫

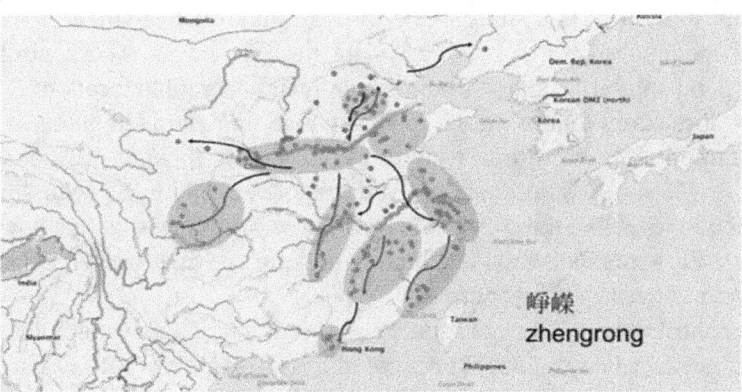

zhengrong 崢嶸

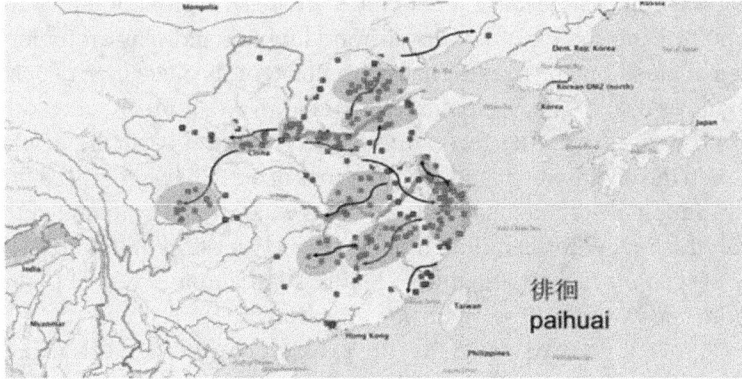

paihuai 徘徊

Figure 8: Comparison of geographical profiles.

The third migration wave took place in the end of the Northern Song (960–1127). Because the Song court could not resist the nomadic invaders, it was forced to flee to the south and abandoned the north in 1127. This migration pattern can be confirmed via the study of ideophones.

5 Conclusion

This paper studies Chinese ideophones in an innovative approach, aiming to combine some issues related to language variation, embodied cognition, language diffusion, migration, and geographical distribution of lexicon. These seemingly different issues converge at one research target, i.e., ideophones in classic Chinese.

A first contribution of this study is the in-depth quantitative study of six corpus-driven ideophones, three of which were near-synonyms. The control set in section 3.4 displayed similar variation as to their geographic location. As a side note, it does stand that of the six relatively high frequent ideophones in Premodern Chinese, only two are in general use nowadays (*paihuai* 徘徊 and *mangmang*$_{GW}$ 茫茫). Future studies should verify if there really is a decline in the use of ideophones,[17] and if this is true it is certainly worth investigating how functions originally expressed with ideophones are expressed now, viz. what has replaced the frequent usage of ideophones?

A second contribution of this case study is the addition of a new methodology in the ever growing body of ideophone research (see, e.g., Akita 2010a; Akita 2010b) – using geographical profiling to trace influence of the environment on the usage, or rather proneness to usage of certain ideophones. The reasoning behind this goes as follows: because ideophones are heavily prone to embodiment (Rohrer 2007; Dingemanse 2011), the surroundings should play an important role in their acquisition and usage. The environment of speakers then deeply influences language usage in a compounded manner. Now, if ideophones are learnt earlier and easier than other parts of the lexicon, and if basic literacy is learnt locally, then the environment and surroundings of one's background could influence the variation of certain ideophones. That is what we have attempted to investigate with this model for handling the diachronic variation and onomasiological study of ideophones, although the identification and function of other factors that influence variation deserve further attention in future studies.

In relation to this, it must be stated that the methodology used in this paper is slightly limited by the selection of possible future candidates: in this study six

---

[17] Or only in certain strata, cf. note 15.

ideophones have been selected that all express vision (dimension) or movement, which score high on previously established iconicity scales (Lu 2006; Akita 2009; Dingemanse 2012). It may prove more difficult to perform similar quantitative analyses with less iconic ideophones (e.g., those that express smell, taste, inner feelings), nor even with the most iconic kind of ideophones, i.e., those that depict sound. However, the selection of visual and movement related ideophones in this case can be defended by the relative frequency in the corpus used to select them: about 62% in the Middle Chinese Tang poetry corpus compiled in Van Hoey (2015).

Lastly, further studies could contrast this kind of quantitative research with more qualitative approaches. Similarly, this kind of onomasiological analyses should be put to the test of semasiological analyses. The combination of these four approaches (Glynn 2010) yields the most interesting and accurate model for understanding the development and structure of ideophones in Chinese, as well as ideophones in general.

References

Academia Sinica 中央研究院. 2015. Scripta Sinica Database (Hanji quanwen ziliaoku jihua 漢籍全文資料庫計畫). Database. *Scripta Sinica Database*. http://hanchi.ihp.sinica.edu.tw/ (accessed 26 June 2016).
Akita, Kimi. 2009. *A grammar of sound-symbolic words in Japanese: theoretical approaches to iconic and lexical properties of mimetics* (日本語音象徴語文法：擬音・擬態語の類像的・語彙的特性への理論的アプローチ). Kobe: Kobe University PhD dissertation.
Akita, Kimi. 2010a. A Bibliography of Sound-Symbolic Phenomena in Languages Other than Japanese. https://sites.google.com/site/akitambo/Home/biblio/bibb.
Akita, Kimi. 2010b. A Bibliography of Sound-Symbolic Phenomena in Japanese. https://sites.google.com/site/akitambo/Home/biblio/bib.
Akita, Kimi. 2012. Toward a frame-semantic definition of sound-symbolic words: A collocational analysis of Japanese mimetics. *Cognitive Linguistics* 23(1). 67–90.
Akita, Kimi. 2013. The lexical iconicity hierarchy and its grammatical correlates. In Lars Elleström, Olga Fischer & Christina Ljungberg (eds.), *Iconic investigations*, 331–349. (Iconicity in Language and Literature volume 12). Amsterdam; Philadelphia: John Benjamins Publishing Company.
Baxter, William H. & Laurent Sagart. 2014. *Old Chinese: A new reconstruction*. Oxford: Oxford University Press.
Baxter, William Hubbard & Laurent Sagart. 1998. Word formation in Old Chinese. In Jerome Lee Packard (ed.), *New approaches to Chinese word formation: morphology, phonology and the lexicon in modern and ancient Chinese*, 35–76. Berlin; New York: Mouton de Gruyter.
Biber, Douglas. 2015. Corpus-based and corpus-driven analyses of language variation and use. In Bernd Heine & Heiko Narrog (eds.), *The Oxford handbook of linguistic analysis*, 193–224. Second edition. (Oxford Handbooks in Linguistics). New York, NY: Oxford University Press.

Bickel, Balthasar, Bernard Comrie & Martin Haspelmath. 2008. The Leipzig glossing rules: conventions for interlinear morpheme by morpheme glosses. https://www.eva.mpg.de/lingua/pdf/LGR08.02.05.pdf (accessed 28 May 2015).

Bodomo, Adams. 2006. The structure of ideophones in African and Asian languages: the case of Dagaare and Cantonese. In John Mugane, John P. Hutchison & Dee A. Worman (eds.), *Selected Proceedings of the 35th Annual Conference on African Linguistics*, 203–213. Somerville, MA: Cascadilla Proceedings Project.

Croft, William. 2001. *Radical construction grammar: syntactic theory in typological perspective*. Reprinted. Oxford: Oxford Univ. Press.

De Sousa, Hilário. 2008. Ideophones in Cantonese – the role of tones. Powerpoint presentation. (Paper presented at workshop Human locomotion across languages, Max Planck Institute for Psycholinguistics).

De Sousa, Hilário. 2011. Ideophonic compounds in East and Southeast Asia. Paper presented at Association for Linguistic Typology 9th Biennial Conference (ALT9). University of Hong Kong 香港大學.

Dingemanse, Mark. 2011. *The meaning and use of ideophones in Siwu*. Nijmegen: Radboud University Nijmegen dissertation.

Dingemanse, Mark. 2012. Advances in the cross-linguistic study of ideophones. *Language and Linguistics Compass* 6(10). 654–672.

Dingemanse, Mark & Kimi Akita. 2016. An inverse relation between expressiveness and grammatical integration: On the morphosyntactic typology of ideophones, with special reference to Japanese. *Journal of Linguistics*. 1–32. doi:10.1017/S002222671600030X.

Dingemanse, Mark, Damián E. Blasi, Gary Lupyan, Morten H. Christiansen & Padraic Monaghan. 2015. Arbitrariness, iconicity and systematicity in Language. *Trends in Cognitive Sciences* 19(10). 603–615.

Esch, Daan van. 2012. Leiden Weibo Corpus. http://lwc.daanvanesch.nl/index.php (26 June, 2016).

Geeraerts, Dirk. 2010. *Theories of Lexical Semantics*. Oxford: Oxford University Press.

Glynn, Dylan. 2010. Corpus-driven Cognitive Semantics: introduction to the field. In Dylan Glynn & Kerstin Fischer (eds.), *Quantitative methods in cognitive semantics: corpus-driven approaches*, 1–42. (Cognitive Linguistics Research 46). Berlin; New York: De Gruyter Mouton.

Hinton, Leanne, Johanna Nichols & John J. Ohala (eds.). 1994. *Sound symbolism*. Cambridge [England]; New York, NY: Cambridge University Press.

Imai, Mutsumi & Sotaro Kita. 2014. The sound symbolism bootstrapping hypothesis for language acquisition and language evolution. *Philosophical Transactions of the Royal Society B: Biological Sciences* 369(1651). 1–13. doi:10.1098/rstb.2013.0298.

Jacques, Guillaume. 2013. Ideophones in Japhug (Rgyalrong). *Anthropological Linguistics* 55(3). 256–287.

Johnson, Mark. 1987. *The body in the mind: the bodily basis of meaning, imagination, and reason*. Chicago: University of Chicago Press.

Kita, Sotaro. 1993. *Language and thought interface: a study of spontaneous gestures and Japanese mimetics*. Chicago: University of Chicago PhD dissertation.

Krois, John Michael, Mats Rosengren, Angela Steidele, & Dirk Westerkamp (Eds.). 2007. *Embodiment in cognition and culture*. Amsterdam; Philadelphia: John Benjamins Pub. Co.

Kroll, Paul W. 2015. *A student's dictionary of Classical and Medieval Chinese*. (Handbook of Oriental Studies. Section 4 China Volume 30). Boston: Brill.

Langacker, Ronald W. 1987. *Foundations of Cognitive Grammar 1: Theoretical prerequisites*. Stanford, California: Stanford University Press.
Langacker, Ronald W. 2008. *Cognitive grammar: a basic introduction*. Oxford: Oxford University Press.
LaPolla, Randy J. 2006. The role of migration and language contact in the development of the Sino-Tibetan language family. In Alexandra Y. Aikhenvald & Robert M. W. Dixon (eds.), *Areal diffusion and genetic inheritance: problems in comparative linguistics*, 225–254. Oxford: Oxford University Press.
Lee, Thomas H. C. 1985. *Government education and examinations in Sung China*. New York : Hong Kong: St. Martin's; Chinese University Press.
Li, Feng & David Prager Branner (eds.). 2011. *Writing & literacy in early China: studies from the Columbia Early China Seminar*. Seattle: University of Washington Press.
Li Jing'er 李镜儿. 2007. *Xiandai Hanyu nishengci yanjiu* 现代汉语拟声词研究 [*Onomatopoeia in Modern Chinese*]. Shanghai: Xuelin publisher.
Liu Guodong 柳国栋. 2008. Lunyu chongdie ci lüelun 《论语》重叠词略论 [A Brief Discussion of Reduplicative Words in the Lunyu]. *Journal of Anhui Vocational Technical College* 安徽职业技术学院学报 7(2). 61–63.
Lockwood, Gwilym, Mark Dingemanse & Peter Hagoort. 2016. Sound-Symbolism Boosts Novel Word Learning. *Journal of Experimental Psychology: Learning, Memory, and Cognition*. doi:10.1037/xlm0000235.
LOPE lab, Graduate Institute of Linguistics, National Taiwan University. 2015. COPENS. Database. http://lopen.linguistics.ntu.edu.tw/copens/search/ (accessed 26 June 2016).
Lu Chiarung 呂佳蓉. 2006. *Giongo, gitaigo no hiyuteki kakuchō no shosō: ninchi gengogaku to reikeiron no kanten kara* 擬音語・擬態語の比喩的拡張の諸相――認知言語学と類型論の観点から [Figurative extensions of onomatopoeia: A Cognitive Linguistic and typological study]. Kyōto: Kyōto University PhD dissertation.
Lu Chiarung 呂佳蓉. 2011. Motivated Aspects of Language: Evidence from ABB-Construction in Mandarin. *Conference Program* of the 11th International Cognitive Linguistics Conference (ICLC-11), 135–136, Xi'An International Studies University, China.
Lu Ping 卢平. 2001. "Shijing" zhong xiangshengci de yunyong 《诗经》中象声词的运用 [The usage of onomatopoeia in The Book of Songs]. *Yindu xuekan* 殷都学刊 2. 103–106.
Lu Yan 陆燕. 2011. Lun yan yin lianmian ci de liang zhong chansheng fangshi – yi Shijing wei li 论衍音联绵词的两种产生方式――以《诗经》为例 [Research on the Two Emerging Ways of Lianmian Words with Derived Syllables with the Book of Songs (Shijing) as a Case Study]. *Qiqihar daxue xuebao: zhexue shehui kexue ban* 齐齐哈尔大学学报：哲学社会科学版 6. 122–124.
Maiese, Michelle. (2011). *Embodiment, emotion, and cognition*. Basingstoke, Hampshire; New York, NY: Palgrave Macmillan.
Mair, Victor H. (ed.). 2001. *The Columbia history of Chinese literature*. New York: Columbia University Press.
Man Fang 滿芳. 2009. Shijing zhong de AABB shi zuhe 《诗经》中的 AABB 式组合 [The AABB structure in the Shijing]. *Shandong jiaoyu xueyuan xuebao* 山东教育学院学报 24(1). 42–44.
Meng, Chenxi. 2012. *A description of ideophonic words in Mandarin Chinese*. Leiden: Leiden University Research Master in Linguistics.
Mok, Waiching Enid. 2001. *Chinese sound symbolism: A phonological perspective*. Hawai'i: University of Hawai'i PhD dissertation.

National Taiwan University Chinese Department 臺灣大學中國文學系 & Academia Sinica 中央研究院. 2011. Hanzi gujin yin ziliaoku 漢字古今音資料庫 [Chinese Character Readings, CCR]. Database. 漢字古今音資料庫. (accessed 26 June 2016).

QGIS Development Team. 2016. *QGIS*. Mac. (QGIS). QGIS.

Rawski, Evelyn Sakakida. 1979. *Education and popular literacy in Ch'ing China*. (Michigan Studies on China). Ann Arbor: University of Michigan Press.

Rohrer, Tim. 2007. Embodiment and experientalism. *The Oxford handbook of Cognitive Linguistics*, 25–47. Oxford; New York: Oxford University Press.

Shin, Jungho. 2012. *A comparative study of symbolic words in Japanese and Korean*. Oslo: University of Oslo MA thesis.

Schneider, Peter. 2002. Computer Assisted Spelling Normalization of 18th Century English. In Pam Peters, Peter Collins & Adam Smith (eds.), *New frontiers of corpus research: Papers from the 21st International Conference on English language Research on Computerized Corpora, Sydney, 2000*, 199–211. Amsterdam: Rodopi.

Sun, Jingtao. 1999. *Reduplication in Old Chinese*. Vancouver: University of British Columbia PhD dissertation.

Tagliamonte, Sali. 2006. *Analysing sociolinguistic variation* (Key Topics in Sociolinguistics). Cambridge, UK: Cambridge University Press.

Three Hundred Tang Poems. 2016. Three Hundred Tang Poems. Wikipedia. *Three Hundred Tang Poems*. Poems (accessed 26 June 2016).

Twitchett, Denis. 1979. *The Cambridge history of China. Vol 3, Sui and T'ang China, 589-906*, Part I. Cambridge: Cambridge University Press.

Van Hoey, Thomas. 2015. *Ideophones in Middle Chinese: a typological study of a Tang dynasty poetic corpus*. Leuven: KU Leuven MA thesis.

Van Hoey, Thomas. 2017. The thunder rolls: iconicity and ideophones in Chinese meteorological expressions. Paper presented at the *CLS-MPI Iconicity Focus Group Workshop: Types of Iconicity in Language Use, Development and Processing*. Nijmegen: Max Planck Institute for Psycholinguistics.

Van Langendonck, Willy. 2007. Iconicity. In Dirk Geeraerts & Hubert Cuyckens (eds.), *The Oxford handbook of cognitive linguistics*, 394–418. (Oxford Handbooks). Oxford; New York: Oxford University Press.

Vande Walle, Willy. 2007. *Een geschiedenis van het Chinese keizerrijk tot 1600: de duurzame zoektocht naar imperium*. Leuven: Acco.

Voeltz, Erhard Friedrich Karl & Christa Kilian-Hatz (eds.). 2001. *Ideophones*. (Typological Studies in Language v. 44). Amsterdam; Philadelphia: J. Benjamins.

Wang Xiuli 王秀丽. 2010. Jinwen dieyin ciyu tanxi 金文叠音词语探析 [A study on the Reduplicated Words in Bronze Inscriptions]. *Guwen zi yanjiu* 古文字研究 117(4). 125–132.

Wu, Mengqi. 2014. *The structure of ideophones in Southern Sinitic*. Hong Kong: University of Hong Kong MA thesis.

Zhao Aiwu 赵爱武. 2005. Xiangshengci: Cong Shijing dao Yuanqu 象声词：从《诗经》到《元曲》[Mimetic word: from "The Book of Songs" to "Yuan Drama"]. *Henan keji daxue xuebao* 河南科技大学学报 (*Sheke ban* 社科版) 23 (2).47–50.

Zhao Aiwu 赵爱武. 2008. Jin 20 nian Hanyu xiangshengci yanjiu zongshu 近20年汉语象声词研究综述 [Chinese onomatopoeia study in recent 20 years: A summary]. *Wuhan daxue xuebao* 武汉大学学报 (*renwen kexue ban* 人文科学版) 61(2). 180–185.

Chihkai Lin
2 A case study of accent shift in the Ryukyuan languages

Abstract: This paper investigates how sound changes take place concurrently with geographical separation. As sound changes and geographical separation are seldom discussed together as a combined factor, I demonstrate that sound changes and geographical separation can be associated. To illustrate this association, I focus on accent shift in the Ryukyuan languages in five regions geographically distributed from north to south: Amami, Okinawa, Miyako, Yaeyama, and Yonaguni. When geographical separation occurs in a sequential manner (A → B → C), sound changes also take place concurrently in a derivational manner (X → Y → Z) by changing one phonological feature step by step.

To explore accent shift in the five regions in the Ryukyuan languages, the data are based on Shimabukuro's (2007) reconstruction of monosyllabic and disyllabic nouns. The results suggest that the five regions show four major regions of pitch accent: Amami, Okinawa, Miyako-Yaeyama, and Yonaguni. The changes in the four regions follow rightward accent shift and correspond to the migration directionality from Amami to Okinawa, then to Miyako-Yaeyama and finally to Yonaguni. When migrants move southward, at the same time, the pitch accent shifts rightward to the next syllable. Finally, the accent becomes atonic. Other phonological processes also emerge locally. In Okinawa, vowels prolong independently, and the long vowels attract accent, especially in disyllabic nouns, even if the accent has shifted to the next syllable. In Miyako-Yaeyama, pitch accent is similar. In Yonaguni, most pitch accent becomes atonic. The results also suggest that register is a crucial feature that distinguishes Northern Ryukyuan (Amami and Okinawa) from Southern Ryukyuan (Miyako, Yaeyama, and Yonaguni).

Keywords: Ryukyuan, accent shift, rightward shift, disyllabic nouns, atonic

1 Introduction

Sound changes are seldom motivated by a single factor. Among various possible causes for sound changes, one factor that triggers different language distributions

Chihkai Lin, Tatung University, Department of Applied Foreign Languages, linchihkai@gmail.com

https://doi.org/10.1515/9783110610895-009

is migration (Dyen 1956). When migration takes place, migrants face different geographical conditions. One condition is geographical separation, such as water intervals and mountains, which might trigger language splitting after the speakers of a language migrate. Dixon (1997) describes two scenarios of language splitting, depending on how migrants connect with their origins. The first scenario, as shown in (1) below, is that a language splits under geographical separation. Some speakers of a language migrate to a new place and reside in the new place without any connection with the people living in the original place. If there is a connection between the two groups of people after X years, it is possible that the two groups of people might be able to communicate with each other. Nevertheless, the longer time the separation is (Z years for example), the less likely that the two groups of people are still mutually intelligible.

(1)

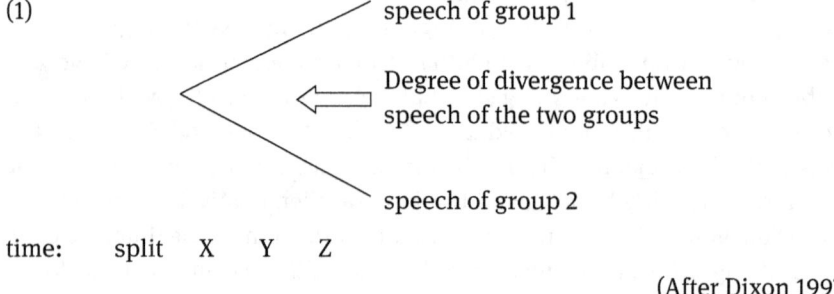

time: split   X   Y   Z

(After Dixon 1997: 59)

The first scenario is exemplified by the languages spoken in the Pacific islands, such as Okinawan (Dixon 1997: 60–61) and Austronesian languages. The migration in the Pacific islands shows a process from one island to another, and then to another until there are no other islands. When living on separate islands without continuous communication with the previous island(s) from which the migrants come, the speakers in the previous and new islands independently develop their linguistic features, and the two groups of people eventually become mutually unintelligible. Take the Austronesian languages as an example. The earliest generation of the speakers moved out of Taiwan (Blust 1988), southward to the Philippines. They gradually migrated to the Philippines, Malaysia, Indonesia, New Zealand, Malagasy and finally reached Hawaiʻi. When moving out and reaching another island, the Austronesian people were separated from each other by water intervals. Consequently, continuous communication becomes difficult. As the migration continues, there are more language distributions.

The second scenario proposed by Dixon (1997) is given in (2) below. A language splits while maintaining geographical contiguity. Two separate groups of people maintain a connected relationship, and thus mutual intelligence is still possible. According to Dixon (1997: 62), linguistic separation is often motivated by a political or social factor for this situation. Suppose that there are dialects A1 and A2, the speakers of dialect A1 tend to be associated more with language B, and the speakers of dialect A2 live closer to language C. The speakers of dialect A1 are easily assimilated by language B, and the speakers of dialect A2 speak more like speakers of language C. Finally, the two dialects A1 and A2 evolve two different but genetically related languages.

(2)

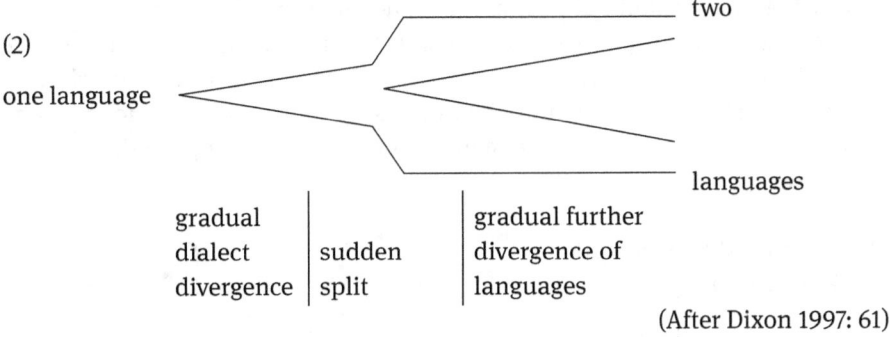

(After Dixon 1997: 61)

The second scenario is illustrated by Gan and Hakka, two of the Sinitic languages. LaPolla (2001) suggests that migration motivated by government encouragement, natural disaster or wars would contribute to the formation of Sinitic languages. LaPolla (2001: 231) points out that due to early contact, Gan dialect is initially formed in an area between Wu and Chu dialects in central and northern Jiangxi. Later migrations from the north brought different groups of immigrants into this area and led to a linguistic split into the Gan and Hakka dialects. Later, Hakka moved to the east and south and finally to the west.[1]

A common issue in sound changes has been the discussion of segmental changes, the English Great Vowel Shift for instance. What is less explored is prosody. Unlike segments, it is not easy to investigate prosody without apparatus that enables precise recording, and sometimes it is notorious to reconstruct prosody (Minkova 2013: 260). Although the difficulty results in far less research assessing prosody, some research has shown the possibility of reconstructing prosody by using different methods: philological data and the comparative method. Minkova (2006, 2013) reconstructs the stress of Old and

---

[1] With sufficient evidence to support the relationship, Chiang (2003) has explicitly explored the phonological affinity between Gan and Hakka.

Middle English by utilizing philological data. On the other hand, Shimabukuro (2007), based on the comparative method, reconstructs the pitch accent of Proto-Ryukyuan. Either philological data or the comparative method makes it possible to reconstruct prosody without using modern apparatus, *praat* for instance.

In this study, I bring together two issues: (a) migration encountering geographical separation due to water intervals and (b) prosodic changes, accent shift in the Ryukyuan languages in particular. I investigate the interaction of migration and accent shift and pay specific attention to whether accent shift reflects the directionality of migration. To facilitate the discussion, I postulate the interaction of migration and accent shift as follows. Suppose that there are three islands A, B, and C, a group of people from island A move to island B and later to island C. Meanwhile, the initial stage of prosody is X, followed by a change to Y, and then to Z. The mapping of migration and prosodic changes looks like (3).

(3) Directionality of migration A → B → C
    Prosodic changes   X → Y → Z

In (3), the migration follows a sequence A → B → C, and the prosodic changes are also in a derivational order (X → Y → Z). People from island A have phonological feature X. When migration takes place from islands A to B, there is a phonological change from X to Y. When migration from islands B to C continues, there is another change from Y to Z.

To illustrate how migration and prosodic changes interact, I explore accent shift in the Ryukyuan languages spoken separately in the Ryukyu archipelago. The data rely on the reconstruction of accent patterns for monosyllabic and disyllabic nouns by Shimabukuro (2007). In particular, I discuss rightward accent shift in the Ryukyuan languages. To show the interaction of migration and prosodic changes in the Ryukyuan languages, section 2 depicts the geography of the Ryukyu archipelago and the reconstruction of accent patterns by Shimabukuro (2007), who classifies five major regions from north to south: Amami, Okinawa, Miyako, Yaeyama, and Yonaguni. The accent patterns of the Ryukyuan languages in the five regions are described and analyzed in section 3 where I probe into monosyllabic and disyllabic nouns. Section 4 explores the parallel development in monosyllabic and disyllabic nouns. Section 5 discusses the interaction of migration and prosodic changes in the Ryukyuan languages and elaborates circular phenomenon and falling tone. Section 6 concludes this study.

2 Geography of the Ryukyu archipelago and the reconstruction of pitch accent in the Ryukyuan languages

This section describes the geography of the Ryukyu archipelago and the five regions used in this study. The reconstruction of accent patterns in the Ryukyuan languages by Shimabukuro (2007) is reviewed in great detail, according to the number of syllables: monosyllabic nouns (section 2.1) and disyllabic nouns (section 2.2).

The Ryukyu archipelago (see Map 1 below, Google Maps, 2018) is located southwest from Kyushu to Taiwan.[2] The island chain includes the Osumi Islands, Tokara Islands, Amami Islands, Okinawa Islands, Miyako Islands, Yaeyama Islands and Yonaguni. Languages spoken in the Ryukyu archipelago are Japanese and the Ryukyuan languages. Residents in the Osumi Islands and Tokara Islands speak Japanese, and others speak the Ryukyuan languages. This study follows Shimabukuro's (2007) five major regions from north to south: Amami, Okinawa, Miyako, Yaeyama, and Yonaguni.[3]

---

[2] The map is retrieved May 22, 2018, from https://www.google.com/maps/@27.4918264,127.6068 882,7z. The place names are marked by the author.

[3] The classification of the Ryukyuan languages has been proposed by Tōjō (1951), Uemura (1963), Nakamoto (1976), Hokama (1977), Thorpe (1983), Nakasone (1987), Hirayama (1992), Ethnologue (2009), and Pellard (2015, 2016). In general, there are two views of classification for the Ryukyuan languages in (i). The first classification is based on Ethnologue (2009), which has two major branches: Amami-Okinawan and Sakishima for (ia), and the second is based on Pellard (2015, 2016), which includes Southern Ryukyuan and Northern Ryukyuan. In (ia), under Amami-Okinawan, there are Amami and Okinawan. Under Sakishima, there are Miyako, Yaeyama and Yonaguni. In (ib), Northern Ryukyuan includes Amami and Okinawa. This branch corresponds to Amami-Okinawa in Ethnologue. Southern Ryukyuan is first divided into Macro Yaeyama and Miyako. Under Micro Yaeyama, there are Yaeyama and Dunan, which is spoken in Yonaguni. The classification in (ib) significantly differs from the one in (ia) in how Miyako is classified. In (ia), Miyako, Yaeyama and Yonaguni are sister languages, while in (ib), Miyako and Yaeyama are not.

(i) a. Ethnologue (2009)

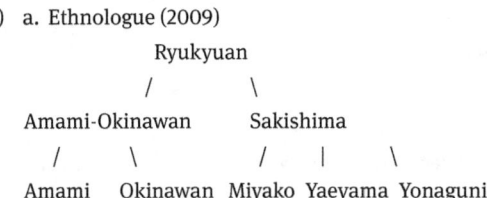

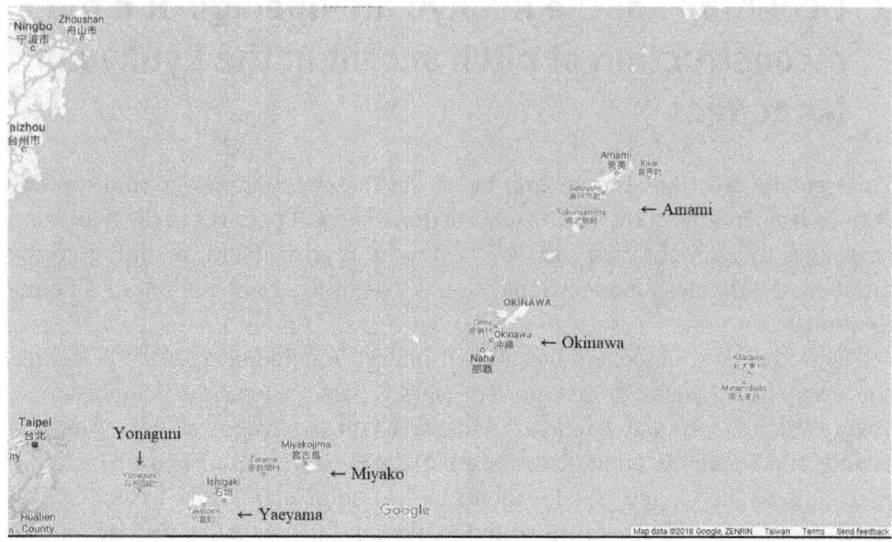

Map 1: The Ryukyu archipelago

Shimabukuro (2007) reconstructs pitch accent for four regions: Proto-Amami, Proto-Okinawa, Proto-Miyako, and Proto-Yaeyama. He selects three sites for each region. To reconstruct Proto-Amami, Shimabukuro (2007) includes Naze dialect, Kamishiro dialect, and Kametsu dialect.[4] Another three dialects from Nakijin, Shuri, and Aguni are used to reconstruct Proto-Okinawa. Ikema dialect, Ôura dialect, and Uechi dialect are used to reconstruct Proto-Miyako. Proto-Yaeyama is reconstructed based on Ishigaki dialect, Sonai dialect, and Kuroshima dialect. As for Yonaguni, Shimabukuro (2007) does not reconstruct Proto-Yonaguni. He only uses the modern forms.

b. Pellard (2016)

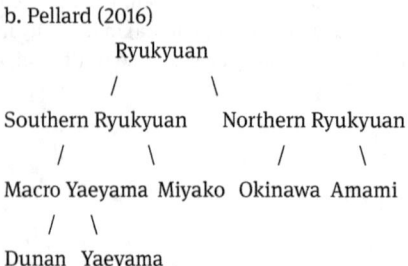

[4] As one reviewer points out, there are updated data for reconstructing Proto-Amami, such as Uwano (2012).

In Shimabukuro (2007), there are two ways of presenting pitch accent in the Ryukyuan languages: phonetic elements, such as high pitch and low pitch, and phonological notations, especially locus and register. Locus refers to the position where pitch falls in a phonological word, and register refers to level pitch (high and low) in the initial position of a phonological word.[5] Examples in (4) from Shimabukuro's (2007) Proto-Amami and Proto-Miyako illustrate how phonological notations and phonetic elements are presented in this study.

(4) Examples of accent in phonological notations and phonetic elements

Myô	Proto-Amami	Proto-Miyako	Myô	Proto-Amami	Proto-Okinawa
1.1	*⁻oo	*_oo˥	2.1/2.2	*⁻OO	*⁻O˥O
	[HH(H)]	[RH(L)]		[HH(H)]	[HL(L)]
1.2	*⁻oo	*⁻oo˥	2.3/2.4/2.5 (a)	*⁻oo˥	*_OO
	[HH(H)]	[HH(L)]		[LH(L)]	[LL(L)]
1.3	*_oo˥	*_oo˥	2.3/2.4/2.5 (b)	*⁻O˥O	*_oo˥O
	[LH(L)]	[RH(L)]		[HL(L)]	[LHL(L)]

In (4), the convention of marking the classes of Japanese nouns follows *Myôgishô*, an ancient dictionary published in 1081CE. Class 1.1 refers to monosyllabic noun (type I) and class 1.2 to monosyllabic noun (type II). In monosyllabic nouns, there are three classes (1.1/1.2/1.3). There are five classes (2.1–2.5) for disyllabic nouns. Likewise, class 2.1 refers to disyllabic noun (type I), and class 2.2 to disyllabic noun (types II).

The pitch accent is presented first in phonological notations and then in phonetic elements. In phonological notations, small o stands for mora, capital O for syllable, superscript - for high register, subscript _ for low register, ˥ for locus, / for rising tone and \ for falling tone. In phonetic elements, H refers to high, L to low, R to rising and F to falling.

The phonological notations and phonetic elements reveal different notions of pitch accent. The phonological notions provide more information for rightward

---

[5] To illustrate Japanese pitch accent, I provide the following examples from Tokyo Japanese, a dialect that implements locus. For example, the pitch accent of *unagi* 'eel' is LHH(H), whose phonological notation is OOO without any locus. In *awabi* 'abalone' (HLL), the locus falls on the first syllable as O˥OO. It is also possible that the locus falls on the second syllable as in *kokoro* 'heart' (LHL, OO˥O). When the locus falls on the final syllable, the pitch accent is LHH(L) as in *huta-tsu* 'two-CL' (OOO˥).

accent shift, and the phonetic elements account for low tone spreading. In this study, I rely more on the phonological notations to seek the interaction of migration and prosodic changes in the Ryukyuan languages.

2.1 Monosyllabic nouns in the Ryukyuan languages

First, the accent patterns of Proto-Amami for monosyllabic nouns are shown in (5). In Proto-Amami, there are two accent patterns. Classes 1.1 and 1.2 have merged into one class, which is reconstructed as *oo, a monosyllabic noun with two moras. The second pattern includes examples from class 1.3 and sporadic examples from class 2.3. The second pattern is reconstructed as *oo⏋ with a locus on the final mora.[6]

(5) Reconstruction of Proto-Amami pitch accent for monosyllabic nouns

		Myô	Naze	Kamishiro	Kametsu	Proto-Amami
(a)			o	⁻oo	oo	*oo
			[H~ L(H)]	[HH(H)]	[HH(H)]	[HH(H)]
'hair'	1.1		kʰï	⁻hi:	kʰï:	*kʰï:
'blood'	1.1		ci	⁻ci:	ci:	*ci:
'leaf'	1.2		ha	⁻ha:	ha:	*ha:
'name'	1.2		na	--	na:	*na:
(b)			o	_oo	oo⏋	*oo⏋
			[H ~ L(H)]	[LR ~ LL(H)]	[LF ~ HH(L)]	[LH(L)]
'tree'	1.3		kʰi	_hi:	kʰi:⏋	*kʰï:⏋
'eye'	1.3		mï	_mi:	mi:⏋	*mï:⏋
'tooth'	1.3		ha	_ha:	ha:⏋	*ha:⏋
'dog'	2.3		ʔin	--	ʔin⏋	*ʔin⏋

(After Shimabukuro 2007: 150)

The accent patterns of Proto-Okinawa for monosyllabic nouns are given in (6).

---

6 In Matsumori (2001), the mergers in monosyllabic and disyllabic nouns are similar to Shimabukuro's system.

(6) Reconstruction of Proto-Okinawa pitch accent for monosyllabic nouns

		Myô	Nakijin	Shuri	Aguni	Proto-Okinawa
(a)			ˉoo	ˉoo	oˈo	*oˈo
			[HH(H)]	[HL(L)]	[HL(L)]	[HL(L)]
'hair'	1.1		ˉkʰi:	ˉhi:	kiˈ:	*kʰiˈ:
'blood'	1.1		ˉci:	ˉci:	–	*ciˈ:
'leaf'	1.2		ˉpʰa:	ˉhwa:	haˈ:	*pʰaˈ:
'name'	1.2		ˉna:	ˉna:	–	*naˈ:
(b)			_oo	_oo	Oo	*oo
			[LH(H)]	[LL(L)]	[LL(L)]	[LL(L)]
'tree'	1.3		_kʰi:	_hi:	ki	*kʰi:
'eye'	1.3		_mi:	_mi:	–	*mi:
'tooth'	1.3		_pʰa:	_ha:	ha:	*pʰa:
'dog'	2.3		(ʔinnukwa:)	_ʔin	–	*ʔin

(After Shimabukuro 2007: 177)

Proto-Okinawa has two accent patterns: *oˈo and *oo. The former includes examples from classes 1.1 and 1.2 with a locus on the penultimate mora; the latter comes from class 1.3 and some other examples from 2.3.[7] In the second pattern, there is no locus.

---

[7] Lawrence (2009, 2016) reconstructs Proto-Northern Ryukyuan as well. His system is presented below (Lawrence 2016: 13), where F refers to foot.

	A	B	C
F	/μμ/μ́μ́:	/μμ/μμ́:	/μμ/μ́:μ́
F+μ	/μμμ/μ́μ́:μ	/μμμ/μμμ́:	/μμμ/μμ́:μ́

In class A, the second vowel is long, and the first two moras are high. In class B, the final vowel is long, and the final mora is high. In class C, the penultimate vowel is long and the final two moras are high. Lawrence's (2016) system differs from Shimabukuro's (2007) reconstruction, which lacks intermediate stage Proto-Northern Ryukyuan. Although the two systems differ in the reconstruction of the Ryukyuan languages, one common feature is that they appeal to mora for tone assignment processes in monosyllabic nouns.

The accent patterns of Proto-Miyako for monosyllabic nouns are shown in (7).

(7) Reconstruction of Proto-Miyako pitch accent for monosyllabic nouns

		Myô	Ikema	Ôura	Uechi	Proto-Miyako
(a)		oo˥	oo˥	oo˥	*_oo˥	
		[LH(L)]	[HH(L)]	[HH(L)]	[RH(L)]	
'sail'	1.1	hu:˥	pu:˥	pu:˥	*_pu:˥	
'child'	1.1	Qfa˥	fa:˥	Qfa˥	*_fa:˥	
'hair'	1.1	ki:˥	--	--	*_ki:˥	
'tree'	1.3	ki:˥	ki:˥	ki:˥	*_ki:˥	
'eye'	1.3	mi: ˥	mi:˥	mi:˥	*_mi:˥	
'tooth'	1.3	ha:˥	pa˥:	pa:˥	*_pa:˥	
'dog'	2.3	in˥	in˥	in˥	*_in˥	
'sea'	2.4	in˥	i˥m	im˥	*_in˥	
(b)		oo˥	oo˥	oo	*⁻oo˥	
		[LH(L)]	[HH(L)]	[LL(L)]	[HH(L)]	
'leaf'	1.2	ha:˥	pa:˥	pa:	*⁻pa:˥	
'name'	1.2	na:˥	na:˥	na:	*⁻na:˥	

(After Shimabukuro 2007: 213)

In Proto-Miyako, there are also two accent patterns. No distinction is made between classes 1.1 and 1.3, and the reconstruction is *_oo˥ with low register and a locus on the final mora. The second pattern includes examples from class 1.2 only. The reconstructed pitch accent is *⁻oo˥ with high register and a locus on the final mora.[8]

---

[8] There are two reconstructions for Proto-Miyako: Bentley (2008) and Matsumori (2015, 2016). Bentley (2008) reconstructs Proto-Miyako with two types of pitch accent as well. Bentley (2008: 88) reconstructs leaf (1.2) as *pa˥ (H.L) and tree (1.3) as *_ke (L.H). Several differences can be found in Bentley's system. First, Bentley does not propose any vowel length for Proto-Miyako, whereas Shimabukuro has two moras for monosyllabic nouns. The second difference is that class 1.2 lacks high register in Bentley's system, as a contrast to Shimabukuro's *⁻oo˥ with high register. Bentley reconstructs class 1.3 without locus, while Shimabukuro reconstructs *_oo˥ with locus on the final mora. The second reconstruction is by Matsumori (2015, 2016). The reconstruction is formulated in terms of phonological words. Matsumori's system postulates that Proto-Miyako is a tone language, and the domain is a phonological word, in which there are three

The accent patterns of Proto-Yaeyama for monosyllabic nouns are presented in (8).

(8) Reconstruction of Proto-Yaeyama pitch accent for monosyllabic nouns

		Myô	Ishigaki	Sonai	Kuroshima	Proto-Yaeyama
(a)			⁻oo	oo	oo	*⁻oo˥
			[HH(L)]	[LL(L)]	[LH(H)]	[HH(L)]
'hair'	1.1		⁻ki:	ki:	ki:	*⁻ki:˥
'blood'	1.1		⁻ci:	ci:	ci:	*⁻ci:˥
'leaf'	1.2		⁻pa:	pa:	pa:	*⁻pa:˥
'name'	1.2		⁻na:	na:	na:	*⁻na:˥
(b)			_oo	o˥o	oo	*_oo˥
			[LL(L)]	[HL(L)]	[LH(H)]	[LH(L)]
'tree'	1.3		_ki:	ki˥:	ki:	*_ki:˥
'tooth'	1.3		_pa:	pa˥:	pa:	*_pa:˥
'eye'	1.3		_mi:	--	mi:	*_mi:˥

(After Shimabukuro 2007: 239)

There are two accent patterns in Proto-Yaeyama. The first one includes examples from classes 1.1 and 1.2, and the reconstruction is *⁻oo˥ with high register and a locus on the final mora. The second one, *_oo˥, is limited to class 1.3 where there is low register and the locus falls on the final mora.[9]

Finally, the monosyllabic nouns in Yonaguni are shown in (9).

---

types of pitch accent: LLH, LHL and HLL. Class A vocabulary takes LLH tone, class B takes LHL tone, and class C takes HLL tone.

9 Bentley (2008: 156) reconstructs Proto-Yaeyama with two types of pitch accent: *⁻pa˥ (H.L) 'leaf' for class 1.2 and *_ke (L.F) 'tree' for class 1.3. As done in Proto-Miyako, Bentley does not reconstruct two moras for monosyllabic nouns. In Proto-Yaeyama, the pitch accent for class 1.2 in Bentley's system resembles Shimabukuro's reconstruction, *⁻pa:˥ 'leaf' for example, with high register and a locus on the final position. With regard to class 1.3, Bentley's system differs from Shimabukuro's reconstruction, *_ki:˥ 'tree' for instance, in the locus. Bentley does not reconstruct locus for class 1.3.

(9) Yonaguni pitch accent for monosyllabic nouns

Phonemic	Phonetic	Myô	Examples
⁻oo	HH(H)	1.1	⁻kʰi: 'hair', ⁻ci: 'blood'
		1.2	⁻ha: 'leaf', ⁻na: 'name'
_oo	LL(L)	1.3	_kʰi: 'tree', _ha: 'tooth', _mi: 'eye'

(After Shimabukuro 2007: 253)

In Yonaguni, classes 1.1 and 1.2 have merged, and the pitch accent is ⁻oo with high register. The pitch accent of class 1.3 is _oo with low register.[10]

2.2 Disyllabic nouns in the Ryukyuan languages

Disyllabic nouns show more complex accent patterns in the Ryukyuan languages. First, the accent patterns of Proto-Amami for disyllabic nouns are given in (10).

(10) Reconstruction of Proto-Amami pitch accent for disyllabic nouns

	Myô	Naze	Kamishiro	Kametsu	PA
(a)		oo	⁻oo	oo	*oo
		[LH ~ LL(H)]	[LH(H)]	[LH(H)]	[HH(H)]
'nose'	2.1	hana	⁻hana	hana	*hana
'cow'	2.1	ʔusi	⁻usi	ʔusi	*ʔusi
'bird'	2.1	tʰuri	⁻tʰui	tʰuɪ	*tʰuri
'loins'	2.1	kʰusi	--	kʰusɪ	*kʰusi
'beard'	2.1	higi	--	sïgi	*higi
'wind'	2.1	hazye	⁻hazi	kʰadɪ	*kʰazï
'stone'	2.2	ʔisi	⁻ʔisi	ʔɪsɪ	*ʔisi
'study'	2.2	kʰabi	--	kʰabi	*kʰabi
'bridge'	2.2	hasi	⁻hasi	hasi	*hasi
'two'	3.2	ta:ci	⁻ta:ci	ta:ci	*ta:cï

---

10 Bentley (2008: 195) also discusses Yonaguni. There is no difference between Bentley's (2008) and Shimabukuro's (2007) reconstructions of pitch accent in Yonaguni. For example, the word for leaf is ⁻ha: (1.2) (HH) with high register, and the word for eye is _mi: (1.3) (LL) with low register.

(b)		OO	_OO	OO˥	*OO˥
		[LH ~ LL(H)]	[LR ~ LL(H)]	[LF ~ (LH(L)]	[LH(L)]
'flower'	2.3	hana	_hana	hana˥	*hana˥
'mountain'	2.3	yama	_yama	yama˥	*yama˥
'cloud'	2.3	kumu	--	kʰumu˥	*kʰumu˥
'shoulder'	2.4	kʰata	[_kata]	kʰata˥	*kʰata˥
'rain'	2.5	ʔamï	_ʔami	ʔamï˥	*ʔamï˥
'sweat'	2.5	ʔasi	--	ʔasɪ˥	*ʔasɪ˥
'board'	2.4	ʔita	[_ʔita]	--	*ʔita˥
'tears'	3.5	nada	--	--	*nada˥
(c)		O˥O	OO˥	O˥O	*O˥O
		[HL(L)]	[LF ~ LH(L)]	[HL(L)]	[HL(L)]
'bone'	2.3	hu˥nï	--	hu˥nɪ	*hu˥nï
'mortar'	2.4	ʔu˥si	usi˥	ʔu˥si	*ʔu˥si
'chopsticks'	2.4	ha˥si	hasi˥	--	*ha˥si
'boat'	2.4	hu˥nï	hi:ni˥	hu˥nï	*hu:˥nï
'needle'	2.4	ha˥ri	[ha:ri˥]	ha˥i	*ha:˥ri
'breath'	2.4	ʔi˥ki	⁻ʔiki	ʔi˥ki	*ʔi˥ki
'sea'	2.4	ʔu˥mi	⁻ʔuni	ʔu˥n	*ʔu˥mi
'shadow'	2.5	kʰa˥gë	haga˥	kʰa˥gï	*kʰa˥gï
'voice'	2.5	kʰu˥i	hui˥	kʰu˥i	*kʰu˥i
'bridegroom'	2.5	mo˥ho	muQkwa˥	(muQkwa)	*mo˥kwa
'bucket'	2.5	u˥hï	wui˥	uki˥	*wu˥kʰï
'fan'	3.4	ʔo˥:gi ~ ʔu˥gi	o:gi˥	ʔo˥gi	*ʔo:˥gi

(After Shimabukuro 2007: 151-152)

In Proto-Amami, there are three accent patterns. The first pattern is *OO for classes 2.1 and 2.2 without register and locus. The second pattern is *OO˥ for classes 2.3/2.4/2.5 with a locus on the final syllable, and the third pattern, *O˥O, is also for classes 2.3/2.4/2.5 where a locus falls on the penultimate syllable. The difference between the second and the third patterns is that examples from class 2.3 are mainly found in *OO˥, while examples from class 2.3 are relatively rare in *O˥O. Examples from classes 2.4 and 2.5 are attested in the second and the third accent patterns.

The disyllabic nouns of Proto-Okinawa are shown in (11).[11]

(11) Reconstruction of Proto-Okinawa pitch accent for disyllabic nouns

		Myô	Nakijin	Shuri	Previous PO	Revised PO
(a)			⁻Ooo	⁻OO	*O˥O	*O˥O
			[LHH(H)]	[HL(L)]	[HL(L)]	[HL(L)]
'nose'	2.1	⁻pʰana:	⁻hana	*pʰa˥na	*pʰa˥na
'cow'	2.1	⁻husi:	⁻ʔusi	*ʔu˥si	*ʔu˥si
'bird'	2.1	⁻tʰui	⁻tui	*tʰu˥i	*tʰu˥i
'loins'	2.1	⁻husi:	⁻kusi	*kʰu˥si	*kʰu˥si
'beard'	2.1	⁻pizi:	⁻hwizi	*pʰi˥zi	*pʰi˥zi
'wind'	2.1	⁻hazi:	⁻kazi	*kʰa˥zi	*kʰa˥zi
'stone'	2.2	⁻ʔisi: ~ ⁻hisi:	⁻ʔisi	*ʔi˥si ~ *hi˥si	*ʔi˥si ~ *hi˥si
'study'	2.2	⁻habi:	⁻kabi	*kʰa˥bi	*kʰa˥bi
'bridge'	2.2	⁻pʰasi:	⁻hasi	*pʰa˥si	*pʰa˥si
'forehead'	3.1	⁻pʰice:	⁻hwice:	*pʰi˥ce	*pʰi˥ce:
(b)			O˥O	_OO	*OO˥	*oo˥O
			[HL(L)]	[LL(L)]	[HH(L)]	[HH(L)]
'bone'	2.3	pʰu˥ni(:)	_huni	*pʰuni˥	*pʰu:˥ni
'mortar'	2.4	ʔu˥si(:)	_ʔu:si	*ʔu:si˥	*ʔu:˥si
'chopsticks'	2.4	--	_ha(:)si	*pʰasi˥	*pʰa:˥si
'needle'	2.4	pʰa˥i	_ha:i	*pʰa:i˥	*pʰa:˥i
'boat'	2.4	pʰu˥ni(:)	_huni	*pʰu:ni˥	*pʰu:˥ni
'sea'	2.4	ʔu˥mi(:)	_ʔumi	*ʔumi˥	*ʔu:˥mi
'breath'	2.4	ʔi˥ci(:)	_ʔi:ci	*ʔi:ci˥	*ʔi:˥ci
'shadow'	2.5	ha˥gi(:)	_ka:gi	*kʰa:gi˥	*kʰa:gi˥
'bucket'	2.5	hu˥kʰi(:)	_u:ki	*u:kʰi˥	*u:kʰi˥
'bridegroom'	2.5	mu˥hu(:)	_mu:ku	*mu:ku˥	*mu:ku˥

---

11 Shimabukuro (2007) provides two versions for disyllabic nouns in Proto-Okinawa. In classes 2.3/2.4/2.5 (a), the earlier version is *O˥O, which is revised as *oo˥O. There is no difference between the earlier and revised versions in other accent patterns.

(c)		_Ooo, _ooO	_OO	*OO	*OO
		[LLH(H)]	[LL(L)]	[LL(L)]	[LL(L)]
'flower'	2.3	_pʰana:	_hana	*pʰana	*pʰana
'mountain'	2.3	_yama:	_yama	*yama	*yama
'cloud'	2.3	_kumu:	_kuma	*kumu	*kumu
'shoulder'	2.4	_hata:	_kata	*kʰata	*kʰata
'board'	2.4	_hica:	_ʔica	*ʔica	*ʔica
'rain'	2.5	_ʔami:	_ʔami	*ʔami	*ʔami
'sweat'	2.5	_hasi:	_ʔasi	*ʔasi	*ʔasi
'fan'	3.4	_ʔo:zi	_ʔo:zi	*ʔo:zi	*ʔo:zi
'tears'	3.5	_nada:	_nada	*nada	*nada
'fat'	3.5	_ʔanda:	_ʔanda	*ʔanda	*ʔanda
'pillow'	3.5	_maQka:	_maQkwa	*maQkwa	*maQkwa

(After Shimabukuro 2007: 186-187)

In Proto-Okinawa, there are three accent patterns. Most examples are from classes 2.1 and 2.2. The first pattern is *O˥O with a locus on the penultimate syllable. In the second pattern, the pitch accent is *oo˥O, where the first syllable has two moras and the locus falls on the penultimate syllable. The third pattern, *OO, lacks register and locus. Examples of this pattern are from classes 2.3/2.4/2.5 and trisyllabic words, classes 3.4 and 3.5.

Examples in (12) are the reconstruction of disyllabic nouns for Proto-Miyako.

(12) Reconstruction of Proto-Miyako pitch accent for disyllabic nouns

		Ikema	Ôura	Uechi	Proto-Miyako
(a)		OO˥	OO˥	OO	*⁻OO˥
		[LH(L)]	[LH(L)]	[LL(L)]	[HH(L)]
'nose'	2.1	hana˥	pa:˥	pa:	*⁻pana˥
'cow'	2.1	usï˥	usï˥	usï	*⁻usï˥
'bird'	2.1	tuï˥	tuï˥	tuï	*⁻tuï˥
'loins'	2.1	kusï˥	kusï˥	kusï	*⁻kusï˥

'beard'	2.1	higi˥	pïgi˥	pïgi	*ˉpïgɩ˥
'wind'	2.1	kadi˥	kazi˥	kazi	*ˉkadi˥
'stone'	2.2	isï˥	isï˥	isï	*ˉisï˥
'study'	2.2	kabi:˥	kabï˥	kabï	*ˉkabï:˥
'bridge'	2.2	hasï˥	pasï˥	pasï	*ˉpasï˥
'centipede'	3.2	nkadi˥	nkazi˥	m:kazi	*ˉmmkazi˥
'mirror'	3.4	kagan˥	kagan˥	kagam	*ˉkagam˥
(b)		OO˥	OO˥	OO˥	*_OO˥
		[LH (L)]	[LH(L)]	[LH(L)]	[LH(L)]
'flower'	2.3	hana˥	pana˥	pana˥	*_pana˥
'mountain'	2.3	yama˥	yama˥	yama˥	*_yama˥
'cloud'	2.3	u:mu˥	fumu˥	fumu˥	*_fumu˥
'board'	2.4	icya˥	icya˥	icya˥	*_icya˥
'rain'	2.5	ami˥	ami˥	ami˥	*_ami˥
'sweat'	2.5	asi˥	asi˥	asi˥	*_asi˥
'calendar'	3.4	kuyun˥	kuyun˥	kuyum˥	*_kuyum˥
'tears'	3.5	nada˥	nada˥	nada˥	*_nada˥
'fat'	3.5	aQva˥	aQva˥	aQva˥	*_aQva˥
'pillow'	3.5	maQfa˥	maQ˥fa	maQfa˥	*_maQfa˥
(c)		OO	O˥O	OO˥	*OO
		[LL ~ HH(H)]	[HL ~ LH(L)]	[LH(L)]	[LL(L)]
'bone'	2.3	puni	pu˥ni	puni˥	*puni
'boat'	2.4	funi	fu˥ni	funi˥	*funi
'needle'	2.4	pai	pi˥ï	pïï˥	*paï
'mortar'	2.4	usï	u˥sï	usï˥	*usï
'breath'	2.4	icï	i˥kï	ikï˥	*ikï
'voice'	2.5	kui	ku˥i	kui˥	*kui
'shadow'	2.5	kagi	ka˥gi	kagi˥	*kagi
'bridegroom'	2.5	muku	mu˥ku	muku˥	*muku

'bucket'	2.5	wu:ki	u:˥ki	u:ki˥	*wu:ki
'pillar'	3.5	hara	pa˥ra	para˥	*para
'life'	3.5	nnucï	nnu˥cï	mnucï˥	*nnucï

(After Shimabukuro 2007: 214-215)

Three accent patterns are proposed for Proto-Miyako. In classes 2.1 and 2.2, the first pattern is reconstructed as *⁻OO˥ with high register and a locus on the final syllable. In the second pattern, in which examples are from classes 2.3/2.4/2.5, the pitch accent is *_OO˥ with low register and a locus on the final syllable. The third pattern is reconstructed as *OO without register and locus, and most examples are from classes 2.3/2.4/2.5.[12]

The accent patterns of disyllabic nouns for Proto-Yaeyama are shown in (13).

(13) Reconstruction of Proto-Yaeyama pitch accent for disyllabic nouns

			Ishigaki	Sonai	Kuroshima	Proto-Yaeyama
(a)			⁻OO	OO	OO	*⁻OO˥
			[HL(L)]	[LL(L)]	[LH(H)]	[HH(L)]
	'nose'	2.1	⁻pana	pa:˥	pa:	*⁻pana˥
	'cow'	2.1	⁻usï	usï˥	usï	*⁻usï˥
	'bird'	2.1	⁻turï	tuï˥	tuï	*⁻tuï˥
	'loins'	2.1	⁻kusï	kusï˥	kusï	*⁻kusï˥
	'beard'	2.1	⁻pïni	pïni˥	pïni	*⁻pïni˥
	'wind'	2.1	⁻kazi	kazi˥	kazi	*⁻kazi˥
	'stone'	2.2	⁻isi	isi˥	isi	*⁻isi˥
	'study'	2.2	⁻kabï	kabï˥	kabi	*⁻kabï:˥
	'bridge'	2.2	⁻pasï̄	pasi˥	pasi	*⁻pasï˥
(b)			_OO	O/O	OO	*_OO˥
			[LH (L)]	[LH(L)]	[LH(H)]	[LH(L)]
	'flower'	2.3	_pana	pa/na	pana	*_pana˥

---

12 Bentley (2008) also reconstructs the pitch accent of disyllabic nouns in Proto-Miyako. Except for segmental differences, Bentley's Proto-Miyako and Shimabukuro's reconstruction are identical in pitch accent. Bentley (2008: 89) reconstructs *⁻pana˥ (HH.L) for 'nose', *_pana˥ (LH.L) for 'flower' and *pone (LL.L) for 'bone'.

'mountain'	2.3	_yama	(yamana)	yama	*_yama˧
'cloud'	2.3	_humu	fu/mu	fumu	*_fumu˧
'dog'	2.3	_in	i/nu	in	*_inu˧
'board'	2.4	_ita	i/ta	ica	*_ita˧
'shoulder'	2.4	_kata	ka/ta	hata	*_kata˧
'rain'	2.5	_a:mi	a/mi	ami	*_a:mi˧
'sweat'	2.5	_asi	a/si	asi	*_asi˧
'tears'	3.5	_nada	na:/da	nada	*_na:da˧
(c)		_OO	O˧O	O˧O	*OO
		[LL(L)]	[HL(L)]	[HL(L)]	[LL(L)]
'bone'	2.3	_puni	pu/ni	pu˧ni	*puni
'needle'	2.4	_parï	pa˧rï, pa˧:ri	pi˧rï	*pa:rï
'mortar'	2.4	_usï	u˧si	u˧sï	*usï
'chopsticks'	2.4	_pasï	pa˧si	pa˧si	*pasï
'boat'	2.4	_huni	hu/ni	fu˧ni	*funi
'breath'	2.4	_ikï	i˧ki	i˧ki	*ikï
'shadow'	2.5	_kai	ka˧i	ka˧i	*kai
'voice'	2.5	_kui	ku˧i	ku˧i	*kui
'bucket'	2.5	_u:ki	u/gi	u:˧ki	*u:ki
'bridegroom'	2.5	_muku	mu˧ku	mu˧ku	*muku
'fan'	3.4	_ongï	on/gi	on˧gi	*ongï
'pillar'	3.5	_para:	pa/ra	pa˧ra	*para:

(After Shimabukuro 2007: 240-241)

Proto-Yaeyama has three accent patterns. Examples from classes 2.1 and 2.2 suggest that the first pattern should be reconstructed as *⁻OO˧ with high register and a locus on the final syllable. The reconstruction of the second pattern is *_OO˧ with low register and a locus on the final syllable. The third pattern, *OO, lacks register and locus. Examples of the second and third accent patterns are from classes 2.3/2.4/2.5.[13]

Examples of the pitch accent in Yonaguni are shown in (14).

---

[13] In Bentley (2008: 157), the reconstruction for the word 'nose' is *⁻pana˧ (HH.L), and the one for the word 'flower' is *_pana˧ (LH.L). As for the word 'voice', the reconstructed pitch accent

(14) Yonaguni pitch accent for disyllabic nouns

Phonemic	Phonetic	Myô	Examples
ˉOO	LH(H)	2.1	ˉuci 'cow', ˉkʰuci 'loins', ˉkʰadi 'wind', ˉŋgi 'beard'
		2.2	ˉhaci 'bridge', ˉkʰabi 'study'
		3.2	ˉta:ci 'two'
	HH(H)	3.1	ˉtai 'forehead'
_OO	LL(L)	2.3	_hana 'flower', _dama 'mountain', _inu 'dog', _mmu 'cloud'
		2.4	_kata 'shoulder', _ita 'board'
		2.5	_ami 'rain', _asi 'sweat'
		3.4	_ku:ru 'bag', _kaŋan 'mirror'
		3.5	_anda 'fat', _nuda 'tears'
OO\	LF ~ LH(H)	2.3	huni\ 'bone'
		2.4	uci\ 'mortar', haci\ 'chopsticks', iti\ 'breath', nni\ 'boat'
		2.5	kʰaɲi\ 'shadow', mugu\ 'bridegroom', ugi\ 'bucket'
		3.5	hira\ 'pillar', nuti\ 'life'
		3.7	cu:ri\ 'medicine'
	HL ~ HH(H)	2.4	hai\ 'needle'
		2.5	kʰui\ 'voice'

(After Shimabukuro 2007: 254)

The disyllabic nouns in Yonaguni have three accent patterns: ˉOO with high register, _OO with low register, and OO\ with a falling tone in word-final position.[14]

3 Migration and accent shift in the Ryukyuan languages

The data in section 2 are used to illustrate the interaction of migration and prosodic changes, focusing on accent shift in the Ryukyuan languages. There are

---

is *koe (LL.L). Regardless of the difference in the reconstruction of segments, it is apparent that Bentley's systems and Shimabukuro's reconstruction are similar in pitch accent.

[14] Bentley's (2008) data for Yonaguni show a similar pattern to Shimabukuro's data. For example, the word 'bridge' is ˉhaci (LH.H) and the word 'flower' is _hana. The word for 'bone' is huni\.

two directionalities for the settlement in the Ryukyu archipelago. It could be from north to south, that is, migration from Amami to Yonaguni. The southward migration can be divided into three hypotheses (Pellard 2015: 25–26). The first one is a strict linear movement from Amami to Okinawa, followed by later settlement in Miyako and then in Yaeyama (cf. Serafim 2003). Finally, the settlement ends in Yonaguni.[15] In a loose sense, it is also possible that the settlers first entered the northern regions of the Ryukyu archipelago, Amami or Okinawa, and then moved to the southern regions, following a directionality from Miyako to Yaeyama and then to Yonaguni. The earlier settlers in Amami or Okinawa became the Northern Ryukyuans, and those who moved to the south became the Southern Ryukyuans. The two hypotheses are rejected by Pellard (2015) because linguistic data do not support such directionality of migration. The third hypothesis is similar to the first one with similar directionality from north to south, but there is a later replacement in Amami or Okinawa. The other directionality of migration is from Yonaguni to Amami, namely northward migration. However, this directionality is rejected by most scholars of Ryukyuan linguistics. It is obvious that northward migration is contradictory to archeology and linguistic paleontology.

In this study, I argue that prosodic changes in the Ryukyuan languages account for which directionality of migration better reflects the historical facts, and I suggest that the settlement should be from north to south. Before discussing the details of how migration and prosodic changes interact, I briefly introduce the historical changes of pitch accent in the Japonic languages. According to Shimabukuro (2007: 115), there are six accentual changes in the Japonic languages, listed in (15).

(15) (i) Leveling of contour tones (Leveling)
     (ii) Lowering of pitch of particles (Lowering)
     (ii) Change from final high to initial-accent (Initial Accent Gain)

---

[15] A strict linear movement from Amami to Yonaguni implies a binary tree for the Ryukyuan languages (Pellard 2015: 25), as shown in (i), and consequently there are no Northern Ryukyuan and Southern Ryukyuan (cf. the tree in footnote 3).

(i) Proto-Ryukyuan
        /\
    Amami /\
       Okinawa /\
          Miyako /\
            Yaeyama Yonaguni

(iv) Change of domain
(v) Low tone spreading
(vi) Rightward accent shift (Accent shift)

The three prosodic changes in (15i), (15ii) and (15iv) are only found in historical materials (Shimabukuro 2007: 115).[16] The other three changes are attested in synchronic materials. The most relevant changes to this study are low tone spreading (15v) and rightward accent shift (15vi). In particular, rightward accent shift provides evidence to southward migration in the Ryukyu archipelago. When the migration takes place from Amami to Okinawa, accent shifts rightward. If similar process is observed from Okinawa to Miyako or from Miyako to Yaeyama, it is certain that migration and prosodic changes interact.

In addition to the six changes in (15), Shimabukuro (2007: 116) suggests that accentual changes follow an ordering: atonic (either high-level, low-level, or final-high atonic) > initial-accent (i.e., HLL) > second-syllable accent (either LHL or HHL) > final-accent (either LHH(L) or LHH(L)) > initial- and final-high (i.e., LHL) > atonic. This ordering also gives insight into the interaction of migration and prosodic changes in the Ryukyuan languages. This issue is discussed in section 5.

3.1 Accent shift in monosyllabic nouns

The data of accent patterns in the five regions in section 2 for monosyllabic nouns are compared in (16).

(16) Comparison of accent patterns for monosyllabic nouns

Myô	Proto-Amami	Proto-Okinawa	Proto-Miyako	Proto-Yaeyama	Yonaguni
1.1	*oo	*olo	*_oo˥	*⁻oo˥	⁻oo
1.2	*oo	*olo	*⁻oo˥	*⁻oo˥	⁻oo
1.3	*oo˥	*oo	*_oo˥	*_oo˥	_oo
1.1	[HH(H)]	[HL(L)]	[RH(L)]	[HH(L)]	[HH(H)]
1.2	[HH(H)]	[HL(L)]	[HH(L)]	[HH(L)]	[HH(H)]
1.3	[LH(L)]	[LL(L)]	[RH(L)]	[LH(L)]	[LL(L)]

---

16 Special thanks go to one of the reviewers, who suggests that leveling of contour tones has been observed in progress over the last few decades in Osaka Japanese.

In Proto-Amami, classes 1.1 and 1.2 are atonic. In Proto-Okinawa, the loci in classes 1.1 and 1.2 fall on the penultimate mora.[17] Classes 1.1 and 1.2 in Proto-Amami and Proto-Okinawa have merged. From Proto-Okinawa to Proto-Miyako, accent in class 1.1 shifts rightward from the penultimate mora to the final mora. Class 1.1 later merges with class 1.3. From Proto-Miyako to Proto-Yaeyama, there is no accent shift.[18] The loci in Proto-Miyako and Proto-Yaeyama fall on the final mora. Later in Proto-Yaeyama, classes 1.1 and 1.2 merge. From Proto-Yaeyama to Yonaguni, the loci in the two classes disappear, and the pitch accent becomes atonic.[19]

Rightward accent shift also takes place in class 1.3 in (16), but it is a partial process from Proto-Amami to Proto-Okinawa and from Proto-Miyako/Proto-Yaeyama to Yonaguni. In Proto-Amami, the locus falls on the final mora. The locus disappears from Proto-Amami to Proto-Okinawa, and the pitch accent becomes atonic in Proto-Okinawa, similar to the change in classes 1.1 and 1.2 from Proto-Yaeyama to Yonaguni. From Proto-Okinawa to Proto-Miyako, the changes are more complex. In Proto-Okinawa, class 1.3 is atonic, *oo. In (16), the pitch accent has a locus on the final mora in Proto-Miyako. As classes 1.1 and 1.3 in Proto-Miyako have merged, the locus in class 1.3 is assimilated to that in class 1.1, *_ooꜗ.[20] From Proto-Miyako to Proto-Yaeyama, there is no accent shift. From Proto-Yaeyama to Yonaguni, the locus disappears, and the pitch accent becomes atonic.

In (16), the phonetic elements also reveal certain patterns of accent shift. As phonetic elements account for low tone spreading, LHH(H) > LLH(H) for example (Shimabukuro 2007: 103), the spreading from the initial low tone to the following high tone is attested in class 1.3 from Proto-Amami to Proto-Okinawa. In Proto-Amami, the pitch accent is LH(L), and the pitch accent is LL(L) in Proto-Okinawa. Low tone in the first mora spreads rightward to the second mora,

---

17 From Proto-Amami to Proto-Okinawa, it seems that the pitch accent shifts rightward, *oo > *oꜗo, in classes 1.1 and 1.2. If the pitch accent for classes 1.1 and 1.2 in Proto-Amami is presented with locus, it would look like *(ꜗ)oo, in which the locus precedes the word. Therefore, the rightward accent shift should be *(ꜗ)oo > *oꜗo
18 Most pitch accent in Proto-Miyako is highly similar to that in Proto-Yaeyama in the data. Due to short geographical distance between Miyako and Yaeyama and frequent mutual communication, the pitch accent in Proto-Yaeyama resembles that in Proto-Miyako.
19 Rightward accent shift from Proto-Yaeyama to Yonaguni can be considered *⁻ooꜗ > *⁻oo(ꜗ). When the locus shifts rightward again, no mora can carry it, and thus the word becomes atonic.
20 Compared with the pitch accent in Proto-Yaeyama, the directionality of merger in Proto-Miyako should be that class 1.1 merges into class 1.3 rather than the opposite directionality.

leading LH(L) to LL(L). Similar spreading process is observed in class 1.3 from Proto-Yaeyama to Yonaguni.

In addition to rightward accent shift and low tone spreading, there is a significant phenomenon in (16). There is no register in Proto-Amami and Proto-Okinawa, while, regardless of high or low, register emerges in Proto-Miyako, Proto-Yaeyama, and Yonaguni. It is apparent that register is a significant feature that separates Northern Ryukyuan from Southern Ryukyuan.

3.2 Accent shift in disyllabic nouns

The disyllabic nouns in the five regions are compared in (17).[21]

(17) Comparison of pitch accent for disyllabic nouns

Myô	Proto-Amami	Proto-Okinawa	Proto-Miyako	Proto-Yaeyama	Yonaguni
2.1/2.2	*oo	*o⌉o	*⁻oo⌉	*⁻oo⌉	⁻oo
2.3/2.4/ 2.5 (a)	*oo⌉	*oo	*_oo⌉	*_oo⌉	_oo
2.3/2.4/ 2.5 (b)	*o⌉o	*oo⌉o	*oo	*oo	oo\
2.1/2.2	[HH(H)]	[HL(L)]	[HH(L)]	[HH(L)]	[LH(H)]/ [HH(H)]
2.3/2.4/ 2.5 (a)	[LH(L)]	[LL(L)]	[LH(L)]	[LH(L)]	[LL(L)]
2.3/2.4/ 2.5 (b)	[HL(L)]	[LHL(L)]	[LL(L)]	[LL(L)]	[LF ~ LH(H)]/ [HL ~HH(H)]

In classes 2.1 and 2.2, the accent is atonic in Proto-Amami, and the accent falls on the penultimate syllable in Proto-Okinawa. In Proto-Miyako and Proto-Yaeyama, the accent falls on the final syllable. Again, it is clear that accent shifts rightward from the penultimate syllable to the final syllable from Proto-Okinawa to Proto-Miyako. As Proto-Yaeyama and Proto-Miyako share similar accent, there is no accent shift. In Yonaguni, the locus disappears, and the pitch accent becomes atonic.

---

21 In disyllabic nouns, three classes 2.3/2.4/2.5 merge into one. Since there are two accent patterns for classes 2.3/2.4/2.5, I term the first type as 2.3/2.4/2.5 (a) and the second type as 2.3/2.4/2.5 (b) in (17).

In classes 2.3/2.4/2.5 (a), the accent of Proto-Amami falls on the final syllable, and that of Proto-Okinawa is atonic. The fact that the locus disappears in Proto-Okinawa suggests that rightward accent shift also takes place from Proto-Amami to Proto-Okinawa. The accent of Proto-Miyako and that of Proto-Yaeyama are *_OO˥ with a locus on the final syllable. In Yonaguni, the pitch accent is atonic. Likewise, there is rightward accent shift from Proto-Miyako/Proto-Yaeyama to Yonaguni.

Rightward accent shift also takes place in classes 2.3/2.4/2.5 (b). In Proto-Amami, the locus falls on the penultimate syllable. From Proto-Amami to Proto-Okinawa, the accent shifts rightward to final syllable, and it should be *OO˥. Nevertheless, the accent falls on the penultimate mora. In Proto-Okinawa, the first syllable in classes 2.3/2.4/2.5 (b) has two moras. The prolongation of the first syllable in classes 2.3/2.4/2.5 (b) in Proto-Okinawa motivates the accent to shift leftward to the heavy syllable. As Shimabukuro (2007: 186) suggests, *oo˥o is a revised version, and the previous form is *OO˥. When the previous form is taken into consideration, the rightward accent shift from Proto-Amami to Proto-Okinawa would look like *O˥O > *OO˥ (> *oo˥o). In Proto-Miyako/Proto-Yaeyama, the pitch accent is atonic, *OO. If the previous form of Proto-Okinawa in classes 2.3/2.4/2.5 (b) is *OO˥, it seems that there is rightward accent shift from Proto-Okinawa to Proto-Miyako. Again, the pitch accent in Proto-Yaeyama resembles that in Proto-Miyako. From Proto-Yaeyama to Yonaguni, the atonic accent turns into a falling tone, which is only observed in Yonaguni.

Low tone spreading is also observed in (17). It is only attested in classes 2.3/2.4/2.5 (a), especially from Proto-Amami to Proto-Okinawa and from Proto-Yaeyama to Yonaguni. In Proto-Amami and Proto-Yaeyama, the accent is LH(L), and in Proto-Okinawa and Yonaguni, the accent is LL(L). The low tone in the first syllable spreads to the second syllable, LH(L) > LL(L).

The distinction between Northern Ryukyuan and Southern Ryukyuan by register is also observed in (17). There is no register in Proto-Amami and Proto-Okinawa. Although there is register in Proto-Miyako, Proto-Yaeyama, and Yonaguni, the register is limited to classes 2.1/2.2 and 2.3/2.4/2.5 (a). Classes 2.3/2.4/2.5 (b) have no register.

4 Parallel development in monosyllabic and disyllabic nouns

The data in section 3 have shown the individual development in monosyllabic and disyllabic nouns in the Ryukyuan languages. In this section, I discuss the parallel development of accent shift in the Ryukyuan languages. If migration indeed interacts with accent shift, the monosyllabic and disyllabic nouns in the Ryukyuan languages should follow the same patterns in accent shift. There are two types of parallel development. The first type includes classes 1.1 and 1.2 and classes 2.1 and 2.2. The second type contains class 1.3 and classes 2.3/2.4/ 2.5 (a). Classes 2.3/2.4/2.5 (b) are independent of the parallel development.

Originally, there are three classes in *Myôgishô* for monosyllabic nouns. The three classes reduce to two classes in the Ryukyuan languages. Except for Proto-Miyako, classes 1.1 and 1.2 in the other four regions have merged. In Proto-Miyako, classes 1.1 and 1.3 have merged. The two accent patterns are compared in (18).

(18) Two accent patterns for monosyllabic nouns

	Proto-Amami	Proto-Okinawa	Proto-Miyako	Proto-Yaeyama	Yonaguni
I	*oo	*o⌐o	*⌐oo⌐	*⌐oo⌐	⌐oo
II	*oo⌐	*oo	*_oo⌐	*_oo⌐	_oo
I	[HH(H)]	[HL(L)]	[HH(L)]	[HH(L)]	[HH(H)]
II	[LH(L)]	[LL(L)]	[RH(L)]	[LH(L)]	[LL(L)]

Reproduced from (16)

As for disyllabic nouns, there are three accent patterns, as shown in (19).

(19) Three accent patterns for disyllabic nouns

	Proto-Amami	Proto-Okinawa	Proto-Miyako	Proto-Yaeyama	Yonaguni
I	*oo	*o⌐o	*⌐oo⌐	*⌐oo⌐	⌐oo
II	*oo⌐	*oo	*_oo⌐	*_oo⌐	_oo
III	*o⌐o	*oo⌐o	*oo	*oo	oo\
I	[HH(H)]	[HL(L)]	[HH(L)]	[HH(L)]	[LH(H)]/ [HH(H)]
II	[LH(L)]	[LL(L)]	[LH(L)]	[LH(L)]	[LL(L)]
III	[HL(L)]	[LHL(L)]	[LL(L)]	[LL(L)]	[LF ~LH(H)]/ [HL ~HH(H)]

Reproduced from (17)

The first parallel development in monosyllabic and disyllabic nouns (type I) is shown in (20).

(20) Parallel development in monosyllabic and disyllabic nouns (type I)

	Proto-Amami	Proto-Okinawa	Proto-Miyako	Proto-Yaeyama	Yonaguni
Mono I	*oo˥	*o˥o	*˗oo˥	*˗oo˥	˗oo
Disy I	*OO˥	*O˥O	*˗OO˥	*˗OO˥	˗OO
Mono I	[HH(H)]	[HL(L)]	[HH(L)]	[HH(L)]	[HH(H)]
Disy I	[HH(H)]	[HL(L)]	[HH(L)]	[HH(L)]	[LH(H)]/[HH(H)]

The data in (20) are consistent in register and locus. Proto-Amami lacks locus and register. In Proto-Okinawa, the locus falls on the penultimate mora/syllable. The accent falls on the final mora/syllable in Proto-Miyako and Proto-Yaeyama. In Yonaguni, there is no accent. In (20), Proto-Amami and Proto-Okinawa differ from Proto-Miyako, Proto-Yaeyama, and Yonaguni in register. As I have discussed in section 3, Northern Ryukyuan lacks register which, however, is a crucial prosodic feature in Southern Ryukyuan. As for phonetic elements, although Yonaguni has a variant in pitch accent, monosyllabic and disyllabic nouns also show a high degree of similarity.

Data in (21) illustrate the second parallel development in monosyllabic and disyllabic nouns (type II).

(21) Parallel development in monosyllabic and disyllabic nouns (type II)

	Proto-Amami	Proto-Okinawa	Proto-Miyako	Proto-Yaeyama	Yonaguni
Mono II	*oo˥	*oo	*_oo˥	*_oo˥	_oo
Disy II	*OO˥	*OO	*_OO˥	*_OO˥	_OO
Mono II	[LH(L)]	[LL(L)]	[RH(L)]	[LH(L)]	[LL(L)]
Disy II	[LH(L)]	[LL(L)]	[LH(L)]	[LH(L)]	[LL(L)]

In Proto-Amami, the locus falls on the final mora/syllable. In Proto-Okinawa, the pitch is atonic. In Proto-Miyako and Proto-Yaeyama, the pitch accent has low register and a locus on the final mora/syllable. In Yonaguni, the pitch accent is atonic. In (21), demarcation of Northern Ryukyuan and Southern Ryukyuan by using register is also observed. In Proto-Amami and Proto-Okinawa, there is no register; in Proto-Miyako, Proto-Yaeyama and Yonaguni, there is low register.

Although the phonetic elements in (21) are similar in monosyllabic and disyllabic nouns (type II), there is a discrepancy in Proto-Miyako. The pitch accent of monosyllabic nouns starts with a rising tone, whereas that in disyllabic nouns is a low tone. The rising tone in monosyllabic nouns could be analyzed as a combination of low and high tones, LLH(L). Hence, LLH(L) in monosyllabic nouns corresponds to LH(L) in disyllabic nouns.

5 Discussion

This section discusses two issues in the Ryukyuan languages. The first issue is whether prosodic changes reflect the directionality of migration in the Ryukyu archipelago. The second issue is concerned with two phonological phenomena: circular effect in the Ryukyuan languages and falling tone in Yonaguni.

5.1 Migration and prosodic changes

In sections 3 and 4, I have suggested that there is rightward accent shift from Amami to Yonaguni in monosyllabic and disyllabic nouns. The process of rightward accent shift roughly corresponds to the migration from north to south through the five regions in the Ryukyu archipelago. To account for the interaction between migration and prosodic changes, there are two ways of formulating rightward accent shift in the Ryukyuan languages. Suppose that there are four locations, A, B, C and D, and the starting point is location A with prosodic pattern x. From locations A to B, there is rightward accent shift, and the accent pattern is x-1 in location B. The accent pattern is x-2 in location C, and x-3 in location D. The first process is depicted in (22).

(22) Process of accent shift (I)

Locations	A	B	C	D
Rightward accent shift	x →	x-1 →	x-2 →	x-3

The second process is that location A is also the starting point, and its accent pattern is x. In location B, there is rightward accent shift, x-1. The accent pattern in location B is x-1, which simultaneously is y. That is to say, location B also functions as a baseline for location C. When rightward accent shift takes place from locations B to C, the accent pattern is y-1 (= z), which is also the baseline for location D, whose accent pattern is z-1. The second process is portrayed in (23).

(23) Process of accent shift (II)

Locations	A	B	C	D
Rightward	x ⟶	x-1		
accent		y ⟶	y-1	
shift			z ⟶	z-1

In this study, I do not adopt the sequential ordering in (22), since it assumes the locations to be in a continuum without any interruption.[22] Instead, I adopt the feeding order in (23). The accent pattern refers back to the previous stage, not to the original pattern in the starting point A. The process in (23) not only better accounts for accent shift in (20) for monosyllabic nouns but also partially elucidates accent shift in (21) for disyllabic nouns.

The process of rightward accent shift reveals two types of chains. A longer chain is in (20) from Proto-Okinawa to Yonaguni. The accent shift looks like *0˥0 > *00˥ > *00 (register is omitted here). This shift is also observed in disyllabic nouns (type III) in (19) from Proto-Amami to Proto-Miyako/Proto-Yaeyama. On the other hand, the rightward accent shift in (21) is a shorter chain, *00˥ > *00 (register is omitted here). The shift is observed from Proto-Amami to Proto-Okinawa and from Proto-Miyako/Proto-Yaeyama to Yonaguni. The two chains of rightward accent shift are summarized in (24).

(24) Two chains of rightward accent shift

a. Longer chain		*0˥0 >	*00˥ >	*00
	Mono and Disy (type I)	Okinawa	Miyako/Yaeyama	Yonaguni
	Disy (type III)	Amami	Okinawa	Miyako/Yaeyama
b. Shorter chain			*00˥ >	*00
	Mono and Disy (type II)		Amami	Okinawa
			Miyako/Yaeyama	Yonaguni

---

22 The process in (22) suggests a strict linear movement from Amami to Yonaguni, corresponding to the tree in footnote 15. The accent shift in (22) has to refer back to the starting point, that is, Amami. On the other hand, the process in (23) does not necessarily refer back to the starting point. In (23), what significantly matters is the previous stage that the following changes have to stick to.

The two chains in (24) clearly reveal that directionality of migration in the Ryukyu archipelago is from north to south, but it is not strictly linear as in Amami → Okinawa → Miyako → Yaeyama → Yonaguni. Pellard (2015: 25–26) has discussed the migration and diversification in the Ryukyuan languages, and a strict linear migration from north to south is not accepted because this directionality does not conform to the fact that there are Northern Ryukyuan and Southern Ryukyuan. I agree with Pellard's argument that it is less likely to follow a strict linear migration, but southward migration in the Ryukyu archipelago is beyond doubt. The rightward accent shift always initiates in a more northern region and ends in a more southern region.

5.2 Circular effect in the Ryukyuan languages and falling tone in Yonaguni

The rightward accent shift in the Ryukyuan languages also involves a circular effect and the emergence of falling tone in Yonaguni. As I have briefly discussed in section 3, the changes of pitch accent in the Japonic languages follow an ordering: atonic (either high-level, low-level, or final-high atonic) > initial-accent (i.e., HLL) > second-syllable accent (either LHL or HHL) > final-accent (either LHH(L) or LHH(L)) > initial- and final-high (i.e., LHL) > atonic. The classes 1.1 and 1.2 and classes 2.1 and 2.2 best illustrate the circle effect in rightward accent shift. First, Proto-Amami is atonic, and Proto-Okinawa is initially accented. In Proto-Miyako and Proto-Yaeyama, the pitch accent falls on the second syllable (or final mora/syllable). Finally, the circle completes in Yonaguni, as the accent becomes atonic again. (25) shows the circle of accent shift for monosyllabic and disyllabic nouns (type I) in (20).

(25) Accent shift in a circle in the Ryukyuan languages

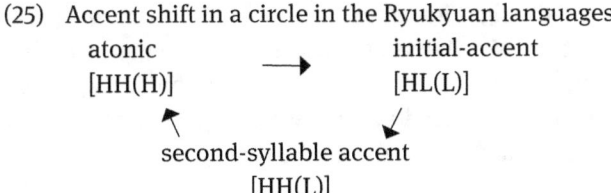

The data in the Ryukyuan languages suggests that there is a circle, as the change starts from atonic and ends in atonic. Whether the accent changes continue remains unknown, nevertheless. When the pitch accent returns to the initial stage, will the next stage be initial-accent again? If the accent shift follows the circle in (25), the initial accent should be attested after the pitch accent becomes atonic. Here, I suggest that the falling tone in Yonaguni provides evidence for the circular effect. The falling tone in Yonaguni consists in classes 2.3/2.4/2.5 (b). As illustrated in (26), the rightward accent shift starts from the second syllable in Proto-Amami. The accent shift renders final accent in Proto-Okinawa, and the first syllable is prolonged. In Proto-Miyako and Proto-Yaeyama, the accent becomes atonic. Until this stage, the process can be accounted for by the circle in (25).

(26) Falling tone in Yonaguni in disyllabic nouns (type III)

	Proto-Amami	Proto-Okinawa	Proto-Miyako	Proto-Yaeyama	Yonaguni
III	*o]o	*oo]o	*oo	*oo	oo\
III	[HL(L)]	[LHL(L)]	[LL(L)]	[LL(L)]	[LF ~LH(H)]/ [HL ~HH(H)]

In (26), accents in Proto-Miyako and Proto-Yaeyama are atonic. If there is no further accent shift, the pitch accent for classes 2.3/2.4/2.5 (b) in Yonaguni should be similar to that in Proto-Yaeyama. Accent shift continues, and a falling tone emerges in Yonaguni. I suggest that from Proto-Yaeyama to Yonaguni, the classes 2.3/2.4/2.5 (b) also follow the circle in (25). Due to the fact that the pitch accent in Proto-Yaeyama has been atonic, the accent returns to initial-accent (HLL) in Yonaguni.

The process in (27) illustrates how a falling tone emerges in Yonaguni. According to the data in (14) where there are two outputs in Yonaguni, HL or LF, the alignment of HL is determined by syllable structure (cf. Yamada, Pellard and Shimoji's (2015) syllable weight), and the directionality of accent alignment. Aligning HL with the first syllable from the right leads to the proper outputs in Yonaguni. When a disyllabic noun has two CV syllables, the accent HL is aligned with the syllable from the right. On the other hand, when the disyllabic word is $CV_1.V_2$, the accent HL is not associated with the second syllable which is comprised of only one vowel. Instead, the accent HL is associated with the first syllable.

(27)		a.	b.
Proto-Yaeyama		[L L(L)]	[L L(L)]
↓				
	initial-accent	HL	HL
Yonaguni		LF	HL
Examples		huni\ 'bone'	hai\ 'needle'

In (27a), when HL is aligned with the first CV syllable from the right, the output is LF (=L(HL)). When HL is aligned with the other CV syllable as in (27b), the output is HL. The process in (27) suggests that the circular effect in the change of pitch accent is possible, depending on the alignment of HL accent in a phonological word.

6 Conclusion

In summary, I have discussed accent shift in monosyllabic and disyllabic nouns in the Ryukyuan languages: Amami, Okinawa, Miyako, Yaeyama, and Yonaguni. The data suggest that migration and prosodic changes indeed interact. The migration should be from north to south; the accent shifts from left to right. When the early settlers move gradually from north to south in the Ryukyu archipelago, the accent shifts rightward to next mora/syllable. Nevertheless, the migration does not follow a strict linear order.

In this study, I have analyzed monosyllabic and disyllabic nouns, and they do not develop separately. The rightward accent shift is best presented in the classes 1.1/1.2 and classes 2.1/2.2. The rightward accent shift is also observed in class 1.3 and classes 2.3/2.4/2.5 (a). Even in classes 2.3/2.4/2.5 (b), rightward accent shift is attested. As the monosyllabic and disyllabic nouns can be stacked together, I have formulated a process for rightward accent shift in the Ryukyuan languages, following an ordering that the previous stage feeds the next stage, e.g. x → x-1 (=y) → y-1, instead of a process referring back to the starting point (x → x-1 → x-2). This process maximally accounts for monosyllabic and disyllabic nouns in the Ryukyuan languages and provides solid support for the interaction of migration and prosodic changes. In addition to the rightward accent shift, I have discussed the demarcation between Northern Ryukyuan and Southern Ryukyuan. Northern Ryukyuan lacks register in its pitch accent, whereas register is crucial in Southern Ryukyuan.

Finally, the rightward accent shift in monosyllabic and disyllabic nouns in the Ryukyuan languages not only shows a continuous process but also forms a circle that starts and ends in atonic. The circular effect has a significant implication for the development of prosody, tone and pitch accent in particular. Hirayama (2005: 289) also has hypothesized a circular effect for Chinese tones following the development 55 > 53 > 51 > 31 > 11 > 13 > 35 > 55 (cf. Matisoff 2001).[23]

---

[23] This is a traditional way of marking tones in Chinese phonology by using numbers: 5 as the highest pitch and 1 as the lowest. For example, 55 is a high level tone, 53 is a high falling tone, and 13 is a low rising tone.

Although Chinese and the Japonic languages are essentially different in prosody, the circular effect in the two language families resembles in the lowering patterns. The change always starts from high level tone 55 or high pitch without locus HH, and then the pitch gradually lowers, generating falling tones, until reaching the lowest. The lowest pitch bounces and turns into rising tones. The pitch again returns to high level. The circular effect in East Asian languages leaves a window open to tonogenesis, and more data are needed for the future research.

References

Bentley, John. 2008. *A Linguistic history of the forgotten islands: A reconstruction of the proto-language of the southern Ryukyus*. London: Global Oriental Publishers.
Blust, Robert. 1988. The Austronesian homeland: A linguistic perspective. *Asian Perspectives* 26 (1). 45–67.
Chiang, Min-hua. 2003. *Kegan fangyan guanxi yanjiu* [On the relationships between Hakka and Gan]. Taipei: National Taiwan University dissertation.
Dixon, R.M.W. 1997. *The rise and fall of languages*. Cambridge: Cambridge University Press.
Dyen, Isidore. 1956. Language distribution and migration theory. *Language* 32 (4). 611–626.
Google Maps. 2018. Google Maps. Available at: https://www.google.com/maps/ @27.4918264,127.6068882,7z [Accessed May 22, 2018].
Hirayama, Hisao. 2005. Hanyu shengdiao qiyuan kuitan [An invespection of the origin of Chinese tones]. In *Pingshan jiuxiong yuyanxue ruwenji* [A collection of linguistics papers by Hisao Hirayama], 288–301. Beijing: The Commercial Press.
Hirayama, Teruo. 1992. *Gendai nihongo hogen daijiten* [A dictionary of modern Japanese dialects]. Tokyo: Meiji.
Hokama, Shuzen. 1977. Okinawa no gengo to sono rekishi [Okinawan and its history]. In Ono susumu & Shibata Takeshi (eds.), *Nihongo 11: Hogen* [Japanese 11: Dialects], 181–233. Tokyo: Iwanami.
Lawrence, Wayne. 2009. The tone system of Proto-Northern-Ryukyuan nouns - a proposal. *Okinawa Bunka* (106). 1–17.
Lawrence, Wayne. 2016. Historical reanalysis in the Nakijin dialect noun accentuation system. *Cahiers de linguistique asie orientale*, 45 (1), 1–25.
LaPolla, Randy J. 2001. The role of migration and language contact in the development of the Sino-Tibetan language family. In Alexandra Y. Aikhenvald & R.M.W. Dixon (eds.), *Areal diffusion and genetic inheritance: Problems in comparative linguistics*, 225–254. Oxford: Oxford University Press.
Lewis, M. Paul (ed.), 2009. *Ethnologue: Languages of the World*, Sixteenth edition. Dallas, Texas: SIL International.
Matisoff, James. 2001. Genetic vs. contact relationship: prosodic diffusibility in South-East Asian languages. In Alexandra Y. Aikhenvald & R.M.W. Dixon (eds.), *Areal Diffusion and Genetic Inheritance: problems in comparative linguistics*, 291–327. Oxford: Oxford University Press.

Matsumori, Akiko. 2001. Historical tonology of Japanese dialects. In Shigeki Kaji (ed.), *Proceedings of the symposium cross-linguistic studies of tonal phenomena*, 93–122.
Matsumori, Akiko. 2015. Minami-Ryūkyū no sankei akusento taikei: sono inritsu tani ni kansuru kousatsu [Three-pattern accentual systems in Southern Ryukyuan and their prosodic unit]. *Departmental Bulletin Study of College of Humanities at Japan Women's University* 64. 55–92.
Matsumori, Akiko. 2016. Seichō gengo toshi no Miyako sogo [Tone language and Proto-Miyako]. In Yukinori Takubo, John Whitman & Tatsuya Hirako (eds.), *Ryūkyū shogoto kodai Nihongo* [The Ryukyuan languages and Old Japanese], 149–169. Tokyo: Kuroshio shuppan.
Minkova, Donka. 2006. Old and Middle English prosody. In Ans van Kemenade & Bettelou Los (eds.), *The handbook of the history of English*, 95–125. Cambridge, MA: Blackwell.
Minkova, Donka. 2013. Reconstructing stress in Old and Middle English. In Manfred Krug & Julia Schlüter (eds.), *Research methods in language variation and change*, 260–278. Cambridge: Cambridge University Press.
Nakamoto, Masachie. 1976. *Ryūkyū hōgen on'in no kenkyu* [A study of Ryukyuan phonology]. Tokyo: Hosei Daigaku Shuppankyoku.
Nakasone, Seizen. 1987. *Ryūkyū hōgen no kenkyū* [A study of the Ryukyuan dialects]. Tokyo: Shinsensha.
Pellard, Thomas. 2016. Nichi-ryū sogo no bunki nendai [The date of separation of the Proto-Japonic language]. In Yukinori Takubo, John Whitman & Hirako Tatsuya (eds.), *Ryūkyū shogoto kodai Nihongo* [The Ryukyuan languages and Old Japanese], 99–124. Tokyo: Kuroshio shuppan.
Pellard, Thomas. 2015. The linguistic archeology of the Ryukyu islands. In Heinrich, Patrick, Shinsho Miyara & Michinori Shimoji (eds.), *Handbook of the Ryukyuan languages: history, structure and use*, 13–37. Berlin: De Gruyter Mouton.
Serafim, Leon. 2003. When and from where did the Japonic language enter the Ryukyus? A critical comparison of language, archaeology, and history. In Osada, Toshiki & Alexander Vovin (eds.), *Perspectives on the origins of the Japanese language*, 463–476. Kyoto: Shobundo.
Shimabukuro, Moriyo. 2007. *The accentual history of the Japanese and Ryukyuan languages: A reconstruction*. London: Global Oriental Publishers.
Thorpe, Maner. 1983. *Ryûkyûan language history*. Los Angeles, CA: University of Southern California dissertation.
Tōjō, Misao. 1951. *Zenkoku hogen jiten* [A dictionary of Japanese dialects]. Tokyo: Tokyodo.
Uemura, Yukio. 1963. *Okinawago jiten* [Okinawan dictionary]. Tokyo: National Institute for Japanese Language and Linguistics.
Uwano, Zendo. 2012. Accent in some Kikai-jima dialects of Ryukyuan with particular reference to nouns in central and southern dialects. *Gengo Kenkyu* 142: 45–76.
Yamada, Masahiro, Thomas Pellard & Michinori Shimoji. 2015. Dunan grammar (Yonaguni Ryukyuan). In Heinrich, Patrick, Shinsho Miyara & Michinori Shimoji (eds.), *Handbook of the Ryukyuan languages: history, structure, and use*, 449–478. Berlin: De Gruyter Mouton.

Hsin-yen Chen and I-wen Su

3 Textual patterns of modern western paintings: A cognitive multimodal exploration

Abstract: This study investigates the textual patterns of a specific multimodal genre, modern western paintings. Specifically, we focus on the examination of the textual flow, or textual directionality, of a spectrum of modern painting categories.

The textual directionality of multimodal texts is discussed notably in Kress and van Leeuwen's (2006) 'Visual Grammar' extended from Halliday (1994), which mainly centered on commercial and applied materials. To fill the gap, we analyze the non-commercial and more autonomous case of modern western paintings, serving to see if they too follow what is proposed in the Visual Grammar. Our data comprise of 90 nonrepresentational modern western paintings ranging from the figurative to the abstract, created by 3 representative artists between 1920 to1980. Painting titles and pictorial contents were co-examined in our multimodal practice.

According to Kress and van Leeuwen (2006), painting compositions generally follow the information structure: The given information resides at the left and the new at the right, in alignment with the left-to-right writing directionality of western languages. In our finding, most figurative paintings indeed display a textual pattern dictated by Information values, determined by both linguistic and visual cues. Nonetheless, such informational pattern declines sharply in semi-figurative paintings, and could not be identified in abstract paintings. Instead, the textual directionality of semi-abstract and abstract paintings is influenced by principles of Diagrammatic Iconicity (Hiraga 2005), a textual pattern less examined to materials outside of language.

Our results brought out what is unseen in previous studies. Information structure can differentiate artistic visuals from other types of visual materials. In addition, Diagrammatic Iconicity influences the textual directionality of all styles of modern paintings sampled.

Keywords: Textual pattern, Textual directionality, Multimodality, Modern paintings, Information structure, Iconicity

---

Hsin-yen Chen and I-wen Su, National Taiwan University

https://doi.org/10.1515/9783110610895-010

1 Introduction

The documentation of linguistic data, pictorial data and the combination of the two – multimodal data – all involve the arrangement of the textual elements within the flat, smooth, two-dimensional text space, such as on papers or on digital screens. As Halliday (1994) proposes a generally left-to-right linguistic textual flow, some have asked whether pictures or multimodal texts contain similar pattern.

For instance, Arnheim (1969) claimed that many western paintings (including but not limited to modern ones) display a heavier left visual weighting, which may be related to the fact that our visual-dominant hemisphere resides at the right. Consequently, the left eye starts the image-scanning/producing most of the time, resulting in the left-weighting. The left-weighting creates, in turn, the psychological impression that images progress from the more "important" left, to the right.

The left-to-right inclination is also credited with other possible mechanisms (Karim and Kojima 2010; Gardner 2011). Inspired by Halliday (1994), Kress and van Leeuwen indicates that such phenomenon is related to the common Information value of most Western cultures. In Kress and van Leeuwen's (2006) 'Visual Grammar', visual compositions are claimed to be generally following the information structure similar to that of linguistic grammar: the given information resides at the left and the new at the right, in alignment with the left-to-right writing directionality of Western languages, as shown in Figure 1:

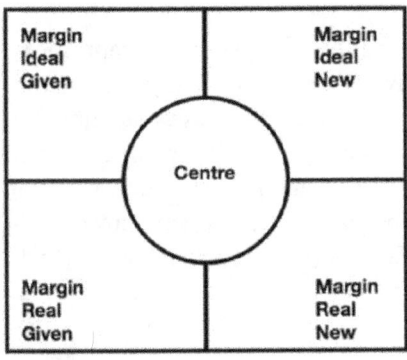

Figure 1: Kress and van Leeuwen (2006).

Put simply, Kress and van Leeuwen's diagram (Figure 1) predicts the general textual composition of visual materials in the context of Western cultures. From the left to the right, there is a pattern of Given to New; from the top to the bottom, there is a pattern of Ideal to Real. It is claimed that a Given-New information pattern could be observed across most Western visuals, postulated to be influenced by the writing-directionality in most Western languages, following Halliday's view. Usually, there would be a left-placing of Given information, while the more "surprising", unexpected information featured at the right, and labeled as the New. The circle in the diagram stands for the sometimes centralized visual focus observed. Kress and van Leeuwen claimed that a centralized visual composition would still follow the overall tendency suggested by this diagram, which is exclusively designed for the two-dimensional nature of pictoriality.

Besides the criteria of Ideal-Real and Given-New, which are based on *Information value*s of in-text pictorial areas, Kress and van Leeuwen mentioned two alternative principles which also play a role in influencing visual compositions: *Saliency* and *Framing*. While Saliency refers to the perceptually salient qualities of a visual, which is often created by stronger contrast in color, tone, size or sharpness of pictorial parts (Kress and van Leeuwen 2006), Framing refers to the compositional separation of textual areas, which is an important feature of applied visual layouts.

Kress and van Leeuwen's (2006) model, though inspiring, is based on an observation of mixed visual genres, ranging from composite pictorials (e.g., magazine layouts, films, photography, picture books), to single pictorials (e.g., paintings, graphic designs, and advertisements). The visual genre of fine art has in fact not been systematically examined, let alone the highly avant-garde and expressive modern paintings which are "nonrepresentational" (Donald 2006; Luhmann 2000), often more theoretical than mimetic, and rich in expressive freedom as well as autonomy.

In order to fill the gap, we investigate the textual flow of nonrepresentational modern western paintings in this study. We would like to explore whether the spectrum of paintings selected follow a directionality flow, as claimed in Kress and van Leeuwen (2006)'s Visual Grammar. Specifically, we will focus on the textual flow by following the left-to-right Information structure, omitting the more subtle distinction of upper-left, upper-right, lower-left and lower-right (Figure 1). The interrelated compositional factors (Saliency and Framing) will not be discussed in detail in this study for the sake of space limitations.

2 Data selection

Pure reality-simulative artworks, in which the creative intention is mainly to capture external scenery or real-world referents, are excluded from our present study. Only nonrepresentational paintings are included as our data, in which the creative intention does not center on faithfully copying the visible world, but with the depicted content created via free association rather than from actual scenery.

Our data consists of 90 nonrepresentational modern Western paintings from the 20th century, including the spectrum (Arnheim 1969) of figurative paintings (paintings that the viewers can easily identify and name the painted elements within), semi-figurative paintings (paintings with identifiable objects, but partly abstracted), and abstract paintings (paintings without real-world depiction, achieving beauty only using colors, textures and shapes). The inclusion of all styles of paintings ensures a comprehensive data pool. We expect the three-group sampling to bring forth possible cross-group comparisons of compositional principles. Each sampling group contains paintings created by one specifically representative painter. For the quality of the data, the sampled paintings are all created by productive painters, selected out of chronological painting albums, and excluding representational pieces, sketches, prints, sculptures, or other miscellaneous pieces. Finally, the amount of samples (30 of each category) is balanced in accordance with the average numbers of paintings sampled in each selected painting albums.

The figurative nonrepresentational group features paintings that are figurative in style and nonrepresentational in intention (the painted events mainly created via free association rather than copying the external world, as noted). Thirty paintings by the Spanish artist Dali are sampled under this category.

The semi-figurative group consists of paintings that are semi-figurative in style, in which the intention of abstraction does not cancel out the identifiable semantics of the depicted items, and the pictorial items still reflect the meaning of the depicted to some degrees. Being somewhat abstracted and nonrepresentational in intention, they demand more "reading" effort. Thirty paintings by another Spanish artist Miro are chosen for this category. While arranging non-abstract elements like human, animals, stars and birds, Miro would almost always simplify these elements. His artistic elements became so abstracted in form and nonrepresentational in intention, that they became sign-like (Corbella 1993). Note that for the sampling of semi-abstract paintings that are nonrepresentational, possible candidates still include artwork done by Cubists, for instance Picasso. However, in his artwork, even if the depicted objects are abstracted and transformed, deliberately flattened till they stuck between figurativeness and mere abstraction, real-world representations are still involved. To be able to select paintings that are most generative and autonomous in expressive processes, we exclude these pictures.

Lastly, the abstract group consists of thirty paintings by the American artist Pollock. Pollock's art pieces are selected due to their impromptus nature known as "action painting". The "forms" in these paintings stand for the visual pleasure they arouse rather than actual concrete referents. His paintings are abstract in style in the sense that the viewers cannot identify nor name any of the pictorial elements. Being nonrepresentational in intention, they do not mimic the real-world objects.

3 Analysis of Information value

Adopting Kress and van Leeuwen's (2006) model, we examine whether the currently sampled paintings display a general textual pattern. In the beginning of our examination, the titles of selected paintings are studied. Second, the New information zones are identified and marked (with the help of the title cues) within the paintings. Finally, we conduct a statistical counting according to our results.

Our investigation is presented in 3.1(figuratve samples), 3.2 (semi-figurative samples) and 3.3 (abstract samples).

3.1 Information value in figurative paintings

The textual pattern dictated by Information value turns out to be highly applicable in the figurative paintings sampled.

As a vivid example, the left side of the *The persistence of memory* (Figure 2) consists of three clocks placing side-by-side, while the right part features an unusual horse-like face (or a face-like horse), with a clock on it. The elongated "horse" form contrasts the more static scenery at the left, extending to the right of the picture, matching the time-extension concept expressed in the title. With the more conceptual and more dynamic area at the right, this arrangement attunes with the "left is Given, right is New" pattern reported (Kress and van Leeuwen 2006). Thus, we identify the New information zone at the right half of this painting, as circled in Figure 2.

3.2 Information value in semi-figurative paintings

In semi-figurative samples, however, we seldom find the principle of Information value applied. For instance, in *Characters in the night*, the title suggests three characters, a bird, and three pictorial signs for "stars" in Miro's invented art

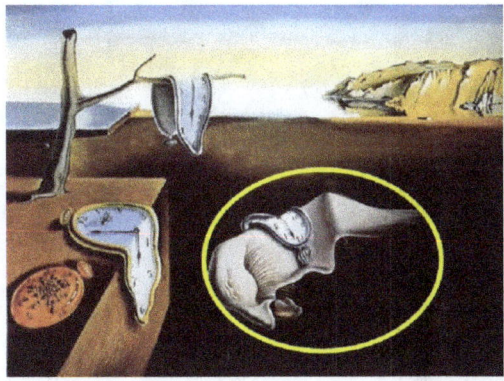

Figure 2: New information zone for *The persistence of memory*.
Note: Salvador Dalí. *The Persistence of Memory*. 1931. Oil on canvas, 9 1/2 x 13" (24.1 x 33 cm). Museum of Modern Art (MoMA), New York City, NY, US. Fair use image taken from https://www.wikiart.org.

language (Corbella 1993). However, no obvious action is seen in this painting, as the picture expresses a state, rather than an event. Hence, no obvious "punch line" or New information zone can be identified in this painting. Put simply, the mostly discussed compositional principle in Kress and van Leeuwen (2006), Information value, fails to apply to this painting and many other semi-figurative samples.

What stands as the hint on reading this picture, instead, is the easy-to-spot visual focus, or Gestalt zone, at the left side of this picture, a huge human figure in its noticeable biggest size, hintly "framed" by two eye-catching red areas. As we start from the large Gestalt (circled in Figure 3), the bright whiteness in the painting-plate next to it smoothly transits our attention to the rhythm created by the white zones changing in size and angles. Our eyes could follow the white zones while reading the painting, though not necessarily with any fixed directionality, for the white zones form a dynamic circulation within the frame (circled in dotted lines).

Despite the non-applicability of Information value, the more eye-catching or stronger visual elements in multimodal texts validate Kress and van Leeuwen's (2006) compositional principle of Saliency. The big Gestalt in Figure 3 is a good example. The noticeable sized figure lands at the left, and the bright color-contrast white parts are arranged at the right.

Thus, in this painting group, the principle of Saliency, though not determining enough in fixating certain directionality, starts to outshine the principle of Information value in determining the flow directionality of paintings.

Figure 3: Saliency zone for *Characters in the night* (Miro).
Note: Joan Miró. *Characters in the Night*. 1931. Oil on canvas, 62 x 80 cm. Private Collection, New York City, NY, US. Fair use image taken from https://www.wikiart.org.

3.3 Information value in abstract paintings

In abstract paintings, similar phenomena are observed: Information value does not serve as a useful criterion for the textual flow of the paintings. Meanwhile, the alternative principle that hints possible reading paths of an abstract painting is the compositional principle of Saliency in Kress and van Leeuwen (2006).

As an example, in *Convergence* (Figure 4), the title adds more emphasis to such a process, in which the most salient dynamics of Gestalt size and color contrasts attract our eyes more easily (circled in Figure 4): this area is arranged

Figure 4: Saliency zone for *Convergence*.
Note: Jackson Pollock. *Convergence*. 1952. Oil on canvas, 393.7 x 237.5 cm. Albright-Knox Art Gallery, Buffalo, NY, US. Fair use image taken from https://www.wikiart.org.

with the largest amount of bright red and bright yellow, which are the colors with highest saturation in this painting. We may more easily "travel" along the visual-perceptual rhythm (circled in dotted lines) created by also salient, bright-toned white lines, wandering about in the painting-frame, because the white "oval" they imply stands out in the grayer-toned background.

4 Results

According to our analyses, what is found so far contrasts the observed in Kress and van Leeuwen (2006). The main difference lies in the low-applicability of Information value as the textual principle of nonrepresentational modern paintings. In our data, the samples do not rely on Information value as the determining factor of compositional directionality. Figurative paintings featured the most instances of Information value applicants, while this feature is almost absent to paintings in the semi-figurative, and completely non-applicable in the abstract group.

To better illustrate the inapplicability of Information value in our data, a visualization of the recorded instances of New information zones among all 90 paintings is shown in Figure 5:

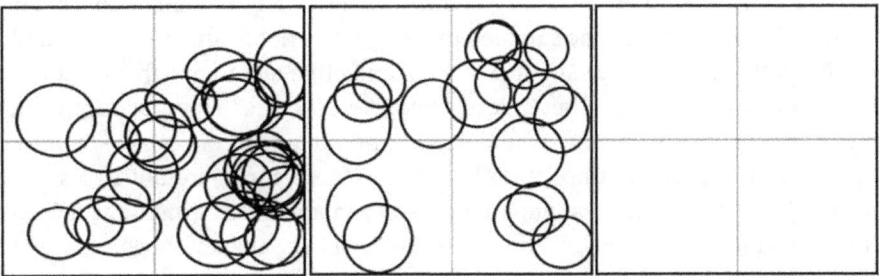

Figure 5: New information zones in figurative, semi-figurative, and abstract samples (left to right).

In the figurative group, the circles representing the New zones remain bountiful. In the semi-figurative case, the applicability of Information value drops, as only 18 paintings could be analyzed according to Information value. Finally, in the abstract group, no sign of Information value could be found.

Our findings so far illustrate what is unseen in the Visual Grammar of Kress and van Leeuwen (2006). In their model, as reviewed, there is a mixture of visual genres, and a methodology involving mostly commercial graphics. This could explain why the textuality of nonrepresentational modern Western paintings does not entirely follow the Visual Grammar, and that modern paintings remain a special category when compared to comics, advertisements, photography and other multimodal texts.

More importantly, the compositional principle of Saliency better outlines the reading paths of the current data. That is, the textual directionality of modern paintings is highly in accordance with the arrangement of visual-perceptual cues, alternative to the dominance of Information value in linguistic grammar (Halliday 1990; 1994) and the applied visual layouts (Kress and van Leeuwen 2006).

5 An alternative view

Meanwhile, Saliency, though helpful, not yet determines a certain textual directionality of paintings, as shown in 3.2 and 3.3. The determinacy of painting flow compositions still requires alternative principles, other than Information value or Saliency alone. We propose here that Saliency (Kress and van Leeuwen 2006) serves as *the basis* for the structural grammar of paintings, rather than as *the grammar itself*, since it does not provide further clue in determining textual directionality.

In fact, we have found that to form a directional textual flow often involves two in-text zones, one formed vaguely by the principle of Saliency (as shown in Figure 2 to 4); the other, by contrast, often opposing to the Salient zones, and lands at the right parts of the sampled paintings. The rightward areas are usually featured with less visually salient elements, and often featured with more space, a relief of visual tension. These "less compacted corners" may not surprise us immediately as the New zones would do, but they do attract our eyes to their less typical existence in paintings. In other words, these zones are not necessarily essential in newsworthiness, but are necessary in appearance, marking a finale of the viewing path initiated by the more eye-catching Saliency zones.

Unique in both form and textual status, such textual mechanism meets the definition of form-meaning alignment, or the grammatical iconicity of "Markeness" in Hiraga's (2005) model. We could illustrate the marked zones here using the very examples back in 3.1 to 3.3 (Figure 6 to 8). Note that in Figure 6, the marked zone overlaps the New information zone discussed: the "fading" horse is comparatively "marked" in the painting comparing to other more enclosed, or more "finished" pictorial outlines in the painting. However, the marked zone is not always protruding in semanticity, as noted before. This is evidenced by the non-applicable Information structure identification in 3.2 and 3.3, and the successful identification of marked zones in Figure 7 and 8.

Textual patterns of modern western paintings — **269**

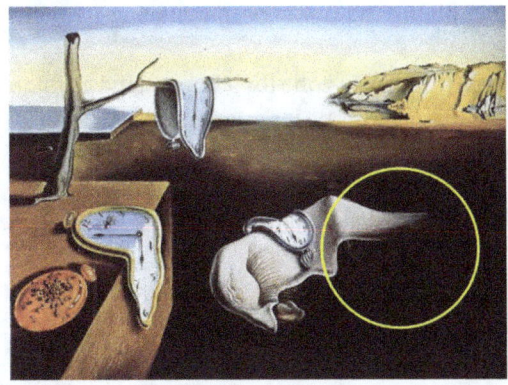

Figure 6: Marked zone for *The persistence of memory*.

Figure 7: Marked zone for *Characters in the night*.

Figure 8: Marked zone for *Convergence*.

In Figure 7, the marked zone is identified because of its visual form – it is the biggest area of color minority, green and blue, of the painting (as the majority painted by red, white and black), marking the end point of the curved visual vector, as if a special textual device implying the finale of the viewing path circulation.

Similarly, in Figure 8, we identified the marked zone for it is arranged right on the bright-colored oral of white and yellow, but in the largest amount of minority color choice of the painting – blue, its uniqueness emphasized by a black spot within. The moment we notice this seemingly unimportant unusualness, our viewing path could rest there, as a less condensed visual zone also accompanies this spot.

The following (Figure 9) displays our manually analyzed instances of both the Saliency zones and the "marked" areas mentioned. Again, each circle represents an instance spotted in the approximate location in its painting-plate represented by a square (following Figure 1). There are a total of 30 circles in each of the three squares standing for the figurative to the abstract grouping:

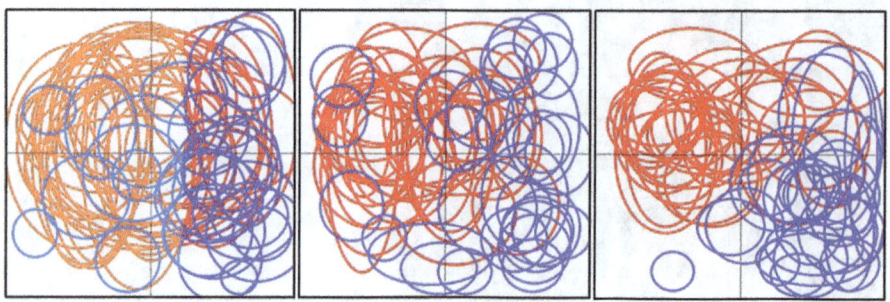

Figure 9: Patterns of Saliency (red) and Marked (blue) in the figurative, semi-figurative, and abstract samples (left to right).

According to this visualization of analysis, it could be observed that the salient zones almost always fall at the left of the paintings in all styles. In addition, the zones that opposing other in-painting elements, which are not default but marked in form and textual meaning, almost always fall at the right of the paintings.

If we consider the psychological impact of Saliency, which is already hinted in Kress and van Leeuwen (2006), it is exactly what attracts our attention easily. It is thus reasonable that the Saliency areas serve as the textual on-sets of nonrepresentational modern paintings, which are regularly arranged at the right.

Our observation further implies a holistic pattern of nonrepresentational modern painting textuality: The Saliency zones serve as the "attention-attracter" of a painting-text. Meanwhile, the visually-marked zones help direct viewer attention to the right of a painting, ending the general viewing flow of the text, and sometimes back to the focus (salient) zone, but less likely the reversed directionality.

The textual patterns of the painting discussed are structurally orchestrated by the collaboration of both visual features and textual functions. Such form-meaning alignments are analogical and grammatical in nature, not simply semantic-based (*i.e.*, Information value) or purely perceptual-based (per Saliency in Kress and van Leeuwen 2006). The systematic form-meaning alignments meet the definition of Grammatical Iconicity in Hiraga (2005), which is a kind of Diagrammatic Iconicity (Nanny and Fischer 1999). Kress and van Leeuwen's Saliency principle, contrastingly, could be said to be a kind of Imagistic Iconicity.

Pierce (1955) defined iconicity as "a continuum of abstractness" formed by the most perceptually-based Imagistic Iconicity, then Diagrammatic Iconicity, finally the most abstract, Metaphors. Hiraga (2005) extends Pierce's notion in her model of grammatical iconicity, exploring further the structural alignment of textual form and textual meaning. The Saliency zones are the parts where the quantity of form systematically accords with its quality (importance) in texts. The Marked zones are the parts that the specific textual arrangements of less-salient zones mark the ending of paintings. The two phenomena, validating Hiraga's Digrammatic Iconicity model, have transcended the most concrete, perceptual level in Pierce's (1955) definition, surpassing to the level of textual pattern.

We have highlighted how the salient and marked aspects of Grammatical Iconicity determine the textual directionality of the current visual corpus. It has outshined the principle of Information value, and directs the textual flow of the paintings from the left (salient form-meaning alignments) to the right (marked form-meaning alignments), forming the generally left-to-right directionality pattern (Figure 10):

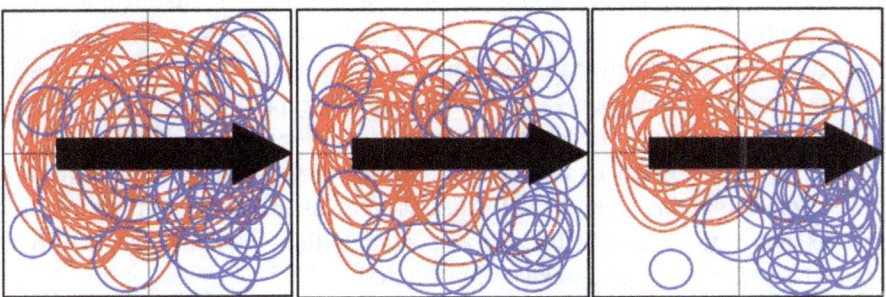

Figure 10: Textual directionality formed by Diagrammatic Iconicity in the figurative, semi-figurative, and abstract samples (left to right).

Diagrammatic Iconicity contrasts Imagistic Iconicity, which merely follows the principles of mimicry. Freeman (2009:172–173) comments that "when diagram takes on the characteristics of image, then iconicity at the more abstract level happens". Through our examination, the principles of Diagrammatic Iconicity, aside from the reported Imagistic Iconicity, serves as the composition principle in the selected paintings.

Our findings, though conforming to the Saliency principle at an Imagistic Iconicity level, further verify the existence of a more abstracted level of Diagrammatic Iconicity. Based on the methodology adopted here, modern paintings could be viewed as a visual genre strongly in favor of structural iconicity stemming from the interplay of form and meaning.

6 Concluding remarks

In this study, we have demonstrated and showed the value of a cognitive multimodal approach in analyzing nonrepresentational modern Western paintings. The selected 90 samples paintings, ranging from the figurative, the semi-figurative, and the abstract, display a high percentage of Diagrammatic Iconicity. Moreover, a textual directionality from left to right could be well observed, regularly structured by the form-meaning iconicity of Saliency and Markedness. The two instantiations of grammatical iconicity co-create a vectoring of textual directionality in all picture-plates, which compensates for the failed principle of Information value in more abstract paintings.

Diagrammatic Iconicity, which is structural in essence, serves as a powerful descriptive criterion for the structuring principles of nonrepresentational modern Western paintings. In addition to the reported "firstness" of Imagistic Iconicity, this study contributes to the revelation of the abstract Diagrammatical iconicity as a structuring textual pattern of nonrepresentational Modern Western paintings. A left-to-right directionality is shown to be generally determined by aspects of Diagrammatic Iconicity, regardless of its painting type.

Due to the scope of this study, however, limitations remain. First of all, our corpus so far only consists of 90 selected nonrepresentational modern Western paintings. It remains unknown if other sources of modern paintings display similar outcome following the present examination, for instance paintings created in other cultural contexts or time periods.

Moreover, the current methodology serves only as a starting point, adopting a textual analysis framework based on qualitative judgments. It remains unexplored whether similar results could be generated by trained co-raters. It would be promising to combine psychological methodologies, e.g. by using eye-trackers, in examining the reading preferences of paintings implied by our results. It remains unknown as to what extent the writing directionality of Western writing systems overlaps with the left-to-right textual directionality observed in our painting corpus, which focused on pictorials created in a certain time period, and does not involve any cross-culturally comparison yet.

In short, the left-to-right directionality pattern in paintings observed involves other possible determinants and explanations, culturally (e.g., context), or biological-perceptually (e.g., the hemispheric dominance). The secrecy of why a left-to-right textual direction exists in nonrepresentational modern western paintings requires more transdisciplinary studies, so as to obtain a complete picture of the visual "grammar" and textuality.

Acknowledgments: The current study is made possible by the research grants provided by The Ministry of Science and Technology, Taiwan, R.O.C. (NSC 100-2410-H-002-160-MY3). We would like to thank our reviewers for their timely help and valuable advice. We would also like to express our gratitude to Graduate Institute of Linguistics at National Taiwan University, Department of Fine Arts at Taipei National University of the Arts, and finally to the organizers and participants of CLDC 2016, who kindly contributed comments.

This study has been presented at The 8th Conference on Language, Discourse and Cognition, Taipei, Taiwan (CLDC 2016), and is based on portions of a 2016 Master's thesis by Hsin-yen Chen at Graduate Institute of Linguistics, National Taiwan University.

The three paintings featured in the current study are accessed from fair-usage websites, with the site organizers acknowledged and copyright experts informed.

Appendix: list of selected paintings

From Shanes, E. (1990). *The Life and Masterworks of Salvador Dalí:*

1. *The lugubrious game*
2. *The enigma of desire-my mother, my mother*
3. *Accommodations of desire*
4. *Illumined pleasures*
5. *Partial hallucination-*
6. *Apparitions of Lenin on a grand piano*
7. *The persistence of memory*
8. *The spectre of sex appeal*
9. *The birth of liquid desires*
10. *The enigma of William Tell*

11. *Atmospheric skull sodomizing a grand piano*
12. *The enigma of William Tell*
13. *Paranoid-critical solitude*
14. *Soft construction with boiled beans-premonition of civil war*
15. *Autumn cannibalism*
16. *The great paranoiac*
17. *The anthropomorphic cabinet*
18. *The metamorphosis of narcissus*
19. *Morphological echo*
20. *Sleep*
21. *Swans reflecting elephants*
22. *Spain*
23. *Impressions of Africa*
24. *Apparition of face and fruit dish on a beach*
25. *The slave market with the disappearing bust of Voltaire*
26. *Visage of war*
27. *Dream caused by the flight of a bee around a pomegranate one second before awakening*
28. *The apotheosis of homer*
29. *Portrait of Isabel Styler-Tas*
30. *The temptation of St. Anthony*

From Malet, R. M. (1984). *Joan Miró:*

1. *Maternity*
2. *Painting with art-nouveau frame*
3. *Woman with fair armpit dressing her hair by the light of the stars*
4. *Women surrounded by the flight of a bird*
5. *The day's awakening*
6. *The beautiful bird deciphering the unknown to the pair of lovers*
7. *Woman and bird at sunrise*
8. *Woman and bird in the night*
9. *The red sun gnaws at the spider*
10. *Characters in the night*
11. *Dragonfly with red wings pursuing a serpent gliding spirally towards the comet-star*
12. *Smile of the blazing wings*
13. *Mural painting for Joaquim Gomis*
14. *Character and bird*
15. *Character and bird*

16. *For E and D Miro*
17. *For E and D Miro*
18. *Women and birds*
19. *Woman iii*
20. *The skiing lesson*
21. *Character and bird in the night*
22. *Characters and birds rejoicing at the coming of night*
23. *Woman and birds*
24. *Women and bird*
25. *Woman and birds in the night*
26. *Woman and birds in the night*
27. *Woman before the shooting star*
28. *Woman and bird before the sun*
29. *Woman before the moon*
30. *Woman before the sun*

From Frank, E. (1983). *Jackson Pollock*; Lewison, J. (1999). *Interpreting Pollock*:

1. *Composition with pouring*
2. *Mural*
3. *Alchemy*
4. *Night mist*
5. *Full fathom five*
6. *Eyes in the heat*
7. *Cathedral*
8. *Number 1 A, 1948*
9. *The wooden horse*
10. *Number 8, 1949l*
11. *Number 13 A, 1948, Arabesque*
12. *Sea change*
13. *Number 14, 1948,Gray*
14. *Number 7A, 1948*
15. *Number 27,1950*
16. *Lavender mist number 1, 1950*
17. *Number 32,1950*
18. *(mural)*
19. *Number 2,1949*
20. *Out of the web, number 7, 1949*
21. *One, number 31, 1950*
22. *Convergence, number 10, 1952*

23. C
24. *Blue poles, number 11, 1952*
25. *Number 28, 1951*
26. *Greyed rainbow*
27. *White light*
28. *Number 1, 1952*
29. *Reflection of the big dipper*
30. *Untitled (Scent)*

References

Arnheim, R. 1969. *Visual thinking*. Berkeley: University of California Press.
Brandt, P. A. 2006. Form and meaning in art. *The artful mind: Cognitive science and the riddle of human creativity*, 171–188.
Chen, Hsin-yen & Lily I-wen Su. 2016. Textual Patterns of Modern Western Paintings: A Cognitive Multimodal Exploration. Presented at The 8th Conference on Language, Discourse and Cognition (CLDC). National Taiwan University, 13–14 May.
Corbella, L.D. 1993. *Understanding Miró: Miró Analysis of Language From the Barcelona Series: 1939–44*. Barcelona: Universitat de Barcelona Publications. Translated by Fen-lan Hsu in 1997. Taipei: Artist.
Donald, M. 2006. Art and cognitive evolution. *The artful mind: Cognitive science and the riddle of human creativity*. Oxford: Oxford University Press.
Erben, W. 1988. *Joan Miró, 1893–1983: The Man and His Work*. Cologne: Taschen.
Frank, E. 1983. *Jackson Pollock*. New York: Abbeville Press.
Freeman, M. H. 2009. Minding: feeling, form, and meaning in the creation of poetic iconicity. *Cognitive Poetics: Goals, Gains, and Gaps*, ed. by Geert Brône and Jeroen Vandaele, 169–196.
Gardner, J. S. 2011. *Aesthetics of spatial composition: Facing, position, and context, and the theory of representational fit*. Berkeley: University of California.
Halliday, M.A.K. 1994. *An Introduction to Functional Grammar 2nd ed*. London: Edward Arnold.
Hiraga, M. K. 2005. *Metaphor and Iconicity*. New York: Palgrave Macmillan.
Karim, A. R., & Kojima, H. 2010. The what and why of perceptual asymmetries in the visual domain. *Advances in Cognitive Psychology*, 6, 103–115.
Kress, G. R., & Van Leeuwen, T. 2006. *Reading images: The grammar of visual design*. London: Routledge.
Lewison, J. 1999. *Interpreting Pollock*. London: Tate Gallery.
Luhmann, N. 2000. *Art as a social system*. Stanford: Stanford University Press.
Malet, R. M. 1984. *Joan Miró*. New York: Rizzoli.
Nänny, M., & Fischer, O. (Eds.). 1999. *Form miming meaning (Vol. 1)*. Amsterdam: John Benjamins.
Peirce, C. S. 1955. *The Theory of Signs. Philosophical Writings of Peirce*. New York: Dover.
Shanes, E. 1990. *The Life and Masterworks of Salvador Dalí*. London: Studio Editions.
Turner, M. 2006. *The artful mind: Cognitive science and the riddle of human creativity*. Oxford: Oxford University Press.

Index

Accent shift 5, 227–258
Aging 4, 149, 155, 156
Atonic 6, 247, 248, 249, 250, 252, 255–257
Auxiliary 57–60, 73

Bilingual 4, 149–172
Bilinguals 155–170
Brabantic 116, 122, 123, 143

Cantonese 4, 6, 177–191
Chinese 15, 17, 19, 21, 23–25, 27, 30, 39, 42, 56–60, 62, 64–69, 71, 73–75, 79, 80, 85, 107, 149, 150, 155–160, 162, 164–165, 167–169, 171, 173, 195, 198–199, 201–202, 204–206, 209–211, 215, 220, 222, 257, 258
Chinese character 21, 30, 52
Classical Chinese 215, 5
Cognition 6, 12, 15, 16, 37, 40, 41, 44, 149, 155, 197–200, 203, 222
Cognitive decline 170–171
Cognitive sociolinguistics 115
Cognitive state verb 4, 177–186
Concept 9, 13, 17, 21, 23, 33, 34, 37, 40, 41, 42, 44, 50, 51, 53, 54
ConceptNet 33, 40, 54
Conceptual space 62, 69, 72, 78
Construal 79
Controllability 2, 76, 77, 79
Conventionalization 9–49
Corpus 9, 13–17, 19–20, 22–24, 30, 37, 42, 49–54
Corpus lexicology 9
Corpus linguistics 2, 3, 5, 13, 16, 200
Corpus-based 14, 200, 202, 205, 215
Corpus-driven 200–201, 205, 207, 222

Diagrammatic iconicity 260, 271, 272
Dialect(s) 116, 117, 122–124, 127, 128, 136, 139, 140, 142, 143
Dialectology 123
Diffusion 5, 14, 18–20, 25–26, 36, 46–47, 211, 215, 216, 222
Discrimination 151, 153, 162, 169, 170, 171, 172

Disyllabic nouns 230, 231, 233, 234, 238–245, 249–257
Dutch 3, 6, 115–148

Embodiment 195–197, 25
Emotion 29, 83, 84, 87, 92, 93, 94, 96, 99, 102, 105, 107, 108, 178, 180
English 83–111
Entrainment 84, 85, 107
Entrenchment 117
Experiential 118, 133, 136, 143
Event/speaker-orientation 56, 79

Familiar(ity) 116, 117, 119, 123, 142
Feedback 3, 41, 46, 84, 86, 87, 90, 91, 92, 94, 96–108
Flemish 116, 122, 123, 140, 142, 143
Frequency 10, 13–17, 20, 23, 26–28, 31, 33–36, 39, 41–43, 49, 51, 117–119, 120–122, 125, 127, 128, 130–135, 136–141, 142–143, 144

Geographical variation 116, 138
German 150, 154–170
GIS 5, 195, 207
Grammatical iconicity 268, 271, 272
Grammaticalization 12, 50, 51, 53, 54, 55

Heteronym 127, 137, 142
Historical linguistics 11, 13, 18, 43, 53

Iconicity 6, 197, 198, 223, 268, 271, 272
Ideophones 5, 195–223
Imagistic iconicity 271, 272
Immediacy 77
Impairment 4, 177–186
Information structure 28, 46, 261, 262, 268
Interaction 4, 5, 37, 38, 39, 41, 46, 84–87, 90–93, 96, 97, 100, 153, 162, 163, 164, 170, 171, 182, 184, 230, 234, 245, 247, 253, 257
Internal uniformity 127–129, 130–135, 136–141
Internet language 25, 26

Japanese 83–111

Language 1–6, 9–13, 16, 17, 19–21, 24–26, 28, 39, 40, 44, 45, 49, 57, 58, 60, 62, 64–67, 69, 72, 77, 79, 80, 83, 85, 86, 91–93, 108, 116–119, 122, 127, 138, 139, 142–144, 150, 151, 154–160, 162–172, 177–186, 195–201, 203, 220, 222, 227–258, 260–262, 265, 273
Language change 9, 195
Language variation 1–3, 6, 117, 144, 195, 196, 200, 222
Learning 4, 43, 149–172, 198
Lexeme 116, 122, 123, 125, 126, 127, 128, 129, 130, 131, 133, 134, 135, 136, 137, 138, 139, 140, 141, 142
(Lexical) diversity 116–119, 125–128, 130–133, 136, 141, 143, 144
(Lexical) heterogeneity 116, 125
Lexical semantics 11, 13, 16, 51
Lexical variation 117, 126, 127, 134, 136, 144, 184, 185, 195–223
Lexicalization 12, 13, 14, 50, 51
Lexicography 10, 13
Life cycle of words 10, 14, 18
Limburgish 116, 122, 123, 124, 143
Literacy 207
Locus 233, 234, 235, 236, 237, 239, 241, 243, 244, 248, 249, 250, 252, 258
Low tone spreading 234, 247, 248, 249

Mandarin 155, 159–160, 9–55, 56–82, 83–111
Markedness 197, 199, 206, 271, 272
Mental lexicon 9, 10, 11, 18, 27, 31, 43, 44, 49, 52
Mental state verb 179
Migration 195, 201, 211, 215, 216, 220, 222, 227, 228, 229, 230, 234, 245, 246, 247, 251, 253, 255
Model 9, 14, 17, 27–30, 32, 36–37, 40–41, 43, 45, 47–49, 50, 52
Modern paintings 262, 267, 268, 270, 272
Morphology 28, 30, 37, 49, 50, 51, 53
(Morpho)syntax 12, 21, 28, 32, 37, 51, 54
Multi-dimensional scaling (MDS) 65, 68–70, 76, 80
Multifunctionality 62

Multimodality 107, 108, 261, 265, 268, 272
Multi-word expression 21

Narrative development 90, 177, 178
Natural language processing 10, 11, 21
NDL 151
Neology 13–14, 18–19, 54
Neologism 10, 13, 15, 19, 24, 27

Onomasiology 118, 122, 199, 200, 203, 220, 222, 223
Onomatopoeia 197–198, 201–202

Paired associate learning 149–172
Passive 60–62, 64, 66, 75–77, 79
Perception verb 179
Phenomime 199
Phonology 28, 30, 37, 53, 55
Phonomime 198
Plant name(s) 116, 117, 137, 143
Pragmatics 28, 33, 34, 37, 40, 50, 52, 55
Premodern Chinese 222
Product word 16, 21
Prosody 84, 86, 87, 88, 91, 94, 96, 107, 108, 197, 229, 230, 257, 258
Psycholinguistics 50, 55
Psychomime 199

Quantitative linguistics 10, 37, 43, 48

Reduplication 198, 199, 201, 211
Referential frequency 117, 118, 143
Register (phonology), 5, 6, 227, 233, 236, 237, 238, 239, 241, 243, 244, 245, 249, 250, 252, 254, 257
Register (pragmatics) 13, 19, 20, 24, 25, 28, 29, 41, 44
Rhythm 83–108, 265, 267
Rightward shift 6, 227
Ryukyuan 5, 6, 227–259

Salience/salient 116–118, 125, 132–133, 142, 143
Saliency 262, 265, 266, 268, 270, 271, 272
Scripta Sinica 195, 202, 205, 207, 208, 211
Semantic map 2, 62–64, 65, 79, 80

Semantic network 13, 46, 53
Semantics 1, 11, 13, 16, 28, 31, 32, 37, 50, 51, 52, 53, 66, 80, 197, 199, 263
Slang word 16, 21
Sociolinguistics 28, 33, 37, 50, 52, 53
Sound symbolism 197, 198, 199
Specific language impairment 178
Spontaneous 76, 79, 84
Standardization 127, 136, 137, 139
Story-retelling 179
Synchrony 3, 83–108

Textual directionality 268, 271, 272, 273
Textual pattern 260–273
Theory of Mind 177
Type-token ratio (TTR) 126–128, 129, 130–139, 141, 143

Variation 9, 25, 30, 37

WordNet 25, 49, 51

www.ingramcontent.com/pod-product-compliance
Lightning Source LLC
Chambersburg PA
CBHW061935220426
43662CB00012B/1912